students of cognitive science at all levels including psychologists, linguists, computer scientists,
philosophers, and neuroscientists—as well as all
readers curious about the latest knowledge on
how the mind works.

Photo by Alan Copeman

Philip N. Johnson-Laird is Assistant Director,
MRC Applied Psychology Unit, Cambridge,
England. He is the author of *Mental Models*,
Language and Perception (with G. A. Miller),
and *Psychology of Reasoning* (with P. C. Wason),
all published by Harvard University Press.

THE COMPUTER AND THE MIND

P. N. Johnson-Laird

THE COMPUTER
AND THE MIND

An introduction to cognitive science

HARVARD UNIVERSITY PRESS
Cambridge, Massachusetts
1988

Library of Congress Cataloging-in-Publication Data

Johnson-Laird, P. N. (Philip Nicholas), 1936–
  The computer and the mind.
  Bibliography: p. 397
  Includes index.
  1. Cognition—Mathematical models.   2. Human information
processing—Mathematical models.   3. Computational
complexity.   I. Title.
  BF311.J58   1988   153   87–29841

  ISBN 0–674–15615–3

CONTENTS

PROLOGUE

Since the Second World War scientists from different disciplines have turned to the study of the human mind. Computer scientists have tried to emulate its capacity for visual perception. Linguists have struggled with the puzzle of how children acquire language. Ethologists have sought the innate roots of social behaviour. Neurophysiologists have begun to relate the function of nerve cells to complex perceptual and motor processes. Neurologists and neuropsychologists have used the pattern of competence and incompetence of their brain-damaged patients to elucidate the normal workings of the brain. Anthropologists have examined the conceptual structure of cultural practices to advance hypotheses about the basic principles of the mind. These days one meets engineers who work on speech perception, biologists who investigate the mental representation of spatial relations, and physicists who want to understand consciousness. And, of course, psychologists continue to study perception, memory, thought and action.

What exactly is going on? Why has it happened? And what discoveries have been made?

A brief answer to the first question is: workers in many disciplines have converged on a number of central problems and explanatory ideas. They have realized that no single approach is likely to unravel the workings of the mind: it will not give up its secrets to psychology alone; nor is any other isolated discipline – artificial intelligence, linguistics, anthropology, neurophysiology, philosophy – going to have any greater success.

A brief answer to the second question is that the invention of the programmable digital computer, and more importantly its precursor, the mathematical theory of computability, have forced people to think in a new way about the mind. Before computation, there was a sharp distinction between brain and mind: one was a physical organ, the other a ghostly nonentity that was hardly a respectable topic of investigation. (Consenting adults

7

could talk about it in private as long as they realized that it didn't really exist.) After computers, there can be no such scepticism: a machine can be controlled by a 'program' of symbolic instructions, and there is nothing ghostly about a computer program. Perhaps the mind stands to the brain in much the same way that the program stands to the computer. There can be a science of the mind.

As to the discoveries that have been made, a brief answer can be found in the chapter headings of this book. We now know something about how human beings perceive the world, how they learn to cope with it, how they reason and make judgements, and how they communicate. Many of these results are already exploited in computer programs that interpret pictures, solve intellectual puzzles, and advise experts on technical problems such as medical diagnosis. But the most important discovery has been to realize how much we do not know. Some people are excited by the possibility of paranormal phenomena, such as telepathy, but they fail to grasp that an apparently effortless process such as ordinary visual perception, which seems so easy to understand, is in fact deeply mysterious: it depends on myriad unconscious processes of which we can never be aware and which we can hope to understand only by scientific investigation. Computation has at last enabled us to formulate with some precision the problems that need to be solved.

A reader who is content with these brief answers need read no further, because the aim of this book is to explain what cognitive science is, to describe its origins, and to spell out what it has achieved. But a word of caution is necessary. That there are sciences that study cognition is undeniable. That there is a single, unified discipline of cognitive science is debatable. Its critics argue that it does not exist; that it could not exist; that it should not exist. New sciences are often invented, they say, as a ruse to gain research funds, and cognitive science is nothing more than six disciplines in search of a grant-giving agency. Intellectual disciplines, however, exist when administrators, recognizing reality, baptise them for administrative convenience. Universities in the United States and Britain contain a growing number of Centres of Cognitive Science.

The discipline is new, and even its practitioners argue among themselves about its essence, though many of them are happy to get on with their research without worrying about the wider perspective. This book presents, I hope, a coherent view of the subject, but it is not a view that would be shared by everyone. Its key concept is computation – a notion that derives from the branch of mathematics known as the theory of computability. Cognitive science, sometimes explicitly and sometimes implicitly, tries to elucidate the workings of the mind by treating them as computations, not necessarily of the sort carried out by the familiar digital computer, but of a sort that lies within this broader framework of the theory of computation.

My aim has been to write a book that could be understood by anyone who is interested in the scientific explanation of mental phenomena. The book is intellectually demanding – how could it not be? – but I have done my utmost to keep it simple. It requires the reader to think, not to come equipped with a large body of technical knowledge. The book may even, I hope, contribute to a subject that is still too new to have inspired any general textbooks informed by the concept of computation.

One final question may be hovering in the reader's mind. Of what use is cognitive science? There was a time when academics were contemptuous of such a question. 'What use is a newborn baby, ma'am?' said Rutherford. The world can no longer afford the luxury of this rejoinder. I shall treat the study of the mind as a scientific end in itself, but the resulting knowledge has already contributed to the practice of teaching and learning, to the diagnosis and treatment of mental disorder, and to the design of a humane technology that augments human intelligence. Ultimately cognitive science may explain our minds in a way that makes a difference to *us* and to how we live together.

PART I

COMPUTATION AND THE MIND

To understand the Turing model of 'the brain', it was crucial to see that it regarded physics and chemistry, including all the arguments about quantum mechanics . . ., as essentially irrelevant. In his view, the physics and chemistry were relevant only in as much as they sustained the medium for the embodiment of discrete 'states', 'reading' and 'writing'. Only the *logical* pattern of these 'states' could really matter. The claim was that whatever a brain did, it did by virtue of its structure as a logical system, and not because it was inside a person's head, or because it was a spongy tissue made up of a particular kind of biological cell formation. And if this were so, then its logical structure could just as well be represented in some other medium, embodied by some other physical machinery. It was a materialist view of mind, but one that did not confuse logical patterns and relations with physical substances and things, as so often people did.

ALAN HODGES

CHAPTER 1

How should the mind be studied?

Nearly everyone believes that their conscious feelings and judgements govern their actions. Thinking determines behaviour. To take a typical example, consider how a friend of mine chose a new car. Since he knew little about cars, he did some research in motoring journals and reached the conclusion that Japanese cars offered the best combination of reliability and price. He also sought advice from other people. Someone told him that the best policy was to buy a new car – that way he was guaranteed a year's trouble-free motoring because new cars are under warranty. Someone else advised him to buy a second-hand car that was still relatively new – that way he would make a saving because of the large initial depreciation on a car. The advice seemed to conflict. But, he finally bought a car that had been used by a dealer as a demonstration model. It combined, he said, all the features that he had been recommended: it was Japanese, it was significantly cheaper than a brand-new model, and it was still new enough to be under the maker's warranty.

I know my friend is sincere, and the reasons for his choice seem entirely logical, but can we be sure that he bought the car for the reasons he stated, or are they *post hoc* rationalizations? He may have confabulated in order to cover his ignorance of the real hinges on which his decision swung. Perhaps what attracted him was the image of the car – its somewhat phallic shape, and the feeling of power he felt behind its wheel – or perhaps he wanted to keep up with his neighbours, who had similar cars.

This case raises a general question: to what extent can people know the reasons for their behaviour? The view that beliefs and desires govern actions may be correct, or it may be part of a naive 'folk psychology' of myths and mystifications that have nothing to do with reality. There is no way to determine the true cause of any particular action: that is the historian's dilemma. Hence, for an answer to the question, we must turn to psychologists, who examine the actions of many individuals in the same experimentally controlled situation.

INTROSPECTION AND THE UNCONSCIOUS

Unfortunately, students of psychology have never agreed about the best way in which to study the mind, or even about whether it is a proper object of study. The difficulties began with René Descartes (1596–1650),* the first recognizably modern philosopher, who drew a sharp distinction between mind and body. You cannot doubt that you have a mind, he argued, because the very act of doubting calls for a mind (cf. his claim: 'I think, therefore I am'). But you can – with a sufficient access of philosophical scepticism – doubt that you have a body. Body and mind are therefore two quite distinct sorts of entity. Reflexes and other bodily behaviours can be understood because the body is a machine, just as animals are machines. But the mind is incorporeal, and it governs voluntary behaviour by way of a mysterious link from the immaterial to the material. The mind is not a machine; there can thus be no science of the mind.

The case is so appealing and has permeated our culture for so long that most people are either confessed or closet Cartesians. Even if you have never heard the arguments before, you probably believe that your mind is distinct from your body, that nothing is easier to know than your mind's contents, that they (like my friend's conscious decision) are the prime-movers in your life and behaviour, and that you have a free will that defies scientific explanation.

Dualism, as Descartes's philosophy is called, is so potent that the history of psychology is, broadly speaking, little more than a series of reactions to it. In the nineteenth century, when

---

* I have not used the scholarly apparatus of footnotes – with this one exception. A reader who wishes to track down a reference should consult the bibliography at the end of the book, armed with the name of the author cited in the text; the details there should be sufficient to identify the relevant work. If no author is cited in the text, then there may be a relevant reference in the further reading at the end of the chapter.

psychologists first attempted to explain mental phenomena sci-
entifically, they agreed that the contents of the mind were
accessible to introspection. They would give each other various
tasks, such as responding to a word with the first word that came
to mind, and after each response they would ruminate about the
mental processes that had led to its production. There were,
however, two challenges to the view that the mind is transparent
to introspection. First, the German polymath Hermann von
Helmholtz argued that vision must depend on unconscious inferences, which, for instance, give rise to the perception of depth.
Second, Freud posited an unconscious system of sexual and
aggressive drives, which if repressed could emerge into consciousness in the distorted form of neurotic symptoms. The repression of hostility towards a loved one, for example, might
subsequently be manifest in the hysterical paralysis of a limb.
Repression itself is a supposedly unconscious process, not to be
confused with the conscious suppression of unpleasant
memories.

These two notions of the unconscious are very different,
though both limit introspection. The Freudian unconscious provides an alternative to our conscious reasons for behaviour: one
buys a car, not (only) because it offers a prudent deal, but
because it satisfies some unconscious wish. The Helmholtzian
unconscious offers no such alternative, but rather provides the
machinery that makes consciousness possible. It therefore presents a more radical challenge to the Cartesian identity of mind
and consciousness. In obedience to the Freudian imperative –
where Id is, let Ego be! – you may recover the contents of your
unconscious motives by free-associating on a psychoanalyst's
couch. Helmholtzian unconscious processes, however, cannot
enter consciousness, since they produce its contents in the first
place. You cannot pick up the introspective process by its own
bootstraps.

A further difficulty with introspection emerged from its
systematic use by a group of psychologists who had gathered
together at Würzburg in the early years of this century. They
discerned in their own introspections a kind of conscious but
unanalysable experience containing neither imagery nor any

awareness of an act of will. One could think about dogs, for example, and decide that they are animals, without forming a visual image of a dog in the mind's eye. There were, as Kant had supposed some two hundred years earlier, 'imageless thoughts', which result from processes functioning below the level of consciousness. The idea provoked those psychologists who believed that thinking was the conscious association of ideas. And, when they examined their introspections, they found, like Hume, that thinking was *always* accompanied by imagery.

The 'imageless thought' controversy lasted for years. There was no way of settling it, because introspection cannot establish *how* one subjective experience leads to another. If you claim that your thinking resembles the interior monologues that James Joyce and Virginia Woolf put into the minds of their characters, and I claim that I never think in this way (except when I am rehearsing how to ask for a pay rise), then there is no way to decide whether one or other of us is deluded.

BEHAVIOURISM

The inability of introspection to resolve the 'imageless thought' controversy prepared the ground for the most radical reaction to Cartesianism, the denial of the mind. This view of the matter arose from a movement known as Behaviourism, and it remains the belief – or whatever the physical equivalent of a belief is – of latterday materialists, such as Paul and Patricia Churchland. In his manifesto for Behaviourism published in 1913, J. B. Watson wrote:

> Psychology as the behaviorist views it is a purely objective natural science. Its theoretical goal is the prediction and control of behavior. Introspection forms no essential part of its method nor is the scientific value of its data dependent upon the readiness with which they lend themselves to interpretation in terms of consciousness.

So psychology was to be objective; it was to be a natural science; it was to control and to predict behaviour; and it was to forget all about consciousness and the mind, which were improper topics for scientific investigation.

These bold slogans had a dramatic effect on many disciplines, especially in the United States. The study of mental processes was abandoned; the introspective technique was replaced by the controlled observation of responses in the laboratory. Psychologists studied how animals learned to run mazes, to press levers to obtain food, and to make other readily observable responses. (It was left to the ethologists to discover how animals behaved in the wild.) Linguists gave up mentalism, and assumed the Behaviouristic view of meaning: words come to stand for objects in the same way that a bell comes to elicit salivation if it is always rung just before a hungry animal is given food – the so-called 'classical conditioning' technique that the Behaviourists borrowed from the Russian physiologist Ivan Pavlov. Philosophers developed this account into a fully fledged theory of meaning. Anthropologists studied behaviour in societies, not how people conceived their cultures. The mind was expelled from its original place in the Dualistic scheme: it was a ghostly mystery that had no role in determining behaviour.

The taboo on the mind was reinforced by a seductive argument made by a number of Behaviourists, notably B. F. Skinner. The argument, which is known as the 'theoretician's dilemma', goes like this: Suppose that there *are* mental states that intervene between a stimulus in the external world and a subsequent response. There are then two possibilities. Either the mental states intervene in a lawful way, or else they do not. If they are lawful, the theoretician can ignore them and formulate a law directly relating stimulus to behaviour. If they are not lawful, then the theoretician must obviously not refer to them. Either way, in framing psychological laws, there is no need to refer to mental states. They are either unnecessary or unmentionable.

The argument is attractive, and even people who resist its allure can be hard put to identify what is wrong with it. In fact, it is based on two false assumptions. The first is that the sole purpose of science is to frame parsimonious laws. Notwithstanding Watson's and Skinner's emphasis on the prediction and control of behaviour, science aims to *explain* phenomena, not merely to describe them in laws. And explanations, of course, take the form of theories. Hence, if mental states exist, a complete psychological explanation should give an account of them even if they could be dropped from laws of behaviour. The second false assumption is that psychology should concern itself solely with the sequence of a stimulus in the external world giving rise to an overt response. Some behaviours are not controlled by environmental stimuli. Many human skills – from spontaneous speech to the solving of intellectual problems – are not governed by events in the environment but depend on complex mental processes. Likewise, perception (the study of which was largely eschewed by the Behaviourists) does not necessarily give rise to any overt behaviour. If perception, thought and communication are to be explained, mental processes must be invoked.

There is a story that after sexual intercourse, one Behaviourist said to another: 'That was fine for *you*, but how was it for *me*?' The joke highlights Behaviourism's antipathy to introspection. That antipathy was a marvellous release from the 'imageless thought' controversy, because introspection could not resolve it. Yet, psychologists should not abandon introspection altogether: not all introspections concern the sequence of subjective experiences. If I ask you to look into a stereoscope, then (provided that I have contrived an appropriate display) you may report seeing a picture in depth. Such introspective reports are crucial for the investigation of perception. It may be true, as Helmholtz argued, that we are never conscious of all the processes underlying perception. It may be also true, as Freud believed, that we can be deluded about the factors that affect our decisions. But the claim that the exercise of conscious judgement has no relation to our behaviour is contrary to common sense. The match between what people say and what they do is good enough to ensure that they go on talking to each other. Moreover, psychologists must study introspective reports if they are to make sense of the discrepancies between a stated claim and the real cause of behaviour. They need to explain, not to ignore, people's introspections about what they have perceived, how they have reached a decision or solved a problem, and why they have chosen to act in a particular way.

When the Behaviourists stuck to the phenomena of animal

learning, they made scientific and technological progress, even though they never succeeded in defining an animal's responses objectively. When they confronted human behaviour, however, they ran up against the difficulty of Watson's slogan that psychology should be done without reference to mental processes. Some Behaviourists invented theoretical devices that enabled them to talk about internal processes without seeming to give up objectivity. This manoeuvre, as Gerald Zuriff (a recent devotee of the movement) has conceded, allowed even mentalistic theories to be accommodated within Behaviourism. What began as an objective science became an ideology.

THE MENTALISTIC TRADITION

Behaviourism prospered until the Second World War, but throughout its hegemony, there were those, especially in Europe, who refused to abandon the study of the mind. After the demise of the Würzburg group, a school of 'Gestalt' psychologists flourished in Germany. It too had arisen in opposition to the philosophical tradition that mental life consists solely in associations between ideas. Its leading members, Wertheimer, Köhler and Koffka, stressed the importance of structural relations (richer than mere associations) in perception. They also argued that insight into a problem depends on grasping its underlying structure. They were right, but they lacked a language in which to make their ideas clear; and they sought laws of structure rather than an explanation of mental processes.

The contrast between Behaviourism and Gestalt psychology led Bertrand Russell to remark that animals tended to display the national characteristics of experimenters:

> Animals studied by Americans rush about frantically, with an incredible display of hustle and pep, and at last achieve the desired solution by chance. Animals observed by Germans sit still and think, and at last evolve the solution out of their inner consciousness.

The truth is that workers from the two traditions set different problems to different species of animals.

19

Another proponent of mentalism was the Swiss linguist, Ferdinand de Saussure, who was the founder of the movement known as Structuralism. In his lectures (1907–11), which were published posthumously, he established the principle that language could be studied independently from its historical origins, contrary to the lore of nineteenth-century philology. He argued that the meaning of a symbol was, not the object that the symbol designated, but a mental entity. A sign or symbol, for Saussure, consisted of a form (the 'signifier') that is mentally associated with a concept (the 'signified'). In language, the actual sound-form that is bound to a particular concept is arbitrary, that is, there is no natural connection between word and concept except in the few cases of onomatopoeia. The particular value that a concept has depends on what other concepts exist. Indeed, Saussure insisted that a concept cannot be defined in its own right, but only in terms of its relations to other concepts. Thus, the French word 'mouton' and the English word 'sheep' have the same signification because they can both be used to refer to sheep, but the concepts differ in value because English contains the word 'mutton' for talking about meat, whereas French has no such counterpart. The concepts for which there are signs differ from one language to another; they are by no means immutable but can change from one generation to another. Hence, while Saussure accepted that language goes beyond what occurs in any particular person's mind, he did not adopt the Platonic view that there is an objective realm of ideal meanings. On the contrary, he recognized that language is a social product – the relations between words and concepts bear the stamp of societal approval.

Structuralism was founded on the notion that the mind contains structures, such as an organized mental lexicon. The anthropologist Claude Lévi-Strauss assumed that the myths, conventions and artefacts of a culture are the manifest consequences of mental structures. The structures are not available to introspection, but they can be revealed by analysis. There are dangers, however, in Lévi-Strauss's methodology. As later cognitive anthropologists discovered, it is difficult to assess the validity of an analysis. One problem is that the theorist imposes a classification on the data in much the same way that

20

numerologists detect what are for them significant patterns in the works of Shakespeare. A theory may be so rich in descriptive possibilities that it can be made to fit any data. Moreover, if some cultural practice is correctly described by a theoretical structure, it does not follow that this structure is in anyone's mind apart from the theorist's. Ordinary members of the culture may use an entirely different representation, since there can never be just a single unique description of any set of data. Indeed, a cultural product such as a myth may be the result of factors, such as errors of translation, that are not represented in anyone's mind.

Structuralism relies on simple classificatory principles – a system of binary oppositions, such as edible/inedible and natural/cultural – which are not powerful enough to explain many types of thinking. The doctrine has had its apotheosis in literary criticism, French psychoanalysis, and aesthestic theory.

The difficulties of Structuralism were paralleled by those of another Swiss mentalist, the late Jean Piaget. He was concerned with epistemology and undertook a study of children in order to elucidate the foundations of knowledge. He carried out many informal studies of children's understanding of the world and of how they think about it. He came to believe that thought develops from 'internalizing one's own actions', and that it passes through qualitatively distinct stages in childhood. These stages, according to Piaget, correspond to the unfolding of new mental structures, which are supposedly precursors to the major branches of mathematics: first, topology (the study of the most general properties of space), next the algebra of relations, and finally formal logic. Once again, the danger is that Piaget has imposed these structures on children's thinking, and that they do not correspond to anything to be found in their heads. Moreover, he never provided an account of the development of mental structures that was explicit enough to be modelled in a computer program. The theory is a clock without a mechanism.

THE RISE OF COGNITIVE PSYCHOLOGY

Gestalt psychology, Structuralism, Piagetian epistemology, and the eclectic work of British psychologists such as Sir Frederic

21

Bartlett ensured that research into human mentality continued throughout the inter-war years. During the Second World War, psychologists were called on to investigate many human skills, from the capacity to recognize speech in a noisy background to the ability to fly a plane. It was impossible to make sense of the phenomena without considering mental processes. After the war, this tendency was amplified by a wholesale importation of ideas from other disciplines. Cyberneticians were studying the role of feedback in achieving goals. When a thermostat maintains a given temperature, it is governed by a goal. It was thus legitimate, as they pointed out, to ascribe teleological principles to human behaviour. Neurophysiologists developed theories of the logic of nerve-cell circuits, and the Canadian psychologist Donald Hebb based a theory of cognition on a hypothesis about the functioning of assemblies of cells. Information theorists provided a statistical measure of the amount of information transmitted over a communication channel such as a telephone line. Roughly speaking, the more improbable a message is statistically, the greater the amount of information it conveys. The measure prompted the American psychologist George Miller to examine the capacity of human beings to process information. It also led the British psychologist Donald Broadbent to analyse the mind as a channel of communication.

The rise of 'information-processing' psychology was helped by an invention: the first digital computer that could store its own program. It was constructed at Princeton in the early 1950s under the supervision of the mathematician John von Neumann. Like the pioneering theorist Alan Turing, he was subsequently to compare the computer with the brain. The challenge was to program computers so that they could perform intelligently, and by the mid-1950s Herbert Simon and Allen Newell had devised a program that could prove logical theorems in a way that resembled human performance. Newell and Simon began to keep systematic records of problem-solvers' introspective reports, and to compare them with a protocol of the computer's attempts at the same problem. Other psychologists, such as Jerome Bruner and his colleagues, developed theories of the strategies that people use when they are learning new concepts, and these strategies were strikingly similar to computer programs.

22

Inevitably, there were reactions against Behaviourism, and it received three decisive blows. First, Karl Lashley, an erstwhile fellow-traveller, expressed his doubts about Behaviouristic analyses of skilled behaviours such as playing the piano or speaking spontaneously. These skills, he argued, must depend on a hierarchy of controls deriving from an individual's intentions, and governing the structure of the sequence of behaviours in progressively finer detail. Speech, for instance, called for an idea, a choice of syntax and a choice of words. It could not possibly be the result of a single chain of associations from stimuli to responses. Second, the linguist Noam Chomsky proved that the treatment of language implicit in Behaviourism is not adequate to specify the syntax of English sentences. Finally, George Miller and his colleagues showed that the concept of hierarchical planning is central to mental life, and is closely related to the concept of a computer program. When, in 1960, Miller and Bruner set up the Harvard Center for Cognitive Studies, the rehabilitation of the mind within American psychology was complete.

As often in a period of rapid scientific growth, not everyone realized what was happening, and perhaps no one at the time grasped its real nature. The mainstream of psychology had certainly returned to the study of the mind, and the computer provided an exciting new metaphor. In the past, the mind had been likened to a wax tablet, to a hydraulic system, and to a telephone exchange. Now, there was a new reaction to Dualism: brain and mind are bound together as computer and program. Yet the full power of the metaphor eluded people. It seemed to reside in the existence of 'machines that think'. In fact, what the computer offered – or rather the theory lying behind the computer – was a new conception of psychological explanation. This conception is much more powerful than the earlier mechanical analogies. Indeed, as we shall see, it has yet to be exhausted.

THE NATURE OF PSYCHOLOGICAL EXPLANATIONS

The bacterium *Escherichia coli*, which lives in the gut and sometimes upsets stomachs, seems to behave like an intelligent

23

organism, because it migrates towards food and away from poisons. One might suppose that it sets its course as the result of a rational decision based on an internal representation of its environment. In fact, D. E. Koshland and other biologists have discovered that *E. coli* has no need for any mental life whatever: no representation, no memory, no choice. Evolution has solved its navigational problems without providing it with an internal map. The bacterium's flagellae rotate – nature does not entirely abhor the wheel – and when they turn in a counter-clockwise direction they propel it forward, whereas when they turn in a clockwise direction they fly apart and cause it to tumble over and over. It has special receptor proteins that can bind a variety of substances (nutrient and toxic) according to the shape of their molecules; and their reception, in effect, shifts the gear controlling the direction of the flagellae's rotation. If food is detected, they rotate counter-clockwise, so that the organism moves in a straight line. But if no further particles of food are detected, the direction of rotation begins to alternate: the organism moves at random, thereby ensuring that it will probably stumble on to the path of the nutrient stimuli again. It is thus able to home in on a target that is emitting particles of food, much like an aeroplane flying, somewhat erratically, down a radar beam.

The bacterium is a Behaviourist's dream. It raises no problems of cognitive psychology because it has no mental life. Its actions can be explained like those of a machine. And, since Descartes, theorists have assumed that there is no problem in understanding how machines work. Indeed, Lord Kelvin, the eminent Victorian physicist, even turned this argument around, and wrote in a letter to a colleague:

> I never satisfy myself until I can make a mechanical model of a thing. If I can make a mechanical model I can understand it. As long as I cannot make a mechanical model all the way through I cannot understand . . .

This is certainly one criterion for what counts as a satisfactory explanation. Because we can make robots that behave in ways analogous to bacteria, we believe that we understand the mainsprings of their behaviour. However, other organisms – human beings at least – do have a mental life, and we need to determine what we may take for granted in order to explain it.

An explanation should spell out what we do not understand in terms of what we do understand. There thus needs to be some consensus about which concepts are well enough understood to be used in explanations. If a psychoanalyst explains my friend's choice of car by asserting that he had an unresolved Oedipal conflict, I am entitled to ask what exactly that means. The analyst may then explain that young boys are sexually attracted to their mothers and therefore jealous of their fathers, and that these unpleasant feelings are repressed and lie dormant in the unconscious. But this explanation takes too much for granted – the notion of the unconscious, for example, needs to be explained. And so we might go on *ad nauseum*, searching for common ground.

Is there any way in which we might make a short-cut by specifying beforehand what can safely be taken for granted in psychological explanations? The question lies at the root of cognitive science. Until recently, there was no acceptable answer to it. Psychological textbooks are littered with technical terms, such as 'set', 'gestalt', 'prägnanz', 'equilibration', 'pure stimulus act'; and psychoanalytical textbooks contain a still greater bounty of jargon, such as 'primary process', 'displacement', 'counter-transference', 'castration anxiety', 'phallo-centricism' and 'libido'. One can hardly forbear to cry out: *What do all these words mean? Why are there so many? And how can we escape from them?* The result of this proliferating verbiage is that theories are often hard to understand, and yield predictions only by an exercise of intuition. Yet, if a theory needs intuition in order to determine what it predicts, it has little explanatory value. It is not a signpost, but a crutch on which the theorist leans in order to use the other arm to point the way.

The answer to the problem is, not the computer directly, but what lies behind it – its mathematical ancestor, the theory of computability. This theory, which was invented by logicians in the 1930s, provides a more powerful notion of mechanism than was dreamt of by Descartes or Kelvin. It shows how an elementary set of building blocks can be used to construct an

25

unlimited variety of complex symbolic processes. These processes have been used to model such domains as the weather, the stock exchange, and the interactions of fundamental particles. They have so far proved applicable to any domain, and they are particularly appropriate for modelling that other device that seems to manipulate symbols, the human brain. Yet the building-blocks of computability are so simple that it is difficult to object to taking them for granted.

The idea that mental life can be explained in terms of a computational process was anticipated by Kenneth Craik in the early 1940s, before the invention of the digital computer. He likened thought to the operation of one of Kelvin's machines, the tidal predictor, which uses an apparatus of gears, cranks and pulleys to model the gravitational forces that affect the heights and times of tides. Craik was evidently ignorant of the theory of computation – at that time a little-known and recondite field – but one of its founders, Alan Turing, entertained much the same ideas about explaining mental processes, though he was not to publish them until later. Moreover, Turing appreciated that the theory of computability provides an excellent foundation for explanations because he knew that it aimed to show which mathematical calculations could be carried out without recourse to intuition.

THE PLAN OF THE BOOK

The goal of cognitive science is to explain how the mind works. Part of the power of the discipline resides in the theory of computability. If an explanation is computable, then *prima facie* it is coherent, and does not take too much for granted. Whether or not it is the right theory depends on whether it fits the facts, but at least it has succeeded in avoiding vagueness, confusion and the mystical incantation of empty verbal formulae. Some processes in the nervous system seem to be computations (though perhaps of a novel sort). Others, such as the retina's response to light, are physical processes that can be modelled in computer programs. But there may be aspects of mental life that cannot be modelled in this way, and that require us to take for granted more than is admitted by the concept of computability. There may even be aspects of the mind that lie outside scientific explanation.

In this book, I am going to explore how much of mental life can be explained by computable theories. The mind's main tasks are:

- to perceive the world
- to learn, to remember and to control actions
- to cogitate and to create new ideas
- to control communication with others
- to create the experience of feelings, intentions and self-awareness.

I have divided the book into separate parts to deal with computational accounts of each of these processes. Before going any further, however, I will outline the central concept of computability.

Further reading

Miller (1966) is the best brief history of the science of the mind. The appendix of Newell and Simon (1972) tells the story of the post-war rise of cognitive psychology. Boden (1977) has written an excellent introduction to computational models of mental processes from the standpoint of artificial intelligence. Gardner (1985) is a stimulating account of the development of cognitive science.

CHAPTER 2

Symbols and mental processes

What do mental processes *process*? The answer, of course, is a vast number of perceptions, ideas, images, beliefs, hypotheses, thoughts and memories. One of the tenets of cognitive science is that all of these entities are mental representations or *symbols* of one sort or another. There is a huge literature on signs, symbols and signals. A psychoanalyst tells us that the occurrence of a staircase in a dream symbolizes sexual intercourse. A structuralist tells us that soap powders symbolize the maintenance of public order. An anthropologist tells us that a society's imagery relating the dead and the living symbolizes the relations between the living. In this chapter, I want to consider, not these claims about symbolism – made by Freud, Barthes and Lévi-Strauss, respectively – but how symbols work. I will start with symbols in the external world, then deal with symbols and computers, and finally try to show that mental symbols are a suitable case for computational modelling.

SYSTEMS OF SYMBOLS

Symbols are seldom, if ever, isolated entities: they come in systems. The simplest systems consist in a small number of distinct symbols, each of which has its own unique interpretation. Thus, the road signs illustrated in Figure 2.1 each pick out a hazard, of which there are many particular instances. The interpretation of a road sign or any other symbol calls for a procedure that retrieves the entity denoted by the symbol. Human beings can obviously carry out such procedures, but animals can also be taught to interpret certain symbols. This method is used when investigating an animal's ability to discriminate between one shape and another.

28

Double bend first to left (may be reversed)	**Slippery road**	**Two-way traffic straight ahead**
Two-way traffic crosses one-way road	**Traffic merges from left**	**Traffic merges from right**

Figure 2.1: Some examples of road signs (with explanations).

The richest symbolic systems have an infinite number of possible symbols. A good example is provided by architects' drawings. A drawing is made up from a repertoire of primitive symbolic elements — lines, vertices and so on. It designates entities in another domain — the various parts of a building. Its relation to these objects depends on a set of principles — the rules of scale drawings and a number of conventions about architecture. Other examples of infinite systems are mathematical notation, musical notation, maps, alphabetic writing in which words are combined to make sentences, and ideographic writing in which symbols designating ideas are combined to make sentences. Like most systems of symbols, they all have three components: a set of primitive symbols, together with principles for constructing complex symbols out of them; a set of entities constituting the domain that is symbolized; and a method of relating symbols to the entities they symbolize, and *vice versa*.

NUMERALS AS SYMBOLS

Any domain of entities can be represented by many different systems of symbols. The point is obvious in the case of numbers, which are abstract entities, and the symbols that denote them, namely, numerals, which are marks that can be made on paper or in some other medium. Numbers are normally written in the

29

decimal numerals devised by the Arabs. But the decimal system is sanctioned only by custom and utility; it is not sacrosanct. Morse code is a notation for the letters of the alphabet, and it is binary because it has only two primitive symbols (a dot and a dash). There is also a binary notation for numbers in which any number is written using only two sorts of primitive symbol (0 and 1). Thus, zero is written as 0, one is written as 1, but two is written as 10, three is written as 11, and four is written as 100. The general principle is that the rightmost digit denotes units (0 or 1), the next digit to the left denotes the number of twos, the next digit to the left denotes the number of fours, the next digit denotes the number of eights, and so on in increasing powers of two. The binary numeral, 1100, for example, stands for the number twelve, as the following scheme shows:

8s	4s	2s	Units
1	1	0	0

Binary numerals are useful because they allow numbers to be represented in devices that have only two internal signals. Thus, the binary primitives can be represented in a computer by the presence (1) or absence (0) of a particular voltage, and a numeral can be represented by an array of such voltages.

There are other ways to symbolize numbers. They can be written as Roman numerals, and even as a simple tally such as a prisoner scratches on the wall to record the days of incarceration. Thus, the number twelve can be written in at least the four following different ways:

XII	(Roman numeral)
12	(Arabic numeral)
1100	(binary numeral)
111111111111	(prisoner's tally)

In fact, there is no limit to the number of different notations that could be used to symbolize numbers.

THE CONSTRUCTION OF SYMBOLS

Systems of symbols can differ in all three of the components that I described earlier: the symbols themselves, the domain that they symbolize, and the principles that relate them to the domain. We need to understand these differences before we consider the sorts of symbols that might be used by the mind.

The first difference concerns the symbols themselves and the principles by which complex symbols are constructed out of the primitives. Thus, different numerical systems differ in the primitive symbols from which they are composed:

I, V, X, L, C, D, M   (Roman primitives)

0, 1, 2, 3, 4, 5, 6, 7, 8, 9 (Arabic primitives)

0, 1   (binary primitives)

1   (prisoner's tally)

They also differ in the principles governing the assembly of complex symbols. Prisoner's tally consists solely in the concatenation of marks (with spaces between separate numerals). The principles for Roman numerals, like those of many systems, assemble symbols according to structural rules. These rules yield complex symbols that have an internal structure, e.g. the digits in XIV have the structure (X) (IV), not the structure (XI) (V). The rules also permit only certain combinations of primitives, e.g. IVX is not an acceptable Roman numeral.

THE MEANING OF SYMBOLS

Any system of external symbols, such as numerals or an alphabet, is capable of symbolizing many different domains. Thus, the binary numeral 1100 can stand for many things. It may stand for the number twelve, for the letter 'Z' as in morse code, or for a particular person, artefact, three-dimensional shape, region of the earth's surface, or many other entities. Numerals are potent because they are each distinct from one another, and there is a simple structural recipe for constructing an unlimited supply of them. Even if a domain contains a potentially infinite number of entities, then a numerical system can be used to symbolize it provided that there is some way to relate the numerals to what they signify. The simplest link is an arbitrary pairing of each symbol to one referent, and each referent to one symbol, as in a numerical code for the rooms of a hotel. A symbol may be well formed, e.g. the Roman numeral XIII, but fail to designate anything – there may be no room with the number thirteen. Rather than arbitrary pairings, it is usually convenient to have some principles for assigning interpretations to symbols. These principles may be a matter of rules, conventions or habits. If symbols are assembled out of primitives according to structural rules, then the *structure* of the symbol may, or may not, be relevant to its interpretation. A Roman numeral has a structure that is relevant to its interpretation as a number. A pile of sand in an hour-glass has a structure that is not relevant to its interpretation as an interval of time – only the volume of sand matters.

THE EXPLICITNESS OF SYMBOLS

Some symbols – poems, perhaps, if Mallarmé is to be believed – are an end in themselves. But most symbols serve some purpose. Here there is a concept of great significance to cognitive science, and one that will crop up throughout the book. Systems of symbols differ in what they make *explicit* about the entities in the domain that is symbolized. It is easy to see what is at stake. Consider, for example, two numbers written in prisoner's tally:

1111

and

1111111

Which number is bigger? You can see at a glance that it is the number designated by the second tally. Now consider two numbers written in Roman numerals:

MCXXX

and

DCCCLII

Which one is bigger? The task is harder because the size of the numbers is made much less explicit by Roman numerals: you have to work out what the numbers are before you can answer the question. A good notation saves work because it makes the required information explicit.

Explicitness is not an absolute quality; it depends on the *process* carrying out the task in hand. A symbol makes explicit whatever information is available to that process with a minimum of work. If the task is to judge the sizes of numbers, then for *us* prisoner's tally is more explicit than Roman numerals. There are procedures where the converse is true, because they can deal only with Roman numerals. When we assess explicitness, we tend to rely on how things strike us introspectively. Anything that we are aware of has indeed been made explicit in our consciousness. Unfortunately, such judgements may be a poor guide to the explicitness of information to some unconscious process.

COMPUTERS AND SYMBOLS

People often imagine that digital computers are machines for 'crunching' numbers, that is, for carrying out long and tedious calculations. This is a double misconception.

First, computers do not work with numbers at all; they work with numerals. Numbers are abstract entities; numerals are symbols that can be interpreted as standing for numbers (or for many other things). You feed in binary numerals, the computer operates on them, and feeds out binary numerals. To make life easier for you, you can feed in data using a keyboard, which converts each character you type into a binary numeral. Likewise, the numerals that the computer produces are normally converted into characters before they are printed out or displayed on a screen. Within the computer, however, everything is electrical patterns of binary numerals.

Second, numerals can be used to symbolize a large variety of different domains, and so computers can cope with data from visual scenes, writing and so on. They can even cope with quantities that vary continuously, such as a sound wave, by making a numerical approximation to them of any required degree of accuracy. But computers have no principles for relating the numerals they use to the external world. Bertrand Russell once remarked that in mathematics one never knows what one is talking about or whether what one is saying is true or false. I am not sure he was right about mathematics, but his aphorism is an apt characterization of current digital computers. As to the meaning of their operations and results, the interpretation is left to the people who use them. Philosophers sometimes conclude from this fact that mental processes cannot be computational. This argument will be less persuasive, perhaps, when computers are provided with the missing link – with processes that relate their symbols to the world.

Although a computer cannot yet interpret its symbols in relation to the world, it does have two symbolic abilities. It can manipulate symbols so as to transform them or to construct new symbols out of them. And its internal operations are controlled by symbols. It can store a program of symbolic instructions and then carry them out one by one. The symbolic instructions are binary numerals, and there is a small set of them that controls the machine's operations. These operations are a set of building blocks that as far as we know suffice to carry out all possible computations, regardless of their ultimate significance (to the people using the machine). All the computer ever does is to manipulate binary numerals, but fifty years of research has failed to find a process that cannot be modelled by these manipulations.

MENTAL SYMBOLS

A major tenet of cognitive science, as I remarked earlier, is that the mind is a symbolic system. It can construct symbols and it can manipulate them in various cognitive processes. It may relate the resulting symbols to something in the world, as when one verifies a description. But a symbol need not correspond to anything in the world. It may, for instance, be an image of a hypothetical state of affairs, such as a fine day in an English summer, or a model of an imaginary entity, such as a fabulous

34

beast. Perception, however, leads to the construction of mental symbols representing the world. The immediate link is a causal one from the world to an internal representation – a link that has evolved as a result of natural selection. The representation makes explicit the information that we need in order to navigate safely around the world: it provides the processes governing our actions with information about *what* is *where*. This information is not explicit in the patterns of light falling on our retinae, but, as I will describe in the next part of the book, it is recovered over several stages of visual processing.

Why should anyone suppose that the brain contains symbols? It is made up of nerve cells, and nerve cells produce impulses, which are electro-chemical changes that propagate relatively slowly down nerve fibres and that leap the junction (or 'synapse') between one nerve and another via other electrical or chemical processes. Mental phenomena depend on the brain, and they can best be explained in terms of symbols. The number of different symbols corresponding to images, beliefs, memories is potentially infinite, but the brain cannot contain an infinite number of pre-existing symbols – no more than a library can contain an infinite number of volumes. The vast diversity of mental symbols must be constructed out of finite means – out of primitive symbols. Nerve impulses and the other electro-chemical events can therefore be treated as the underlying primitives – perhaps analogue in form – out of which the symbols are constructed. Here the computer and the power of numerical symbols provide the crucial idea. No matter how complicated the computer's performance, no matter what the domain, no matter how profound the results, all that a computer can do is to carry out a few sorts of basic operations on binary numerals. In consequence, computational processes should be able to model mental symbols and their manipulations.

Further reading

The idea of treating the mind as a symbol-manipulating device can be found in Craik (1943) and in the work of Turing (see

Hodges, 1983). Newell and Simon (1976) provide a recent formulation of the concept of a physical symbol system. Different types of symbolic representation are discussed by the philosopher Nelson Goodman (1968). Sutherland and Mackintosh (1971) discuss the ability of animals to learn to discriminate symbols.

CHAPTER 3

Computability and mental processes

Theories of the mind should not take so much for granted that their content is obscure. A useful constraint is to express them in a computable form, because the mathematics of computation was originally developed to show what could be computed starting from principles that are entirely transparent. The essence of computability is simple, as I will demonstrate by a series of examples. The first two concern the elementary arithmetical operation of addition. Then, I will show how to make computation more powerful, using two examples of robots that can take excursions into their respective universes. The robots also illustrate the relation between machines and grammars. Finally, I will consider the ultimate computational machine. The point of the exercise is to establish that computation relies on just a few intuitive building blocks, which are easily realized in physical devices such as computers. Readers who find the mathematics too austere can take this conclusion on trust and proceed to the next chapter.

INSTRUCTIONS AND PROGRAMS

You know at once the sum of any two digits, and so when you are asked: 'What's nine plus eight?', you can immediately reply: 'Seventeen.' In order to do the following sum:

$$139$$

$$+288$$

you exploit this knowledge, but you also have to carry digits from one column to the next. The digits in the rightmost column sum to 17, and so you must carry 1 forward to the next column to be included in its sum.

This procedure for addition is simple but effective. It consists in a finite number of instructions which, if properly followed, will yield the sum of any two natural numbers in a finite number of steps. You may wonder: why fuss about the finite nature of things? But, if a procedure requires you to know an infinite number of instructions or to carry out an infinite number of steps, then it is not going to be of any practical use. An effective procedure, like a recipe or a knitting pattern, must reach the desired goal in a finite number of steps, using only a finite amount of knowledge. I shall use the word 'program' to refer to an explicit description of an effective procedure of this sort. Mathematicians sometimes use the word 'algorithm'.

THE DESIGN OF A PROGRAM

Suppose that we want to devise a program that will carry out addition. The program will be simpler if it uses the binary numerals that I described in the previous chapter. It will then need only the rules for binary addition, which are straightforward: the sum of two 0s is 0, and the sum of 1 and 0 is 1. Since the number 2 is written as 10 (see the previous chapter), the sum of 1 plus 1 has to equal 0 with a carry of 1 to the next column to the left. Consider the sum 3 + 2 as carried out in binary arithmetic:

$$
\begin{array}{r}
1\ 1 \\
+1\ 0 \\
\hline
1\ 0\ 1
\end{array}
\qquad
\left(
\begin{array}{r}
3 \\
+2 \\
\hline
5
\end{array}
\right)
$$

We start with the rightmost column, and the result of adding 1 to 0 is obviously 1. The next column requires us to add 1 to 1, and here the result is 10, and so we must carry the 1 forward to the next column. This column contains no other digits so it sums to 1. The result is the binary numeral 101, which corresponds to 5.

The program has to cope with carrying a digit forward. One solution is to keep track of whether or not a carry has occurred, and to specify a separate set of instructions for addition with a carry. The program has the following instructions:

In the no-carry state:

$$0 + 0 = 0$$
$$0 + 1 = 1 \quad \text{stay in the no-carry state}$$
$$1 + 0 = 1$$
$$1 + 1 = 0 \quad \text{shift to the carry state}$$

If there are no more digits to be added, the machine halts.

When a carry occurs, the program enters into a carry state and uses an appropriately modified set of rules to include the carry:

$$0 + 0 = 1 \quad \text{shift back to the no-carry state}$$
$$0 + 1 = 0$$
$$1 + 0 = 0 \quad \text{stay in the carry state}$$
$$1 + 1 = 1$$

If there are no more digits to be added, the machine outputs 1, and halts.

There are many ways to build a machine that would carry out this program: it could be made out of cogs and levers like an old-fashioned mechanical calculator; it could be made out of a hydraulic system through which water flows; it could be made out of transistors etched into a silicon chip through which an electrical current flows. It could even be carried out by the brain. Each of these machines uses a different medium to represent binary symbols – the positions of cogs, the presence or absence of water, the level of the voltage and, perhaps, nerve impulses. But what matters is the program rather than the physical structure of the machine. Figure 3.1 summarizes its design: the two circles stand for the two states of the machine, and the arrows stand for instructions and show the shifts from one state to another. The program produces the result digit by digit as pairs of digits from the numerals to be added are fed in column by column.

From a computational standpoint, the machine is an instance of the simplest possible design: it has a finite number of primitive symbols, instructions and states of memory. Any such device is known as a 'finite-state' machine. There are many sorts, ranging from combination locks to knitting machines.

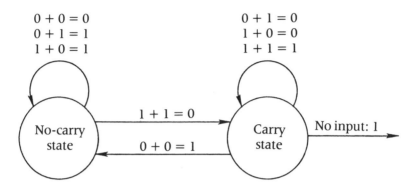

Figure 3.1: A finite-state machine for the addition of two binary numerals. The machine has two states represented by the circles: one state for where a carry has occurred, and one for where no carry has occurred. The arrows represent shifts from one state to the next, and the equations above the arrows are the instructions that are carried out: the left-hand side of each equation represents the input of the two digits to be added, and the right-hand side represents the machine's output. Thus, starting in the no-carry state, the result of 1 + 1 is 0 and a shift to the carry state.

HOW TO INCREASE COMPUTATIONAL POWER

Imagine a robot that can explore its world like a bacterium. It can move, however, only by taking a series of steps of a standard length, and at each point in an excursion it can step only North, South, East or West. Whenever it makes an excursion it must always return to its home. Figure 3.2 shows an example of an acceptable journey. How can we design a system of 'dead reckoning' by which the robot could navigate its way home, and find the shortest route there, solely from a record of the steps that it has taken? Because there is no limit to the length of an excursion, this problem calls for more computational power than is available to a finite-state machine.

The concept of computational power refers to what a computation can do rather than to its speed or efficiency. You might imagine that its secret lies in some new and potent types of

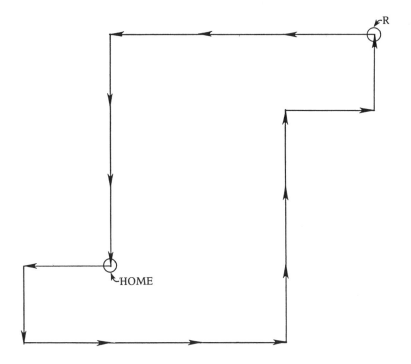

Figure 3.2: An excursion made by a robot that returns to its 'home'. Its
path from point R is amongst the set of minimal return
routes, i.e. it takes the fewest possible steps.

instruction. In fact, somewhat surprisingly, the crucial modification does not call for novel instructions, but for a better
memory. What is needed is an unlimited memory for the intermediate results obtained during computations. Memory is
power.

The simplest form of unlimited memory works like a stack of
plates. The only plate to which you can have direct access is the
one on the top of the stack, and the only place to put a new plate
is on the top of the stack. A stack of symbols provides a similar
form of memory with access to the item on top. If a program
needs to get to a symbol stored lower down in the stack, the items

41

above it have to be removed. But, once a symbol is removed from the stack, it is no longer in memory. It must then be used at once or it is forgotten.

To solve the robot's navigational problem, I will begin with a simpler device, one that can move only forwards or backwards along a single dimension. Obviously, if its excursions must always finish up at its home, they must contain the same number of steps in both directions. We need to equip the robot with a navigational program that acts like a counter, and we can do so by using a *stack* to keep a record of the journey. We will designate a step forwards by the symbol 'forward', and a step backwards by the symbol 'back'. These symbols can be represented in binary code.

The program starts with nothing in its stack, and, in general, when the robot takes a step, the program puts the symbol corresponding to that step on top of the stack. But there is an exception. A step in one direction is cancelled out by an immediate step in the opposite direction. Hence, whenever such a sequence occurs, the symbol at the top of the stack is removed, e.g. if the robot steps backwards and there is a 'forwards' on the top of the stack, the program removes it from the stack. It is erased because the two moves cancel each other out. There is then a simple way to determine whether the robot has returned home: it is there whenever its stack is empty.

We can see how the program works by following the state of the robot's stack as it makes a journey out into its universe and back again. It starts with an empty stack, takes a step forwards away from base, and so the program places the symbol 'forward' on the top of the stack:

$\longrightarrow$ 'forward'

It takes another step forwards, and so the program places another 'forward' on the stack:

$\longrightarrow$ 'forward'
'forward'

It now takes a step back towards home. This move cancels out the previous one, and the 'forward' on the top of the stack is removed:

42

'forward' ⟵

It takes a further step backwards, removing the symbol from the stack:

⟵

At this point, since the stack is empty, the robot is home.

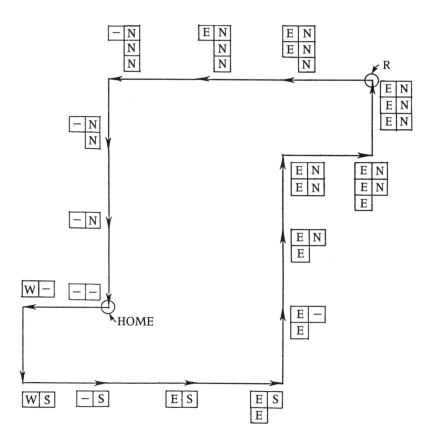

Figure 3.3: The contents of the stacks used by the navigational program as the robot makes an excursion. There is, in fact, no need for two stacks, since their contents can be combined in a single composite symbol that is stored in a single stack. From point R, the robot takes a shortest route home.

43

The navigational program for the robot that moves in two dimensions, North-South and East-West, should now be obvious. It uses two stacks: one records the steps Northwards and Southwards, and the other records those Eastwards and Westwards. At any point in a journey, the position of the robot with respect to home is directly represented by the contents of the two stacks. The shortest routes home are those that empty the stacks as quickly as possible: each step should be opposite to the symbol currently at the top of a stack. Figure 3.3 shows the contents of the robot's two navigational instruments (its stacks) as it takes the journey illustrated in the previous figure.

Strictly speaking, the program does not need two stacks. Their contents can be collapsed into a single composite symbol, because there is only a finite number of possible combinations, e.g. 'N E', '— E', 'E —'. A single stack holding such pairs is sufficient.

PROCEDURES THAT ARE NOT DETERMINISTIC

What determines the direction in which the robot moves on each step? There are no instructions in the navigational program that make such decisions. It merely evaluates whether a given journey is acceptable or not. The robot returns home by choosing any route that empties its stacks as quickly as possible. Such a program has a curious property. The program for addition is *deterministic*: at each step in its calculations, there is only one instruction that it can carry out, and the choice is entirely determined by the input and the current state of memory. Most programs are deterministic, but a program that allows the robot to choose among different routes is not deterministic. On the return part of the journey, there may be more than one alternative instruction that can be carried out: it can choose to take a step that empties one stack or the other (granted that they both contain symbols).

Occasionally, in daily life one comes across an apparently non-deterministic machine. My telephone, for example, recently developed an intermittent fault: it would suddenly start ringing for no apparent reason. In fact, it was not operating outside deterministic principles. There was a loose wire in the circuit.

44

Perhaps the only truly non-deterministic behaviours, if quantum theory is correct, are those of fundamental particles. Machines (including computers) are intended to follow their working principles deterministically. If we want them to simulate apparently random behaviour, such as a robot (or bacterium) moving haphazardly through its universe, we can borrow a procedure from the casino in Monte Carlo and use an event that is determinate but not predictable. However, it is often convenient to ignore how a decision is made. The result will be a specification that is not deterministic. This tactic is useful in the analysis of creative processes (see Chapter 14).

GRAMMARS AND PROGRAMS

A complex symbol can be assembled out of primitive symbols according to rules that govern acceptable combinations. Thus, there are rules for Roman numerals that specify the acceptable sequences of their primitive symbols. A grammar is a set of rules for a domain of symbols (or language) that characterizes all the properly formed constructions, and provides a description of their structure. Grammars so defined, as first suggested by the linguist Noam Chomsky, are intimately related to programs. The nature of the relation can be illustrated by returning to the robot that moves in one dimension. Any of its journeys can be represented by a string of symbols, e.g.:

Forward Forward Back Forward Forward Back Back Back

and we can construct a grammar that specifies all the acceptable journeys, which end with the robot at home.

There are two acceptable minimal journeys, a step forwards followed by a step backwards, or *vice versa*. Hence, the first two rules in the grammar are obvious:

1. JOURNEY = Forward Back

2. JOURNEY = Back Forward

where 'JOURNEY' denotes an acceptable journey, and '=' means that the symbol on its left has the analysis on its right.

Now we run into a major difficulty. There are no bounds on

the number of steps in a journey. Given any acceptable journey, no matter how long, we can always preface it with a step forwards and end it with a corresponding step backwards, and the result will still be acceptable. Similarly, we can preface any acceptable journey with a step backwards and end it with a corresponding step forwards, and the result will also be an acceptable journey. The problem is to capture these possibilities in the grammar. Logicians working on the theory of computation came up with an ingenious idea: we state rules that capture these two possibilities directly. Thus:

3. JOURNEY = Forward JOURNEY Back

4. JOURNEY = Back JOURNEY Forward

Rule 3 says that if you add a forward step in front of any acceptable journey and a backward step at its end, the result is still an acceptable journey. Rule 4 allows the converse additions. These rules are circular, because the symbol, 'JOURNEY', occurs on both sides of the equality sign. But this circularity, which is known as 'recursion', though subtle, is not vicious. It will become clearer if we use the grammar to analyse a journey.

Consider the journey represented by the string of symbols:

Forward Forward Back Back

Rule 3 tells us that a journey is acceptable if it can be analysed as:

Forward JOURNEY Back

Thus, rule 3 provides an analysis that can be illustrated using a diagram like an inverted tree:

The symbol at the top of the diagram, 'JOURNEY', corresponds to the symbol on the left side of Rule 3, and the three symbols at the bottom of the diagram correspond to those on the right-hand side of the rule. Of course, this analysis is incomplete. We have to ensure that the 'JOURNEY' at the bottom of the diagram also

46

refers to an acceptable journey. In fact, it corresponds to the sequence 'Forward Back' in the original string, and Rule 1 specifies that they make up an acceptable journey. Hence, the analysis of the complete journey can be illustrated in a tree diagram:

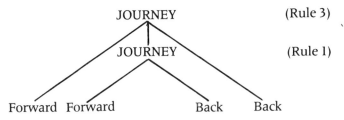

Instead of a tree diagram, we could equivalently bracket the symbols of the journey together and label the bracketings appropriately:

(Forward (Forward Back) $_{\text{JOURNEY}}$ Back) $_{\text{JOURNEY}}$

There is no limit on the number of times an acceptable journey may be embedded within another in this way.

One final rule is necessary:

5.   JOURNEY = JOURNEY JOURNEY

This rule states an obvious generalization: if two acceptable journeys are combined one after the other, the result is also an acceptable journey. If we combine three or more acceptable journeys, the result is still acceptable, but we do not need any further rules to capture this fact. Recursive rules, such as Rule 5, can be used again and again:

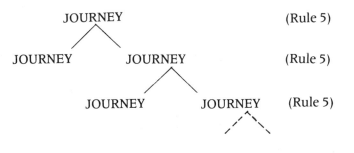

so as to analyse journeys made up of any number of constituent journeys.

There is a general relation between programs and grammars. The output of any program can be captured in a grammar. But a grammar by itself can *do* nothing: it is waiting to be used to produce symbols or to analyse them. Programs, however, *are* capable of doing things. They can use a grammar to produce strings of symbols or to produce a tree diagram analysing them according to the grammar.

Although a navigational program could be based on the grammar for journeys, there is no need to use it. The program that I described earlier makes no use of grammatical rules. This is an important point: there are always limitless ways of devising different programs to carry out the same computation. We can navigate with or without the grammar; we can add two numbers together using decimal or binary numerals. There are many ways to skin a rabbit; and there are many ways to design a program.

TURING MACHINES

As more powerful programs are introduced, so grammars of increasing power are needed in order to characterize their outputs. Conversely, as more powerful grammars are introduced to characterize languages, or domains of symbols, so programs of increasing power are needed to analyse their structures or to assemble them. Power, as I have already remarked, depends on memory for intermediate results. Finite-state machines have a memory for only a finite number of them, which they treat as states of the machine. They are not able to execute the navigational programs, because there is no bound on the length of a journey. With the addition of a single stack-like memory, however, the resulting machine is of a more powerful species: it can store unlimited intermediate results, and so find its way home. The obvious question is: how can memory be still further improved?

A natural step is to remove the constraint that memory operates like a stack, and to allow unlimited access to any amount of memory. There are several equivalent ways in which to conceive of such a memory. Alan Turing had perhaps the simplest idea. He imagined a machine that has a memory consisting of a tape divided into cells like a strip from a child's arithmetic notebook. The tape can move to and fro under a device that can read the contents of one cell, and, if need be, expunge the current symbol and replace it with another. If the machine gets to one end of the tape, then a further length can be added so that it never runs out of memory. Since a symbol is lost from memory only when it is expunged by the machine, this system escapes from the constraints of the stack. Two stacks, however, can simulate an infinitely extendable tape by shunting symbols between them.

Since the supply of tape is unlimited, one and the same tape can be used to feed into the machine any initial data, to store intermediate results, and to feed out any final result. The tape acts as a combined input, memory and output. Using separate tapes for these different purposes does not increase the power of a machine; nor indeed does using several tapes in parallel or using two-dimensional, three-dimensional, or multi-dimensional forms of representation. These modifications can affect *how* something is done – the sort of program that is used, and its speed and efficiency – but not *what* can be done.

When a finite-state machine is equipped with an unlimited tape, the result is the most powerful computational device: a Turing machine. It can carry out just four elementary operations: it can rewrite a 0 on its tape as a 1, it can rewrite a 1 on its tape as a 0, it can shift the tape one square to the left, or it can shift the tape one square to the right. It is controlled by a program of instructions, like those for a finite-state machine except that they can obviously call for intermediate results to be written on the tape. Each instruction specifies a condition and an action to be carried out if the condition is satisfied. The condition is determined by the symbol on the tape and the state of the machine, and the action is one of the four operations and a shift to the next state of the machine. Here are part of the instructions for a Turing machine that adds together two numbers represented in prisoner's tally (see Chapter 2):

Condition		Action	
Present state	Symbol scanned	Operation	Next state
1	1	Replace symbol by 0	1
1	0	Move tape left	2

In 1936 Turing conjectured that anything that can be computed at all can be computed by a program for a finite-state machine equipped with a single, one-dimensional tape, bearing binary code with one digit per cell. This conjecture cannot be proved, because the notion of computation is not a clear-cut one. Indeed, what Turing offered is an explicit analysis of a vague notion. He succeeded in taking the minimum possible for granted. As the subsequent development of digital computers shows, he took no more for granted than would have satisfied Lord Kelvin's demand for 'mechanical' explanations. Yet Turing's conjecture would be falsified if someone developed an alternative form of computation, which also takes a minimum for granted, but which yields results that cannot be obtained by a Turing machine. Many alternative conceptions of computability have been proposed, but so far they have all turned out to be equivalent in power to Turing machines.

A UNIVERSAL MACHINE

The program for a Turing machine is its set of instructions. Each instruction can in turn be symbolized as a binary numeral, using a standard code for the states of the machine and its four types of operation on the tape. (We observe again the potency of numerical symbols.) It follows, of course, that each Turing machine can be represented as a single, though very long, binary numeral constructed by placing the binary numerals of each of its instructions one after another. (Many authors are attracted by the analogy with the representation of genetic information in DNA.) Given this coding system, it is possible to construct a so-called 'universal' machine that can simulate the operations of any particular Turing machine. A universal machine reads data followed by the binary numeral encoding the instructions of a particular Turing machine. The instructions of the universal machine enable it to interpret the instructions encoded in the binary numeral, and to carry them out on the data. It is a universal machine because it can thereby simulate any Turing machine. It is the abstract ancestor of the modern digital computer.

Computers work in a very different way from Turing machines: their memories are not just one-dimensional tapes, and they have a much richer set of basic operations. But a computer program is analogous to a particular Turing machine, and the computer is analogous to a universal machine because it can execute any program that is written in an appropriate code. Anything that can be computed by a digital computer can be computed by a Turing machine.

Not everything, however, can be computed. There are many problems that can be stated but that have no computable solution. It is impossible, for example, to design a universal machine that determines whether any arbitrarily selected Turing machine, given some arbitrarily selected data, will come to halt or go on computing for ever. Hence, there is no test guaranteed to decide whether or not a problem has a computable solution.

SOME MORALS FOR COGNITIVE SCIENCE

Is the mind a computational phenomenon? No one knows. It may be; or it may depend on operations that cannot be captured by any sort of computer. If these operations are nevertheless effective procedures, they would demonstrate the falsity of Turing's conjecture about the nature of computation. *Theories* of the mind, however, should not be confused with the mind itself, any more than theories of the weather should be confused with rain or sunshine. And what is clear is that computability provides an appropriate conceptual apparatus for theories of the mind. This apparatus takes nothing for granted that is not obvious – any computation can always be reduced, if need be, to a finite set of instructions for shifting a tape and writing binary code on it. Yet, granted Turing's conjecture, any clear and explicit account of, say, how people recognize faces, reason deductively, create new ideas or control skilled actions can always be modelled by a computer program.

There are three morals to be drawn for cognitive science.

First, since there is an infinity of different programs for carrying out any computable task, observations of human performance can never eliminate all but the correct theory. There will always be some alternative theories that are equally plausible. Theories are vastly underdetermined by empirical data: they invariably go beyond what has been, and what can be, observed.

Second, if a theory of mental processes turns out to be equivalent in power to a universal machine, then it will be difficult to refute. As we shall see later, such a theory would be able to accommodate any pattern of observed responses.

Third, theories of the mind should be expressed in a form that can be modelled in a computer program. A theory may fail to satisfy this criterion for several reasons: it may be radically incomplete; it may rely on a process that is not computable; it may be inconsistent, incoherent, or, like a mystical doctrine, take so much for granted that it is understood only by its adherents. These flaws are not always obvious. Students of the mind do not always know that they do not know what they are talking about. The surest way to find out is to try to devise a computer program that models the theory. A working computer model places a minimal reliance on intuition: the theory it embodies may be false, but at least it is coherent, and does not assume too much. Computer programs model the interactions of fundamental particles, the mechanisms of molecular biology, and the economy of the country. The rest of the book is devoted to computable theories of the human mind.

Further reading

Turing's (1936) classic paper on computability is highly technical. The best and shortest introduction to the subject for the lay reader is by Trakhtenbrot (1963). The link between grammars and computation was established in a technical paper by Chomsky (1959). Turing (1950) in a very readable paper raised the question of whether a machine could think. The only way he could see to settle the issue was by way of an operational test: can a computer imitate the performance of a human being so well that one cannot tell the difference between them? Many of these issues are discussed in an entertaining book by Hofstadter (1979).

PART II

VISION

... the true heart of visual perception is the inference from the structure of an image about the structure of the real world outside. The theory of vision is exactly the theory of how to do this, and its central concern is with the physical constraints and assumptions that make this inference possible.

DAVID MARR

CHAPTER 4

The visual image

Consider three beliefs about vision. The first, which is often expressed, is that it is trivially easy. The eye is like a television camera. You point it at a particular scene, it registers that scene, and projects a picture of it inside your head.

The problem with this tale from 'folk psychology' is simple: who looks at the picture, and how do they see it? Clearly, the end result of perception cannot be a picture, because that in turn would have to be perceived, just as a picture hanging on a gallery wall makes no sense until it has been perceived. The explanatory problem has merely been thrust backwards a single step. In computational terms, this way of regarding vision is useless because it fails to deliver the right result.

The second belief is that vision is impossible. The eye is like a television camera. You point it at a particular scene, and it registers that scene. But many different arrangements of things can produce the same image, and so the brain is unable to work out which particular arrangement you are looking at.

This more sophisticated argument can be illustrated by an example. Suppose that the eye views a single thin bar that appears upright. In fact, the bar could be leaning towards the viewer or leaning away and yet project virtually the same image on the retina. Figure 4.1 illustrates three possibilities: each of the bars creates the same image since from top to bottom they all project the same visual angle. Although the figure contains only three possibilities, the eye would receive the same image from an infinite number of different bars provided that their lengths, thicknesses and positions combine to produce the appropriate visual angle.

A natural response to this sceptical argument is to say: I have two eyes, they receive slightly different images of the bar, and I can use this disparity to work out its true orientation. Similarly, if

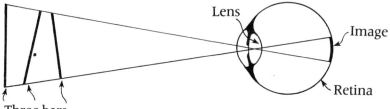

Three bars

Figure 4.1: Three different bars that project the same image on the retina.

I walk around, or move my head from side to side, I will see the bar from different viewpoints, and the resulting images will be consistent with only one particular orientation. To which the sceptic replies: very well, perception is impossible if you close one eye and stand motionless; and, by the way, you owe me explanations of how the brain does stereopsis, that is, how it recovers depth from the slight disparities between the two retinal images, and of how it combines images from different viewpoints.

The third and most helpful view is that vision is easy for the brain to do, but difficult for us to understand. You normally see things automatically and with no effort at all. This ease yields the subjective experience of direct contact with the world, which has an enormous evolutionary advantage. If you see a tiger, you avoid it. You do not stop to inspect the processes of vision to check whether they are working properly. What is advantageous to the species, however, creates a problem for cognitive science. It is hard to discover how vision works.

To solve any such problem, we must bear in mind a lesson from computation: we need at least three different levels of explanation. We need a theory of *what* is computed – what the input to the process is, what has to be recovered from it, and what constraints may guide the process. We need a theory of *how* the system carries out the computations, that is, a computable theory of the procedure that it uses. We need a theory of the underlying neurophysiology (the 'hardware' of the nerve cells in which the procedure is embodied). Investigations that are restricted to only one of these levels are unlikely to yield a correct explanation. A theory of vision that embraces them all has been framed by the late David Marr and his colleagues, particularly Keith Nishihara, Tomaso Poggio and Shimon Ullman. It is their account that I shall mainly follow, because they have modelled it in computer programs that will be useful for the robot's vision.

THE COMPUTATIONAL PROBLEM OF VISION

The hapless robot, which we left in the previous chapter wandering about its universe, finds its way home solely by 'dead reckoning'. Vision would enable it to see where it is going, but for that it will need eyes. The function of an eye is twofold. It must contain an array of light-sensitive elements – a retina – to convert the energy in quanta of light into an internal symbolic code. Light is reflected by surfaces in all directions, and so the eye must also ensure that the light from each point in a scene falls on to a single point of the retina, not on to all of them. A small pin-hole, or a lens, focuses the light in this way. That's the theory, but alas, the human eye, as Helmholtz remarked, is not a perfect instrument.

The illumination, arrangement of the surfaces in the scene, and the amount of light they reflect, cause a particular pattern of light to fall on to the retina. The cells in the retina convert this energy into nerve impulses. These nerve impulses depend on the physics of light and lenses and on the biochemistry of the nerve cells in the eye. Cognition is therefore not wholly a matter of computations that transform mental symbols: symbols can be created by physical interactions with the world. These inter-actions are hardly mysterious. Electronic cameras, which the robot will use, depend on sensors to convert the energy in light into electrical impulses, albeit in a much cruder way than the human eye. We shall not be concerned with these details, but with what happens afterwards.

For the robot, what is ultimately to be computed is a symbolic representation of the three-dimensional world that can guide its behaviour. As it moves its eyes over a scene, the representation will make *explicit* where the robot is in relation to the objects in the scene, and where they are in relation to one another. (The reader will recall from Chapter 2 that a symbol makes information explicit to a process if that information is available without further computation.) The representation will also make explicit shapes, colours, textures and illumination. If the robot moves through the world, then the representation will be kinematic, indicating that the robot is moving (and the scenery is not). The robot will be able to use the representation to navigate its way around objects without bumping into them or falling down holes. If the things in the scene are moving, then the robot will be able to use its representation to predict their future positions. If two things collide, then the representation will be dynamic: the robot will see that one thing *causes* another to move. If things are familiar to the robot, it will recognize them for what they are. It will even be able to identify objects that it has never seen before, such as a tree of an unfamiliar sort or a bookcase of an unconventional shape. In sum, the robot's vision, like that of a human being, will construct a *model* of the world from the patterns of light falling on its retinae.

CONSTRAINTS ON THE VISUAL PROCESS

Empiricists think of the mind as a blank slate, and of the information that makes vision possible as out there in the real world. Rationalists think of the mind as containing knowledge that it imposes on the world. The truth appears to be that both are right. There is information in the patterns of light that fall on the eyes, but visual processes also depend on assumptions about the nature of the physical world. Vision is rather like the problem of finding the value of x in the equation:

$$5 = x + y$$

The equation is plainly not well posed, since there is no way of determining how much of the 5 comes from x and how much from y. If, from prior knowledge, you can assume that y is likely to have a value less than 1, then you can infer that x is likely to have a value greater than 4. In vision, assumptions about the world make an ill-posed problem soluble.

The late J. J. Gibson emphasized that light reflected from surfaces and focused on the retinae contains a large amount of information. The proposition has been demonstrated by an analysis of the projective geometry of two images. Christopher Longuet-Higgins has shown, amongst a number of such proofs, that if just five points on the surface of an object can be matched from one photograph to another taken from a different angle, then the complete three-dimensional geometry of the situation can be established – the orientation of the surface with respect to the two cameras, and the relative positions of the cameras to each other. Berthold Horn and his colleagues have constructed analogous proofs about shapes: the shape of something can be recovered from the intensity values of its image provided that its surface is smooth, matte so that it reflects light in a uniform and diffuse way, and has a known orientation at certain points in the image.

No matter how much information is in the light falling on the retinae, there must be mental mechanisms for recovering the identities of things in a scene and those of their properties that vision makes explicit to consciousness. Without such mechanisms, retinal images would be no more use than the images produced by television cameras, and, contrary to the naive view, *they* cannot see anything. If the robot is to travel over a dangerous terrain, it needs to process the images produced by its cameras so as to recognize and to locate obstacles and pitfalls. These processes must rely on certain assumptions about the world.

Assumptions about the world can be acquired in two ways. They can be built into the nervous system as a result of millions of years of evolution, or they can be learned during a person's lifetime. Both sorts of assumption play a part in perception, but in different ways. In this chapter, I shall concentrate on the initial stages of vision that lead to the construction of a visual image; in the next chapter, I will describe the perception of depth. Both depend on general constraints that are inborn. In Chapter 6, I will turn to knowledge acquired in a lifetime and how it enters perception.

THE FIRST STAGE OF VISION: THE GREY-LEVEL ARRAY

The first stage of vision is the physical interaction between light focused on the retina and the visual pigment in retinal cells. The human retina is composed of over 100 million light-sensitive cells. A small proportion of them near the centre (about 6

Figure 4.2: A grey-level image: a point-by-point representation of the intensity values of a scene (576 × 454 pixels).

(From T. Poggio, Vision by man and machine. *Scientific American*, April 1984, p. 70)

million) are specialized to respond maximally to light from one of three wavelengths, and these three sorts of cells – the so-called 'cones' – are maximally sensitive to red, green and blue respectively. The full range of perceived colours is based purely on these inputs. The remaining cells in the retina – the so-called 'rods' – are less specialized, responding to light over a wide range of frequencies.

The responses of retinal cells and of an electronic camera comprise, in effect, a two-dimensional array of the intensity values at

Figure 4.3: The intensity values for the part of Figure 4.2 inside the rectangle on the right-hand side.

225	221	216	219	219	214	207	218	219	220	207	155	136	135	130	131	125
213	206	213	223	208	217	223	221	223	216	195	156	141	130	128	138	123
206	217	210	216	224	223	228	230	234	216	207	157	136	132	137	130	128
211	213	221	223	220	222	237	216	219	220	176	149	137	132	125	136	121
216	210	231	227	224	228	231	210	195	227	181	141	131	133	131	124	122
223	229	218	230	228	214	213	209	198	224	161	140	133	127	133	122	133
220	219	224	220	219	215	215	206	206	221	159	143	133	131	129	127	127
221	215	211	214	220	218	221	212	218	204	148	141	131	130	128	129	118
214	211	211	218	214	220	226	216	223	209	143	141	141	124	121	132	125
211	208	223	213	216	226	231	230	241	199	153	141	136	125	131	125	136
200	224	219	215	217	224	232	241	240	211	150	139	128	132	129	124	132
204	206	208	205	233	241	241	252	242	192	151	141	133	130	127	129	129
200	205	201	216	232	248	255	246	231	210	149	141	132	126	134	128	139
191	194	209	238	245	255	249	235	238	197	146	139	130	132	129	132	123
189	199	200	227	239	237	235	236	247	192	145	142	124	133	125	138	128
198	196	209	211	210	215	236	240	232	177	142	137	135	124	129	132	128
198	203	205	208	211	224	226	240	210	160	139	132	129	130	122	124	131
216	209	214	220	210	231	245	219	169	143	148	129	128	136	124	128	123
211	210	217	218	214	227	244	221	162	140	139	129	133	131	122	126	128
215	210	216	216	209	220	248	200	156	139	131	129	139	128	123	130	128
219	220	211	208	205	209	240	217	154	141	127	130	124	142	134	128	129
229	224	212	214	220	229	234	208	151	145	128	128	142	122	126	132	124
252	224	222	224	233	244	228	213	143	141	135	128	131	129	128	124	131
255	235	230	249	253	240	228	193	147	139	132	128	136	125	125	128	119
250	245	238	245	246	235	235	190	139	136	134	135	126	130	126	137	132
240	238	233	232	235	255	246	168	156	141	129	127	136	134	135	130	126
241	242	225	219	225	255	255	183	139	141	126	139	128	137	128	128	130
234	218	221	217	211	252	242	166	144	139	132	130	128	129	127	121	132
231	221	219	214	218	225	238	171	145	141	124	134	131	134	131	126	131
228	212	214	214	213	208	209	159	134	136	139	134	126	127	127	124	122
219	213	215	215	205	215	222	161	135	141	128	129	131	128	125	128	127

(From T. Poggio, Vision by man and machine. *Scientific American*, April 1984, p. 70)

each point on the light-sensitive surface. These values can be represented as numerals (the larger the numeral, the more intense the light). If we ignore colour, these numerals can be converted back into shades of grey and thus into a picture known as the 'grey-level image'. Figure 4.2 presents a grey-level image from an electronic camera, and Figure 4.3 presents the numerals corresponding to the intensities from a small area of this grey-level array. The human retina yields an array with vastly more elements (or 'pixels', which stands for 'picture elements').

The grey-level image is a long way from a representation of what is in a scene. All that it makes explicit is the intensity of light at each point in the array, relative to some arbitrary scale. The next stage of processing recovers more useful information.

THE SECOND STAGE OF VISION: LOCATING CHANGES IN INTENSITY

If you squint at the scene in front of you through half-closed eyes, you will see that it is made up of regions of different light intensity. There are bright patches and dull patches, depending on the direction of the light and on how much of it is reflected into your eyes. The intensity tends to change at the edges of objects, and such edges – as the effectiveness of line drawings demonstrates – are important cues to perception. Hence, the visual system must analyse the grey-level array to determine where the boundaries between regions of different intensity occur. However, many boundaries arise from changes in illumination and reflectance rather than from edges, and conversely some edges do not produce clear intensity boundaries. The visual system has to determine which boundaries correspond to the edges of objects.

The information in a grey-level array, such as Figure 4.3, contains a certain amount of 'noise' – random fluctuations occurring in the light itself and within the eye. A simple technique for reducing noise is to replace each value in the array by its local average, that is, the average of it and its neighbouring values. The idea can be illustrated on a small one-dimensional strip taken from a grey-level array (with deliberately simplified values), such as:

4   5   4   3   6   9   8   7   9

The strip corresponds to the following graph of intensities:

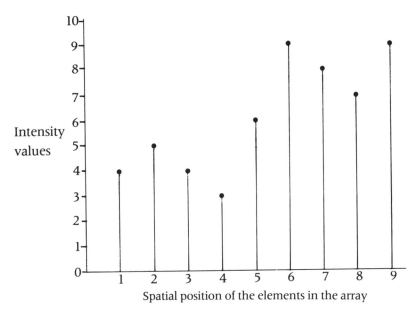

Spatial position of the elements in the array

A crude local averaging technique is to set each value equal to the average of it and one value either side of it. Thus, the value 3 near the middle of the array is set to its average with its adjacent neighbours: ⅓ (4 + 3 + 6), which rounding to the nearest integer equals 4; and the 4 at the left-hand end of the strip is set to the mean of 4 + 5, which with rounding equals 4. This procedure is a form of weighting in which we start at one end of the array and work along it from left to right, adjusting each value according to a mathematical operation, yielding a local average. The application of a mathematical operation to an array is known as 'convolution'. Convolving the averaging operation with the array above yields to the nearest integer:

4   4   4   4   6   8   8   8   8

corresponding to the following graph:

65

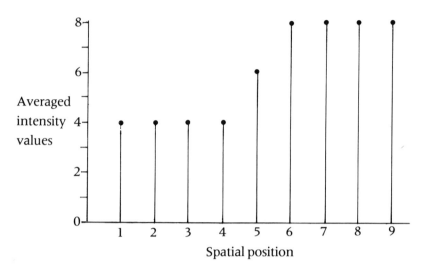

Smoothing away the local irregularities begins to reveal that there may be a boundary between two different levels of intensity, one region at a level of 4 and one at a level of 8.

A more sensible averaging function takes account of a wider range of neighbours but weights them so that the further away they are, the smaller their contribution to the average. There are many possible operations, but a useful one is based on the *normal distribution*, which often arises in connection with measurements. Figure 4.4 shows its bell-shaped curve.

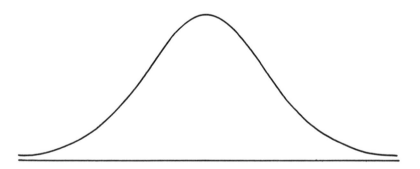

Figure 4.4: The bell-shaped curve of the normal distribution.

Given that the values in the grey-level array are smoothed out by local averaging, how are the intensity boundaries to be detected? The boundary between a bright region and a dull region corresponds to a relatively abrupt shift from values of one size to those of another size. A strip from the relevant part of the array will have values like those in the previous graph. If you were to walk along a surface supported by the bars in that graph, it would be flat at both ends but have a steep gradient in between:

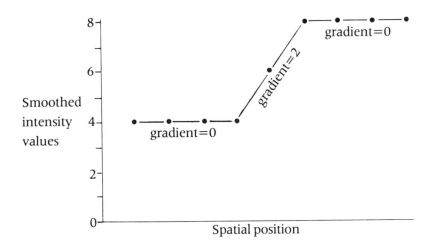

A simple way to measure the steepness of the gradient between any two adjacent values is to multiply the one on the left by −1 and the one on the right by +1, and to sum the results. Two adjacent intensity values near the middle of the graph are 4 and 6, and so the gradient between them is: $(4 \times -1) + (6 \times +1) = 2$. We can work along the array above applying this operation:

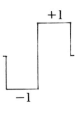

The resulting values of the gradient are as follows:

0   0   0   2   2   0   0   0

and we can plot them in a graph:

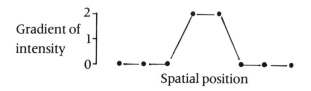

The boundary between the two regions of different intensity corresponds here to a local highpoint in the values of the gradient of intensity. The boundary also shows up in the *changes* in the gradient of intensity. At the left-hand end of the surface above, the gradient is constant, then its values go up (from 0 to 2), stay constant in the middle (from 2 to 2), and then go down (2 to 0). Finally, the slope is constant once again at the right-hand end of the array. Our operation above measures these changes in gradient, and it yields the values:

0   0   2   0 −2   0   0

which we can plot in a graph:

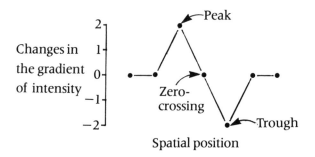

68

The point in the middle where the value is zero and the curve crosses from a peak of positive values to a trough of negative values is called a 'zero-crossing'. It and its adjacent peak and trough provide excellent evidence for the existence of a boundary between two regions of different intensities.

The operations of local averaging and finding changes in gradient have to be carried out in two dimensions, not just on a single one-dimensional strip. However, the two operations can be combined into one. This combined operation looks like a Mexican hat; Figure 4.5 shows a cross-section through it.

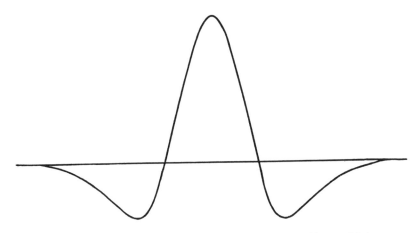

Figure 4.5: A cross-section through the 'Mexican hat' filter, which combines local averaging with the detection of changes in the intensity gradient.

Each value in the grey-level array is averaged with its neighbours weighted according to the Mexican hat. As the figure shows, the weights will be positive for near neighbours, decline to negative for more distant neighbours, and taper off to zero for points so distant that they need not be taken into account. When all the numbers in the grey-level array are filtered through the Mexican hat, the result is an array containing positive and negative values. The boundaries between these areas yield a map of the zero-crossings. Figure 4.6 shows a grey-level image and a map of the zero-crossings obtained from it.

Figure 4.6: (a) A grey-level image. (b) A map of zero-crossings: the intensity of the lines here varies with the contrast in intensity between the two regions on either side of the zero-crossing.

(a)

(b)

(From D. Marr, *Vision.* San Francisco: W. H. Freeman, 1982, p. 61)

VISUAL FILTERING

What size Mexican hat should be used in filtering the grey-level array? All sizes will detect sharp and clearly separated intensity changes. A large hat extending over many elements in the array will also reveal gradual changes in intensity over a large area,

Figure 4.7:
(a) A grey-level image (320 × 320 pixels).
(b) The zero-crossings obtained from it with a small filter (with an excitatory region of about 9 pixels in size).
(c) The zero-crossings obtained with a larger filter (with an excitatory region of about 18 pixels in size).

(From D. Marr, *Vision*. San Francisco: W.H. Freeman, 1982, pp. 58 and 72)

(a)

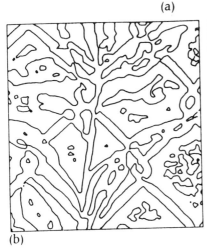

(b)

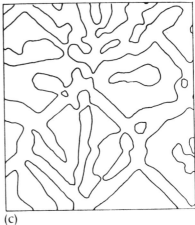

(c)

perhaps as a result of the illumination. A small hat extending over a few elements will reveal many small changes in detailed intensity. Since human beings are sensitive to a wide range of changes, we will design our robot to be similarly sensitive and to process the grey-level array with a series of different sizes of filter (i.e. Mexican hats). Figure 4.7 shows a picture (a grey-level image) and two maps of zero-crossings obtained from it, one using a small filter and the other using a filter of twice the size.

A NOTE ABOUT THE MATHEMATICS

Readers familiar with the differential calculus will recognize that calculating the gradient of intensity in the smoothed grey-level array corresponds to taking the first spatial derivative, and that calculating the changes in the gradient corresponds to taking the second spatial derivative. This second derivative can be carried out in two dimensions isotropically, i.e. giving equal weight to all paths extending away from a pixel, by the so-called Laplacian operator. The two-dimensional Gaussian normal distribution smooths the data, with importance decreasing with distance. The Mexican hat combines the two functions: it is this Laplacian of a Gaussian, which is convolved with the intensity array.

THE NEUROPHYSIOLOGY OF VISION

Trying to understand vision by studying only nerve cells, as Marr remarked, is like trying to understand bird flight by studying only feathers. One of the striking features of his account is that it fits together what the visual system does, how it does it, and which cells carry out the computations.

There are cells in the human retina (see Figure 4.8) which gather information from a set of retinal receptors lying in a roughly circular field. Some of these 'ganglion' cells are excited by light falling on the receptors in the centre of their field, and inhibited by light falling on those in the surround. Other ganglion cells have exactly the opposite characteristics: they are inhibited by light in the centre and excited by light in the surround. These two sorts of cells are just what are needed to carry out the

72

computations of the Mexican hat. The first sort calculate the positive values in the centre of the hat, and the second sort the negative values of the brim. Every nerve cell fires spontaneously from time to time. A cell normally registers significant information by departing from its spontaneous rate of firing, and cannot directly report both positive and negative values. They are therefore signalled by separate cells. Hence, zero-crossings correspond to locations where activity in the two sorts of ganglion cell is about equal.

The neurophysiologists David Hubel and Torsten Wiesel, who received the Nobel Prize for their work, discovered cells in the visual cortex at the back of the brain that are excited by bright lines or bars at particular orientations in the visual field. One erstwhile interpretation of these cells is that they detect edges, borders and other features of objects. A more plausible interpretation is suggested by Marr's theory: they detect zero-crossings. They are excited by a line of neighbouring retinal ganglia, which in turn are excited by a change in the gradient of intensity aligned with their fields of receptors.

THE THIRD STAGE IN VISION: THE PRIMAL SKETCH

The grey-level array is filtered through a set of different sized Mexican hats. The results can be interpreted taking into account a fact that evolution is likely to have 'wired into' the brain: one thing cannot be in two places at the same time, whether it is an edge of an object, a change in the reflectance of a surface, or a change in illumination. Hence, if any one of these phenomena creates a zero-crossing in a filtered image, there is likely to be a corresponding zero-crossing not too far away in images produced by filters of other sizes. However, thin bars and other details may yield two zero-crossings from a small filter that become blurred together by larger filters. Similarly, two different phenomena may produce intensity changes at the same place but on different scales. A comparison of the filtered images is therefore highly informative. In general, where they concur, a zero-crossing is a result of the same physical phenomenon.

What the visual system extracts from a comparison of the

Figure 4.8(a): A diagram of the eye.

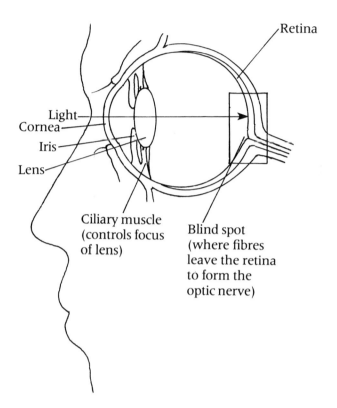

(A black and white version of Plate 9 from J. P. Frisby, *Seeing: Illusion, Brain and Mind.* Oxford: Oxford University Press, 1979)

filtered images is a matter of controversy. For Marr, as I have explained, the correspondences of zero-crossings are the critical data. But at curves and corners the zero-crossings from different sizes of filter do not lie in the same position in the array (see Figure 4.7). Moreover, as we shall see in the next chapter, human vision seems to be sensitive to the peaks and troughs adjacent to zero-crossings. Roger Watt and Michael Morgan have argued that some zero-crossings are the spurious results of noise,

Figure 4.8(b): A schematic detail from 4.8a showing the positions of the receptor cells and the retinal ganglion cells. The light passes through the nerves and ganglion cells before it strikes the receptors.

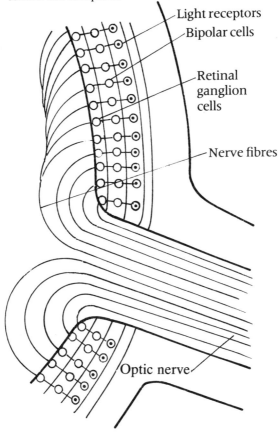

Light receptors

Bipolar cells

Retinal ganglion cells

Nerve fibres

Optic nerve

(A black and white version of Plate 9 from J. P. Frisby, *Seeing: Illusion, Brain and Mind.* Oxford: Oxford University Press, 1979)

and that it is better to rely on peaks and troughs. A program that they have devised keeps the positive and negative values of the filtering process separate, working out their averages from different sizes of filter. It locates the centres (and sizes) of the peaks in the positive averages and the centres (and sizes) of the troughs in the negative averages, which it then uses to construct a symbolic representation of bars, edges and regions of the same intensity.

Bars, edges and blobs are the basic elements out of which the visual image is constructed. They are the sorts of primitive that artists who etch pictures have at their disposal. Each has a specified position, orientation, length, width and contrast in intensity with its surrounding region. Marr makes this information explicit by using symbolic descriptions with appropriate numerical values, such as:

BLOB
(POSITION 146 21)
(ORIENTATION 105)
(CONTRAST 76)
(LENGTH 16)
(WIDTH 6)

They are attached to locations in the map summarizing the results of filtering the grey-level array. This particular description applies to the blob below the wire in the top left-hand corner of Figure 4.7(b).

Such information captures the local details in the visual image, and provides the raw data for what Marr called the 'primal sketch', which makes explicit the complete organization of the visual image – roughly, what you are aware of when you screw up your eyes and look at the world slightly out of focus. The primal sketch is constructed by grouping similar elements together to form lines, larger blobs and structured groups, and the process is progressively repeated on an ever larger scale. These principles, however, have yet to be implemented in a program. They are difficult to isolate because they organize visual images automatically with no conscious effort. Thus, Figure 4.9 seethes with potential groupings, and as soon as a potential organization arises it is succeeded by a rival candidate, particularly if you allow your eyes to wander from place to place. The primal sketch should reveal what is crucial to locating discontinuities in the physical surfaces of the things in the scene. Once again, the underlying principles are not well understood, but presumably depend on inbuilt assumptions about the world.

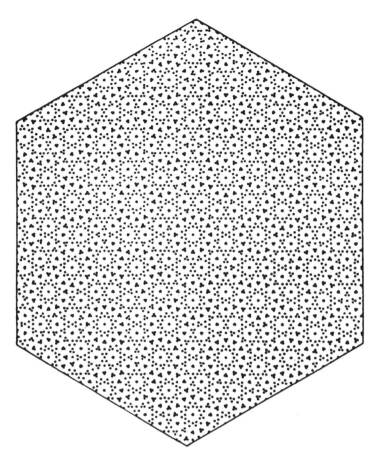

Figure 4.9: A figure with many potential organizations.

(From J. L. Marroquin, Human visual perception of structure. Master's thesis, Department of Electrical Engineering and Computer Science, MIT, 1976)

When you view things through half-closed eyes, you lose information. Paradoxically, this manoeuvre can help you to see something otherwise not apparent. The checkerboard picture in Figure 4.10, which was devised by Leon D. Harmon, reveals an identifiable person only if you blur its image by squinting at it from a distance. This procedure reduces the information about the sharp edges of the blocks, which otherwise interferes with the interpretation of the large-scale changes in intensity. They suffice for you to recognize Abraham Lincoln.

77

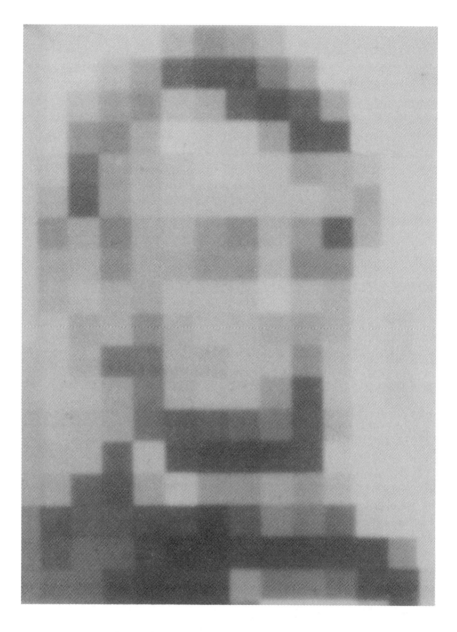

Figure 4.10: A checkerboard picture devised by Leon D. Harmon. It should be viewed at a distance through half-closed eyes.

(From L. D. Harmon, The recognition of faces. *Scientific American*, November 1973, p. 75)

THE COST OF EARLY VISUAL PROCESSING

Present-day technology can equip a robot with an eye containing about a million light-sensitive elements, though they take up a larger area than the much more densely packed human retina. Nature has mastered small-scale wiring in three dimensions and the parallel execution of myriad computations. Each cell in the nervous system has thousands of connections to other cells and carries out its own computations. Electronic components such as the micro-chip, however, are restricted to an essentially two-dimensional wiring of components, with far fewer interconnections than occur between nerve cells. Most digital computers carry out just a single sequence of computations, and parallel computers are a recent innovation. Hence, the major problem in equipping a robot with a program to construct the primal sketch is to ensure that it works fast enough. A computation that takes two seconds is no use if you are travelling at fifteen miles an hour. By the time you are aware of a large black patch in the image, you will be falling down the hole that caused it.

The major computational cost is the filtering of the grey-level array. Each pixel in the 1000×1000 array produced by an electronic camera has to have a mathematical operation applied to it that takes into account the values of its neighbours, and this process has to be repeated for all the different sizes of filter. Special electronic devices have been built to carry out this operation, but have yet to rival the efficiency of the nervous system.

A robot whose vision of the world was solely a primal sketch would be comparable to a common housefly. Despite its amazing aerial agility, the housefly probably does not form a three-dimensional model of the world. Its flight pattern, as Werner Reichardt and his colleagues at Tubingen have shown, is controlled by rapid and automatic mechanisms. One mechanism puts the fly into its landing routine if its visual field suddenly expands at a high speed. Wherever the looming surface is, the fly turns its feet towards the centre of expansion, and as soon as they touch the surface, the power to its wings is cut off. Another mechanism allows the fly to track its mate. This system is sensitive to a small black patch moving against a background. The relative power provided to the left and right wings is governed by the patch's position in the visual field and by its angular velocity, and the fly thereby keeps the target centred in its visual field and flies towards it. The real size of the target, however, is not critical. All that matters is its size in the visual image. Thus, the argument that vision is impossible, which I outlined at the start of the chapter, applies to the fly. It cannot tell the difference between a nearby mate and a distant passing bird if they each project an image of the same size on its eye. However, the mechanism controlling its flight path is innately tuned for small, nearby objects. If the fly attempts to intercept a distant bird, it will fail; the converse, alas, may not be true.

The fly's visual system is adapted to its world. It needs to home in on mates, to land on surfaces, and to take off rapidly if another looming surface hurtles towards it. If our robot is to inhabit a richer world, it will have to perceive it in three dimensions just as people do. It will have to treat the visual image – the information made explicit in the primal sketch – as a precursor to the recovery of information about the physical surfaces giving rise to it.

Further reading

Poggio (1984) is an excellent short introduction to Marr's work. Frisby (1979) has written an attractive book on vision, full of splendid illusions and embued with the computational approach. Mayhew and Frisby (1984) give a more technical account of computer vision. Watt (1988) is an advanced monograph on the initial stages of human vision.

CHAPTER 5

Seeing the world in depth

Hold one thumb a few inches away from your nose and your other thumb almost in line with it but at arm's length. Now look at your thumbs with one eye closed, and then with the other eye closed. You will notice that their apparent distance apart differs from one eye to the other. The effect arises, of course, because the eyes view the world from slightly different positions. The early stages of vision, which I described in the previous chapter, produce an image – a primal sketch – that is an organized representation of the major regions of different intensities. The views of your thumbs illustrate the disparity between the two images produced by your eyes. The visual system uses this disparity to work out how far from you things are. *Stereopsis* – the fusion of the disparate images so as to see the world in depth – is one of the main components of human vision, and in this chapter I am going to examine both it and other cues to depth.

THE COMPUTIONAL PROBLEM OF STEREOPSIS

Figure 5.1 is a diagram illustrating disparity. Whatever the point the eyes fixate, its image falls on the centre of each retina, where the density of receptors is at a maximum. Any other point visible to both eyes will also project on to both retinae, and, as the figure illustrates, the distance and direction of its projections from the centres of the two eyes are uniquely determined by its spatial position in relation to the fixation point. A nearby point, for example, projects on to the two retinae at slight distances from the centres, but the distances or directions differ from one eye to the other because of their differing viewpoints. Once the size and direction of the disparity is known, trigonometry suffices for the recovery of the relative depth of the point.

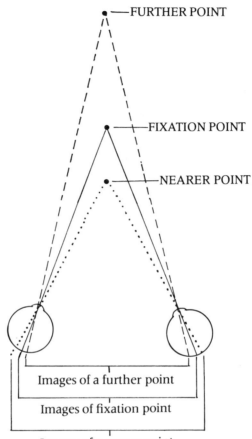

Figure 5.1: A diagram of the disparities between points projected on to the retina.

You might suppose that stereopsis is easy to explain, but it is *not* — for one very good reason. Before the disparities can be measured, the corresponding projections of each point in a scene must be matched from one visual image to the other. This step is puzzling: it is no use looking at the same place on the retina, precisely because of the disparities between the two images. One way to proceed might be to identify the objects in the scene and then to match their various parts in the two images. This method uses the structure of objects to guide the low-level task of matching points in images. It is an instance of what, in general terms, is known as 'top-down' processing. However, it is hard to imagine that objects could be identified *before* stereopsis had established the relative depths and orientations of their surfaces. Another procedure might be to match the intensity values in the pair of grey-level arrays. This method uses the lowest form of data, and it is an instance of what, in general terms, is known as 'bottom-up' processing. Unfortunately, there is no method that could work with intensity values, since the intensities of matching points may be quite different at the two eyes. If you put a sunglass lens over one eye, you still see the world in depth even though the lens reduces the intensity of the light entering one eye.

TOP-DOWN AND BOTTOM-UP PROCESSING

The question of top-down or bottom-up processing, or some combination of the two, arises whenever a program is used to assign structure to data according to certain principles. Programs can be designed to operate in either mode, or to alternate from one to another, or even to carry them out together in parallel. Working top down, a program uses the principles to predict the details to be found in the data, e.g. it uses the structure of objects to predict retinal disparities. Working bottom up, a program uses the principles to predict high-level structure, e.g. it uses retinal disparities to predict the structure of objects. If there is any uncertainty about how to proceed, both modes are predictive, but they predict different things.

Which mode is best? There is no general answer, and computational considerations alone cannot decide which mode has been adopted by a cognitive system. What we need is evidence, and there are two experimental tactics we can use. First, we try to find out whether the system can still cope if there is no possibility of exploiting high-level knowledge. If it can, the process can be carried out bottom up. Second, we try to find out whether the system can still cope if the input data are badly corrupted. If it can, the process is not entirely driven by data, and it can exploit high-level knowledge to work top down. We will encounter examples of both tactics in due course, but the first one proved decisive in the study of stereopsis.

RANDOM-DOT STEREOGRAMS

The stereoscope is a Victorian invention that allows two pictures of a scene (taken from slightly different viewpoints) to be presented separately to the two eyes. The visual system fuses the two images so that the viewer sees a single scene in vivid depth. You can construct a simple stereoscope by taping two small rectangular mirrors together, and then viewing the pictures on the following pages in the arrangement shown in Figure 5.2. Take care to ensure that the left eye sees the left-hand picture and the right eye sees the right-hand picture, and that the two images can be fused. If you view Figures 5.3 (a) and (b), they should spring sharply into relief. You should also try turning the book upside down, and the depth effect should reverse. For some people, depth takes a minute or two to appear; and for others – about 10 per cent of the population, who suffer from slight squints, 'lazy eye' and other minor defects – it may never appear at all.

A key discovery about stereopsis was made by Bela Julesz. He found that pictures composed of random dots could produce depth effects when they were viewed in a stereoscope. The pictures themselves are constructed by a computer program that introduced appropriate disparities. If you view Figures 5.4 (a) and (b), then you should eventually see a central square displaced in depth.

The implication of Julesz's discovery is, of course, that stereopsis can work bottom up from simple disparities alone and in the absence of the visible structure of objects. You cannot see the square within Figures 5.4 unless stereopsis occurs, because the random dots do not otherwise produce any cues to it. Conversely, explicit high-level knowledge does not help stereopsis. John Frisby and John Clatworthy found that telling people what they should see, or even presenting them with a three-dimensional model, did not speed up the perception of depth

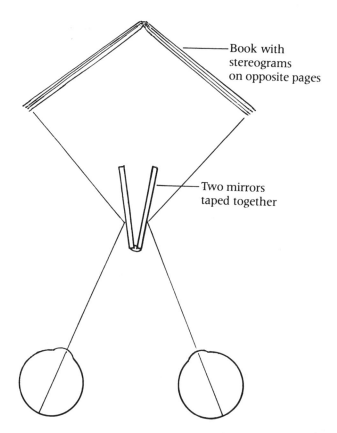

Book with
stereograms
on opposite pages

Two mirrors
taped together

Figure 5.2: A diagram of a home-made stereoscope for viewing the
stereograms in this book: the left eye (at the bottom of the
diagram) views the left-hand picture and the right eye views
the right-hand picture.

from random-dot stereograms. Stereopsis may be largely independent of other visual processes. It may be a separate module of
the visual system.

Left eye's view

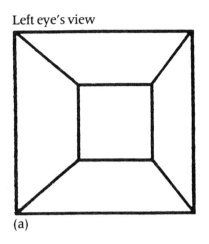

(a)

Figure 5.3: A pair of geometric figures to be viewed stereoscopically.

TWO CONSTRAINTS ON STEREO-MATCHING: UNIQUENESS AND CONTINUITY

There are two facts about the world that, as Marr emphasized, could be wired into the brain so as to guide the matching process in stereopsis. First, a constraint that we encountered earlier: one thing cannot be in two places at the same time. It follows from this *uniqueness* constraint that a point in one image can normally

(a)

Figure 5.4: A pair of random-dot stereograms.

86

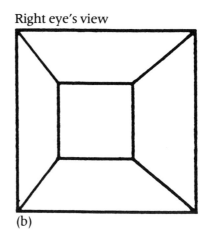

(b)

be matched with one and only one point in the other image. Second, the surfaces of objects are usually opaque and relatively smooth, and so their depth from an observer varies continuously rather than leaping from one extreme to another. It follows from this *continuity* constraint that adjacent points in an image will tend to represent points in the scene at about the same depth from the eye.

(b)

87

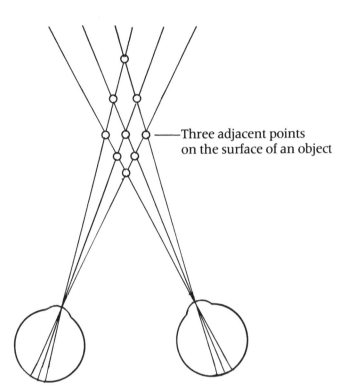

Three adjacent points on the surface of an object

Figure 5.5: Three lines of sight from each eye yield nine possible points of fusion.

To illustrate the two constraints, imagine that an observer is looking at an object, and consider three adjacent points on its surface. There are three lines of sight from each eye corresponding to the three points, as is shown in Figure 5.5. The lines of sight have nine potential points of fusion. The matching problem is to determine which of them are genuine matches representing actual points on the object's surface. The uniqueness constraint implies that no more than one point is along each line of sight. Hence, there can be only three genuine matches, and only one match for each line of sight. The hypothetical match illustrated in Figure 5.6 (a) is feasible, but the hypothetical match illustrated in Figure 5.6 (b) is ruled out by this constraint. The continuity constraint, which reflects the fact that

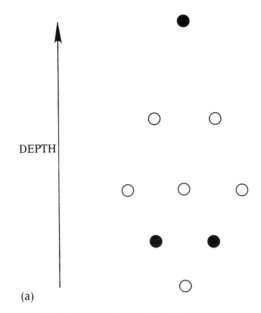

(a)

Figure 5.6: (a) A possible fusion indicated by the three solid dots on the lines of sight in the previous figure. (b) A fusion violating the uniqueness constraint.

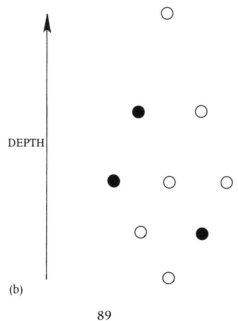

(b)

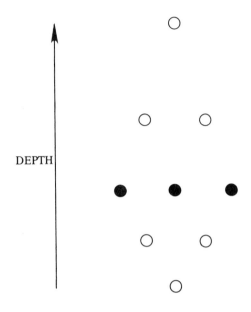

Figure 5.7: The only fusion of the lines of sight in Figure 5.5 that is consistent with both the uniqueness and continuity constraints.

the surfaces of objects vary smoothly, rules out the interpretation in Figure 5.6 (a). The only interpretation consistent with both constraints is shown in Figure 5.7. The three adjacent points lie on the surface of an object at about the same depth from the observer.

The possible points of fusion illustrated in Figure 5.5 can be represented by a mental array of processors – one for each possible fusion. If each processor is either active or inactive, with the degree of its activity representing the likelihood of a fusion, then the constraints can be implemented by wiring up the processors appropriately. The uniqueness constraint requires inhibitory links between those processors in the same line of sight so that whenever one indicates a possible fusion it inhibits the others. This scheme is shown in Figure 5.8. The continuity constraint is

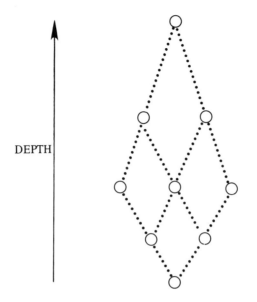

DEPTH

Figure 5.8: In an array representing all possible points of fusion of lines of sight from the two eyes, the uniqueness constraint can be implemented by inhibitory links down each line of sight. Each link in the figure is inhibitory, and so if one fusion point is active it inhibits all those to which it is connected.

wired up in an analogous way: whenever a processor indicates a possible fusion, it excites all the other processors representing the same depth from the observer. This scheme is illustrated in Figure 5.9. These diagrams show only a single horizontal set of points from a scene. A complete system would require processors for every horizontal level (or for every horizontal row in random-dot arrays).

A PROGRAM FOR RANDOM-DOT STEREOGRAMS

Marr and Poggio devised a computer program for stereopsis that relies on the uniqueness and continuity constraints. It works directly on elements representing random dots. The problem, accordingly, is to find a way of matching a dot in one array with its

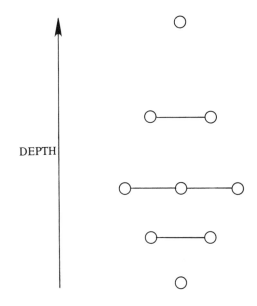

Figure 5.9: In an array representing all possible points of fusion of lines of sight from the two eyes, the continuity constraint can be implemented by excitatory links between fusion points at the same depth from the eyes. Each link in the figure is excitatory, and so if one fusion point is active it excites all those to which it is connected.

mate in the other array even though the two may be in slightly different horizontal positions in their respective arrays. (The disparities producing the perception of depth create such differences.) Thus, a fragment from a row in the left-hand array might consist in the sequence:

whereas the same fragment from the right-hand array might be:

The program requires a large number of computations, but in theory they can be carried out at the same time in parallel. The idea is to use a vast array of processors, each of which does the same computation on the particular values local to it, that is, its own value and those of its neighbours. The output from each processor is then used in a fresh cycle of activity, and the whole system continues to compute until it settles down to stable values at each processor. This form of computation is known as 'relaxation': the system gradually relaxes into a stable configuration of values. Spreadsheet programs for microcomputers, which allow one to make financial computations, can be used in the same way.

The relaxation program for stereograms takes as its initial input the rows from the pair of stereograms, and an array of processors works out the set of possible fusions. The array is three-dimensional, and each two-dimensional slice from it corresponds to one horizontal row from the two stereograms. It represents, as Figure 5.10 shows, all the different depths of possible fusions of the dots in the two rows. Each processor in the array is a finite-state device (see Chapter 3) with some resemblance to a nerve cell. It is either active or inert. If it is active, then it currently represents a point of fusion between the two dots that are inputs at the edge of the array. If it is inert, then it currently represents a point that is *not* a fusion. The uniqueness and continuity constraints are implemented directly. Processors receive excitation from their neighbours in the same depth plane including those in other horizontal slices (according to the continuity constraint). They receive inhibition from processors in the same line of sight (according to the uniqueness constraint). The processors have a threshold, and are active only if the combination of excitation and inhibition exceeds their threshold value. After the stereograms have been fed into the array, it goes through a series of cycles, which continue until it settles down into a stable configuration. This configuration represents the appropriate matches of the two stereograms, making explicit the relative depth of each dot in the stereogram.

A graphic sequence of cycles that gradually reveals the depth interpretation of two stereograms is presented in Figure 5.11. The planes in this figure correspond to different depths and they are therefore at right angles to the slice from the stereograms illustrated in the previous figure.

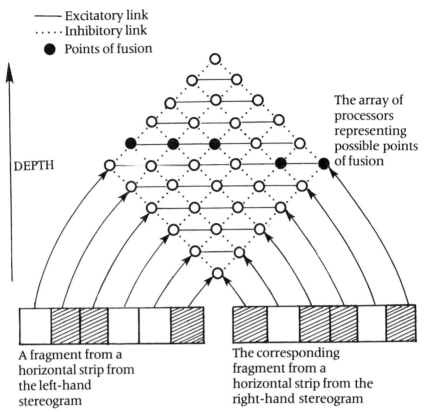

— Excitatory link
····· Inhibitory link
● Points of fusion

DEPTH

The array of processors representing possible points of fusion

A fragment from a horizontal strip from the left-hand stereogram

The corresponding fragment from a horizontal strip from the right-hand stereogram

Figure 5.10: An array of processors for computing the points of fusion from horizontal strips from two stereograms.

In theory, the program enables a large amount of computation to be carried out in parallel, because each processor needs information only about the outputs from its neighbours. Even so, the process requires a number of cycles, and given that actual nerve cells are rather slow (say, 1/100th of a second for each cycle), it may take too long for mammalian vision.

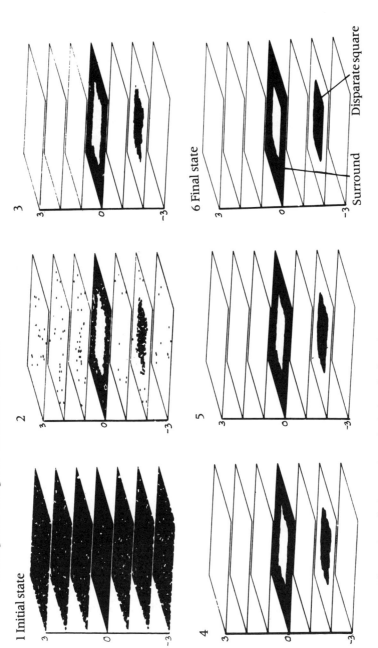

Figure 5.11: The sequence of cycles of a three-dimensional array of processors working out the depths in random-dot stereograms using the 'relaxation' method.

(From J. P. Frisby, *Seeing: Illusion, Brain and Mind.* Oxford: Oxford University Press, 1979, p. 151)

REAL STEREOPSIS

The random-dot program illustrates an interesting computational principle and a way to implement the constraints on matching. To develop a psychologically plausible procedure, however, we need to discover the input to human stereopsis. They are low-level data of some sort, but what elements are actually matched? The intensities in the grey-level array are affected by variations in illumination, and so do not correspond directly to physical features of surfaces. Yet it is surfaces to which the continuity constraint applies. Hence, the elements to be matched must be something closer to the representation of surfaces. Marr and his colleagues conjectured that zero-crossings are the obvious candidate, and they devised a program that matches zero-crossings, which are given a positive or negative sign depending on whether they mark a boundary that shifts from a dark to a bright region (moving from left to right) or from a bright to a dark region.

The program initially matches zero-crossings (of the same sign) obtained from filtering the grey-level array through a large-sized Mexican hat. It proceeds point by point along the zero-crossings, but it is quite tolerant about their positions. The reason for starting with a large filter is that it yields a coarse image in which zero-crossings are relatively rare. The probability of making a false match is much smaller if one searches only within a region of about the width of the central peak of the Mexican hat. If a zero-crossing in one image has two possible matches in the other, then within this search area one match will correspond to a point closer to the observer than the fixation point, and the other will correspond to a point further away. The ambiguity can be resolved by making a match of the same sort as the nearest one that has already been made. This tactic implements the continuity constraint: if one part of a surface is at a particular depth from the observer, then a nearby part of the same surface should be at roughly the same depth. The matching procedure leads to an initial registration of the coarsely filtered images. It can then be repeated on zero-crossings obtained from a smaller sized Mexican hat; and finally a matching of the images from the smallest size filter can be used to calculate the precise size of the disparities from which the relative depths are computed.

The program is psychologically more plausible than the relaxation method for random dots. It is suitable for robot vision, and Eric Grimson has extended it to deal with aerial stereophotographs so as to produce an explicit representation of the relative distances of the surfaces they depict. (Depth can be excellent at unmasking camouflage.) Yet, it is uncertain whether human stereopsis uses the same procedure. Obviously, the human system is responsive to disparities; and the neurophysiologist Colin Blakemore has reported the existence of columns of cells in the mammalian visual cortex in which each cell in a column responds to a different disparity in the same line of sight (cf. Figure 5.1). But quite what the disparities are between remains a mystery. The problem is that Marr's candidate – zero-crossings – does not seem to be the answer. John Mayhew and John Frisby have demonstrated that there are cases where the nearby peaks in the change of gradient, rather than the zero-crossings themselves, are used for stereopsis. Richard Gregory and his colleagues have likewise found that the edges of objects (zero-crossings *par excellence*) do not always correspond to the elements that are matched in stereopsis. And, if Roger Watt and Michael Morgan are right in their analysis, which I outlined in the previous chapter, then zero-crossings do not play a major role in seeing the world in depth. The only safe conclusions are that stereopsis can be carried out on low-level elements in the primal sketch, and that the matching procedure must be guided by innate constraints deriving from the nature of the physical world. Once the elements have been matched, the rest of stereopsis is largely trigonometry.

OTHER CUES TO DEPTH

James J. Gibson argued for many years that gradients in texture, such as the ones illustrated in Figure 5.12, are a major source of information about the depth and orientation of surfaces. A texture gradient is created by the presence of objects or marks of roughly the same shape and size lying at regular intervals on a surface. The gradient indicates the orientation of the surface, both the degree and direction of its slant in relation to the viewer. The connection between depth and surface orientation is obvious: given the depth of each part of a surface from an observer, then its orientation is determined too. The visual system may therefore respond directly to information in texture gradients. It could calculate the tilt of a surface, for example, by setting the axis of the tilt perpendicular to the direction in which the density of the elements varies most. Although there are computer programs that use such methods, little is known of how the human visual system interprets texture gradient.

Figure 5.12: Two examples of texture gradients.

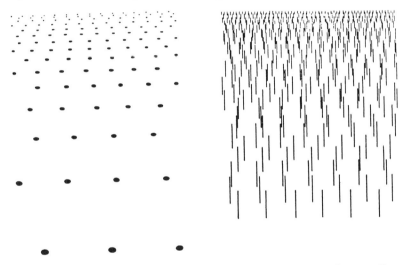

(From J.J. Gibson, *The Perception of the Visual World.* Boston: Houghton Mifflin, 1950; pp. 84, 86. Copyright © 1950 by James J. Gibson, renewed 1977 by Houghton Mifflin Company.)

There are other potential cues to depth. Some are more informative about distance than shape or orientation. Thus, distant objects are hazier, bluer and usually higher in the visual field; and parallel edges, such as railwaylines or the sides of buildings, converge with distance. But other cues do reveal the shape of objects. Thus, the motion of an object, or of an observer, affords more than one view of the object, which can help to determine its three-dimensional shape. The visible boundaries of an object against its background – its external contour – are similarly a major cue to its shape. I will examine these cues in more detail.

MOTION AND THE THREE-DIMENSIONAL STRUCTURE OF OBJECTS

The motion of objects can reveal their shapes. Shimon Ullman has an ingenious demonstration of this point: a set of dots is projected on to a screen. When the dots are stationary, an observer sees merely a screenful of randomly distributed dots. When they move, however, the display springs to life, and the observer sees two cylinders rotating in opposite directions. The effect occurs even if the axis of rotation changes abruptly from moment to moment. In fact, there are no cylinders: the display is manufactured by a computer program, which projects nothing but an animated sequence of pictures of dots (see Figure 5.13). It is their movements that create the shapes of cylinders.

The problem of recovering the shape of an object from its movement resembles stereopsis. The visual system has to match the corresponding points on the object in two images separated by a moment in time, and then use the amount each point has moved to determine the depths of the corresponding parts of the object (and their direction of movement). As in stereopsis, the matches should be unique because of the temporal version of the uniqueness constraint: one thing can only move to one place at a time. Of course, things appear and disappear, just as in stereopsis, they may be visible or invisible to one eye. Yet there is an important difference between stereopsis and the perception of motion. At any moment in time, the two eyes view the same shape; but the shape of an object can change continuously in time, as, for example, when you clench and unclench your fist.

Ullman has formulated a computational theory of how the matches between moving images could be established, but, as with stereopsis, there are some unsolved problems. The input to

Figure 5.13: Ullman's rotating cylinders of random dots (only the dots are projected on the screen).

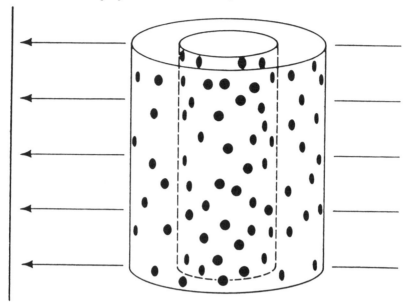

(From S. Ullman, *The Interpretation of Visual Motion.* Cambridge, Mass.: MIT Press, 1979)

the system cannot be the grey-level array, but quite what it is remains an open question. Marr hints again that perhaps zero-crossings are used, but there are difficulties with this idea.

When the matches from one image to the next have been established, the next step is to interpret them. This process calls for constraints on the possible interpretations. One constraint is that objects tend to be relatively rigid or to be made up from relatively rigid parts. The importance of rigidity has been demonstrated by the Swedish psychologist, Gunnar Johansson. He found that in a pitch-dark room tiny lights fixed only to the major joints of a person are sufficient to enable observers to perceive someone walking even though nothing is visible except for the trajectories of the tiny lights. When the lights are placed in the middle of the limbs, however, it is no longer possible to make sense of their movements. Evidently, the visual system assumes that adjacent lights are connected by rigid entities, and when they are not – as in the second case, it cannot perceive a human figure from their motions.

Ullman has shown that the assumption of rigidity also suffices for inferring the structure of moving objects from images of them separated in time. Given that one can match four points on a rigid object over three successive views, then their static three-dimensional configuration can be reconstructed. The four points must not be in the same plane, and because they are assumed to be projected on to the visual image in parallel rather than in perspective, there is an ambiguity over which are the closer points, and which the more distant ones. Although certain configurations require less information, only three views of four points guarantee a solution.

Ullman's proof does not apply to points lying in the same plane, and just this arrangement arises in the case of 'optical flow'

Figure 5.14: The optical flow field for a pilot approaching an aerodrome.

(From J.J. Gibson, *The Perception of the Visual World.* Boston: Houghton Mifflin, 1950. Copyright © 1950 by James J. Gibson, renewed 1977 by Houghton Mifflin Company.)

when an observer is moving in relation to a large surface, e.g. the situation that confronts a pilot landing an aeroplane, as shown in Figure 5.14. The mathematics of optical flow has been definitively established by Christopher Longuet-Higgins. In principle, the orientation of a rigid surface, and the motion of the eye in relation to it, can be determined from the instantaneous velocities of the changing image on a single eye. The computation checks the rigidity assumption on which it is based. As yet there is no evidence on whether such computations occur in human vision.

CONTOUR AND SHAPE

I hold my hand between a light and a wall, manipulate it appropriately, and what you see on the wall is the shadow of a rabbit. The phenomenon raises again the argument about the impossibility of vision: there are an infinite number of different three-dimensional shapes that can give rise to the same two-dimensional shadow. How is it, then, that you see a rabbit?

The same question arises not just with shadows, but with silhouettes and the visible contours of objects against their backgrounds (where there is a major discontinuity in the depth of surfaces from the viewer). Once again, the issue is whether vision relies on a knowledge of such things as rabbits or uses low-level assumptions to work bottom up from the visual data.

Marr argued that there are low-level inborn constraints on the interpretation of shadows, silhouettes and the contours of objects. The visual system assumes that each point in the image of a contour can be mapped one-to-one on to the actual contour of the object giving rise to it, that adjacent points in the image of the contour arise from adjacent points on the object, and that these points on the object lie in a single plane. In other words, when you look at the silhouette of your hand, each line of sight grazes it at just one point on its surface, and these points make up a continuous external contour running round the object in the same plane.

Of course there are exceptions to these principles. Two separate parts of an object may create exactly the same visible contour from a particular point of view. If you look at your hand edge-on with your fingers closed, then several fingers may yield a coinciding silhouette at various parts. Likewise, if you turn your hand away slightly, then adjacent points of its silhouette may belong to two quite different fingers, one behind the other. And, of course, its silhouette will not consist of points that all lie in the same plane. In general, when such violations occur, it is impossible to see the true three-dimensional shape of an object from its silhouette unless it *is* as familiar as the back of your hand. Where the assumptions do hold, however, then the visual system can usually perceive the true shape of an object.

THE TWO-AND-A-HALF-DIMENSIONAL SKETCH

Whenever the mind accomplishes a seemingly impossible task, it must have independent information about the world. Vision appears to be impossible, but evolution has equipped the visual system with inborn constraints that enable it to cope. Uniqueness, continuity of surface, rigidity and the constraints on contours all play a role in recovering the depth and orientation of surfaces from the primal sketch. There are other cues that are biologically important, e.g. the brightness and hue of a surface, and its shading and surface contours. They too probably rely on such built-in constraints, which operate automatically and unconsciously, and are relatively unaffected by a knowledge of objects. They are part of what one might call *pure* perception: the set of visual modules that operate in bottom-up mode to transform the grey-level array into the primal sketch, and that then carry out stereopsis, interpret motion, recover shape from contour, and perform all the other processes underlying the perception of surfaces.

The cornerstone of Marr's theory of vision is that the last stage of pure perception delivers an explicit representation of the relative depths and orientations (with respect to the observer) of each visible surface in a scene. He calls this representation the 'two-and-a-half-dimensional sketch' (or 2½ D sketch). The expression should not be taken literally: it merely designates a representation that does not make explicit the full three-dimensional relations among objects, since the depths are relative to the observer. The representation is sometimes depicted in a diagram that looks like a pin-cushion in which each pin represents the depth and orientation of a region of a surface (see Figure 5.15). The sources of the two-and-a-half-dimensional sketch are stereopsis, motion, contour and all the other depth cues that I have discussed in this chapter. It is supposed to integrate the information that they yield, establishing consistency and filling in missing parts of surfaces. Whether, in fact, the human visual system constructs such a representation is not known.

Figure 5.15: An illustration of the two-and-a-half-dimensional sketch.

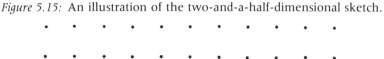

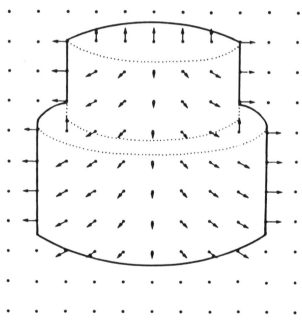

(From D. Marr, *Vision.* San Francisco: W. H. Freeman, 1982, p. 129)

Although computer programs for many of these sources of information have been implemented, it is not yet possible – unfortunately for our robot – to model all the processes that

104

enable us to see the world in depth. Moreover, the two-and-a-half-dimensional sketch is not sufficient for a robot to navigate safely through the world, since it makes explicit only the appearance of surfaces from the robot's point of view. A sensible representation of a scene, as we shall see in the next chapter, should enable objects to be identified, and therefore needs to be independent of any particular point of view. Identification is no longer a matter of pure perception, since it depends on assumptions that are the result of a person's own experiences.

Further reading

Marr (1982) and Ullman (1979) are the best sources for the topics of this chapter. Special issues of the journals *Artificial Intelligence* (1981, Vol. 17) and *Cognition* (1984, Vol. 18) have been devoted to vision. Koenderink (1984) gives an advanced account of the role of contour as a cue to shape, and also points out errors in Marr's analysis. Brady (1983) considers the analysis of shape from the standpoint of machine vision. Marr's notion of a visual module, as exemplified by the mechanism for stereopsis, has led Fodor (1983), along with other considerations, to propose a modular architecture for much of the mind.

CHAPTER 6

Scenes, shapes and images

Our goal is to understand human vision and to implement, if possible, a similar system in a robot. What needs to be computed is a symbolic representation of the three-dimensional world that makes explicit *what* is *where*. You walk into a room, recognize that it contains a table and other items of furniture, and can make your way to the table. You can carry out this action even if you have never been in the room before. There are three problems that your visual system solves: it perceives the three-dimensional shapes of objects, it identifies the objects on the basis of their shapes (the *what* in the symbolic representation), and it perceives their relative locations in space (the *where* in the symbolic representation).

The perception of the shapes of objects and of the spatial relations among them are not two independent tasks, but the same task on two different scales: a scene is simply a complex object made up of many component objects, and most objects in turn are made up of component parts, and so on and on. Just as one object can move in relation to another, so one part of an object can move in relation to another, as when you open and close your hand. Where a difference emerges is that objects (and their parts) tend to have names and functions, but few scenes (with the exception of rooms) have either. I shall begin with the perception of shapes, and defer the naming of parts until later.

THE CONSTRUCTION OF A THREE-DIMENSIONAL MODEL
OF THE WORLD

Suppose that a robot has computed a symbolic representation of the relative depths and orientations of all surfaces lying within its view – the two-and-a-half-dimensional sketch that I described in the previous chapter (though some modern robots cheat by using

106

lasers to measure these distances). This representation does not make explicit the shapes of objects or their spatial relations, and it changes when the robot moves, because the orientations of the surfaces change in relation to the robot. A more useful and stable representation would make explicit the intrinsic three-dimensional shapes of objects and the spatial relations among them.

Confronted with the scene in Figure 6.1 – a seventeenth-century world of blocks similar to a domain beloved by workers in artificial intelligence – the robot needs to construct a representation that is independent of its particular point of view and that would enable the program controlling its movements to ensure that it does not collide with any obstacles. The representation must therefore be a *model* in three dimensions of the scene, which, like an architect's model, makes explicit the shape of everything in the scene – the regions that are filled and the empty spaces. Such a structure does not call for a three-dimensional layout in the hardware of the computer. Its physical embodiment merely has to function as three-dimensional so that elements can be accessed and manipulated by specifying their positions on three coordinates. Such structures are commonplace in programs.

The construction of the model depends on a geometrical transformation of the two-and-a-half-dimensional sketch. A similar task arises in constructing computer models of terrains from radar scans or from stereo photographs. There are programs that convert such data into three-dimensional models within the computer, and that can present projections of the scene from different viewpoints. The programs are relatively straightforward, but how the human visual system carries out the analogous transformations is not known.

THE INTERPRETATION OF LINE DRAWINGS

A number of workers in artificial intelligence, notably the late Max Clowes, David Huffman and David Waltz, set out to solve an analogous problem. They noted that line drawings make explicit the edges of objects, and that people interpret such drawings as

Figure 6.1: A drawing from a book on perspective published in 1604 by the Dutch artist Jan Vredeman de Vries.

(From J. V. de Vries, *Perspective*. New York: Dover, 1968)

depicting three-dimensional scenes. They attempted to devise programs that could make similar interpretations.

What Clowes and Huffman independently realized is that knowledge of the world constrains the interpretation of the primitive symbols in a line drawing, and so enables a sensible three-dimensional interpretation to be made. Since their ideas are similar, I shall describe only Clowes's program. It takes as its input line drawings of a simple world of blocks. Each block has plane-faced surfaces and only three surfaces can meet at a corner. The program delivers an interpretation of the drawing in which each primitive symbol (lines and junctions of lines) receives a label representing its appropriate three-dimensional interpretation. At the heart of the program is a dictionary that defines the set of possible meanings for each sort of primitive symbol that can occur in a drawing. A single straight line, such as:

---

has only four possible meanings. It may stand for an external edge that bounds an object in the scene. If so, one side of the line corresponds to a surface of the object and the other side corresponds to the background or to some surface occluded by the object. There are obviously two interpretations here, depending on which side of the line the surface of the object lies. But the line may also depict an edge that is the meeting place of two surfaces of a single object. In this case, the edge can be either convex as on the top of a block or concave as on the inside of a box.

In drawings of the Clowes–Huffman world of blocks, only four sorts of junctions between lines can occur: an L-shape, a T-shape, a Y-shape and an arrow-shape. They can be seen on the beam lying across the boxes in Figure 6.1: there is an L-shape at the point labelled *f*, T-shapes at each intersection between the line depicting the bottom of the beam and the lines depicting the top of a box, a Y-shape at the point labelled *d*, and an arrow-shape at the point labelled *c*.

Since there are four possible interpretations for a single line, you might imagine that there should be sixteen possible interpretations for an L-junction (the four for one line multiplied by the four for the other). In fact, many of the combinations are ruled out as nonsensical by the nature of the blocks world. For instance, at least one of the two lines in an L-junction must denote the edge of an object that occludes another surface or the background. There is a similarly constrained set of interpretations for the other sorts of junctions.

The interpretation of a drawing exploits a higher level form of constraint: the need for a consistent interpretation of all the primitive symbols (lines and junctions) in the drawing. Even if each primitive in a drawing is initially assigned only physically possible interpretations, there will still be a massive number of potential interpretations of the drawing as a whole. Most of them, however, will denote objects that are impossible, such as the one in Figure 6.2. If the interpretation of a junction treats one line as an occluding edge of an object, then that line must also be an occluding edge in the interpretation of the junction at its other end. The object in Figure 6.2 violates this constraint: if you look at the front of the object alone, or its back alone, what you see is sensible. The two parts, however, call for incompatible interpretations of the lines connecting them.

Figure 6.2: A line drawing of a figure that is recognized as physically impossible by Max Clowes's program for interpreting drawings.

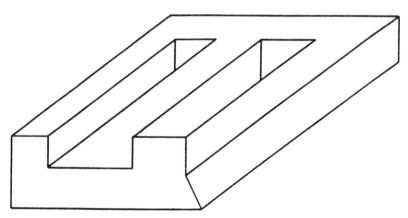

(From M. Clowes, On seeing things. *Artificial Intelligence*, 2, 1971, p. 105)

The procedure for interpreting the drawings first assigns all legal interpretations to each primitive, and then checks the consistency of the interpretations of a neighbouring pair. When it has eliminated all but the consistent ones, it considers the interpretations of another neighbouring primitive, establishes a consistent interpretation for all three, and so on, until every primitive in the drawing has been pulled into the process. When the program finally stabilizes – it is using the 'relaxation' method discussed in Chapter 5 – the result will be those interpretations that make sense of the drawing. If, in fact, it denotes an impossible object then there will be no resulting interpretation for it.

David Waltz showed that a step that seemed to complicate matters – the introduction of shadows, more complex blocks, and more complex configurations of blocks (see Figure 6.3) – led in fact to a simplification. His program allows that a line may denote a crack where one block lies next to another or on top of a surface, or that it may denote the edge of a shadow with shade on one side and light on the other. Shadows give information that is

Figure 6.3: A line drawing of blocks to be interpreted by a computer program.

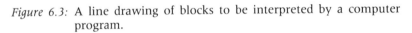

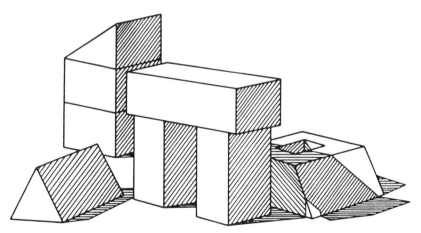

(From D. Waltz, Understanding line drawings of scenes with shadows. In P. Winston, ed., *The Psychology of Computer Vision*. New York: McGraw-Hill, 1975)

Figure 6.4: The labelling of a line drawing according to David Waltz's program.

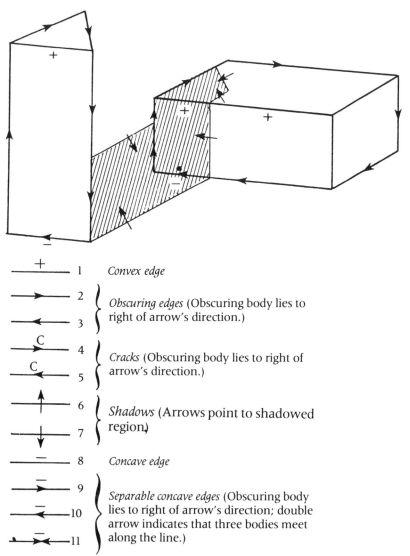

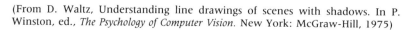

——**+**—— 1	*Convex edge*
———▶——— 2 ⎫ ———◀——— 3 ⎬	*Obscuring edges* (Obscuring body lies to right of arrow's direction.)
——**C**▶—— 4 ⎫ ——**C**◀—— 5 ⎬	*Cracks* (Obscuring body lies to right of arrow's direction.)
——▲——— 6 ⎫ ———▼— 7 ⎬	*Shadows* (Arrows point to shadowed region.)
——**‖**—— 8	*Concave edge*
———▶— 9 ⎫ ——◀—10 ⎬ ▶—◀—11 ⎭	*Separable concave edges* (Obscuring body lies to right of arrow's direction; double arrow indicates that three bodies meet along the line.)

(From D. Waltz, Understanding line drawings of scenes with shadows. In P. Winston, ed., *The Psychology of Computer Vision.* New York: McGraw-Hill, 1975) analogous to another viewpoint, and can reveal whether an object is resting on a surface or is merely close to it. Figure 6.4 illustrates some of these possibilities in a labelling of a drawing according to Waltz's program. Although there are now more primitive symbols and many more meanings for them, the program arrives at an interpretation of a drawing as a whole more rapidly (and less ambiguously) than in the simpler blocks world.

Other workers, such as Alan Mackworth, have devised still more advanced programs, which can label drawings using general principles rather than a dictionary of interpretations for individual primitives. Yet there remain problems in working within a blocks world. The programs give a sensible interpretation to certain drawings that depict impossible objects (see Figure 6.5). Marr criticized the approach on the grounds that it fails to deal properly with the question of what should be computed. The output of a program, if it is to resemble human vision, should be a three-dimensional interpretation of the scene depicted in the drawing. Such a representation needs to make explicit the shapes of objects, but the programs that label lines recover only the orientations of connected surfaces.

Nevertheless, the research was valuable. It clarified the distinction between form and function. Thus, Stuart Sutherland,

Figure 6.5: A line drawing of a figure that is not recognized as physically impossible by programs for interpreting line drawings.

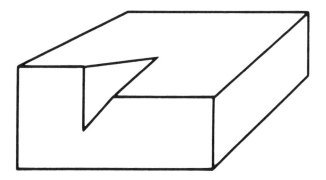

(From J. Mayhew and J. Frisby, Computer vision. In T. O'Shea and M. Eisenstadt, eds., *Artificial Intelligence*. London: Harper and Row, 1984)

who had studied the way in which animals discriminate shapes, distinguished three separate domains: the domain of the picture, e.g. lines, regions and junctions; the domain of the scene, e.g. surfaces, edges and shapes; and the domain of functional objects, e.g. chairs, tables and people. The research also convinced many psychologists that there were mundane aspects of perception that could be investigated without having to carry out elaborate experiments: simple intuitions about drawings were enough to raise questions that no one knew how to answer.

THE IDENTIFICATION OF OBJECTS

The construction of a mental model can call for more than a transformation of the two-and-a-half-dimensional sketch. There are often insufficient data in the sketch for a complete model. For instance, only two edges of the table-top in Figure 6.1 are visible, yet if you are familiar with Western furniture you will identify the object as a table and represent its top as rectangular. You depend on your knowledge of the shapes of tables gained from your experience of the world, but the machinery of identification is unconscious in the Helmholtzian sense. Your visual system constructs a description of the perceived object and compares it with some sort of mental catalogue of the three-dimensional shapes of objects. It can recognize them from particular viewpoints and then make automatic extrapolations about the rest of their shapes.

The pioneer of computational models of the process was L. G. Roberts, who devised a program that interprets photographs of objects in a blocks world by identifying them with stored prototypes. Artists such as Cézanne and the Cubists were inspired by the Platonic doctrine that all shapes could be decomposed into a primitive vocabulary of elementary solid forms; and Roberts's program works on a similar principle. It is based on three space-filling prototypes: the cube, the right-angled wedge and the hexagonal prism (see Figure 6.6). It first converts a photograph into a line drawing by using a crude line-finder – a rudimentary precursor to the machinery of the primal sketch. It then works bottom up using particular junctions of lines as cues to a relevant

114

Figure 6.6: The three prototypes used in L. G. Roberts's program.

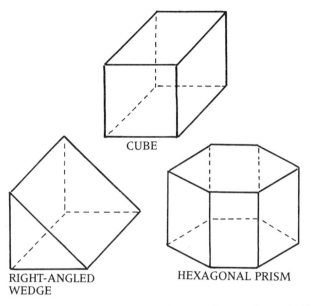

(From K. Oatley, *Perceptions and Representations*. London: Methuen, 1978, p. 178)

prototype. Thus, a Y-junction cues the prototype of the cube, since it occurs at a top corner on the front of the cube.

The final stage of the program uses the prototype in a top-down process to interpret the rest of the object in the drawing. The operations that carry out this matching process can project the internal prototype (specified in terms of coordinates in three dimensions) on to two-dimensional images, and they can stretch or shrink the dimensions of the prototype, rotate it, or translate it from one position to another, so as to fit the actual object in the scene. The program can also join prototypes together in order to analyse more complex objects.

The use of prototypes was taken a step further by David Marr and Keith Nishihara. Since the identification of an object can occur from many different viewpoints, they argued that the shape of the object must be specified, not in a coordinate system centred on the observer (such as the two-and-a-half-dimensional sketch), but in coordinates that are determined by the shape of the object itself. The visual system creates a representation of a folded umbrella that makes explicit that it is a long cylinder. This model is independent of viewpoint, and indeed people can imagine the appearance of an umbrella from different points of view. This ability to rotate mental images is one that I shall come back to presently.

A powerful system for capturing the shapes of objects is based on the idea of moving a two-dimensional cross-section along an axis. If a circle, for example, is moved at right-angles along a straight line, it sweeps out the solid shape of a cylinder. If it shrinks continuously as it moves along, it defines a cone. In general, we can use a cross-section of any shape, it can change size continuously as it moves, and the axis need not be a straight line but can curve in any way. The resulting class of shapes are known, somewhat misleadingly, as 'generalized cones'. Thus, the shape of a banana can be described reasonably accurately by a generalized cone, and the shape of a human being can be described reasonably accurately as made up from a number of generalized cones. Marr and Nishihara proposed that the mind contains a catalogue of shapes of objects represented as generalized cones. Figure 6.7 shows the sort of catalogue they envisaged, which works on the same representational idea as the 'stick figures' of children's drawings. It makes explicit the lengths and arrangements of the component axes, which is why it is useful for the identification of complex objects. Although Figure 6.7 represents the shapes as simple cylinders, the mental catalogue is supposed to employ generalized cones. They are the class of shapes that are recovered from silhouettes meeting the constraints described in the previous chapter. However, there are certain shapes, ranging from Origami to crumpled newspapers, that violate those constraints and that are not generalized cones.

Marr and Nishihara's catalogue represents complex objects in a hierarchical organization. The top level captures their gross structure of objects; the lower levels make the details explicit. Figure 6.8 shows the hierarchical representation of the shape of a human being. (Cylinders are again used for illustrative convenience.) The axis of the body provides a coordinate system centred on the body itself, and this system can be used for

Figure 6.7: A fragment of the catalogue of shapes proposed by Marr and Nishihara.

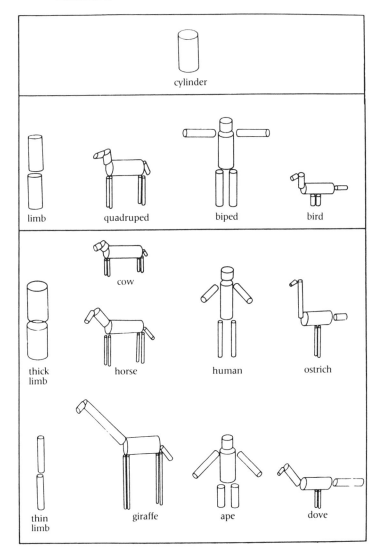

(From D. Marr and H. K. Nishihara, Representation and recognition of the spatial organization of three-dimensional shapes. *Proceedings of the Royal Society,* B, 1978, 200)

117

specifying the relations of the axes of the head, arms and legs. Their axes in turn provide coordinates for the next level down, and so on. The catalogue can be searched in a variety of ways. Like Roberts's program, a specific cue about a key part of an object may provide bottom-up access to a prototype. The prototype can then be used top-down to try to match the rest of the figure. Specific information about the orientation of the principal axis in relation to other axes may also be used in the matching process.

Figure 6.8: The hierarchical organization of a human being's shape according to Marr and Nishihara.

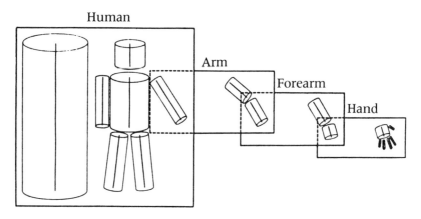

(From D. Marr and H. K. Nishihara, Representation and recognition of the spatial organization of three-dimensional shapes. *Proceedings of the Royal Society*, B, 1978, 200)

David Hogg has extended some of these ideas to cope with movement. He has developed a program that interprets films of a man walking. The program has an internal prototype of a man, like the one in Figure 6.8, which it can project on to the moving image using principles like those of Roberts's program. The prototype also contains constraints on the variables that control the various angles of the joints so that the man can only cycle through the specified sequence of postures that occur in walking. The program operates on the raw data in the grey-level array, and the matching process is triggered by the detection of a difference between successive frames of the film. In essence, the program draws a rectangle around the area of change and assumes that its major axis corresponds to the major axis of the prototype. Once it has established this relation, it switches to a top-down mode of operation in order to fit the details of arms and legs to the picture, allowing for the camera's point of view.

The theme of these approaches to recognition is the use of high-level knowledge of the shapes of objects. The theories assume that your experience enables you to build up such knowledge and to exploit it in procedures that make sense of the visual world. Is the assumption warranted? The reader will recall that earlier I described a relevant experimental tactic: if a process

Figure 6.9: A picture illustrating the role of top-down processes in perception.

(From J. Thurstone and R. G. Carraher, *Optical Illusions and the Visual Arts.* New York: Litton, 1966. Copyright © Van Nostrand Reinhold Co.)

occurs even though the low-level data are corrupted, then it can be guided by higher-level knowledge. Figure 6.9 is a classic illustration of just such a phenomenon. At first glance, the figure may appear to be random patches of black and white. It is, in fact, a picture of a dog sniffing the ground under the dappled shadow of a tree. This knowledge should be enough for you to identify the dog.

FORM, FUNCTION AND IDENTIFICATION

Your concept of a table must contain information for the perceptual identification of tables. But, when George Miller and I undertook an analysis of concepts, we soon realized that tables, unlike human beings, do not have a canonical shape: they come in a profusion of shapes. Moreover, you can recognize an object as a table even if it has a shape unlike any table you have ever seen. We were forced to conclude that an artefact can be identified as a member of a category, not because of any intrinsic aspect of its three-dimensional shape, but because its form, dimensions and other visible properties, whatever they may be, are perceived as appropriate for a particular *function*. You can see the possibilities inherent in the artefact. It is a table because it has a surface on which you could rest utensils. This sort of advanced recognition is, so far, beyond the competence of any computer program. It depends on high-level knowledge – the knowledge, for example, of the particular functions served by tables. It also depends on inferences from form to function. You perceive the shape of an object and infer its likely purpose. In some cases, unfortunately, you perceive the shape of an object – an unknown wedding gift, perhaps – but are unable to project a function on to it.

Striking evidence about visual recognition has come from the field of neuropsychology. Neuropsychologists study the psychological effects of damage to the brain caused by accidents, strokes, toxins and surgery. Their aim is to elucidate its normal operations, and where possible to ameliorate any debilitating effects of the damage. A leading British neuropsychologist, Elizabeth Warrington, and her associates have obtained good evidence for a distinction between the mechanisms for perceiving form and function. They found that damage to one part of the brain (the left parietal lobe) can impair a patient's ability to discern the function of an object, though the patient can still perceive its three-dimensional shape. Conversely, damage to another part of the brain (the right parietal lobe) yields exactly the opposite effects. When some patients are impaired in one ability but not in a second, and other patients are impaired in the second ability but not the first, neuropsychologists are then able to say that there is a 'double dissociation' between the two abilities. It implies that they are handled by different modules since they can be independently disrupted by brain damage. In the case of form and function, the double dissociation confirms the distinction between their underlying perceptual mechanisms.

VISUAL IMAGERY

The ability to imagine the use of an object may be related to visual imagery. Most people are able to form an image in their mind's eye of a familiar person, room or scene. And if they are presented with a picture such as the one on the left of Figure 6.10, then, as Roger Shepard and his collaborators have demonstrated, they can decide whether or not it depicts the same object as the one on the right-hand side of the figure. The comparison appears to depend on a mental rotation of the image of the first object: the greater the degree of rotation, the longer (in exact proportion) the time to respond. People take about a second for each 60 degrees that they have to rotate an image of this shape, and the relation holds even when the rotation is in depth and not just in the plane of the picture. Marcel Just and Patricia Carpenter recorded the eye movements of people carrying out this task, and Figure 6.10 shows a typical pattern of fixations, which suggests that the subjects find the major axis (fixations 1 and 2), mentally rotate it, and then check their judgement, first at the ends of one object (fixations 3–5), then at the other (fixations 6–7), and so on.

An image is like a perception except that, as David Hume put it, the two differ in the force and liveliness with which they

Figure 6.10: Does the drawing on the left depict the same object as the drawing on the right? An example of a trial from Shepard's mental rotation task. The numbers record the pattern of fixations of the eye movements made by one subject in an experiment carried out by Just and Carpenter.

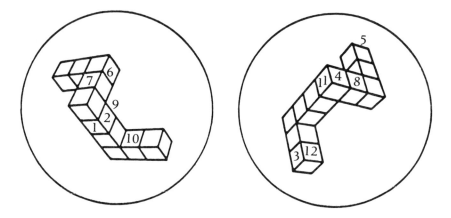

(From M. A. Just and P. A. Carpenter, Eye fixations and cognitive processes. *Cognitive Psychology,* 8, 1976).

strike upon the mind'. Indeed, a classic experiment of 1910 demonstrated the similarity between the two experiences: C. W. Perky asked people to imagine a common object such as a banana and to 'project' their image on to a pane of glass mounted on the wall. Unbeknownst to them, the experimenter projected a picture of a banana on to the pane from the other side of the wall and gradually increased its intensity. The subjects were fooled into believing that they were experiencing an intense image, even though it was clearly visible to anyone else in the room.

There is neuropsychological evidence for a common mechanism underlying vision and imagery. Brain damage can cause a curious phenomenon known as 'visual neglect' in which patients do not register consciously one side of the visual field. There is nothing wrong with their eyes and they are not aware of their problem. Hence, for example, they eat the food on one side of their plates and ignore everything on the other side as though it does not exist. Eduardo Bisiach has observed that when such patients are asked to describe scenes from memory, such as a familiar piazza, they similarly neglect one side of the image. When they are asked to imagine standing at the other end of the piazza, they again ignore one side – the opposite side to the one they neglected in their first description.

The major issue about imagery is its underlying nature. Stephen Kosslyn, a leading theorist in the area, has argued that an image corresponds to a view of an object, and that various mental processes can be applied to it. For example, in one of his experiments he asked people to draw a map of an imaginary island and to place various landmarks on it. When they had memorized the map, it was removed and they had to imagine it and to focus on a particular location. The experimenter gave them the names of various landmarks, and for each landmark that was on the map they scanned their images until they reached it, and then pressed a button. The time that it took them to respond depended on the distance of the landmark from the starting point. This finding and others suggest that people can scan internal images.

Kosslyn's hypothesis is that images are represented in a two-dimensional internal array. He has implemented a computer program based on this hypothesis. The program generates an image as a pattern of activation in the cells of an array. The pattern corresponds to the shape of the visible surfaces of an object. It begins to fade as soon as it is generated unless it is refreshed. It may overflow the array, which has a finite size; conversely, it may be too small to be resolved in the array, which has a finite 'grain' determined by the amount of information that each cell can hold. The array can receive information either directly from visual processing or else from memory. Kosslyn assumes that we remember either an object's literal appearance (akin to its two-and-a-half-dimensional sketch) or a more abstract structural description (akin to the three-dimensional model used for its recognition). Both sorts of memory may be used to generate an image. The pattern of activated cells in the array can be moved from one place to another, rotated or re-scaled; and the results of these transformations can be examined by operations that find particular shapes, scan across the array, or zoom in on it for a closer look at details. One prediction to which the program gave rise was that small images should take less time to rotate than large images; the prediction was confirmed experimentally.

A program modelling imagery must contain procedures for constructing and manipulating images. However, if images are specific views of objects (akin to the two-and-a-half-dimensional sketch), then perhaps they are generated from three-dimensional models of the objects. In mental rotation, the model is manipulated, and then the image is derived from it by a projective process. Another possibility has been suggested by Geoffrey Hinton. He argues that there is no need for an internal array whatsoever. Imagining an object consists in accessing its structural description (akin to its three-dimensional model) and then adding to it temporary information about its appearance from a particular viewpoint. The procedures for manipulating the image can then directly transform these coordinate values, and the new values that they produce can be used by procedures for finding significant relations.

The Canadian cognitive scientist Zenon Pylyshyn goes one step further. He has long argued that images play no causal role in mental life. The phenomena of imagery arise because people are using their general cognitive abilities to simulate physical events. There is no process of rotating or transforming internal arrays, but merely manipulations of strings of symbols – the standard medium of mental representation, according to Pylyshyn. There is a trivial sense in which Pylyshyn is bound to be right: any computer program is reduced to strings of binary numerals in the code that controls the machine, and presumably any mental process reduces to nerve impulses or some other primitive code. Yet the functional organization of these primitive symbols may make explicit high-level relations, such as the three-dimensional structure of an object or its visual appearance from a particular point of view. A mental image would indeed be similar to an array in a programming language. It would make certain relations easy to establish – just the sort of relations that the various procedures in Kosslyn's program are designed to recover.

CONCLUSIONS

In what pattern does light reflect from objects on to a surface? This problem in optics is well formed: it can be solved much as a set of equations can be solved. Vision is inverse optics. It has to establish what objects caused the patterns of light projected on to the retinae. This problem is not well formed: it is almost impossible to solve, because there are too many unknowns – too many different ways in which the pattern of light could have been created. When the mind solves a seemingly impossible task, it must have a secret weapon, and, as I remarked, that secret weapon is knowledge. Knowledge comes in two main varieties that are used in two main ways, top down or bottom up.

One sort of knowledge arises from evolution, and its wisdom is built into the processes of the nervous system. This knowledge is not really knowledge at all. It is never made explicit, and it is encapsulated in the computations of a low-level module. Such modules neither reveal their mode of operation to introspection nor are much affected by conscious control.

The other sort of knowledge accrues during the lifetime of an individual. You have experience with tables, and so you learn about their shapes and functions, and you can use this explicit knowledge, which is available to introspection, to deliberate about the identity of an object. In fact, you are not always aware either of using such knowledge or of its nature. What is rapidly bearing down on you as you stand musing in the middle of the road? It's a motor-bike. Fortunately, you do not have to engage in a long-winded analysis to reach this conclusion. You have leapt out of the way before you could describe how you carried out your identification. This immediacy of perception has led Gibson and his followers to doubt the story that I have told in this chapter – the story of how vision constructs three- dimensional mental models, and of how personal knowledge is used to make unconscious inferences that identify objects. The story, however, has the enormous advantage that a beginning has been made in translating it into a computational framework. It is even possible to equip our robot with a crude ability of the same sort.

The distinction between the two sorts of knowledge may mark the boundary between pure perception and cognition. Marr drew this boundary between the two-and-a-half-dimensional sketch and the three-dimensional model. The neuropsychological evidence suggests that the boundary could be drawn between the three-dimensional model and the identification of objects and their functions. It may be that there is no clear-cut boundary. There are just two certainties. First, when we perceive the world, the information about the relative depths of surfaces (the two-and-a-half-dimensional sketch) cannot be recovered without the use of innate constraints. Second, the identification of objects cannot occur without the use of personal knowledge. The accumulation of this knowledge depends on learning and on the ability to recall what has been learned. The theories that I have discussed have had nothing to say about these abilities. They are the topic of the next part of the book.

Further reading

Gregory (1970, 1981) has long championed the role of unconscious inference, and likens perception to the formation and testing of scientific hypotheses. Oatley (1978) gives a stimulating account of the role of top-down processes in vision and of computer programs that interpret line drawings. Details of many of these programs can be found in Winston (1975). Pinker's (1984) tutorial essay concentrates on imagery and the perception of shape. Biederman (1987) presents experimental evidence corroborating a theory of the recognition of objects, which is based on generalized cones and invariant cuès to them. The main studies of imagery are to be found in Shephard and Cooper (1982) and Kosslyn (1980, 1983). Pylyshyn (1984) presents his general views on cognitive science and his scepticism about images as functional representations. Block (1981) is a useful anthology of papers on imagery from a philosophical standpoint. Farah (1984) presents a brief review of the neuropsychology of imagery.

PART III

LEARNING, MEMORY AND ACTION

We can now see why the problem of central control in brains is linked with that of long-term memory. It is obvious that no animal, let alone man, carries out a simple and predictable sequence of operations on the inputs which stimulate it. We must suppose therefore that the control exercised over the brain's operations is one which varies not only with the nature of the input but also with the results of past operations.

DONALD BROADBENT

CHAPTER 7

Learning and learnability

Some organisms are born with an innate repertoire of behaviours for coping with their particular 'niche' in the environment. They can survive and reproduce on the basis of inborn responses that are automatically triggered by specific events. The advantage of such responses is that they do not have to be learned and so can be ready as soon as the organism enters the world. Their disadvantage is that apart from some fine tuning, they may be mindlessly repeated whenever the circumstances that trigger them reoccur. A sand wasp constructs its nest by performing a chain of innate responses, and if part of the nest is removed the wasp automatically returns to the appropriate earlier stage in the chain to build it again. As long as an experimenter repeats the partial destruction, the wasp repeats the construction: it never learns that its Sisyphean efforts are futile. Not all inborn behaviours, however, have this unfortunate characteristic.

Every organism has some innate behaviours. A new-born baby, for instance, has a grasping reflex strong enough to support its own weight. This reflex subsequently disappears, but others, such as the protective blink of the eyelid, last a lifetime. Yet innate behaviour is suitable only for life in a simple world. It dooms a species if its environment changes drastically, whereas a species that can *learn* may acquire new behaviours that enable it to adapt. Human beings are so adaptive that they can learn to live in almost any environment.

But what is learning? Everyone is familiar with it, but it is difficult to define. It is normally a relatively permanent change that occurs when, as a result of experience, you become able to do something that you could not do before, or able to do it better. You can learn facts such as a person's name, general concepts and principles such as the theory of relativity, and habits and skills such as driving. Learning also occurs in various regimes. You can

129

learn how to open a lock as a result of trial and error; you can learn how to use a word processor as a result of following instructions; you can learn how to ski by imitating your instructor.

Once you have some internal model of what ought to happen, you can learn by practising the skill until your performance converges on the desired model. You begin by paying attention to what you are trying to do, but as you grow more practised, you need to monitor only the trickier parts of performance. Many skills become so automatic that you can perform them without conscious attention at all. As the philosopher Alfred North Whitehead wrote:

> It is a profoundly erroneous truism . . . that we should cultivate the habit of thinking what we are doing. The precise opposite is the case. Civilization advances by extending the number of important operations which we can perform without thinking about them.

What automatic performance shows is that the brain can do different things in parallel: one part is devoted to the skill whilst another part mediates conscious experience. I shall return to this phenomenon on several occasions.

LEARNING AS THE CONSTRUCTION OF ASSOCIATIONS

Despite the diversity of learning, theorists have traditionally sought its fundamental 'building blocks'. The answer that emerged from Aristotle's couch and from the psychologists' laboratory is that all learning depends on *associations*. One experience becomes associated with another. The organism may be a passive observer of the two experiences, or it may come to associate a particular piece of its own behaviour with a subsequent class of events. Associations are supposed to be links in the brain that lead from one thing to another. They can link the same stimulus to several alternative responses with differing probabilities that depend on the strengths of the associative links.

Psychologists have demonstrated that animals learn to predict certain events in their environment. They will form an associative link from one event to another provided that the second event is significant, or surprising, and is predicted by the first. The prototypical case of such learning is Ivan Pavlov's 'classical conditioning', in which an animal learns that an event such as the ringing of a bell predicts the arrival of food. The bell alone then triggers the reflex of salivation. George Bernard Shaw said that Pavlov had tormented dogs to show that their mouths water at the sound of the dinner gong. (The best prophylactic for such despicable behaviour, he added, would have been singing lessons from Shaw's mother.) In fact, Pavlov did not discover the conditioned reflex, which had been known for at least a century, but rather some of its subtler principles.

An associative link can also be established from a voluntary response to an event that acts as a reward. The standard example occurs in 'operant conditioning', to which B. F. Skinner devoted much study. For example, a hungry pigeon is put into a box containing a disc-shaped key. Sooner or later it pecks the key, and, as soon as it does, its response is 'reinforced' with food. This regime increases the rate at which the pigeon pecks the key. It establishes a link between the response of pecking and the rewarding event.

Simple associative theory has been overtaken by developments on several sides. On one side, ethologists, who study animals in the wild, have discovered that behaviours are as diverse as species and as intimately related to an animal's environment as its bodily structure. They have called attention to inborn *constraints* on what a species can learn. Some behaviours are easily learned, whereas others are not. For example, if a rat drinks a sweet-tasting liquid and later becomes ill, it learns immediately never to drink that liquid again. But, if the liquid is tasteless and its poisonousness is signalled by some other concurrent event, such as a flashing light, then the animal fails to learn to avoid the liquid. Natural selection has sensitized it to certain causal relations, not others. Similarly, a newly hatched gosling learns to follow the first large moving object that it sees. It treats this object as the mother goose − even if it happens to be the ethologist, Konrad Lorenz. There are again innate constraints underlying this rapid form of learning, which is known as 'imprinting'.

On another side, modern animal psychologists have become

131

dubious about direct associations between stimuli and responses, and have taken an increasingly cognitive view of learning. Even in animals, learning can occur without any immediate signs in behaviour. It changes an internal cognitive state, and its effects become apparent only later.

There is still another difficulty. You can learn to press a button if one light comes on or else if another light comes on, and not to respond if both lights come on. There is no way, however, in which this exclusive disjunction (respond only to one light or the other, but not both) can be set up in a direct association from stimuli to response. If the associative links are strong enough to elicit a response to a single light, they are bound to elicit it to both lights. The task demands an internal representation that mediates between stimuli and responses so as to inhibit the response to both lights.

Doubt about associations has led cognitive scientists to approach learning from other, more abstract, points of view. Some have set out a comprehensive theory of how learning might occur. Others have developed computational models of human learning. Still others, in the vein of artificial intelligence, have sought a universal procedure that could learn any fact, concept or skill. It would be most convenient if, instead of people having to program a computer, the machine could be equipped with a learning program so that it could learn how to do every-thing for itself. There are limits on the feasibility of such a scheme, and they are highly informative about the limits of learning. Before we can examine them, we need to consider learning as a computational exercise.

LEARNING FROM A COMPUTATIONAL STANDPOINT

When you learn a fact, you learn to think about something in a different way: sometimes the difference is trivial, sometimes not. When you learn a concept, you learn how to treat different things as instances of the same category. Without this classificatory procedure, thinking would be impossible because each event or entity would be unique. When you learn a skill, you acquire a program that enables you to do something that you could not do before. Hence, in general terms, learning is the construction of new programs out of elements of experience. It follows that you cannot learn anything unless you already have some abilities, because programs cannot be constructed out of thin air. The methods of construction themselves must be a special program, or suite of programs, that take experience as input and build or modify programs governing performance. A program that learns may itself have been learned – you can learn to learn, but then that learning would depend on another program, and so on. Ultimately, learning must depend on innate programs that make programs.

Only a small set of procedures needs to be innate before there exists a basis for constructing any possible program. This conclusion follows because only a small number of building blocks are needed to construct a universal Turing machine, i.e. a device that can compute anything that is computable (see Chapter 3). Moreover, as I will now show, there are only three possible classes of program that could learn.

Consider some arbitrary task that is feasible to learn, and ask yourself by what principles its learning might proceed. The learning has to converge on a program that carries out the task, and so it must be possible for someone – learner or teacher – to assess whether progress is being made. Without such 'feedback', the learner will be stumbling around in the dark. One method of learning is to assemble the program by combining existing elements arbitrarily, using the feedback to assess the usefulness of the result. This method of pure 'trial and error' resembles the evolution of species according to modern neo-Darwinian theory. It will work only if there is a reasonable chance of converging on the required program by a series of gradual steps, which each have a reasonable probability of occurring by chance, and which can each be successfully maintained so as to lead to the next improvement. The chances of acquiring any significant ability using an unconstrained neo-Darwinian method are neglible, as workers in artificial intelligence discovered in the 1960s when programs based on the method failed to make progress.

The second method of construction is governed by information which ensures that only viable programs are produced – a method that resembles a neo-Lamarckian theory of evolution. Such a program is highly efficient, but it calls for considerable knowledge (or instruction) about a domain. In practice, it is feasible only where the task is trivial or an individual has learned to learn. If the task is a new dance step, for instance, then a skilled dancer can master it rapidly.

The third method of construction is only partially constrained by existing information. In daily life, this method is the most common. When you learn to open a lock by trial and error, you already possess the main components of the skill, together with constraints on how they are likely to be combined: the set of possibilities from which you select is highly restricted. When you learn to ski, you go through a long series of alternating cycles of construction and evaluation, which gradually improve your competence. You may get stuck on a plateau of ability from which you can lift your performance only by prolonged practice: the reorganization of each successive program becomes progressively harder.

My goal now is to use a computational analysis to set up some boundaries on the domain of what, in principle, can be learned. At one end of the domain, I shall repudiate the sceptical philosophical thesis that concepts cannot be learned. At the other end, I shall show that a universal procedure that could learn any imaginable task is indeed a phantasy. Learning is possible, but only if there are constraints on the class of possible concepts or skills to be acquired.

CONCEPTUAL LEARNING IS POSSIBLE

The most pessimistic view about learning is that, apart from the acquisition of simple facts and skills, it is impossible. This thesis has been advanced most provocatively by the philosopher Jerry Fodor. He claims that all concepts are innate – perhaps the most extreme version of the Rationalistic doctrine of innate ideas that anyone has ever proposed. Fodor's argument is ingenious and instructive, but I shall try to show that it is not decisive.

Fodor starts with the hypothetical problem of how children who know an elementary form of logic could learn a more powerful logic. He imagines that the children have mastered the logic of the words 'and', 'or', 'not' and 'if', which enables them to make such inferences as:

If it isn't raining, then the horse is in the meadow.
The horse isn't in the meadow.
Therefore: it's raining.

The more powerful logic admits the use of such words as 'any' and 'some', and it enables inferences of the following sort to be drawn:

If it hasn't rained at any time today, then there will be some horses in all the meadows.
There aren't any horses in some of the meadows.
Therefore: it has rained at some time today.

Fodor argues that children cannot learn to make the transition from one logic to the other. To learn the more powerful logic, they would first have to learn what is *meant* by such expressions as:

There aren't any horses in some of the meadows.

But, says Fodor, the meaning of such a sentence cannot even be formulated within a child's mind at the earlier stage, because the only available concepts are those of the elementary logic, and these concepts are not powerful enough to express the meaning of 'any' and 'some'. If children cannot even represent the meanings of statements in the more powerful logic, then they will not be able to learn it.

The argument is quite general, and leads to the conclusion that complex concepts cannot be constructed out of simpler ones, because the simpler ones are not rich enough to allow the complex ones to be represented. And thus ineluctably Fodor is drawn to his extreme view that all concepts are innate: 'There literally isn't such a thing as the notion of learning a conceptual system richer than the one that one already has.'

One sign that Fodor's argument is wrong is that it proves too much, namely, that logic and concepts could not even be innate, because they could not have *evolved*. If the construction of new ideas out of old and feedback from the environment cannot lead to the learning of new concepts, then analogous neo-Darwinian processes on an evolutionary scale could not work either. Conversely, if neural hardware is changed by maturation, mutation, bombardment by cosmic rays or any other agent, then what grounds are there for assuming that such a process cannot be mimicked computationally by a device that has universal Turing machine power?

Where Fodor's argument goes wrong is in the ambiguity of its claim that learning cannot increase power. Learning cannot increase computational power, but it can increase logical and conceptual power: the two notions are quite distinct as I shall now explain.

A learning system as a whole has a certain degree of *computational* power. Suppose that it has the power of a finite-state machine, then nothing that happens subsequently by way of learning will increase its computational power – for that to occur, it needs to be equipped with a better memory. Yet, at one stage, such a system may not be able to carry out addition, whereas at a later stage it may have mastered the ability. To demonstrate the point, I shall assume that at the earlier stage it is able to compute only a single mathematical operation, one that delivers the successor to any integer:

$$\text{successor } (0) = 1$$
$$\text{successor } (1) = 2$$
$$\text{successor } (2) = 3$$

and so on. It can construct the operation for addition by forming the right combination of its existing building blocks. For example, it can represent addition using any arbitrary novel symbol, e.g. '+', and it can capture its meaning in the following two-clause definition:

$$x + 0 = 0$$
$$x + \text{successor } (y) = \text{successor } (x + y)$$

with a second recursive clause (see Chapter 3). Since it can already compute the successor of any integer, it can use this definition to carry out the addition of any two integers.

Here, for example, is how it can compute 1 + 1:

$$1 = \text{successor } (0) \qquad \text{(from successor operation)}$$
$$\therefore\ 1 + 1 = 1 + \text{successor } (0)$$
$$1 + \text{successor } (0) = \text{successor } (1 + 0)$$
$$\text{(from second clause)}$$
$$1 + 0 = 1 \qquad \text{(from first clause)}$$
$$\therefore\ 1 + \text{successor } (0) = \text{successor } (1)$$
$$\text{successor } (1) = 2 \qquad \text{(from successor operation)}$$
$$\therefore\ 1 + 1 = 2$$

Hence, the system has advanced from an elementary to a more advanced concept.

The moral of all this mathematical 'knitting' is what matters: a system with a fixed computational power may nevertheless increase its conceptual power. The argument is quite general: it is possible to *learn* more complex concepts.

WHY THERE CAN BE NO UNIVERSAL LEARNING PROCEDURE

A second lesson to be drawn from a computational analysis is that there are limits on what can be learned: not just any procedure can be acquired, even granted the most powerful learning system that is possible – one with the power of a universal Turing machine. To demonstrate this point, I need to remind you of the relation between programs and grammars.

In Chapter 3, I showed how different sorts of programs vary in computational power because they vary in their use of memory for the results of intermediate computations. I also showed that the behaviour of any program can be characterized by a grammar, and so grammars also vary in their power. We can ask: is it possible to learn any grammar whatsoever? If not, then it follows that the corresponding programs cannot be learned either. In short, the argument is going to rest on the close relation between programs and grammars.

The question of the learnability of grammars was first raised by Noam Chomsky, who was interested in how children could acquire the grammars of their native languages. However, I shall deal with the general question of learning any sort of grammar, including those that characterize the programs' underlying skills. Suppose there are two grammars, A and B, and you know that one of them characterizes, say, the improvisations of a particular musician. No matter how powerful the grammars, you may be able to decide which is the correct grammar quite easily – a few bars of music may contain a sequence that obviously cannot be generated by one of the grammars, and so the other grammar must be the right one. Unfortunately, it is rather rare for there to be a small set of grammars known *a priori* to be the only relevant candidates. It may also be difficult to discover whether or not a particular string of symbols can be generated by a certain grammar. Hence, suppose instead that all you know is which particular *class* of grammars is appropriate. Since there are infinitely many grammars in the different classes corresponding to programs of different computational power, it is not obvious how to proceed. E. M. Gold, however, has proved some highly pertinent theorems.

Gold assumed an idealized form of learning, which takes place over a series of trials. On each trial, you are presented with a single string of symbols. In a simple learning regime the strings are always grammatical. But if your task is to learn a grammar selected arbitrarily from a class of grammars, then, as Gold proved, this regime suffices only for grammars that admit just a finite number of grammatical strings. Most grammars of any use, however, admit a potentially infinite number of grammatical strings. If there were a finite list that was supposed to contain every grammatical English sentence, one could always add another by conjoining a clause with 'and' to the longest sentence in the list.

In a more powerful learning regime, you are presented with either a grammatical or an ungrammatical string, which is properly identified, and you use this information to formulate a hypothesis about the grammar governing the grammatical strings. You can examine only a finite number of sentences or strings of symbols in a lifetime, and any such corpus can always be characterized by an indefinite number of different grammars – they all agree on the status of the strings you have seen, but they disagree about the status of other strings. Yet, perhaps after a finite number of strings, you will always hypothesize the same grammar. This is an interesting state of affairs. You have, in effect, mastered the language, and Gold introduces a piece of jargon to label your achievement: you have identified the language 'in the limit'. You will not change your mind about its grammar ever again. Of course, you can never know if (or when) you have reached this state, but then you can never be certain that you have completely mastered any language. There are, however, two distinct sorts of failure: you may stabilize on the wrong grammar, or you may fail to stabilize at all and keep changing your mind.

Gold proposed a general learning program, which, though purely hypothetical, enabled him to prove some theorems about what classes of grammar could be learned. Because any grammar consists of a finite number of rules, it follows that the infinite set of all possible grammars of a given computational power can be put into a single numerical order. (We convert the rules into, say, binary numerals, concatenate them into one grand numeral representing each grammar as a whole, and order the numerals by their size.) This list continues *ad infinitum*, but it is in numerical order. The learning program starts with the hypothesis that a grammar it is trying to learn corresponds to the first grammar in the list. It maintains this hypothesis until the grammar fails to predict the correct status of a string. At this point, the program adopts the next grammar in the list until it fails, and so on. Since the correct grammar is somewhere in the list, once it is reached it will never have to be abandoned. The language will have been identified 'in the limit'.

The simplest grammars correspond to finite-state programs, which have no recourse to memory for intermediate results. At the next level up in computational power, there are grammars, such as the one for the robot's navigational system, that correspond to programs needing access to a stack-like memory. Both classes of grammar can be identified in the limit. However, if a grammar is arbitrarily selected from the set corresponding to programs with the power of a universal Turing machine, then there can be no regime guaranteed to learn it in the limit. If there is no guarantee that a grammar can be learned, there is no guarantee that the program that it characterizes can be learned either. Hence tasks exist for which learning cannot be guaranteed: there is no universal learning procedure.

The atmosphere in this domain of pure mathematics is a little rarified, so let us come down to earth. Suppose your task is to learn to predict a sequence of dots and dashes, and that the source of these symbols is some *deterministic* device, then there is no guarantee that you or anyone else will be successful – not even with the assistance of the most advanced computing facilities. The source of the signals may be a Turing machine that has been arbitrarily selected from the set with universal power. If we ever succeed in picking up radio signals from outer space, there is no guarantee that we will be able to learn the grammar of the entities transmitting them.

THE NEED FOR CONSTRAINTS IN LEARNING

A final lesson to be drawn from the computational analysis is the need for constraints on what is to be learned. This need follows directly from the lack of a universal learning procedure. There are various ways in which to react to Gold's theorems: his idealization of the learning process is psychologically unrealistic; his learning procedure takes an impossibly long time to learn even a simple grammar; his criterion of successful learning – identification in the limit – is too strong. Since learning must succeed in a reasonable time, there is a need for one or more of the following:

—— a more efficient learning program
—— severe constraints on the set from which the grammar to be learned is drawn
—— a weaker notion of what constitutes success.

However, if the grammar to be learned could be any member of the set of grammars of a particular computational power, then there is no method that can in general out-perform Gold's program. We therefore need to examine the other two possibilities.

If the constraints on the class of relevant grammars suffice to eliminate all but a *finite* number of candidates, then the task of acquiring a grammar is feasible regardless of the power of the relevant grammars. Gold's program will clearly converge on the correct grammar after a finite number of trials, and it will work just as well for the most powerful of grammars. Thus, it is desirable to have access to a representation of the different, but finitely many, candidate grammars from which the one to be learned is drawn.

Noam Chomsky drew this conclusion in connection with children's mastery of their native tongues. A major aim in his programme of research has been to show that the variety of grammars for natural language is severely curtailed. He argues that there is only a finite number of possible human languages, and that they are captured in an innate set of principles (a so-called 'universal grammar'). Any particular language is represented by specific choices within this general framework, and children tune in to their particular language by setting these choices (or 'parameters') to their appropriate values.

Where there are only finitely many candidates, learning becomes a species of deduction: as evidence comes in, it is used to eliminate hypotheses until just a single surviving candidate remains. In some cases, however, learning takes an inductive form, which is much less certain and which therefore satisfies a weaker criterion of success than identification in the limit. Nevertheless, constraints are essential for successful learning, and, as the ethological studies of animals have shown, the nature of the constraints determine what it is possible to learn.

In this chapter, I have outlined a computational analysis of learnability and drawn some conclusions about the nature of what can, and cannot, be learned. And I have described the three general classes of procedure by which learning could occur. Before I discuss some specific procedures that have been proposed by cognitive scientists, I want to consider the nature of memory. All forms of learning depend on memory, and I shall begin my enquiry with the different components of memory that are required for remembering facts.

Further reading

Innate behaviours and ethological studies of learning are discussed by Hinde (1982). The standard psychological text book on learning is Hilgard and Bower (1974) – a new edition is under preparation. Early psychological studies of how animals learn are described in Boakes (1984); Dickinson (1980) provides an excellent account of modern studies and emphasizes the role of cognitive representations. The attempt to achieve artificial intelligence by simulated and unconstrained evolution is outlined by Fogel, Owens and Walsh (1966). The theory of learnability is introduced informally by Pinker (1979), enlarged in technical detail by Osherson, Stob and Weinstein (1986), and its applications to the acquisition of natural language are discussed by Pinker (1984) and Berwick (1985).

142

CHAPTER 8

The components of memory

Because there are few advantages to holding on to red-hot objects, your innate reflex to drop them has an obvious value. Life, however, can seldom be anticipated with such certainty, and so an ability to learn and to remember is advantageous. If you discover a source of food and can recall its location rather than needing to rediscover it, you are more likely to survive. This is an example of learning a fact: an experience is laid down in memory and later called to mind when it is needed. The ability seems commonplace, but it is the envy of workers in artificial intelligence, who have yet to devise programs that retrieve facts with the same sensitivity to context. You may go through life complaining about the fallibility of your memory, but take comfort from the thought that no one knows whether the normal tendency to forget is an unfortunate flaw in the design of human memory, or a feature that improves its overall efficiency.

The complexity of memory is revealed as soon as one thinks about what is needed to remember a fact. The memory system must do at least five things. First, it registers the experience and evaluates whether it is worth remembering. Second, it lays down a representation of the experience. Third, it maintains the memory, perhaps for a long period of time. Fourth, it retrieves the memory rapidly and efficiently when required to do so, either as a result of a deliberate act, as when you have to recall your telephone number, or spontaneously, as when one thing reminds you of another. Fifth, it retains the retrieved memory for a short time in consciousness while it contributes to thought.

I am going to scrutinize the memory system. I shall begin with one sort of memory that is well understood – memory in computers – and compare it with human memory, trying to reach a conclusion about the number of different components of memory that the mind relies on. I will then confront the question of whether these different components are linked up in a series of stages or in a freely interacting parallel system. The story of the experiments that have been carried out to answer this question is itself a lesson in the difficulty of doing psychology. Finally, I will draw some conclusions about what components of memory our robot is likely to need. I shall leave until the next chapter the most perplexing puzzle of all – how unconscious mental processes control the retrieval of memories.

THE ORGANIZATION OF COMPUTER MEMORY

Memory is crucial in computation. Earlier in the book I described how the power to make certain computations depends on the right sort of access to memory. Now, I want to examine how memory works in an actual computer.

In practice, a computer has three main components:

—— a central processor, which controls the actions of the machine;

—— a memory, which stores programs, data and results;

—— an input and output system, which communicates with peripheral devices such as a keyboard for typing in information.

A computer takes data from its input, manipulates them according to a program in its memory, and outputs the results. The program is executed by the central processor, which fetches the next instruction from memory and executes it. This action depends on the three components of the central processor: the arithmetic-logic unit that performs the operations, the control unit that synchronizes them, and a set of registers that are small temporary memories. Thus, to remember the current position in the program, there is a register called the program counter, which contains the address in memory of the next instruction to be executed. Another register, which is called the accumulator, is used to hold a numeral to which the contents of registers can be added, subtracted etc. Other registers are used for general purposes, such as to indicate the status of some result, e.g. that there is a carry. For the computer, everything consists of binary

144

numerals represented as binary patterns of voltages; and there is a set of a hundred or so basic instructions 'wired into' the central processor and initiated by different binary numerals. They carry out arithmetical or logical operations on numerals (in registers or in memory), shift data from one location to another, transfer control from one part of a program to another (by operating on the program counter), input and output data, and control the processor itself, e.g. halting it at the end of a program.

A computer's memory is organized like a set of pigeon-holes. Each location has a specific numerical address and holds a fixed amount of information in the form of a binary numeral. There are three sorts of memory. Read-only memory (ROM) is permanent because the information in it is not lost when the machine is switched off; it contains programs that are vital to the machine. Random-access memory (RAM) has contents that can be changed by the central processor; it is used to store a program that is being executed, any data required by the program, and its results. Secondary memory, such as a magnetic tape or disk, is used for the long-term storage of programs and data that are not currently in use.

Central processing unit

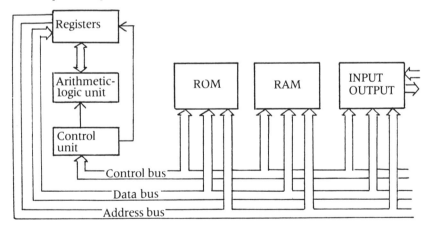

Figure 8.1: A simplified diagram of the architecture of a computer.

145

The components of the computer communicate by three separate highways, or 'buses'. The address bus carries the binary addresses of locations in memory; the data bus carries information to and from these locations; and the control bus carries instructions generated by the control unit of the processor to synchronize such transfers. The overall architecture of the machine is summarized in Figure 8.1.

Memory in a computer serves different functions. There is a repository of basic 'skills' available to the machine at all times, which cannot normally be changed (ROM). Permanent records of programs and other information are held in long-term memory (on tape or disk). They can be transferred to the main memory (RAM), whose contents can be readily changed by the execution of programs. Finally, the intermediate results of computations and other parochial data of no permanent value are held in a short-term memory (the accumulator and other registers of the central processor).

There are many other possible architectures for computers. The one that I have described exemplifies the architecture drawn up by the mathematician John von Neumann. It is a descendent of the universal Turing machine in that program and data are stored alike in the same memory, and the central processor operates serially. Machines with radically different architectures in which a number of processors operate in parallel are becoming more common. They still employ short-term, main and long-term memories, though program and data are often held in separate memories.

THE ORGANIZATION OF HUMAN MEMORY

Cognitive psychologists have been trying for many years to discover how human memory is organized. They used to think that there was a single monolithic memory in which all experiences are retained for lengths of time that depend on how well they have been learned. Gradually psychologists have come to believe that there are at least three distinct memory systems: a set of sensory stores, a short-term memory and a long-term memory.

146

The first development occurred in the 1950s, and led to one of the major precursors to cognitive science: the idea that the mind is a device for processing information. George Miller in his classic paper of 1956, 'The magical number seven, plus or minus two', observed that many phenomena point to the existence of a short-term memory with a limited capacity for holding information. On average, you can remember a seven-digit telephone number for a few seconds without too much difficulty. Your ability to retain binary numerals is little better. If you read the sequence:

101000100111

and then turn away and try to repeat it, you will find the task quite difficult. You can improve your performance by grouping the digits into bigger chunks according to some mnemonic code. For example, after each group of three, translate them into the decimal equivalent. Thus,

$$101 = 5$$
$$000 = 0$$
$$100 = 4$$
$$111 = 7$$

Now all you have to remember is 5047. If you can learn to chunk digits into groups of five and to translate the results into their decimal equivalents, you will be able to repeat back a string of about forty binary digits. Yet, as Miller noted, the number of chunks that you can retain remains roughly constant at about seven items (plus or minus two). In contrast, the capacity of your long-term memory is so large as to seem limitless.

In 1958, Donald Broadbent in his book *Perception and Communication* proposed a theory of the flow of information between the senses and short- and long-term memory. He summarized the theory in a way that was novel at the time, using a block diagram, which is presented in Figure 8.2. The essence of the theory is that there is far too much information impinging on the senses for it all to be processed in full. A selective filter therefore operates to determine which information shall pass through a 'channel' of limited capacity for further processing. If you are at a cocktail party, for example, the selective filter enables you to concentrate on one particular conversation and to ignore all the others in earshot. The filter is controlled by long-term memory, so that if your name is mentioned in another conversation then the filter immediately switches your attention to that conversation. If you are hungry, then the filter will be tuned to select information pertinent to your bodily need, and the system controlling your behaviour will act to increase your chances of coming across such states of affairs. Your behaviour is governed by your memories of past experiences, which are stored in the form of knowledge about the probability of one event occurring given that some other event has occurred. Your short-term memory holds incoming sensory information for a few seconds until it is selected by the filter or replaced by other incoming information. Alternatively, information that has passed through the limited channel can be recirculated by way of short-term memory: this route allows material to go round and round in a loop as you rehearse it mentally. Whilst you are rehearsing, however, the limited channel will have still less capacity to handle anything else.

This early blueprint has been progressively modified as a consequence of further experimental findings. It assumed that a

Figure 8.2: Broadbent's 1958 diagram of the flow of information from senses to memory.

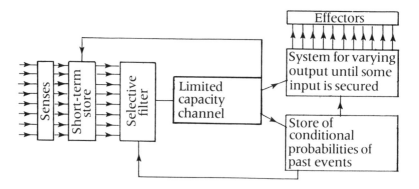

(After D. E. Broadbent, *Perception and Communication.* Oxford: Pergamon, 1958, p. 299)

conversation to which you are not attending is processed only minimally. Subsequent studies have shown that there can be rather more processing of such material. For example, the interpretation of an ambiguous sentence presented to one ear can be biased by material presented so softly to the other ear that you are not even aware of its content. Theorists, such as Anne Treisman, have therefore argued that a more flexible mechanism exists for attenuating the processing of unattended material.

The next innovation was the splitting of short-term memory into two separate components. The phenomenon that led to the split is easy to demonstrate. If you are in your living room at night and switch the light out, you will retain an evanescent visual impression of the room for a fraction of a second afterwards. In an experimental analogue of the situation, George Sperling showed that although people are unable to report the entire contents of an array of letters flashed momentarily before them, they have actually seen and briefly registered the entire array. If they are prompted to recall any particular part of it immediately after its presentation, they can usually do so. The longer the prompt is delayed, however, the more their performance declines. There is evidently a sensory memory for a visual image that persists for about a quarter of a second. This memory might be useful for reading a newspaper in a lightning storm – as one sceptic, Ralph Haber, remarked – but what could its function be? The answer is: to retain the primal sketch long enough for the computations needed to recover the next representation from it. Indeed, there must be separate and continuously updated memories for each sort of representation (primal sketch, two-and-a-half-dimensional sketch, three-dimensional model) required for vision, and the persistence of an image after the lights go out probably depends on them in a complicated way. Similar effects have been demonstrated for hearing – you retain a brief 'echo' of what someone has just said, which fades rapidly. Each sense must have its own memory system whose contents are continuously replaced by new incoming information and cannot be rehearsed. These sensory memories are separate from the short-term memory that holds information for several seconds.

NEUROPSYCHOLOGICAL EVIDENCE FOR DIFFERENT MEMORY SYSTEMS

The differences between short- and long-term memory are shown up starkly by certain patterns of brain damage. The tragic case of a patient known as 'H.M.', described by Brenda Milner, is particularly telling. He suffered damage to the hippocampus (an organ of the brain lying beneath the cortex) and as a result ceased to be able to lay down experiences in his long-term memory. He could recall events before the damage, but thereafter he lived solely in the present tense. He never recognized his doctors from one day to the next; he read the same magazines repeatedly without realizing that he had read them before. Yet, his short-term ability to remember a telephone number was unimpaired, and he was still able to learn new manual skills.

The case of 'K.F.', who was studied by Tim Shallice and Elizabeth Warrington, presents almost the opposite configuration of symptoms. This patient, again as a result of brain damage, had virtually no short-term memory for words or digits, yet he was able to lay down experiences in his long-term memory and to recall them. His ability showed that laying down and retrieving long-term memories may not depend on much processing in short-term memory.

You might wonder whether K.F. could cope with language. On one occasion I had the opportunity to talk to him. He could certainly maintain a conversation without difficulty. There was, however, one tell-tale sign. When I asked him to repeat back the sentence:

The dog bit the man and the man died

he was able to do so perfectly. But when I asked him to repeat the sentence:

The man the dog bit died

he was unable to do so. This sentence requires a listener to hold its subject, 'the man', in memory – whilst processing the embedded relative clause, 'the dog bit' – until the main verb, 'died', occurs. Sentences of this sort do indeed place an additional load on short-term memory. Michael Power has demonstrated that people make more errors in tracking a moving target with a

150

pointer when they happen to utter such a sentence while telling a story. K.F.'s limited short-term memory presumably led to him forgetting the subject of the sentence by the time the main verb occurred, and so he was unable to understand the sentence, and therefore unable to repeat it back.

Since long- and short-term memory can each be independently disrupted by brain damage, there is a 'double dissociation' between them, which suggests that they depend on separate modules within the brain.

WORKING MEMORY

You may have noticed a number of discrepancies between computer memory and human memory. Computers have a main memory (RAM) that stands midway between permanent long-term storage (on tape or disk) and the fleeting short-term record of the intermediate results of computations (in registers). People, however, appear to be equipped with a long-term memory that is both easy to access (like RAM) yet relatively permanent (like tape or disk). They also have sensory memories, whereas computers, which for the most part lack sense organs, have no such memories. Our robot, which is equipped with vision, will certainly need a large memory in which to hold the various visual representations that it computes.

The analogy between human and computer memory has grown closer in a recent theory put forward by Alan Baddeley and Graham Hitch. They observed that when people are asked to rehearse eight digits – a task that ought to preoccupy short-term memory entirely – they can still carry out various tasks. They can understand and verify sentences, albeit at a slower rate than usual, and they can even perform another independent memory task in which they have to recall a list of items. Baddeley and Hitch argue that what has hitherto been treated as short-term memory is better conceived of as a 'working memory' containing several distinct components: a central executive, which can process a limited amount of data of any sort, and which controls the system as a whole; a short-term store for visual or spatial information; and a short-term store for speech, which can function

151

like the 'loop' used to rehearse verbal material in Broadbent's original model.

One of the consequences of this theory is that your limited capacity for remembering telephone numbers, binary digits and so on depends on how much material you can rehearse during a period of two to three seconds. This capacity is usually about seven words, but, as Baddeley has confirmed, the greater the number of syllables in the words, the poorer your performance. The effect of chunking, which I described earlier, is to reduce the number of items to be rehearsed. Since you cannot rehearse visual shapes (unless you can name them), your ability to retain them is much poorer – only two or three. The theory has been neatly corroborated in a recent experiment by Guojun Zhang and Herb Simon. They asked some Chinese people to remember sets of two different sorts of written Chinese characters: both sorts were merely parts of a full character, but one sort had names, whereas the other sort did not. The subjects in the experiment were able to retain about six of the characters with names, but not even three of the nameless characters.

PARALLEL AND SERIAL PROCESSING

The brain, unlike the conventional digital computer, is not a device with a single processor. Many processes occur in parallel, though the stream of conscious experience seems to be serial. Broadbent's original theory assumed that there is a flow of information through a series of stages from the senses to long-term memory (see Figure 8.1). It postulates a production line with a series of processors lined up along it so that one thing happens after another to the 'product' that is being assembled. The concept of working memory, and Broadbent's own current theory, imply that several processors can operate on the same information simultaneously, like robots operating on a single car at the same stage on the production line. Similarly, information can be transmitted directly from one sort of memory to another.

How can one tell whether processing is serial or parallel in any particular mental task? Thereby hangs a cautionary tale about the difficulty of interpreting experimental results, which I shall tell because it hinges on how the contents of short-term memory are used to make a decision. The story begins with a simple experiment.

If I ask you whether or not a particular digit occurred in a list that I have just given you, you will be able to respond without difficulty. Thus, if I give you the list 4 1 7, and then probe your memory with the digit 1, you will respond 'yes'. Saul Sternberg, then of the Bell Telephone Laboratories, observed that, not surprisingly, the time it takes to respond goes up with the number of digits in the list. For each additional digit, people took about a twenty-fifth of a second longer to respond. If they stop mentally scanning the list as soon as they detect a match, they would be slowed down less for a 'yes' response than for a 'no' response where they obviously have to scan the entire list to ensure that it does not contain the probe digit. In fact, however, both the 'yes' and the 'no' responses were slowed down by the same amount for each additional digit. Sternberg therefore concluded that people carry out the task in a series of stages: they scan the entire list even after a positive match, and they do so *before* they respond.

A traditional way to check whether a task calls for a series of stages is to design a variant on it that omits a stage, and then to measure how much faster the variant can be performed. If the same probe digit is used throughout an entire experiment, then it would soon be known by heart, and the task would cut out the stage of identifying the digit. The subjects should respond faster, and the saving in time would provide an estimate of how long it takes to identify the probe digit. Such estimates of the different stages should add up to the duration of the task as a whole. However, the 'subtraction' of stages from a task is a dangerous method. Its estimates will make sense only if the resulting task still calls for precisely the same operations in those stages that remain. In fact, the remaining stages may change considerably – or so one assumes, because sometimes the subtraction of a stage yields a task that takes longer to perform!

This problem led Sternberg to devise a new 'additive' method. If a task depends on a series of independent stages, then something that interferes with one stage should have effects that are independent of something that interferes with another stage. For example, the effect of making the probe digit harder to identify will be to slow down responses, and the effect of adding an extra digit to the list will be similar, and these two effects should be additive and predict how much people are slowed down if both occur. When the experiments were done, Sternberg discovered that the effects of degrading the probe digit and increasing the size of the list were indeed additive. These and other findings appeared to confirm that the task depended on serial stages of processing.

Unfortunately, as Sternberg recognized, his analytical method is not watertight. The interpretation of additive effects only makes sense if a task depends on independent serial stages. But that, of course, is what one wants to find out. The stages may not be independent and there may be parallel processing.

The 'additive' method launched a thousand experiments. And, as often in cognitive psychology, a small change in procedure had a big impact on the pattern of results. When people are given a list of digits to remember and are then asked to search a *visual* display of digits and letters to determine whether it contains any of them, there is one condition in which the length of the list has no effect at all. If the only digits that ever occur in a display are ones that are in the list, then, as Walter Schneider and Richard Shiffrin observed, the response time is not affected by the length of the list. All the subjects have to do is to recognize a digit in a display of letters, and the distinction between digits and letters becomes so highly practised in the experiment that the subjects can respond automatically. If there can be digits in the display that are not in the list, then the task requires a conscious decision, and the size of the list once again affects the time to respond. Even here the results differ from Sternberg's findings. As the list becomes longer, it has a much more costly effect on the 'no' responses than on the 'yes' responses. This finding suggests that people scanning a visual display respond 'yes' just as soon as they find a positive match, but they still have to scan the entire display in order to respond 'no'.

Donald Broadbent has developed a computer model that shows how all the diverse results could arise from a single underlying *parallel* mechanism. He proposes that the mind accumulates and weighs the evidence for making a 'yes' or 'no' response, like a statistician reaching a decision in the face of uncertainty. The strength of evidence accumulates in parallel in a set of registers, with one register for each item in the list: each incoming item is compared with all the items in the list, and a positive match increases the numerical value in the relevant register by a certain amount, and a negative match decreases the value of a register by this same amount. What complicates matters is the presence of random 'noise' in the system; after each comparison is made in the computer simulation, every register also has a different random number added to or subtracted from it. Whenever the strength of evidence in any register exceeds a certain criterion value, the system responds with a 'yes'. Should this response be an error as a result of the random fluctuation, then the criterion is set to a much higher value so as to prevent such premature responses. On every subsequent correct trial, the criterion is gradually reduced a little until another error occurs. The 'no' responses depend on a similar criterion: whenever all the strengths are below its value, the system responds 'no'. An error causes a big drop in the value of the criterion. On subsequent correct negative responses, the criterion is gradually increased in value again.

What Broadbent discovered by running his computer simulation was that different patterns of performance emerged as he manipulated the relative size of the noise in the system. With a modicum of noise, the simulation produced results like those that Sternberg obtained, but as noise was reduced there ceased to be much effect from the number of items in the list and the results were like those of subjects searching for digits in a visual display of letters. Practice thus might have the effect of reducing the noise in the system rather than producing a shift from conscious control to automatic responses. When Broadbent allowed other factors to affect his program, including differences in the discriminability of visual items, the addition of an item to the list had a greater retarding effect on 'no' responses than on 'yes' responses – exactly the result observed by Schneider and Shiffrin. Hence, a single underlying mechanism – the parallel accumulation of evidence – can explain the different patterns of results.

And the moral of this cautionary tale? It is, of course, that the mode of processing in any particular mental task is very difficult to pin down. The difficulty has been demonstrated here for memory, but it is ubiquitous.

CONCLUSIONS

Our ultimate goal is to equip a robot with a system of remembering comparable to human memory. The research that I have discussed in this chapter provides us with some clues about how to set up such a system, but we are not yet in a position to complete the job. We have learned something about the different components of memory, and it has emerged that we shall need five main components:

—— a central executive to control the system as a whole

—— a set of sensory stores to hold the various representations needed by the perceptual system

—— a working memory to hold the intermediate results of the central executive, including spatial representations, and to provide a verbal loop for rehearsal

—— a permanent memory for essential skills

—— a long-term memory for experiences and knowledge.

The evidence suggests that the human cognitive system selects just certain impinging information for further processing and retention in memory, and that it can do so in two different ways: one depends on deliberate decisions emanating from the central executive, and the other reflects the automatic 'attention-grabbing' effects of certain classes of events.

There are two outstanding problems. First, in what sort of format is information represented in long-term memory? Does it consist in propositions in some mental code, in images, in associations between mentally represented events, or in some alternative format? Second, how does the central executive control the sequence of operations for laying down information

156

in long-term memory, for retrieving it, or for manipulating it in working memory? You are not born with the automatic ability to carry out Sternberg's memory task. You go to the laboratory, the experimenter explains what you have to do, and you are able to translate these commands into processes that enable you to perform the task. But you are aware neither of how your mind controls the requisite flow of information, nor of how it is able to set up the appropriate sequence of operations. During the course of the experiment, you become more practised and various changes of which you are hardly conscious may enable you to perform more efficiently. Different people may develop different strategies, which may also change during the course of the experiment.

A major subplot in this chapter has been the difficulty of pinning down answers to such questions from the results of psychological experiments. The theories that I have discussed have tried to explain such results by postulating an appropriate sequence of mental operations; they have little to say about how the sequence is set up, developed and modified. Allen Newell has said of research that is driven by particular experimental paradigms, such as Sternberg's task: 'You can't play 20 questions with nature and win.' In other words, the control processes of the mind, which adapt it so flexibly to strategic demands, cannot be isolated simply by studying this or that task in the laboratory. We must consider in addition the overall architecture of the memory system.

Further reading

For an excellent introduction and 'user's guide' to memory, see Baddeley (1983). Halsall and Lister (1980) describe the standard architecture of memory in microcomputers. The notion of a 'double dissociation' in patients suffering from brain damage is discussed in Shallice (1978). Sacks (1985), in an evocative set of case histories, presents 'The Lost Mariner', a patient who, like 'H.M.', lives only in the present tense. The distinction between intentional and automatic behaviour is discussed in many places in the psychological literature, e.g. Norman and Shallice (1980), Reason and Mycielska (1982) and Johnson-Laird (1983).

CHAPTER 9

Plans and productions

Learning, memory and all higher mental processes may be different manifestations of the same general principles governing the mind. If so, a sensible research strategy is to develop a theory of such a mental 'architecture', and then to implement a programming language based on that architecture in which specific programs can be written to model mental processes. There are two main conjectures about the architecture of the mind: one is that it is based on a 'production system', and the other that it is based on 'parallel distributed processing'. They both have important things to say about learning and the retrieval of information from memory. And I shall describe them both, beginning in this chapter with production systems, and dealing in the next with parallel distributed processing.

There was a time when psychologists believed that behaviour was controlled by external events. Karl Lashley, as I wrote in Chapter 1, pointed out that this hypothesis could not explain the rapid execution of skills which call for an internal organization. In 1960, George Miller, Eugene Galanter and Karl Pribram sealed the coffin of Behaviorism with the publication of their book *Plans and the Structure of Behavior*. They defined a plan as: 'any hierarchical process in the organism that can control the order in which a sequence of operations is to be performed', and they demonstrated that planning is a major part of cognition. Production systems have their roots in planning and in the work of Allen Newell and Herbert Simon, who pioneered the computational modelling of mental processes. I will start my description of productions by considering their origins in the study of plans.

PLANS AND THE PROCESS OF SEARCH

When you develop a plan, Newell and Simon argued, you have in mind an *initial state* and a *goal*, and your task is to devise a sequence of *operations* that will get you from one to the other. Suppose your task is to prove a theorem in geometry. The initial state is a set of conditions, often summarized in a diagram; the goal is a conclusion; and the operations consist of various axioms and rules of inference that you are allowed to use. The set of all possible sequences of these operations is vast, and what you have to find within this hypothetical 'problem space' is a route through the space from initial state to goal:

initial state $\longrightarrow$ state 2 $\longrightarrow$ state 3 $\longrightarrow$ . . . $\longrightarrow$ goal

where each arrow symbolizes one of the permitted operations.

There are many different ways in which you can search for a route through a problem space, and many have been implemented in computer programs. You can start at the initial state, apply all feasible operations to it to yield a set of alternative second states, and then do the same thing to each of these states, and so on. If a problem is intrinsically insoluble, or you do not know all the essential operations, your efforts are bound to fail. Otherwise, sooner or later, this so-called 'breadth-first' search will arrive at the goal. The trouble is that the number of routes to be explored grows exponentially: it doubles at each step even if there are only two possible operations that can be applied at any point. It soon ceases to be feasible to explore all the routes – even if you have a computer as big as the universe and running at the speed of light. The search problem is intractable. Still worse, as we shall see in Chapter 12, it has been proved that in certain domains any search procedure may fail to discover that there is no successful route: the procedure, in effect, goes into the problem space, gets lost, and never emerges with an answer. Hence, no matter what procedure is used, constraints are needed to keep the search to a manageable size. Once again, they play a critical role in a mental task.

Another class of search procedures explores one route at a time in a 'depth-first' search, just as you do in trying to find a way

159

through a maze. When you come to a choice of routes, you plump for one on the basis of whatever means are at your disposal. In trying to solve a problem, you might choose by assessing the potential values of each of the alternatives. Of course, if you have an absolutely certain method of assessment, there is no difficulty: you choose the best option at each point and will thereby arrive at your goal without ever exploring any blind alleys.

Many problems of planning, alas, are like the Hampton Court maze. You are forced to choose with only an uncertain guide to the value of any alternative, and you proceed in this way until you reach either the goal or a dead end. If you come to a dead end, you can go back to the previous point of choice and try a different alternative. If you exhaust all the options at this point to no avail, then you can go back one step further, and so on. If, eventually, you exhaust all possibilities at all choice points, then the problem is insoluble. This procedure of working back through the choice points is called, appropriately enough, 'backtracking'. To use it, you must be as prudent as Theseus, who unwound Ariadne's ball of thread as he made his way through the Minotaur's labyrinth: you must lay down a record of each choice that you make. Like the robot's navigational system (see Chapter 3), programs typically use a stack as a memory for this purpose.

'Those who know no history', it is said, 'are doomed to repeat its mistakes.' Thus it is with simple backtracking, which does not take into account the *reason* that a particular choice failed. If you pick up a red-hot poker with one hand, then it will lead you to try the other hand.

You do not necessarily have to start at the initial state in a problem 'space' and search blindly forwards for a route to the goal. Newell and Simon devised a program based on an idea of the mathematician George Polya (he was anticipated by Plato). It looks for an operation that reduces the difference between the goal and the initial state. Thus, if you are trying to find a plan to mend the hole in your bucket, a relevant operation for reducing the difference between goal and initial state is to put a stopper in the hole. However, it may be impossible to carry out such an operation because one of its preconditions is not satisfied, e.g.

you do not have a stopper. At this point, Newell and Simon introduced an ingenious idea. You create a new subgoal – to find a stopper – and you put this subgoal on the stack above your main goal. You now use exactly the same procedure to try to achieve this subgoal: you search for an operation that is relevant to reducing the difference between it and the initial state. If you succeed in finding a stopper, you remove the subgoal from the stack because it has been achieved. This removal reinstates the main goal by bringing it to the top of the stack, and you can carry out the operation that provoked the diversion, i.e. you put the stopper into the hole in your bucket. The search for a solution to a subgoal may create a further sub-subgoal, and so on, so that subgoals pile up on the stack to a considerable depth. Of course, their creation must not be allowed to go on forever. Similarly, one subgoal must not lead round to the same subgoal as part of its own solution. Unlike the song, you do not want to arrive at the subgoal of carrying water in the bucket in order to mend the hole in it.

Newell and Simon's program, which is known as GPS (for 'general problem solver'), has to be equipped with a knowledge of all the operations relevant to solving a problem in a particular domain, and with constraints on the situations in which they are likely to be useful. It plans a course of action using a general search procedure, which, as I have explained, is also used to solve subparts of the problem. Such a scheme is another example of 'recursion', which here builds up a hierarchical plan to solve a problem.

HOW PRODUCTION SYSTEMS WORK

When people plan, they have to bring to mind knowledge about relevant operations. But, what program controls the retrieval of knowledge from long-term memory, and in what form is the knowledge stored there? In a more recent theory, Newell and Simon have proposed that knowledge is represented by a vast set of conditional rules (or 'productions') that have this form:

$$\text{condition} \longrightarrow \text{action}$$

Conditional rules, such as 'if there is a hole in the bucket and you have a stopper, then put the stopper in the hole', might seem a rather impoverished representation for general knowledge. In effect, however, they constitute a grammar, which can be equivalent in power to a universal Turing machine. Indeed, the American logician Emil Post originally devised production rules in order to define what could be computed. They are a psychologically oriented theory of computation in which one can construct specific theories of cognition.

A grammar, as I remarked in Chapter 3, cannot do anything. It needs a program to make use of it. Production rules similarly must rely a program before they can do anything. Newell and Simon assumed that they are stored in long-term memory, and the program for retrieving and using them runs in working memory. Whenever the state of affairs described in the *condition* of a rule occurs in working memory, then the rule is triggered and its *action* is carried out. Hence, the current contents of working memory are matched against the conditions of all the rules in long-term memory – a comparison that in human beings is presumably done in a single parallel step – in order to trigger a rule. The action of a rule can be a physical response, but it can also change the contents of working memory and in this way control which rule is triggered next. The principles that determine how one rule is followed by another are therefore built into the rules themselves. The system solves the problem that I mentioned at the end of the last chapter: it controls the performance of a task. This abstract recipe is hard to grasp at first, but it will become clearer from an example.

To illustrate a production system at work, I will outline one devised by my colleague, Richard Young, which models children's performance in a simple task. They have to put a set of wooden rods into order according to their length. As Jean Piaget and his collaborators observed, children pass through several stages in their competence to perform the task. Four-year-olds succeed in getting just the occasional pair of rods into the right order. This limited ability requires only a simple set of production rules, which I shall paraphrase in English. They depend on a working memory in the form of a stack on which goals are placed and from which they are removed as they are achieved.

The initial step is to put the main goal (to form the ordered

162

series) on to the stack. The rest of the performance is governed by the rules. There are rules that ensure that the first rod is placed in position:

1. If the current goal (i.e. the one at the top of the stack) is to form a series and no rods have been placed in position, then add to the stack the goal of placing the first rod.

2. If the current goal is to place the first rod, then pick up a big rod.

3. If the current goal is to place the first rod and a big rod has just been picked up, then put it down at the far left and remove the goal from the top of the stack (because it has been achieved).

This last step satisfies the goal of adding the first rod to start the array, but the main goal of forming a series still remains at the top of the stack. A second set of rules enables the cycle of placing rods to continue:

4. If the current goal is to form a series and at least one rod has been placed in position, then add to the stack the next goal, which is to place another rod.

5. If the current goal is to place another rod, then pick up the nearest rod.

6. If the current goal is to place another rod and a rod has just been picked up, then put it down on the right of the series and remove the goal from the stack.

7. If the current goal is to form a series and at least one rod has been placed in position and there are no rods left to place, then remove the goal from the stack and stop.

A program that has these seven rules will first pick up a big rod – perhaps the biggest – and thereafter add rods willy-nilly to the series, just like the youngest children that Piaget observed.

Young has shown how the transition from one stage to another in children's development can be modelled by adding new rules. Thus, the addition of the following rules improves performance by switching round a newly formed adjacent pair of rods if they are in the wrong order:

8. If the current goal is to place another rod and a new configuration of rods has just been formed, then check whether the rod that is in a new position is bigger than its adjacent rod in the series.

9. If the current goal is to place another rod and the rod that is in a new position is smaller than its adjacent rod, then remove the goal from the stack (because it is satisfied).

10. If the current goal is to place another rod and the rod that is in a new position is *bigger* than its adjacent rod, then switch the two rods around.

The effects of this last rule propagate throughout the entire series of rods. The rule is initially triggered when a rod just added to the array is bigger than the adjacent rod, as in the series:

The rule acts to produce a new arrangement:

This new arrangement triggers rule 8, which notes that the rod in a new position is bigger than its adjacent fellow to the left, and this fact triggers rule 10 again. It yields:

This new arrangement triggers rule 8, which records that the new rod is *smaller* than the one on its left, and this fact‘triggers rule 9 which removes the goal of placing the rod from the stack.

164

This system of rules will ultimately arrange the rods correctly, much like the performance of five- and six-year-olds, who can do the task but only by continually rearranging the rods to get them into the right order. Eight-year-olds can usually put the rods into the right order without making mistakes, and can even insert an additional rod into its rightful position. Young modelled this stage by still further rules, which ensure that the order in which the rods are picked up depends on their size.

The program stacks up goals in a hierarchy, and the task has the structure:

Form a series

Place first rod   Place another rod

where the goal of placing another rod continues until there are no further rods to be added. Thus, the plan is a simple hierarchy in which a goal dominates two subgoals. In principle, plans may contain subgoals that dominate sub-subgoals, and so on – not *ad infinitum*, but until it reaches a set of basic actions that accomplish low-level goals.

Production systems are just one way of generating and executing hierarchical plans. The theories that are most naturally framed within them work on the basis of explicit patterns. The conditions of the rules contain variables, such as 'rod' that can designate many different rods, and so it is the *pattern* of the information in working memory, rather than its particular content, that triggers a rule.

Newell and Simon originally used a production system to formulate a theory of how people solve problems in logic, chess, and other domains. Since then, a variety of programming languages have been based on production systems. They have been used to develop practical programs that embody the knowledge of human experts (the so-called 'expert systems', which I shall discuss in Chapter 12). They have also been used to construct a number of psychological theories. The major differences in these theories concern, not the production rules, but the programs that manipulate them. There is controversy about whether or not working memory is a stack, be-

165

cause people have difficulty with many tasks that would be trivial for such a memory, e.g. understanding highly embedded sentences. Some programs therefore make use of a working memory that works as a loop, or 'buffer', in which items are accessed in the order in which they enter memory: the first one in is the first one out.

Another difference between the theories concerns something that may have been troubling the reader: what happens when more than one production rule matches the contents of memory? Young's system triggers the rule that matches the contents of memory in most detail. Rules can also be put into an order of priority by the programmer so that when a conflict occurs, the rule with the highest priority is chosen. Alternatively, the resolution can take into account how frequently a rule has been used, or how recently it has been triggered.

THE **ACT** THEORY OF MEMORY

John Anderson has developed a comprehensive theory of memory and learning based on a production system. This theory, which he calls ACT, has been implemented in an evolving series of computer simulations. A recent one is ACT*, which is outlined in Figure 9.1. The theory recognizes two types of long-term memories: those for facts and experiences, and those for skills. You remember experiences, calling them to mind and perhaps savouring them again. But you do not so much remember skills, or even re-enact them: you carry them out in ways that fit the circumstances. As we saw in the previous chapter, brain damage can impair memory for experiences but leave memory for skills almost intact. Some psychologists, notably Endel Tulving, have argued that a further distinction can be drawn between memory for specific autobiographical experiences and memory for items of general knowledge, such as the meanings of words. Anderson, however, posits just three memory components: a working memory that varies in capacity from moment to moment, a long-term memory for skills (production memory), and a long-term memory for propositions, images and representations of the order of events (declarative memory).

Figure 9.1: The main components of John Anderson's ACT* theory of memory.

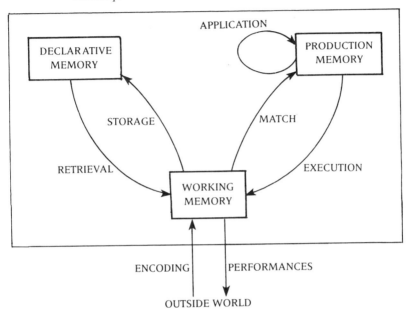

(From J. R. Anderson, *The Architecture of Cognition.* Cambridge, Mass.: Harvard University Press, 1983, p. 19)

The theory introduces several complications into the architecture of production systems. The items in all three memories can vary in their degree of 'activity' (like the processors in Marr and Poggio's program for random-dot stereopsis). If the contents of working memory match more than one rule in production memory, then whichever is the most active is triggered. Moreover, if one pattern is active, it excites its other, more specific versions and inhibits alternative patterns. Thus, ACT combines the normal 'bottom-up' mode of matching patterns with a subsequent 'top-down' processing that leads from active high-level structure to predictions about low-level detail. The top-down process may trigger a rule that does not completely match the contents of working memory – a procedure that can be useful, but that can also lead to errors in performance similar to the errors that people make.

167

A central assumption of Anderson's theory is that all knowledge is initially propositional, but it can be converted into procedures. You start off learning to drive, for example, by being told certain facts, which you can interpret in a slow-witted way as a guide to actions. As a result of practice, this knowledge is converted into procedures in the production system that are executed rapidly and automatically. This idea raises again the topic of learning, and in particular how it can occur in a production system.

LEARNING AND PRACTICE

The learning of complex skills, particularly intellectual skills such as planning, takes a long time. Simon has pointed out that children take five or six years to get ready for school, and then a further twenty years of education to become competent doctors, scientists or professionals. One wonders whether the slowness is inevitable, and what it reflects about the mind during the processes of accumulating facts and becoming practised in the use of knowledge.

One clue is the 'power' law of learning, which relates the time it takes to perform a task to how much the task has been practised. Obviously, practice makes perfect, and the more you practise the faster you get. But, as a result of examining many studies of learning – from making cigars in a factory to reading text presented upside down in the laboratory – Allen Newell and Paul Rosenbloom have found a ubiquitous quantitative law: if you plot the logarithm of the time that it takes to perform a task against the logarithm of the number of times that it has been performed, the result is a straight line. Figure 9.2 shows a typical example. The major constraint on the law is that the task should be one that people can immediately perform without error. There is a physical barrier to how fast any task can ultimately be performed, which also places a limit on the law.

What does the law mean? Suppose that the time taken to perform a task depends on the sum of the times taken to perform each of its separate components. If practice caused each of these components to get faster at the same constant rate, then it would

168

Figure 9.2: An illustration of the 'power' law of learning: the logarithm of the time taken by a single individual to read a page of inverted text is plotted as a function of the logarithm of the number of pages that the individual has already read. The data were originally reported by Paul A. Kolers.

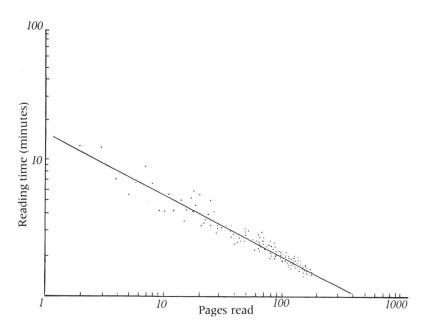

(From A. Newell and P. S. Rosenbloom, Mechanisms of skill acquisition and the law of practice. In J. R. Anderson, ed., *Cognitive Skills and their Acquisition.* Hillsdale, NJ: Lawrence Erlbaum, 1981, p. 7. The data were originally reported in P. A. Kolers, Memorial consequences of automatized encoding. *Journal of Experimental Psychology: Human Learning and Memory,* 1, 1975)

lead to a saving directly proportional to the current time taken to perform the task. This principle is far too efficient: it yields a so-called 'exponential' law. What the power law shows is that the rate of learning is not constant, but gradually slows down. It is as though the possibilities for improvement are gradually exhausted as practice continues. But what might these possibilities be?

One idea, due to George Miller as I noted in the previous chapter, is that practice can enable a learner to organize the elements of a task into ever larger units or 'chunks'. Chess novices, for instance, have difficulty in remembering the details of a chess position if they are allowed to examine it for only a few seconds. Yet, after the same brief exposure, chess masters recall the position of each piece. They have developed an enormous memory for chess positions, stored in 'chunks' that correspond to meaningful relations between pieces. They have built up some 50,000 chunks, Simon estimates, as a result of years of experience. The larger the scope of a chunk – that is, the more pieces it includes – then the rarer its occurrence in games. A new chunk of a larger size can be formed only out of occurrences of the patterns making up its constituents. Newell and Rosenbloom use productions to simulate the growth of chunks, and, as they point out, the occasions for such learning become rarer and rarer as the size of the chunks grows larger and larger. The inevitable slowing down of the rate of learning may account for the power law.

THE CONSTRUCTION OF NEW PRODUCTION RULES

We now come back full circle to the treatment of learning as a program that constructs new programs, but with the proviso that the resulting programs should take the form of production systems. A production system is a set of rules, and so learning can occur merely by adding a new rule to the existing set. There are many possible mechanisms for constructing such rules. There can be special rules that have the power to construct new rules, or to add new rules, or, as Clayton Lewis has suggested, to combine different existing rules into one.

Another source of productions could be facts. Suppose, for instance, that among the facts in your long-term memory, there is an ordinary addition table, which you learned at school. This table will include the fact:

$$3 + 5 = 8$$

Such facts have the advantage that they can be used to do several things, e.g. to find the sum of $3 + 5$, or to work out what number must be added to 3 in order to obtain 8. But, of course, to use facts one needs procedures that will interpret them, and

170

this interpretation takes time. If you have only the addition table, and procedures for interpreting it, your performance will be relatively slow. The transition from the early hesitant execution of a skill to its highly practised performance corresponds, at least for John Anderson, to the transformation of a set of facts into a set of production rules. Productions have the advantage that they can be immediately executed, and so if you can convert the facts of the addition table into productions, you will be able to perform more rapidly. Here is an example of a special production rule paraphrased in ordinary English that will create the sort of productions that you need:

If the addition table contains a fact of the form A + B = C, then build a new rule with the condition: (GOAL to add A and B) and the action: (ANSWER C).

This rule can construct a new rule, such as:

If the goal is to add 3 and 5, then the answer is 8.

This mechanism may well be unrealistically good at certain forms of learning.

John Anderson has also proposed an alternative method of learning. He has introduced a special mechanism that transforms facts into rules. This transformation resembles the translation, or 'compilation', of a program written in a high-level programming language into the machine code that directly controls a computer. Just as compilation depends on a special program to carry it out, so the conversion of propositions into procedural rules calls for special machinery that is built into the architecture of the production system. One of the nice features of this account, as Anderson has pointed out, is that it explains some of the negative aspects of practice. When a skill has become automatic, it is executed without thinking and without conscious access to some of its hitherto intermediate stages. The result is sometimes foolish. If you have learned a certain formulaic way in which to behave, then you may overlook an obvious short cut that occurs in a novel situation. Your performance may even lead you into error, as the following children's riddle demonstrates. How do you pronounce 'M', 'A', 'C', 'H', 'A', 'M', 'I', 'S', 'H'? How do you pronounce 'M', 'A', 'C', 'H', 'E', 'N', 'R', 'Y'? How do you pronounce 'M', 'A', 'C', 'H', 'I', 'N', 'E', 'R', 'Y'?

CONCLUSIONS

A production system is an elegant, uniform way in which to construct a theory about the learning, representation and retrieval of knowledge. A specific theory, such as ACT, can obviously be shown to be false. In principle, however, production systems have the unlimited power of a universal Turing machine. Hence, as an hypothesis about the architecture of the mind, they are unlikely to be refutable by any empirical evidence. They can accommodate any consistent pattern of results. They are more like a programming language than an empirically testable theory.

What, if anything, do the theorists who have constructed production systems hold in common? The answer appears to be three main principles. First, the theorists are committed to a unitary mental architecture. Second, they argue that the control processes governing the performance of mental tasks should be relatively simple: in essence, the contents of a working memory trigger procedures stored in a long-term memory, which in turn can govern what is selected next by way of their effects on working memory. Third, they assume that the processes governing learning and memory depend on symbolic rules. The significance of a particular symbol in a production system depends entirely on the rules in which it occurs, and these rules have to be spelt out with an explicit structure within the system. You might think that it is rather odd that such rules, which are so easily paraphrased in English, lie beneath the surface of your mental life. If you could lift the lid off the mind and peer in, would you really find a set of principles laid out like an Act of Parliament, and could such principles cover all eventualities? Perhaps not. These doubts, in part, lie behind the alternative conception of mental architecture that I shall describe in the next chapter.

172

Further reading

Newell (1973) gives an account of production systems from the standpoint of psychology, Simon (1981, Ch. 4) provides a stimulating essay on remembering and learning, and Winston (1984, Ch. 6) outlines the programming procedures. A recent book of papers on the use of production systems to model learning and children's development has been edited by Klahr, Langley and Neches (1986). Studies of children's performance in the seriation task are described by Piaget (1952) and Inhelder and Piaget (1964).

CHAPTER 10

Parallel distributed processing

There is a recent and revolutionary idea about mental architecture that is sometimes called 'connectionism', and sometimes 'parallel distributed processing'. Unlike the theory of production systems, it does not use rules with an *explicit* structure. And in this theory, memory is still more remote from a set of numbered pigeon-holes each containing its particular contents. Instead, like a hologram, a long-term memory for an experience is distributed over many processing units, and each of these units participates in the representation of many experiences – an idea that will become clearer as we proceed. The processing units of the system are a little like idealized brain cells. They can perform only the same simple computation. The power of the system comes from how the units are connected. One of its major features, which I shall explore, is the ability to learn.

THE RECONSTRUCTIVE NATURE OF HUMAN MEMORY

The difference between the purposes of human and computer memory is not so striking as the difference in their performance. A computer never forgets – unless it malfunctions or you switch it off or you program it to forget – but the contents of its memory are ultimately accessed by instructions that contain a numerical address and that copy data from that address to the central processor. Human memory has its occasional lapses and foibles, but it is equipped with a remarkable ability that is so familiar to us that we scarcely notice it: one thing reminds us of another. To illustrate the subtlety of this ability, let us play a game.

I am thinking of something that you will probably have heard of, and I am going to give you a series of clues about it. Your task is to guess what the object is as soon as you can. Here are the clues:

It is a navigational instrument.
It is not a compass.
It is used to measure the angle of the sun or other celestial bodies above the horizon.
It enables you to determine your geographical position.
It contains a telescope, a triangular frame and a mirror.

You are now likely to be in one of three states of mind. You have identified the object, or you know that you have no idea what it is, or you have its name on 'the tip of your tongue'. In this last case, you may be able to say how many syllables the word has (two) or what its initial consonant is ('s'), and you may also have been reminded of one or two words that are similar in meaning ('theodolite') or in sound ('sexton') or both ('secant'). I need hardly continue: I was thinking of a *sextant*. You may have thought of the right object after only one or two clues even though the description was incomplete. You could probably have coped even if I had included a misleading clue. Somehow your memory delivers an item that satisfies a set of constraints. This retrieval system, which operates outside your conscious awareness, does not examine the contents of a set of pigeon-holes one by one. If it did, you would take a long time indeed to decide that you had never heard of the object.

Figure 10.1, which is based on one devised by Peter Lindsay and Don Norman, shows a word that has been partly obliterated by ink blots. What is the word? Again you are likely to realize at once that it is: RED. In this case, your memory acts in a recon-structive way. The first letter could be K or R, the second letter could be E or F, and the third letter could be B or D. There are therefore eight different possible strings of letters, but only one of them is an English word. You did not have to consider each possibility in a cold-blooded way – the right word came to mind with little effort. Once again, the retrieval system automatically copes with separate constraints and retrieves an item that matches them.

Figure 10.1: What word is here partly obliterated by ink-blots?

(After P. Lindsay and D. Norman, *Human Information Processing*. First edition, New York: Academic Press, 1972, p. 142)

PARALLEL PROCESSING OF LOCAL REPRESENTATIONS

How can we explain the efficiency of the human retrieval system in recognizing printed words? One hypothesis is that cues can be matched simultaneously to all the contents of memory, like sticking knitting needles through a pack of punched cards. A better theory was proposed by Jay McClelland and Dave Rumelhart. They assumed that each possible word is represented by a separate processing unit. Likewise, each letter at each position in a word is represented by a separate unit. The units are small-scale processors that are connected to each other and that compute in parallel. They each have a certain level of activity that can vary from moment to moment, and that corresponds to how much current support exists for the item that a unit represents. Some pairs of units represent mutually supporting possibilities, e.g. that the first letter of the word is 'R' and that the word as a whole is 'RED'. Such units are wired up so as to excite each other: when one is activated then it increases the level of activation of the other. Other pairs of units represent inconsistent possibilities, e.g. that the first letter of the word is 'R' and that the first letter of the word is 'B'. Such pairs are wired up so as to inhibit each other: when one is activated then it reduces the level of activation of the other.

A fragment of the overall design is shown in Figure 10.2. For clarity, I have left out most of the connections, including all the inhibitory ones between units at the same level. The connections between the levels of word and letter are either excitatory or inhibitory, depending on whether the items they represent are mutually consistent or inconsistent. There is a third level of units, which represent parts of letters, such as a vertical line or a horizontal bar, and which excite or inhibit the units representing letters.

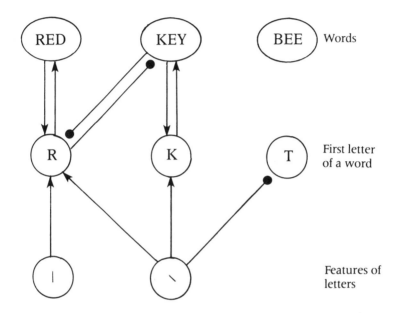

Figure 10.2: A fragment of the McClelland and Rumelhart device for recognizing words. Arrows correspond to excitatory connections, and blobs correspond to inhibitory connections. Only a few such connections are shown.

The theory explains how we perceive words that are partly obliterated by ink blots. In the case of Figure 10.1, the unit representing the word 'RED' will be excited by those units representing 'R' in the first position, 'E' in the second position, and 'D' in the third position. Although other words will be slightly excited by, for example, 'K' in the first position, no word will receive so much activation as 'RED'. It in turn will feed activation back to the units representing individual letters that excite it; they will further excite it, and so on, until the word unit is sufficiently active to reach a threshold corresponding to recognition.

Experiments have shown that it is easier to recognize a letter in the middle of a word than in the middle of a nonsense string. It is easier to recognize, say, 'K' if it occurs in:

ANKLE

than if it occurs in:

XMKTF

The theory explains this phenomenon. It occurs because the unit representing the word, 'ANKLE', feeds back activation to the units representing its component letters, including 'K', but no such feedback can occur with the nonsense string since it is not a word and will not be represented as a whole by any processing unit.

Instead of pigeon-holes with numerical addresses, there are active units that are addressed by the actual components of the word that is to be recognized. This arrangement seems like a step towards human memory, but how is the system of interconnections set up in the first place? And is it necessary that each word, letter and part of a letter has a separate, local pigeon-hole in memory? In the next section I will show how their representations can be distributed across many memory units, each of which enters into the representation of many items. This idea, which is due to a number of theorists including James Anderson, Geoff Hinton and Tuevo Kohonen, will prepare the way for an account of how the connections in memory could be learned.

LINEAR ASSOCIATIONS BETWEEN PATTERNS

Suppose that two sets of processing units are to be connected so that when one set is stimulated with a particular pattern of activity the other set will respond with an appropriate pattern of activity. For example, when the pattern representing the printed word 'red' is fed into one set of units, then the pattern corresponding to the sound of the word will be produced by the other set. We shall assume that each unit can be at only one of three levels of activation: active ($+1$), neutral (0) or inhibited

(−1). This scheme may seem too rudimentary to represent words, but, as we know, we can represent just about anything by a string of binary numerals (0 or 1), and so we can do just as well in this ternary notation. However, such coding systems may not make *explicit* what is most significant in the item that is represented.

The associations between patterns can be set up in three steps. The first step is to establish the strength of connections between the two sets of units. (The reader must keep this concept distinct from that of the levels of activity of units.) We can represent the strengths of connections in a wiring diagram, or in an array in which a row stands for a unit in one set, a column stands for a unit in the other set, and the cell where row and column intersect contains the strength of the connection between the two units. In practice, there would be many units but all the principles of the system can be illustrated in a small-scale example with just two units in each set:

Visual units

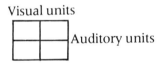Auditory units

The strength of the connection between two units is the same in both directions. Like McClelland and Rumelhart, we will assume that the strength can be excitatory, neutral or inhibitory; and thus it can have any value between +1 and −1. One unit transmits to another an activation equal to its own activation multiplied by the strength of the connection, e.g. an active unit (+1) with an inhibitory connection of −0.5 to another unit transmits to it a value of −0.5.

The second step is to implement the principle that a unit's level of activation is equal to the sum of all the activations that it receives from other units. We can use this principle to set the strengths of the connections so that, for example, the visual pattern +1 −1 automatically produces the auditory pattern −1 −1, and *vice versa*. Here are the strengths of connection that establish this association:

179

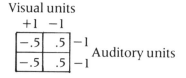

Consider the auditory unit in the top row. Its level of activation is the sum of the values (activation × strength of connection) that it receives from each visual unit:

$$(+1 \times -.5) + (-1 \times .5)$$

which equals -1. The activation of the auditory unit in the bottom row is determined in the same way. The arrangement is symmetrical: if the auditory pattern is the input, then the visual pattern is the output. In general, the strength of the connection between two units needs to be positive when both of them have levels of activation of the same sign; otherwise, it needs to be negative. The numerical values of the strengths depend on the overall number of connections.

We can use the same principles to construct an array that establishes an association between a different pair of patterns. The following array establishes an association between the visual pattern $+1$ $+1$ and the auditory pattern -1 $+1$:

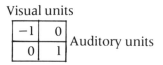

Now comes the third, and remarkable, step. We add together the two arrays of strengths of connection to obtain:

Visual units

−1	0
0	1

Auditory units

This one array suffices to make either association: feed in the first visual pattern, and you get out the first auditory pattern; feed in the second visual pattern, and you get out the second auditory pattern. Both associations are encoded in a single set of connections between the two sets of units. The system is what mathematicians refer to as 'linear', because separate operations – in this case, strengths of connection – have effects that can be combined additively.

There is obviously a limit to the number of different associations that can be represented in a single set of connections, and it is equal to the number of units in either one of the sets. Hence, with just two units in each set, only two associations can be established, but an actual network of nerves in the brain could represent millions of associations. Similar input patterns give rise to similar outputs, and so if it is desirable to avoid interference, the input patterns should be unrelated to one another. (This notion has a precise mathematical formulation: any pair of input patterns should be 'orthogonal', i.e. the cross-products of the pair should sum to zero, e.g. for the two visual inputs, $+1 -1$ and $+1 +1$, the cross-product is $(+1 \times +1) + (-1 \times +1) = 0$, and so the equation holds.)

Several interesting properties emerge from a large system of this sort. The activity of any single unit is relatively unimportant. If it malfunctions or is destroyed, the system will not be drastically impaired. Similarly, if a small part of an input is missing or obliterated, the system can still yield the correct output. Indeed, if an array is based on associating each input with itself, it will be able to complete fragmentary inputs with their missing parts. Numerical addresses have been replaced by a system in which the *symbols* in the input themselves address memory. Such a memory has only vague boundaries between recall, reconstruction and complete confabulation.

This blurring of the categories of memory resembles human recall. In the 1930s, Sir Frederic Bartlett observed that people remember stories by reconstructing them. They highlight certain points and omit others, depending on their interests. Without realizing it, they make plausible inferences in order to reconstruct a missing detail. The same phenomena occur for events in real life, as Ulric Neisser has shown in an ingenious study. He compared John Dean's testimony about the events leading up to the Watergate scandal with the transcripts of the tapes made in the White House. The comparison showed that Dean had a correct recall of the gist of past conversations, but could not relate it accurately to specific episodes. It was as though his memories of many related discussions had merged together into a single composite, like a set of superimposed photographs of the same individual. The picture was accurate overall, but its details were fuzzy and sometimes erroneous.

Our capacity to retain gist is reflected in a striking ability to recognize what we have seen before. Lionel Standing has measured this ability experimentally. He presented small groups of people with ten thousand pictures at a rate of one every five seconds. Then, as a test, he presented pairs of pictures, one from the original set and one from a set of similar pictures that had not been presented. Even after an interval of two days, people could pick out which of the two pictures they had seen before with an accuracy of 80 per cent.

LEARNING IN PERCEPTRONS

How might the appropriate strengths of connection be learned as a result of experience? This question is almost as old as the idea of associative learning. Its modern formulations go back to the first investigations of the properties of networks of units resembling nerve cells. The late Donald Hebb, a pioneer in this field, suggested a simple learning principle: whenever two connected units are active at the same time, they increase the strength of the connection between them. Another pioneer, Frank Rosenblatt, proposed that patterns could be identified using a device that he called a 'perceptron'. It consists of an artificial retina connected to a set of input units, which in turn are connected to output units. The units have a threshold, and only if the sum of the values that a unit receives exceeds its threshold does it become active.

The introduction of thresholds creates a unit in which inputs no longer have additive effects: if the activation of a unit is increased by repeatedly adding the same amount, then there is no effect until the accumulation exceeds the unit's threshold and it springs to life. Such 'non-linear' units can carry out complicated computations if activation is recycled through them. Recycling activation through a system of linear units, however, yields only trivial results, because (as matrix algebra shows) the same computation can always be carried out by a single pass through some other linear network.

Figure 10.3 presents a simple perceptron containing two input units with neglible thresholds connected to an output unit with a threshold of 0.5. The strengths of connection from the two input units to the output unit are both +1. Hence, if one input unit is active, it will transmit a value of +1 to the output unit. This exceeds its threshold and so it will fire. It only fails to fire if neither input is active. The network thus recognizes an inclusive disjunction, i.e. activity in one or other (or both) of the input units.

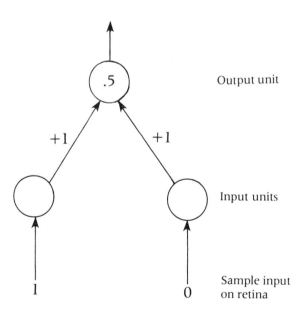

Figure 10.3: A perceptron that recognizes when one or other (or both) of its inputs is active.

In order to enable a perceptron to learn, Rosenblatt adopted the crucial idea of giving it feedback about its performance – in effect, telling it when it had made an error. The following principle enables it gradually to converge on the correct settings for thresholds and strengths of connection: if the perceptron fails to detect the pattern when it is there, then all the strengths of connection from active units are raised, and the threshold of the output unit is lowered. Conversely, if the perceptron erroneously responds that the pattern is present when it is not, then all the strengths of connection from active units to the output unit are reduced, and its threshold is raised. Marvin Minsky and Seymour Papert proved that this procedure will work for any pattern that a perceptron can recognize. Alas, there is a snag. There are certain patterns that perceptrons cannot recognize. For example, there are no values for the thresholds and strengths of connection for the network in Figure 10.3, or for any other perceptron, that will enable it to respond to an *exclusive* disjunction, i.e. to respond when one input or else the other is active, but not both.

NETWORKS WITH HIDDEN UNITS

The trouble with perceptrons, like the trouble with traditional associative theories, is that they rely solely on direct links from input units (stimuli) to output units (responses). They make no use of internal representations. That is why they cannot cope with exclusive disjunctions or other complex concepts, and why they cannot account for the power of human memory.

Given a network architecture, the need for representations can be met by introducing units that lie hidden between the input and output units. These 'hidden' units can represent relations between the different parts of an input. The device in Figure 10.3 could recognize an exclusive disjunction (either one input unit or the other is active, but not both) if only it could be prevented from firing when both inputs are active. Hence, we interpose a hidden unit that recognizes when both inputs fire and then inhibits the output unit. Figure 10.4 displays such a device. If just one of the inputs is active, the output unit fires because its threshold is exceeded. If both inputs are active, however, then the hidden unit fires and transmits sufficient inhibition to the output unit to cancel out its excitation by the input units. The device recognizes an exclusive disjunction.

Figure 10.4: A network with a 'hidden' unit that recognizes when one but not both of its inputs is active.

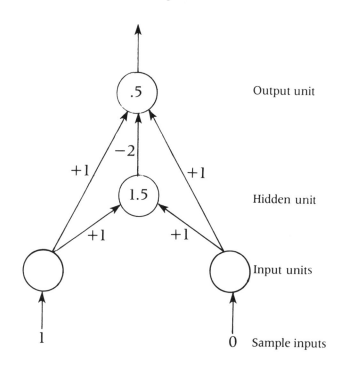

(After D. E. Rumelhart, G. E. Hinton and R. J. Williams, Learning internal representations by error propagation. In D. E. Rumelhart, J. L. McClelland and the PDP Research Group, *Parallel Distributed Processing: Explorations in the Microstructure of Cognition.* Vol. 1: *Foundations.* Cambridge, Mass.: Bradford Books, MIT Press, 1986)

Hidden units were used by the pioneers of network theory, but no one knew how to modify the strengths of their connections to produce learning. One of the achievements of connectionism is to have found some solutions to this problem.

185

There are several ways in which to set up networks with hidden units so that they can learn. The most efficient current method is 'backward error propagation', which was devised by Dave Rumelhart, Geoff Hinton and Ron Williams. The idea is easiest to understand in networks that are arranged in layers with the input units at the bottom, the output units at the top, and any number of intermediate layers of hidden units. Each unit is connected only to units in higher layers, and so activation spreads up through the network (cf. Figure 10.4). A unit does not have an all-or-none threshold as in a perceptron, but a threshold bias that reduces the net size of its input. It is not a linear device either, because linear units, as I mentioned earlier, can carry out only trivial computations. Hence, the output of a unit increases continuously as the sum of its inputs increases, but the relation is not linear: a given increase in input activation has effects on the output of different sizes depending on the overall size of the input.

Learning depends on three operations. First, there is an initial test phase in which an input activation is introduced at the bottom of the network and propagates up through it to yield an output. Second, this output is compared with the required output as indicated by some external source (or teacher). If there is no difference between them, then no learning occurs. If there is a discrepancy, then an error signal is calculated. Third, the strength of each connection to an output unit is adjusted in the direction – excitatory or inhibitory – that reduces the error, and in proportion to its effectiveness to do so. The procedure is a generalization of the principle used in perceptrons. A similar process of adjustment occurs at the next layer down. In general, the contribution that a hidden unit makes to the overall error depends on its level of activation, and its strengths of connection to each unit at the next level up (and those units' contribution to error). Hence, it is possible to work back down the hierarchy of units adjusting the strengths of connection at each level so as to reduce the error. A program for back-propagation is surprisingly simple (less than two hundred lines of LISP), and Table 10.1 summarizes the procedure for the benefit of programmers.

Table 10.1. Back-propagation of error: a summary for programmers.

After assigning initial random values (between $+1$ and -1) to the strengths of connections, the main function loops through each input-output pair calling three main functions: propagation of activation up the network, calculation of error, and back-propagation of change in strengths. There are five main calculations.

1. For the propagation of activation:

> Input to a unit = (Sum of activations × strengths from units below) − Threshold bias

The threshold bias of a unit is created by another unit that is connected to it and that is always active.

2. For the error signal of an output unit:

> Output error = (target − activation) activation (1 − activation)

where 'target' refers to the required activity of the output unit, and 'activation' refers to its actual activity.

3. For the error signal of a hidden unit:

> Hidden error = (Sum of strengths of connection to each output unit × output unit's error) activation (1 − activation)

where 'activation' refers to the hidden unit's activation.

4. For the change in the strength of connection from a hidden unit to an output unit:

> Change = (Learning rate × output error × activation of hidden unit) + (momentum proportion × previous change)

where learning rate is a global variable (usually set somewhere between 0.3 and 0.7) and momentum proportion is another global variable (usually set at around 0.9) which smooths out changes.

5. For the change in strength of connection from an input (or lower level) unit to a hidden unit:

> Change = (Learning rate × hidden error × activation of lower unit) + (momentum proportion × previous change)

The strength of connection from a unit acting as a threshold bias is made according to calculation 4 or 5 except that the unit's activation = 1.

In order to learn, say, an exclusive disjunction, a network with hidden units is set up and started with small, arbitrarily determined strengths of connection. The three operations of learning are applied through a number of cycles for the different input-output patterns, and, typically, the system will converge on strengths of connection that solve the problem after some hundreds of cycles. The greater the number of hidden units, the faster the solution will be discovered. Rumelhart and his colleagues have modelled the procedure in computer programs and shown that they are able to learn a variety of other sorts of task, e.g. to distinguish between the letters 'T' and 'C' regardless of the orientation in which they are presented. In most problems, the internal representation of the 'problem space' develops in a distributed way over the hidden units.

One potential drawback of the procedure is that it may get stuck at a local minimum to which all small changes in strengths are for the worse even though their values are a long way from those that yield the real minimum of error. The procedure is analogous to moving a ball-bearing around a two-dimensional surface with the goal of finding the lowest point: the ball-bearing may get stuck in a local pocket far from the real minimum, as depicted in cross-section in Figure 10.5. There are distributed systems that solve this problem, though they do not use backward error propagation. However, at least in the programs that have been developed, the danger of getting stuck in a local minimum has not proved to be too serious.

An impressive demonstration of the power of backward error propagation has been devised by Terry Sejnowksi and Charlie Rosenberg. Their network learns the correct pronunciation of English words. The problem with written English is, of course, the existence of irregular pronunciations. A typical way to solve this problem is to use a set of rules that captures the regular pronunciations, such as 'gave', 'omen' and 'penny', and to supplement it with a list of irregularly pronounced words, such as 'have', 'women' and 'deny'. The network, however, is merely trained on a large corpus of phonetic transcriptions from ordinary speech, and gradually builds up a parallel distributed representation mapping written elements to the features of speech. These

188

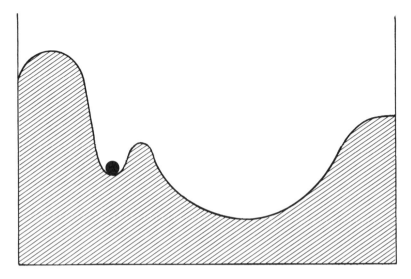

Figure 10.5: A cross-section through a surface on which a ball-bearing is stuck in a local minimum.

features are then fed into a commercially available program to synthesize the sound of the word (see Chapter 17 for a description of such programs).

SOME LIMITATIONS OF BACKWARD ERROR PROPAGATION

Since backward error propagation is essentially deterministic, it must embody principles that lead to viable outcomes, and so it is a species of what I referred to in Chapter 7 as a neo-Lamarckian program. Such a learning program calls, as I said, for considerable knowledge or considerable instruction. Since a network can start with no knowledge at all, the secret of its learning regime lies in the nature of its instruction, that is, the amount of information that it receives from feedback. This insight reveals some of the limitations of backward error propagation.

When you learn to skate, could your performance be controlled by backward error propagation? Almost certainly, not. There is no way in which falling over can yield sufficient information about what has gone wrong in your performance. The procedure needs a more sensitive index of performance than a crude 'right' or 'wrong'.

Even if a task yields an accurate and quantitative measure of error, there may still be problems. The procedure is feasible for any finite mapping from input to output binary numerals and for any infinite mapping for which a finite sample is sufficiently representative to permit safe generalizations. Unfortunately, in real life inductive generalizations must be guided by a knowledge of which similarities are important and which are spurious (see Chapter 13). Suppose we try to teach a network the principles of arithmetic by providing it with pairs of binary numerals, one encoding an arbitrarily selected expression, such as:

$$(15 \times 2) + 6$$

and the other its value. The system is unlikely to be able to learn the rules of arithmetic. It is put at risk because the domain has a potentially infinite number of input-output pairs and any sample may contain disparate examples with little in common, and because it has no knowledge of the structure of the input expressions and thus of the priority and significance of the different arithmetical operations. The only way for it to master arithmetic is for it to be taught each arithmetical operation separately in a domain that has only a finite number of possible input-output pairs.

CONNECTIONISM OR PRODUCTION SYSTEMS (OR BOTH)?

Simple processors connected up in parallel, and communicating levels of activity alone, can carry out complex computations. Some of the emergent properties of these computations are surprising and psychologically plausible. They can perform tasks that might be thought to depend on rules with an explicit structure governing the manipulation of mental symbols. They can also produce phenomena that are difficult to explain in terms of explicit rules.

Consider, for instance, what happens when a distributed representation suffers the equivalent of brain damage. Hinton set up distributed associations between words and features of their meaning. He then knocked out some of the hidden units used in establishing the associations. There was a rise in errors of interpretation for several words rather than a complete loss of meaning for any specific word. Many of the errors consisted of elements of meaning appropriate to a word other than the one that had been presented. This phenomenon is reminiscent of the 'deep dyslexia' that occurs in certain cases of brain damage. Neuropsychologists such as Max Coltheart, Karalyn Patterson and John Marshall have observed that when such patients are asked to read a word, they sometimes respond with a semantically related word. Given the word 'thunder' to read, they say, 'lightning'. It is not obvious how the effect could arise from damage to a system based on structural rules.

Some connectionists hint that perhaps there are only distributed representations in the mind, and that structural rules like those of production systems play no causal role in mental life, and are at best approximate descriptions of the underlying reality. If they are right, then cognitive science is likely to become a dull subject: the only answer to how the mind carries out some task will be to point to a network that has acquired the appropriate strengths of connection. There would be no simpler model of the brain, as John von Neumann once fearfully surmised, than the brain itself. However, since any computable process according to Turing's conjecture can be computed by a Turing machine, which is a device controlled by structural rules (see Chapter 3), production systems are not doomed to be approximate descriptions. In principle, they can always give an accurate account of any computational process.

The issue of explicitness is the crux. You may recall from Chapter 2 that this notion is not an absolute one, but depends on whether information is available to some process with a minimum of work. When I played rugby, my knowledge of the rules was not explicit, but was a composite derived from many experiences. Referees, however, are obliged to possess an explicit knowledge of the rules. Thus, on the one hand, certain rules, principles and facts can have structures that are explicit to consciousness. These contents of consciousness can govern behaviour. If I ask a referee the penalty for a certain infringement, he can make a deliberate act of recall to retrieve the rule. The input to the retrieval mechanism is high-level symbolic information, and it will produce further explicit symbols. On the other hand, the processes that occur outside consciousness during the retrieval may be parallel distributed patterns of activity. Since they depend on many simultaneous events, these patterns cannot be explicit to consciousness.

One resolution of the competing theories is therefore to postulate different levels of representation: high-level explicit symbols and low-level distributed symbolic patterns. The high-level structural processes are translated into low-level distributed processes, much as a computer program written in a high-level language, such as LISP, is ultimately translated into a low-level machine code. David Touretzky and Geoff Hinton have shown how such a translation from a production system to a parallel network can be carried out. The low-level processes implement the high-level rules. Of course, certain low-level processes occur in the absence of symbolic activity in consciousness and may yield important emergent properties. The central crux remains: at what level is the mind organized by structural rules?

CONCLUSIONS

The most serious technical problem confronting connectionism is to determine the power of the different systems. We know relatively little about the speed with which learning can proceed in networks, their propensity to fall into local minima, or the class of tasks that they can learn. One point is certain. No distributed learning procedures can by-pass the limitations on learning that I described in Chapter 7: not every imaginable task can be learned. Likewise, parallelism does not magically convert an intractable problem into one that can be solved in a reasonable time. There is no search procedure that can overcome exponential demands.

Particular theories in the framework of connectionist networks, or production systems, are open to empirical test. The puzzle is how to assess the architecture itself as opposed to such theories framed within it. Connectionists sometimes claim that their networks are closer to the 'hardware' of the brain. Its cells respond slowly, fatigue rapidly, and often die. Yet mental life continues apparently unaffected, with a grace under pressure that is mirrored by parallel networks. Unfortunately, whatever sort of computations brain cells carry out – and little is known of their nature – they are not satisfactorily idealized by network units. The brain is not wired up in a way that resembles any of the current connectionist proposals. It does not appear to contain any mechanism like backward error propagation. Unlike this procedure, it can also learn from correct responses (see the 'power' law described in the previous chapter). Neuroscience provides scarcely any more evidence for a connectionist architecture than for one based on a production system.

Zenon Pylyshyn has proposed that mental architecture should have the property of what he calls 'cognitive impenetrability', that is to say, it should always operate in the same way and so the phenomena it yields should not be influenced by beliefs, goals or any other high-level aspects of cognition. If a phenomenon arises from the architecture of the mind, it should be so robust that merely taking thought should have no more effect upon it than upon the thinker's height. Although there are examples of cognitive systems that seem to be impenetrable, e.g. the module that carries out stereopsis (see Chapter 5), there are many mental components that are hard to assess, e.g. working memory. Moreover, beliefs, goals and other high-level aspects of cognition must themselves depend on mental architecture, and, by definition, they are cognitively penetrable.

Connectionism is in a state of explosive development, and theorists are beginning to explore networks that contain internal loops and that can therefore carry out complex computations. Yet, its importance for cognitive science may turn out to be, not its current accounts of psychological phenomena, but its value in helping us to understand that symbols need not necessarily be represented as separate entities. Conscious processes may depend on the manipulation of such symbols, but unconscious processes may not be covert operations on the same sort of symbols. They may instead be the parallel processing of distributed representations created by the merging of many separate experiences.

Further reading

There is no introductory book on connectionism. There are books of readings edited by Hinton and Anderson (1981), McClelland and Rumelhart (1986) and Rumelhart and McClelland (1986), and a special issue of the journal *Cognitive Science* published in 1985, Volume 9, part 1. The pioneering studies and some recent programs are described in the chapter; an important paper that kept the topic alive during the intervening years was published by Willshaw, Buneman and Longuet-Higgins (1969). An alternative approach to connectionism using local representations has been proposed by Feldman and Ballard (1982). Backward error propagation was preceded by probabilistic networks known as Boltzmann machines (Hinton, Sejnowski and Ackley, 1986), and other similar systems to be found in Geman and Geman (1984) and Smolensky's (1986) 'Harmony' theory. Pinker and Prince (1987) defend the thesis that language depends on structural rules and demonstrate the inadequacies of a connectionist model (albeit one without hidden units) of how children learn the past-tense endings of English verbs. The properties of nerve cells are described by Kandel and Schwartz (1981) and Crick and Asanuma (1986). The design of massively parallel computers is reviewed in Gabriel (1986). An experimental study of the 'tip of the tongue' phenomenon is reported by Brown and McNeill (1966). The result that letters are easier to recognize in words than in nonsense strings has been obtained by several authors including Wheeler (1970).

CHAPTER 11

Action and the control of movement

A robot that can perceive, learn and remember is a fine thing, but it will be useless unless it can *do* something. Knowing, as the philosopher C. I. Lewis remarked, is for doing. What the robot does will be based on its goals and plans. Ultimately, however, its actions will depend on its capacity to move. Likewise, human actions ultimately depend on an ability to move various parts of the body – from limbs for walking to lips for talking. A hierarchical plan for action cannot be extended indefinitely into finer and finer details or else action would be postponed for ever. The buck must stop: the plan must end in movements – in instructions for muscles to contract.

You are unlikely to be aware of the contractions of individual muscles (unless perhaps you practise yoga). You cannot monitor the state of all 792 muscles in your body. Most of what you do in carrying out a skilled action is not accessible to introspection; conversely, if you are told what to do, it will not mean much. It is not very helpful in learning to ride a bicycle to be given the instruction:

> Turn the handle bars so that the curvature of your trajectory is proportional to the angle of your unbalance divided by the square of your speed.

As Michael Polyani put it, the skill is tacit. It is carried out by unconscious processes, presumably because they must occur in parallel to control the simultaneous contractions of muscles, and their number would defy the monitoring capacity of the 'central executive' of consciousness. It is these parallel workings, of course, that need to be examined in order to grasp how plans are translated into instructions to muscles. Cognitive scientists understand something of their nature, and have contributed to the development of programs that control the movement of robots.

195

Human movements fall into a number of categories. There are reflexes, such as the knee-jerk or the protective blink of the eyelid. There are sequences that depend on an innate program that can be modulated by voluntary control, such as the movements of walking or the movements of the vocal apparatus. There are acquired skills, such as skiing or playing the piano, which can be performed automatically, though again consciously modulated if need be. There are voluntary movements, which divide up into two main sorts: rapid 'ballistic' movements, as when you shoot your hand out to swat a fly, which depend on a program that is run off automatically with no opportunity for correction; and slower controlled movements, as when you thread a needle, which can be guided by visual and tactile information. Of course, movements may call for both modes in successive phases, as when you bring your finger to your nose as rapidly as possible. If you try out this action, you will confirm the long-standing observation that it terminates, at pain of missing the target, with a slower controlled phase after the initial ballistic phase.

My plan in this chapter is to begin with what has to be computed in order to move, that is, trajectories, both those for navigating from one place to another and those for moving a limb. This topic leads naturally to a discussion of how a limb is actually moved through a particular trajectory, and thus to the ubiquitous phenomenon of feedback, which enters into much more than the control of muscles. The chapter closes with an analysis of skilled actions and the ability to do two things at once.

COMPUTING A TRAJECTORY

Normally, before an organism moves, it works out where it wants to go – its path through the world or the trajectory of one or more of its appendages. The need for such a computation is clear if you are about to climb the North face of the Eiger. It is less obvious, however, if you are about to pick up a cup. All you seem to do is . . . pick up the cup. But consider what you see in a slow-motion film of the action. The hand reaches out towards the cup in what is, in fact, a rapid ballistic movement, and as it moves, the fingers accommodate themselves to the handle's shape and size and the wrist turns to adjust to its orientation. There is a brief interval as the hand coasts towards the cup. When it is near, some final adjustments occur, and as soon as contact with the handle is made, the hand adapts to its shape under the control of tactile sensations. It grasps the handle: the thumb exerts a downward force on top; the fingers within exert an upward force; those below help to stabilize the grasp; and the arm raises the cup. The manoeuvre is as exquisite as the docking of the lunar module with the mother ship.

The computation of a trajectory needs to solve several problems. The movement must get the appendage to the intended destination. And the dynamics of the trajectory may be critical, as, for example, when you are picking up a delicate object: you must not use too much force. The trajectory must avoid any obstacles, including other parts of the body. Robots have been known to commit the automated equivalent of *hari-kiri* when their designers failed to solve this problem. It is exacerbated when several parts can move simultaneously: who has not bitten their tongue by mistake? Finally, the movement of a limb must not put the organism into unstable positions for too long, or else it will topple over.

To ensure that you do not bump into obstacles, vision provides you with a three-dimensional model of the world. Plainly, your navigational system must represent your body itself in order to determine whether it can pass between obstructions. The form of these computations with the 'body image' is not known, but several possibilities are suggested by procedures for robot navigation. Consider the robot in Figure 11.1. Its goal is to get from its base to the destination avoiding all the obstacles, which are represented in its perceptual model of the world. It can compute the required trajectory by adding to its model a hypothetical barrier round each object with a thickness equal to the radius of its body. Such a model is represented in the Figure. No viable trajectory can allow the centre of the robot to transgress any barrier. There are three possible ways of starting the route: to points A, B or C (as shown in the Figure); and the possible ways of continuing can be examined until each of the different routes

197

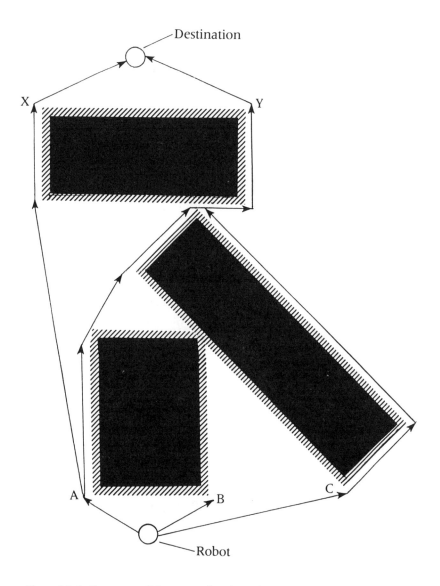

Figure 11.1: Some possible routes for the robot to take to its destination. The penumbrum round each object represents an imaginary boundary over which the centre of the robot must not cross.

to the destination has been constructed and evaluated. An optimal path can be found by a variety of standard search procedures (see Chapter 9).

If a robot is not circular in shape, then a safe route must take into account its dimensions and manoeuvring capabilities. At one extreme, the route can be tried out by trial and error either in reality – as people tend to do when shifting pieces of furniture around – or, more prudently, in an internal model. There are techniques, however, that enable a robot's turning geometry to be taken into account. They chart the channels between obstacles, and generate a path which ensures that the permissible positions of the robot at the end of one segment of the route allow for at least one acceptable transition to a permissible position at the start of the next segment.

MOVING A LIMB: COMPUTING THE ANGLES OF THE JOINTS

The robot arm illustrated in Figure 11.2 has three degrees of freedom in its movements: like an angle-poise light, it can rotate about its base, move its arm up and down on the horizontal axis of its shoulder, and move its forearm up and down on the horizontal axis of its elbow. From a knowledge of the angles of its joints, the position of the tip of the arm can be worked out by trigonometry. The inverse problem is to work out the angles required to position the tip at a particular place. This problem is hard if there can be different configurations of limbs for the same position of the tip. However, if the robot arm is not double-jointed, only one set of angles corresponds to each position of the tip. There is a one-to-one mapping between the 'space' of possible angles for joints and the space represented in the model of the world. Given a starting position and a destination in the model, one possible trajectory consists in transforming all three angles simultaneously from their initial positions to those of the destination.

The human arm has more degrees of freedom than this robot arm. The shoulder joint allows movement up and down, movement forwards and backwards, and rotation of the whole arm

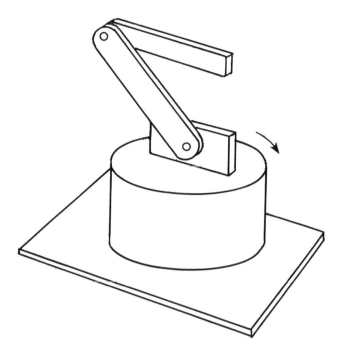

Figure 11.2: A schematic robot arm that has three degrees of freedom in movement.

along its axis; the forearm can move towards and away from the upper arm and it can rotate along its axis independently of the upper arm; the wrist can move up and down and slightly from side to side. There are thus seven degrees of freedom, which is an embarrassment of riches, because there are so many possible ways in which the hand can be held at a particular location. To check this claim, hold your hand in a fixed position and see how your elbow is still free to move into a variety of positions. There is no way in which a trajectory can be worked out by a direct mapping from the model of the world to the angles of the joints.

There are further complications. Complex joints, such as the shoulder, are controlled by many muscles, and which pairs work antagonistically is not fixed but changes with the direction of the movement. In addition, separate movements often have to be coordinated so as to satisfy several concurrent goals. If you reach out to grasp something, you may have to move your legs so as to keep your centre of gravity over your feet.

One way out of these difficulties was suggested by the Russian physiologist Nicolai Bernstein, and more recently by Mike Turvey, Scott Kelso and a group of psychologists at Storrs, Connecticut. Their hypothesis is that the body exploits fewer degrees of freedom than are theoretically available to it. There are 'synergies', that is, groups of muscles that act together as units rather than independently. The hypothesis therefore distinguishes between movements that occur and movements that are physically possible but that do not occur.

Another way to cope with some of these problems has been modelled computationally by Geoff Hinton. Figure 11.3 shows a stick figure that inhabits a two-dimensional 'flatland'. It has one arm, one leg and five joints. It has more degrees of freedom than it needs, because any position of the tip of its arm is defined by

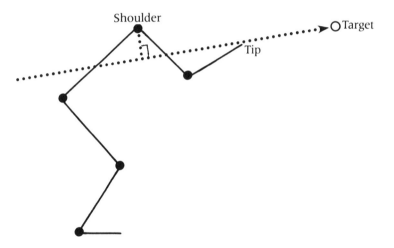

Figure 11.3: Hinton's stick figure that inhabits a two-dimensional 'flatland'. The angle through which a joint turns as the tip moves to the target depends on the distance of the line from tip to target and on the perpendicular distance of the joint from this same line (as shown for the shoulder).

only two spatial coordinates. There are many different ways by which its arm can move in a straight line, e.g. it can use just its shoulder and elbow or it can bend at the waist too. So, how should it move? Consider a rudimentary physical model of the figure made out of cardboard, with inverted drawing pins as joints, and an elastic band attached from the tip of its arm to an intended target. When the arm is pulled away from the target and then released, the elastic band snaps its tip straight at the target. If this line is extended so that the perpendicular distance of a joint from it can be measured (see Figure 11.3), the angle of the joint changes at each moment by a small amount proportional to this perpendicular distance multiplied by the distance from the tip to the target.

Hinton's program implements this rule. It has another rule for changing the angle of a joint to maintain the centre of gravity over the figure's foot. It also has rules that work like synergies. Unlike Turvey's scheme, they do not eliminate degrees of freedom, but rather allow for interactions between joints so that an appropriate trajectory can be found faster. Suppose you want to move your hand from your shoulder to a target, then opening your elbow will have something of the desired effect, but it may also move your hand down from the straight line to the target. This undesirable effect can be cancelled out by simultaneously raising your upper arm at the shoulder joint. Provided that the two movements are properly coordinated – with the shoulder changing its angle at half the rate at which the elbow does – then your hand will travel straight to the target. This interaction is represented by a separate rule that is triggered only when the direction of the target from the tip of the arm lines up with the shoulder.

Figure 11.4 shows the simulation of the stick figure reaching for an object whilst maintaining its balance. The trajectory is generated little by little by a set of simulated parallel procedures (cf. the connectionist architecture of the previous chapter). On every step of the program, the new angles are worked out by a separate procedure for each joint. Each rule suggests how the angle should be changed, and the procedure merely adds together all the suggestions. This method enables the program to satisfy different goals at one and the same time. The computations depend on the current distance of the tip from the target, the current location of the centre of gravity, and other global information. Hence, there is a model of the current configuration of the stick figure, which, like a blackboard, is available for inspection by all the procedures.

Figure 11.4: Hinton's simulation of the stick figure reaching for an object (+) while maintaining its centre of gravity (o) over its foot. The head of the figure was not part of the simulation and is included only to help the reader to perceive the sequence of movements. The figure is shown on every second iteration of the program.

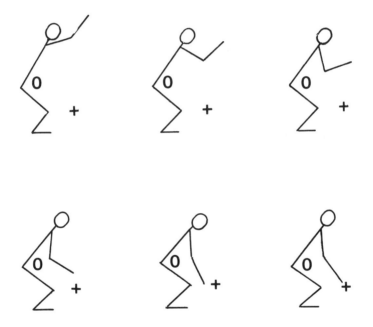

(From G. E. Hinton, Parallel computations for controlling an arm. *Journal of Motor Behavior*, 16, 1984, p. 182)

MOVING A LIMB: COMPUTING THE FORCES

Once a sequence of angles of joints has been computed, the next task is to work out the forces needed to move the limbs through this trajectory. If known forces are applied to a body of a given mass, then Newton's three laws of dynamics can be used to predict its trajectory. The present problem is the inverse: to work out the forces that move a body through a desired trajectory.

Imagine that your arm is a single rigid link rotating your hand in a circle around your shoulder. Newton's first law states that a body moves in a straight line (or remains at rest) unless it is acted upon by an outside force. Your hand is moving in a circle, and so there must be a force that is pulling it away from a straight line. This centripetal force is exerted by your arm and acts to accelerate your hand directly towards your shoulder. The second law states that force is proportional to mass times acceleration – the bigger the mass, the harder you must pull it to accelerate it. The third law states that if one body exerts a force on a second body, then the second exerts an equal force in the opposite direction on the first. Thus, your rotating hand exerts a centrifugal force on your arm to displace it from its position. People often think a rotating object flies off at a tangent when it is released, because there is a centrifugal force acting on it. In fact, the centrifugal force is not a force on the object, but one that it exerts on whatever is rotating it. The object flies off in a straight line, according to Newton's first law, because the centripetal force has ceased to act upon it.

In order to move your hand in a straight line, you must unbend your elbow and raise your upper arm at the shoulder. The rotational force (or 'torque') that is needed to unbend your elbow is affected by the rotation of your upper arm since this movement causes a force on the lower arm. (There will be an equal and opposite force on the upper arm.) If you also have to move your wrist, the force that is needed will be affected by the movement of your forearm. In general, the force needed at one joint depends on the angles of the other joints in the limb, and on the angular velocities of its other parts. The problem of computing the required forces, and in turn the forces that muscles should generate to produce them, is difficult. Indeed, it is sufficiently difficult that the designers of robots sometimes rely on a massive table of previously computed equations for particular configurations. An alternative possibility, however, is to make use of feedback.

FEEDBACK AND SERVO-MECHANISMS

Feedback occurs whenever the value of a varying quantity depends in part on its value a moment ago. When a microphone is too near to a loudspeaker, for example, it picks up its own output, and the feedback creates a howl. Feedback can also have a corrective function when a system has a goal, since behaviour can be governed by a comparison between feedback from the current situation and the goal. The goal may be a value of some physical quantity, such as body temperature, or a *representation* of a desired state. 'Biological clocks' that enable organisms to synchronize their activities with time and tide seem to have evolved, as Keith Oatley has suggested, from feedback in biochemical processes that originally had no representational purpose.

The role of a representation of a goal is illustrated by the servo-mechanisms that govern the power-assisted controls of modern aircraft. The pilot exerts a small rotational force on the rudder control, which is amplified by an hydraulic system and exerted on the rudder. If there were no more to controlling the rudder, then any vagaries affecting its position would not be corrected until their effects had been noticed by the pilot. The resulting corrections to corrections would soon cause the plane to oscillate in an erratic path. The solution is to feed back information to the servo-mechanism about the position of the rudder. It compares this information with the representation of the intended position, as indicated by the rudder control, and then adjusts the rudder to minimize the discrepancy. A delay in the feedback would lead again to an oscillation in the flight path. Hence, the adjustments are continuous and on a fine scale: they correct for perturbations in the plane's environment and it flies smoothly in the required direction. Figure 11.5 presents a block diagram of the feedback system.

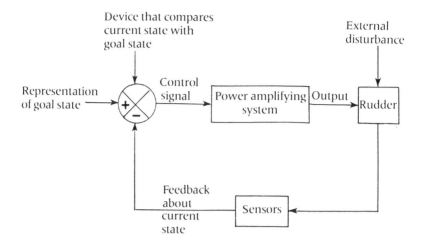

Figure 11.5: A simple block diagram of a feedback system.

The idea that the brain functions as a servo-mechanism stimulated a number of workers during and after the Second World War. It lay at the heart of Norbert Weiner's conception of 'cybernetics' – the science of control and communication in living organisms and machines. A controlled movement is guided by the discrepancy between the goal and feedback from what has been achieved. If you ride a bicycle, then you have become accomplished at using such feedback. You might imagine that you perform almost continuous corrections, but Kenneth Craik showed experimentally that people act at a voluntary level as *intermittent* servo-mechanisms. They do not modify their actions continuously, but must wait until they detect a discrepancy and then act to reduce it.

THE CONTROL OF MUSCLES

Feedback governs movement at many levels from voluntary control down to the contraction of muscles. Each muscle can exert a force in only one direction, and muscles are arranged in pairs that work antagonistically in opposing directions.

Nerve cells in the spinal cord receive signals from that part of the cortex in the brain that controls movement. These 'motoneurons' transmit impulses to the muscle fibres causing them to contract. The motoneurons controlling an antagonistic pair of muscles are connected by inhibitory links in the spinal cord so that when one muscle in a pair contracts, the other relaxes. Certain special muscle fibres contain sensors called 'muscle spindles', which respond to changes in the length and tension of these fibres. The circuitry is summarized in Figure 11.6. If your arm is in a position in which the spindles are unstretched and I put a weight in your hand, the whole muscle will be stretched including those fibres containing spindles. Their signals feed back to the motoneurons in the spinal cord, which as a result stimulate the muscle fibres to contract. The discrepancy between the actual and the intended position of your arm is reduced at once. Thus, feedback maintains the arm in a position that does not cause the spindles to respond beyond a basic resting level.

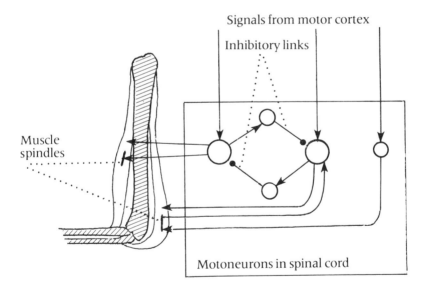

Figure 11.6: A diagram of the feedback circuits controlling movements of the arm: only a few neurons are shown.

How can an arm be moved to some other position? The answer is simple: contract the fibres containing spindles so the resting-level response is also at this new setting. There are accordingly other motoneurons (see the right-hand side of Figure 11.6) that stimulate these fibres and cause them to contract. The circuitry enables the arm to move to a new position. The cortex stimulates the main motoneurons to contract the muscle by roughly the right amount, and at the same time it stimulates the specialized motoneurons to set the fibres containing spindles to the same amount. Feedback from the spindles then fine-tunes the gross contraction of the muscle.

The reflex that withdraws your hand from a hot poker before you have time to think about it occurs because the temperature receptors in your skin are wired up to the main motoneurons. When the receptors detect heat, they stimulate the motoneurons, which in turn cause the muscle to contract involuntarily.

FEEDBACK AND MOVEMENT

As we saw earlier, it is difficult for a robot to work out the forces needed to move a limb through a particular trajectory. One possibility to obviate such computations is to exploit the feedback that is needed to maintain the robot in a fixed position. If its joints are frictionless, then forces on them are necessary to counteract gravity, otherwise all its limbs will slump into a relaxed position. The size of the force on a joint depends on the mass of the limb (and its parts), but feedback has to be used to compensate for error. Any discrepancy between the actual and intended position will trigger a correction. A primitive method for moving the robot's arm is merely to reset its desired position. The discrepancy between this and its current position will trigger a corrective movement. Because the discrepancy is large, the resulting force will also be large, with the consequent danger of overshooting the target. Moreover, the trajectory of the movement will be unpredictable and uncontrollable. The result is the characteristic jerky movements beloved of 'break' dancers.

A better method is to compute a trajectory as before, then to break it into a series of small segments, and finally to move the arm successively through their starting points using the feedback system. The procedure works satisfactorily for slow movements. But, if speed is called for, then the large forces that are needed can be generated only by large discrepancies, and skilled movements become impossible. In fact, the control of a movement solely in terms of a sequence of positions is useless for many tasks. But if the dynamics of the movement are to be controlled, there are a number of problems to be solved. If a robot has to open a door, for example, and the hinges are not true, then there is a danger that it will succeed only in pulling the knob off the door. It is necessary to control both the position of the arm and the direction of the force it exerts.

The force necessary for a ballistic trajectory could be computed using Hinton's blackboard method. The computations will need an internal model of the dynamics of the situation, which is based on objects rather than on an egocentric representation of the angles of joints. The model's frame of reference can move, and the choice of axes should be based on the nature of the task so that, for example, the forces on the doorknob can be minimized in all directions others than its turning arc. Ideally, a trajectory should be smooth, use as little force as necessary, and put a minimum of stress on the joints. The difficulty in working out such a trajectory is the need to examine its entire course. However, feedback about the smoothness of a trajectory could be used as a corrective if it is impossible to carry out all the computations beforehand.

There is one final form of feedback, which, as Hinton points out, depends not on a representation but on the fact that the force generated by a given setting of antagonistic muscles depends on the current angle of the joint. A given rotational force bends the limb with a certain acceleration. If its trajectory lags behind the intended path in the model, the same muscle contraction will generate a slightly different force because the angle of the joint is lagging behind its proper position. Because the angle is different, the resulting force is larger and will bring the limb back into line on its correct trajectory. This feedback is in the physics of the situation.

209

HIERARCHY IN THE CONTROL OF SKILLS

The nineteenth-century view of skilled performance – deriving principally from the neurologist Hughlings Jackson – was that there is a hierarchy of control: you decide, say, to ride a bicycle, this conscious decision is passed to the brain centres that govern the separate modules of the skill, such as steering and pushing the pedals, which in turn pass on instructions to the lower brain centres that govern the control of the limbs, and so on down to the instructions to motor nerves. The construction of such a hierarchy was demonstrated by W. Bryan and N. Harter in a classic nineteenth-century psychological investigation of how telegraphers learn morse code. They do not show a smooth increase in competence, but after much practice a relatively abrupt shift to a new level of mastery. They first learn to encode individual letters, next they develop an ability to treat words as single units, and finally they are able to run off whole phrases as units. A similar pattern occurs in learning to type. A hierarchy of control is built up from elementary units to high-level con-stituents. The process of 'chunking', which I described earlier, yields just such a hierarchy.

Another example of hierarchical control occurs in walking and other forms of locomotion. People have the knack of nearly always moving so that their centre of gravity does not depart too long from above their feet. Even infants have a stepping reflex: if you pull an infant towards you so that her centre of gravity is in front of her feet, she will automatically take a step forwards so as to regain her balance. Walking is a succession of such unstable states. The only easy way in which to achieve static stability with two legs is to have large feet, as is illustrated by the familiar mechanism of Figure 11.7 which is used in toys. Dynamic stability, however, can be achieved even with one leg, as has been demonstrated by some enterprising robot designers who have built an animated pogo-stick that maintains its balance by continually jumping in the direction in which it is falling.

People talk of children learning to walk; in fact, the motor program unfolds according to an innate recipe, but calls for practice to bring it into operation and to fine-tune it. The pro-

Figure 11.7: A robotic mechanism for achieving static stability with two legs.

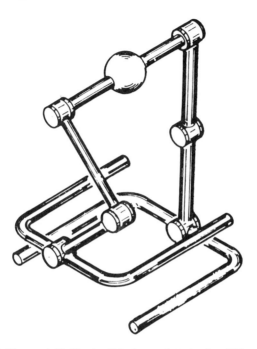

(From D. McCloy and M. Harris, *Robotics: an Introduction*, Milton Keynes: Open University Press, 1986, p. 72)

gram is hierarchically organized with separate modules for each leg. A single leg moves through four main positions: it directly supports the body's weight, the body moves forward until the leg is extended backwards, the leg flexes upwards bending at the knee, and it is then extended forwards to land in front of the body. This routine changes surprisingly little for running. Thus, the speed with which the knee is flexed remains almost constant, and only the phase in which the body swings over the front leg is significantly faster. The timing of the two legs (and the swinging of the arms) has to be coordinated at a higher level.

The millipede is right not to worry about how it walks: as the number of legs goes up, so the number of theoretically possible gaits increases exponentially. The different gaits of four-legged

211

animals, such as horses, are merely different ways of coordinating at a higher level the separate programs for each leg. In galloping the front legs move together, as do the rear ones; in trotting they move alternately and each is synchronized with the rear leg on the opposite side; in pacing they move alternately and each is synchronized with the rear leg on the same side.

Hierarchy is better than anarchy. However, the wisest government of both body politic and body corporeal is obtained by feedback from lower levels. As we saw in the blackboard method, there may even be advantages to a *heterarchy* in which all levels contribute equally to control. Yet, not everything can be achieved by such a democracy. When conflicts arise, their demands cannot be blended. One task can interfere with another.

DOING TWO THINGS AT ONCE

The extent to which you can do two different things at once is an excellent clue to mental organization. There have been many psychological investigations of this intriguing problem. Gertrude Stein, author of the imperishable observation, 'a rose is a rose is a rose', trained as a psychologist at Harvard and published a paper on the topic in 1896. She and her co-author, L. Solomons, discovered that with practice one could listen attentively to a story and at the same time write without attending to what one was writing. This 'automatic writing' resulted in fragmentary and strangely repetitive phrases, such as 'a rose is a rose is a rose'. Modern research has confirmed the phenomenon: one can listen and write at the same time, but pay conscious attention to only one of the two.

You might think, as some psychologists do, that the central executive is capable of processing a certain amount of information and no more: tasks differ in their demands, and so they will interfere with one another as their joint demands exceed its limited capacity. This view is simplistic. The logic of the argument against it has been neatly spelt out by Herbert Heuer and Alan Wing. Consider three tasks: say, tapping a foot, writing and listening. Tapping a foot and writing interfere with one another more than tapping a foot and listening do. It follows, according to the limited-capacity argument, that if tapping a foot is replaced by some other task, such as speaking, then speaking and writing should interfere with one another more than speaking and listening. Almost certainly, the prediction is wrong: what matters are the interrelations between the tasks.

Conflicts can occur at any level. Those between conscious goals are resolved in ways that depend on one's feelings and on an exercise of will. How such decisions are taken is a matter that I shall defer until the final chapters of the book. Once a compatible set of goals has been created, however, then plans to achieve them may be initiated at a high level. If two simultaneous actions are integrated within the same plan, then as its execution becomes habitual and automatic there will be little interference between them. They may well be implemented using the blackboard method of parallel computation. If two independent plans have to be carried out simultaneously, there may be problems. Novel actions often call for conscious monitoring and a deliberate use of feedback. But two tasks cannot both be given continuous attention. Hence, there tends to be a 'see-saw' relation between them: a good performance of one pushes the performance of the other one down. Even in the case of highly practised skills, a conflict can occur at a lower level in the hierarchy if they contain elements that depend on a common mental component. It is disruptive, as Peter McLeod has shown, to have to carry out different tasks with different hands even though there may be no interference when one of the tasks is carried out verbally instead of manually.

CONCLUSIONS

Vision provides us with a three-dimensional representation of the world. In order to act, as we have seen in this chapter, a similar model, enriched with dynamic information, can help us to move through the world and to move our limbs to specific locations. Simple reflexes depend on the properties of neural circuits that interconnect sensors and motoneurons in the spinal cord. Other movements, such as walking, are governed by innately determined programs. Still others may be computed beforehand

and executed ballistically, or else carried out slowly with deliberate corrections to their trajectories. The organization of movement depends ultimately on a hierarchy of control, but it is tempered by numerous forms of feedback. The computations at different levels are carried out in parallel, and there may be occasions where information from different levels is integrated within a common representational scheme.

Where do the prescriptions for actions come from? I have talked of instructions descending from the motor cortex, but where do *they* come from? Isn't there a danger that the theory is relying on some little man or woman in the head who decides what to do? Is it this homunculus who examines the model of the world and tries to determine a sensible course of action? In the next part of the book, I shall begin to show why there is no need to postulate this particular ghost in the machine.

Further reading

Smyth and Wing (1984) have edited an excellent introduction to the study of human movements, which surveys experimental work from psychology, physical education and neurophysiology. A different perspective is provided in readings edited by Kelso (1982), which include three chapters by Turvey and his colleagues on such matters as synergies, walking and the gaits of horses. Aleksander and Burnett (1983) is a popular account of robotics; McCloy and Harris (1986) is a technical introduction. The problems of robot motion are discussed at an advanced level in Brady, Hollerbach, Johnson, Lozano-Pérez and Mason (1982). Wiener (1947) provides the original account of feedback and cybernetics; Porter (1969) provides an introduction. Walking machines, including animated pogo-sticks, are described in Raibert and Sutherland (1983). A modern replication of Gertrude Stein's automatic writing was carried out by Spelke, Hirst and Neisser (1976).

PART IV

COGITATION

My hypothesis then is that thought models, or parallels, reality – that its essential feature is not 'the mind', 'the self', 'sense-data', nor propositions but symbolism, and that this symbolism is largely of the same kind as that which is familiar to us in mechanical devices which aid thought and calculation. . . .

. . . If the organism carries a 'small-scale model' of external reality and of its own possible actions within its head, it is able to try out various alternatives, conclude which is the best of them, react to future situations before they arise, utilize the knowledge of past events in dealing with the present and future, and in every way to react in a much fuller, safer, and more competent manner to the emergencies which face it.

KENNETH CRAIK

CHAPTER 12

Deduction

Thinking occurs in such a dazzling variety that some cognitive scientists have despaired of understanding it. There is, at one extreme, the free flow of ideas in daydreams. James Joyce re-created this stream of consciousness in the final pages of his great novel *Ulysses*:

> Yes because he never did a thing like that before as ask to get his breakfast in bed with a couple of eggs since the *City Arms* hotel when he used to be pretending to be laid up with a sick voice doing his highness to make himself interesting to that old faggot Mrs Riordan that he thought he had a great leg of and she never left us a farthing all for masses for herself and her soul greatest miser ever was actually afraid to lay out 4d for her methylated spirit telling me all her ailments she had too much old chat in her about politics and earthquakes and the end of the world let us have a bit of fun first . . .

Joyce chose not to punctuate Molly Bloom's soliloquy, in order, perhaps, to catch its fleeting, inchoate nature. The process generating daydreams is rapid, involuntary and, apart from its results, outside conscious awareness. You recall an episode:

she never left us a farthing [in her will]

and the memory triggers a judgement:

greatest miser ever

which, in turn, reminds you of something else:

was actually afraid to lay out 4d for her methylated spirit

and so on and on. William James likened the stream of consciousness to the trajectory of a bird – a sequence of alternating flights and perchings. The flight of ideas in daydreams, however, has no goal.

At the other extreme, there is mental arithmetic. You deliberate in a voluntary and consciously controlled way. You are not aware of how you retrieve a particular arithmetical fact or of how the numbers and processes are mentally represented, but you are aware of what is going on. You may choose how to do the calculation (or whether or not to carry it out at all), but once you have chosen a procedure you have no freedom about what to do to get the answer right. Your thinking is deterministic and it has a precise goal; at each point, the next step in the calculation is determined by its current state.

Perhaps most thinking lies between these two extremes. It has a goal, but it is not carried out like a calculation. When you are trying to create a new idea – a work of art, a scientific hypothesis, or even something as prosaic as a novel turn of phrase – there is a goal, but it is not precisely defined: there is not just one correct answer, and you do not follow a strictly determined procedure. Different people tackle the same problem in different ways. You yourself, if you could step backwards in time and make another attempt in ignorance of your first one, might take a different path the second time around. Nothing constrains you to just a single option at each step in the process. It is creative, not deterministic.

Reasoning is different yet again. When you are confronted with a social or intellectual problem, your goal may be precise, but there is seldom a routine procedure for arriving at it. Yet you can reason from a set of premises to a conclusion. Suppose you know the following fact: if Fred is at work, then he is probably in his laboratory, and someone tells you, 'Fred is at work.' Then you can couple your knowledge with this assertion to infer: he's probably in his laboratory. You have made a *deduction*, and you may put the conclusion into words or merely act upon it. Reasoning relates premises to conclusion. In the case of a deduction, the relation is supposed to be one of validity, i.e. that the conclusion must be true, given that the premises are true. Validity does not mean that the premises *are* true, but only that if they are, then so is the conclusion.

There are other forms of reasoning, and here the concept of *semantic information* helps to draw a major distinction. The more possible states of affairs that a proposition eliminates from consideration, the more semantic information it contains. For example, the assertion, 'It is freezing but there is no fog', excludes more states of affairs than the assertion, 'It is freezing', because the former rules out the presence of fog, whereas the latter does not. Whenever reasoning occurs, one can ask: does the conclusion contain more semantic information than the premises? More precisely, does it rule out some additional state of affairs over and above those ruled out by the premises? If not, then the inference is a valid deduction: its conclusion is true in any situation in which the premises are true. But, if the conclusion does rule out additional states of affairs, it is not valid. *Induction* can be defined as a systematic way of reasoning that increases the given information.

I have now distinguished five main varieties of thought. Daydreams are mental processes that have no goal. Calculations have a goal and are deterministic. Other processes are not deterministic. If their goal is precise, they are varieties of reasoning, which divide up into deduction or induction depending on whether or not they increase semantic information. If there is no precise goal, they are varieties of creation. Since you can carry out a calculation in the midst of a daydream, or daydream in the midst of a calculation, these names are merely convenient labels to reflect underlying distinctions. Figure 12.1 summarizes the taxonomy.

Are there any other forms of cogitation? I suspect not, though the taxonomy can be refined into many subvarieties. I shall say no more about its two extremes – the clocks and clouds of the mind – but I shall examine deduction, induction and creation, in this and the next two chapters.

DEDUCTION IN EVERYDAY LIFE

If you read in a paper:

> The victim was stabbed to death in a cinema. The suspect was on an express train to Edinburgh when the murder occurred

you would probably conclude that the suspect was in-

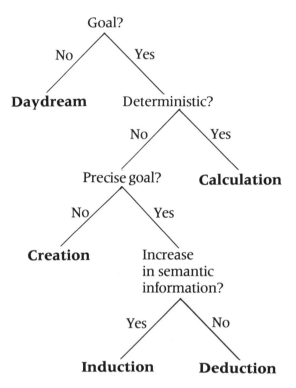

Figure 12.1: A taxonomy of thought.

nocent. This is a typical piece of everyday reasoning, and it illustrates three important phenomena. First, it depends not just on the premises but also on general knowledge, e.g. one person cannot be in two places at the same time, there are no cinemas on express trains to Edinburgh. You forge these links in the inferential chain so rapidly and automatically that you are hardly aware of them. Indeed, the need for them was discovered only when cognitive scientists tried to devise computer programs that understood discourse. Second, you drew an informative conclusion, that is, one that is not stated explicitly in the premises and that does not throw semantic information away. There are infinitely many valid conclusions that follow from any set of premises, but most of them are totally trivial, e.g.:

The victim was stabbed to death in a cinema *and* the suspect was on an express train to Edinburgh when the murder occurred.

Since people do not draw such banal, though valid, conclusions, they must be guided by some principles outside logic. Third, although your conclusion is invalid, if it is challenged, you can test its validity. When Tony Anderson and I queried such conclusions in an experiment, our subjects searched for alternatives and often produced scenarios in which the suspect *is* guilty, e.g. he (sic) may have had an accomplice, he may have used a spring-loaded knife or a radio-controlled robot. There is a further devilish possibility, which I shall reveal later to allow you an opportunity to discover it for yourself.

What mental processes led to the initial conclusion that the suspect is innocent? It is difficult to say because we are not aware of how we reason. We can observe only the consequences in our conscious thoughts. For many years, however, psychologists took for granted that deduction depends on a mental logic containing formal rules of inference like those of a logical calculus. Recently, however, cognitive scientists have divided into two camps in both psychology and artificial intelligence. On one side there are indeed those who favour formal rules of inference, and on the other side are those who favour rules containing specific knowledge. I will outline these two schools of thought, and then – in the best tradition of British compromise – argue that both of them are wrong.

FORMALISM: USING FORMAL LOGIC TO REASON

Validity is a semantic concept; modern logic specifies rules for deriving just those inferences that are valid. But the rules are formal and work in a purely syntactic way that does not depend on the meanings of expressions. Leibniz dreamed of such a system – an *ars combinatoria* – but it was not realized until in 1879 Gottlob Frege published a logic powerful enough to express just about all of mathematics, a logic which is known as the predicate (or quantificational) calculus. This calculus embraces both the logic of sentences connected by such terms as 'and', 'or' and 'not', and the internal logic of sentences containing quantifiers such as 'any' and 'some'.

The traditional view in psychology is that people are able to make valid deductions because they have a formal logic in their heads. Bärbel Inhelder and Jean Piaget, the Genevan psychologists, argued that deductive reasoning, which they believed children master in their early teens, is nothing more than a logical calculus. There is a need, however, to clarify what is meant by formalism here.

Consider the earlier example of a deduction that you can make:

If Fred is at work, then he is probably in his laboratory.
Fred is at work.
Therefore, Fred is probably in his laboratory.

A formal explanation of your performance is that you matched the premises with those of a well-known formal rule of inference:

If p then q
p
Therefore, q

and drew the corresponding conclusion. Hence, the doctrine of mental logic assumes that the deductive mechanism operates, not on the meanings of statements, but on their abstract form. Since a logical calculus can be formalized in many different ways, the crucial issues for the doctrine are: what logic does the mind contain, and how is it formalized? Because people can reason with quantifiers, most theorists assume that mental logic must be some version of the predicate calculus. The question of its mental formalization is much harder to answer. As a starting point, I will consider formalism in computer programs that embody the predicate calculus.

A major intellectual discovery was made by the logician Alonzo Church in 1936. He proved that there can be no formal procedure guaranteed to determine the status of an inference in the predicate calculus. If the inference is valid, there are procedures guaranteed to find a proof. But, if it is not valid, then any procedure may fail to reveal this fact – it may get lost in the 'space' of possibilities, wandering round for an eternity. A computer program must therefore minimize the time it takes to discover the validity of an inference, because as it grinds away there is no way of knowing whether it will yield a decision or go on computing for ever. One economy is to use just a single formal rule of inference. This rule is apt to seem obscure at first, but it is a combination of familiar principles.

Imagine that there are two alternatives, A and B, which might be, say, my watching TV and my listening to the radio, and that it is a fact that last night:

I watched TV or I listened to the radio (or both).

(This assertion, and others henceforth, are inclusive disjunctions in which both propositions could be true.) Later I introduce a third possibility, C, which is reading the paper, in a further fact about my behaviour:

I didn't watch TV or I read the paper.

Well, either I watched TV or I didn't. If I did watch it, then the first part of this new assertion is false, and so the second part must be true:

I read the paper.

And if I didn't watch TV, then the first part of my initial assertion is false, and so you can conclude:

I listened to the radio.

Since you don't know whether or not I watched TV, you can validly infer only that at least one of these two possibilities holds:

I listened to the radio or I read the paper.

To summarize the deduction, its premises are:

I watched TV or I listened to the radio.   [A or B]

I didn't watch TV or I read the paper.   [not-A or C]

And its conclusion is:

I listened to the radio or I read the paper.   [B or C]

If you look at its abstract form, you will notice that it obeys a simple principle. Whenever one proposition and another that is inconsistent with it occur in separate inclusive disjunctions, they cancel each other out and the conclusion is a disjunction of whatever remains. This principle is called the 'resolution' rule of inference. It suffices for the derivation of any inference in the predicate calculus, though it may have to be used many times in the same derivation.

Before the resolution rule can be used, all the premises must be converted into disjunctions, and something must be done about any quantifiers in them. These technical problems are readily solved. Indeed, the programming language, PROLOG, which has been adopted by the Japanese in their quest for a 'fifth generation' of intelligent computers, is based on a combination of the resolution method and backtracking (see Chapter 9).

Resolution is intelligent, but artificial. It provides cognitive scientists only with a standard of comparison, because people are hardly likely to translate all premises into a standard disjunctive form and to use only a single rule of inference. A more plausible conjecture is that the mind contains a logic in which each logical term has its own formal rules of inference. Thus, the connective 'if' will have the rule I described earlier, and there will be other rules for 'and', 'or', and the quantifiers 'any' and 'some'. Martin Braine, Daniel Osherson, Lance Rips and others (including myself at one time) have put forward different proposals about which particular rules the mind contains. When people attempt to reason formally, then as Rips has shown, their performance can be modelled by a program based on such a system.

There are, however, some severe problems for purely formal theories of human reasoning. First, as I have already noted, formal logic permits an infinite number of different valid conclusions to be drawn from any set of premises. But people are fussy about what conclusions they draw, and will often refrain from drawing any conclusion at all if nothing new follows from the premises. At the very least, formal theories will have to be supplemented by some semantic principles to account for the conclusions that people actually draw. Second, human reasoners are affected by the semantic content of problems. One such effect, which Peter Wason and his colleagues have observed, is that content can affect the following task. You are presented with four cards showing, respectively, 'A', 'B', '2' and '3'. You know from previous experience that every card in the pack from which they are drawn has a letter on one side and a number on the other side. Your task is to decide which cards you need to turn over to determine the truth or falsity of the rule:

> If there is a vowel on one side of a card, then there is an even number on the other side.

Most people choose to turn over the card bearing 'A', and some people in addition select the card bearing '2'. But few select the card bearing '3', even though if it had a vowel on its other side, it would falsify the rule. People are much less susceptible to this error of omission when the rules and materials have a sensible content, e.g. when they concern postal regulations (see below). Hence, the content of a problem can affect reasoning, and this phenomenon is contrary to the notion of formal rules of inference.

'EXPERT SYSTEMS' AND RULES OF INFERENCE WITH A SPECIFIC CONTENT

The effects of content would be immediately explained if mental rules of inference had a specific content. A person who possessed the following knowledge:

> If a letter has a stamp less than 50 lira on it, it must not be sealed

would be able to perform the postal version of Wason's selection task without difficulty. Since there is no such knowledge for the abstract version of the task with letters and numbers, its performance will remain poor. Such rules are conditionals that can be represented within the framework of a production system (see Chapter 9), and computer programs of this sort have been developed in order to capture aspects of human expertise. Their rules of inference have a specific content extracted from human experts. The resulting 'expert systems' provide advice on medical diagnosis, the molecular structure of compounds, where to drill for oil, and several other domains. Such a program navigates its way through the rules to yield a solution to particular problems provided by the person using the program.

The programs for reasoning in expert systems vary considerably. Some use the conditional rules to work bottom up from the initial data to their consequences, which in turn may trigger further rules enabling further consequences to be drawn, and so on until the program produces a final diagnosis. Other programs work top down from hypotheses about the diagnosis to specific predictions about the data. Some programs use estimates of the probabilities of hypotheses, and of the likelihood of particular observations given each relevant hypothesis. There is a well-known principle of the calculus of probabilities – Bayes theorem – which then enables the program to work out the most likely hypothesis, given the data. Many expert systems allow the user to ask why a particular datum is required, or how a particular diagnosis was reached. They may even allow a user to change the conditional rules. But, whatever the method, a system is only as good as the knowledge it embodies, and the task of formulating knowledge explicitly is difficult because so much of it is not immediately available to introspection.

Although current expert systems differ strikingly from human experts – if only because the latter make better excuses for being wrong – there are cognitive psychologists who propose that the mind contains content-specific rules of inference. As a complete theory of reasoning, however, the hypothesis has a crucial defect. It provides no machinery for general inferential ability – after all, people can make valid deductions in domains with which they are not familiar. Content-specific rules swing too far away from formal procedures. What is needed is the best of both worlds: general ability coupled with sensitivity to content.

MENTAL MODELS IN REASONING

People understand the meanings of statements, and so it is odd to suppose that when they reason they throw their understanding away and work with formal rules that are purely syntactic. There is, in fact, a semantic procedure that they can use to reason deductively. An inference is valid if its conclusion cannot be false, given that its premises are true. One way in which a valid inference can therefore be made is to imagine the situation described by the premises, then to formulate an informative conclusion which is true in that situation, and finally to consider if there is any way in which the conclusion could be false. To imagine a situation is, I have argued, to construct a 'mental model' along the lines suggested by Kenneth Craik in the quotation at the beginning of this Part. Thus, you build a model based on the meaning of the premises, not their syntactic form, and on any general knowledge triggered by their interpretation. Next, you draw, if possible, a conclusion from the model that is not stated explicitly in the premises and that does not discard the semantic information in the model. Finally, you search for alternative models of the premises that falsify the conclusion. If there is none, the conclusion is valid.

Logicians are familiar with such 'model-theoretic' procedures. What complicates matters psychologically is that there are usually many alternative situations that are compatible with the premises. If I tell you that there are some scientists and some sceptics in a room, and that:

All the scientists are sceptics

how can you build a single model that captures all the different ways in which my statement could be true? This problem has haunted philosophers for centuries in the guise of how it could be possible for a geometrical proof to be based on just a single diagram. The answer in both cases is to make some bold assumptions, which if need be can be revised later. Thus, you can imagine that the relevant set of scientists consists of, say, just two individuals:

scientist
scientist

You may be the sort of reasoner who forms a vivid image of, say, two people in white coats holding test-tubes, but the theory assumes that what matters is not your subjective experience, but the structure of the model, which may not be available to you for conscious inspection: a finite set of mental tokens represents a finite set of individuals. Since the premise asserts that all the scientists are sceptics, you must include this information in your model:

> scientist = sceptic
> scientist = sceptic
>   (sceptic)

where the token in parentheses represents a sceptic who is not a scientist – an individual who may or may not exist in the relevant situation, because the premise and your general knowledge leave this possibility open. Given the further premise, 'Anne is one of the scientists', then you can add this information to the model:

> Anne = scientist = sceptic
>   scientist = sceptic
>   (sceptic)

Your next task is to find a relation in the model that was not explicitly expressed in the premises, and to formulate a conclusion to express it:

> Anne is a sceptic.

Finally, you must search for an alternative model of the premises that falsifies this conclusion. If there is no such model, then the conclusion is valid; if you cannot find such a model but your search is not exhaustive, the conclusion *may* be valid; if you find such a model, then your conclusion is not valid, and you must consider the new model together with any previous ones to see whether they support a new conclusion, and then in turn test that conclusion, and so on.

The example does not depend on general knowledge, and since the model is finite you can easily check that the premises do not support any variant of it that falsifies the conclusion. Hence, the conclusion is valid.

The main prediction of this theory is obvious: the greater the number of different models that have to be constructed to draw a valid inference, the harder the task will be. Here is an example of a difficult inference.

Imagine that in a room there are some archaeologists,

228

biologists and chess-players, and that the following assertions are true:

None of the archaeologists is a biologist.
All the biologists are chess-players.

What, if anything, follows validly? If you want to test your deductive ability, you should commit your answer to paper. Few people respond correctly; the right answer for the right reasons calls for the construction of at least three models. The first model is exemplified here:

archaeologist
archaeologist
_____

biologist = chess-player
biologist = chess-player
(chess-player)

The reasoner imagines some arbitrary number of archaeologists, and demarcates them as not identical to biologists (as indicated here by the barrier). The second premise calls for each biologist to be identified as a chess-player. Of course there may be chess-players who are not biologists. They are represented by the token within parentheses, and the theory assumes that they are initially put on the same side of the barrier as the biologists: people do not realize at once that such a chess-player could be an archaeologist. This first model yields an informative conclusion:

None of the archaeologists is a chess-player (60%)

and I have shown the percentage of university students who drew this conclusion in one of our first experiments. If the model is scanned in the opposite direction to which it was constructed – a procedure that is relatively difficult – it yields the converse conclusion:

None of the chess-players is an archaeologist (10%)

Neither of these conclusions is valid, since they can be refuted by a second model:

```
archaeologist
archaeologist          =              chess-player

                biologist = chess-player
                biologist = chess-player
                (chess-player)
```

The two models together support the informative conclusions:

Some of the archaeologists are not chess-players   (10%)
Some of the chess-players are not archaeologists   (0%)

Finally, a third model refutes the first of these conclusions:

```
archaeologist          =              chess-player
archaeologist          =              chess-player

                biologist = chess-player
                biologist = chess-player
                (chess-player)
```

Granted that people tend to scan models in the direction in which they construct them, reasoners who have got this far have moved from a model in which none of the archaeologists is a chess-player to one in which all the archaeologists are chess-players. They may well respond:

There is no valid conclusion   (20%)

In fact, if the models are scanned in the opposite direction, then there is a conclusion that holds in all three:

Some of the chess-players are not archaeologists   (0%)

This is the only valid conclusion relating the two terms, and the difficulty in drawing it is nicely predicted by the theory.

There are, of course, other possible forms of mental model, such as the various geometrical diagrams invented by logicians. People who have learned these techniques often try to use them – usually with disastrous results, but experiments with logically naive individuals corroborate the present theory. In the experiment from which the data above were drawn, American university students made 92 per cent correct valid conclusions to those problems that required only one model to be constructed, 46 per cent correct valid conclusions to those problems that required two models to be constructed, and only 28 per cent correct valid conclusions to those problems that required three models to be constructed. The comparable results for eleven-year-old English school children were: 63 per cent correct for one-model problems, 26 per cent for two-model problems, and 2 per cent correct for three-model problems.

The theory has been implemented in several computer programs, which make no use of formal or content-specific rules of inference. They depend instead on procedures that construct models from the meanings of the premises, and that scan the models to produce informative descriptions of them. These tasks are easy to program for certain domains, such as spatial relations and inferences that depend only on the meanings of connectives and quantifiers. Whenever an account can be given of the meaning of expressions – that is, of how to construct models of them – the theory can be immediately applied to reasoning in the domain.

CONCLUSIONS

People could perhaps reason using all three of the methods that I have described – formal rules of inference, content-specific rules and mental models. Such a hypothesis, however, is neither economical nor easy to test. Of the three approaches, the most parsimonious is the one based on mental models. Vision yields mental models, and the control of movement depends on mental models. Similarly, I shall argue later that the process of understanding discourse leads to models of the states of affairs that are described. Language enables people to experience the world vicariously since they can imagine it on the basis of a description. That description in turn is produced from the speaker's model of the world. Granted the need for procedures that map models into words, and words into models, all that is necessary for an account of deduction is the machinery that searches for models which are counterexamples to putative conclusions. Although the mind could be equipped in addition with rules of inference, either formal or content-specific, there is no good reason to postulate them.

The theory has further advantages. It accounts for both logical competence – the human potential for rationality – and for errors in performance. Errors may occur because of the bottleneck created by working memory. Its limited capacity may lead a reasoner to fail to generate, or to hold in mind, all the models that may be counterexamples to a conclusion. The erroneous conclusions that subjects draw in experimental studies are consistent with this thesis. Over and over again, they produce conclusions that are compatible with only some of the possible models of the premises. Similarly, the theory provides a uniform mechanism for different sorts of inference and for the effects of content. In particular, the information available to you in daily life is often insufficient to lead to a valid conclusion. Yet, as in the case of the murder in the cinema, you can imagine a state of affairs that satisfies the available facts. You can draw a conclusion from this model, and then assess its likelihood in terms of alternative models. If you are fiendishly imaginative, you may even have thought of the following scenario, which I promised to reveal: the murderer gave the victim a post-hypnotic suggestion to stab himself during a certain climactic scene in the film.

Theories based on formal rules of inference are not yet able to explain either the particular errors that reasoners make or the many everyday inferences that are not warranted deductively. They also run into a further problem. There may not be any formal rules that people are prepared to follow regardless of the content of the premises. The earlier rule:

> If p then q
> p
> Therefore, q

strikes most formalists as indispensable. But premises of the form:

> If Philip is interested, the Queen has abdicated
> Philip is interested

hardly warrant an inference. There is no need to infer that the Queen has abdicated: it is asserted in the second clause of the conditional. Conversely, as my colleague Ruth Byrne has shown, people given the premises:

If it is raining, then she will get wet

It is raining

are not likely to draw the conclusion:

She will get wet

when they have been told in addition:

If she goes out for a walk, then she will get wet.

This additional premise presumably suggests that it may rain without her getting wet provided she does not go out for a walk. The phenomenon is readily explained if reasoners are imagining states of affairs, because the additional premise sensitizes them to possibilities not explicitly asserted in the original premises.

Further reading

Hunter (1977) describes the mental arithmetic of a calculating prodigy. The concept of semantic information was developed by Bar-Hillel and Carnap (1952); for its use in an analysis of reasoning, see Johnson-Laird (1983, Ch. 2). The inferences needed to understand discourse are discussed in Part V of Johnson-Laird and Wason (1977). Hodges (1977) is an introduction to logic; Kneale and Kneale (1962) describe Leibniz's quest for an *ars combinatoria* and Frege's work. Robinson (1979) describes resolution theorem-proving in technical detail. There is a booming literature on expert systems: Feigenbaum and McCorduck (1984) provide a proselytising introduction, and Michie (1979) a book of readings. Wason and Johnson-Laird (1972) is an introduction to the psychology of deduction; and Evans (1982) is the standard textbook. Wason (1983) describes recent work on his selection task. For the theory of mental models, see Johnson-Laird (1983), and for experimental evidence on their use in reasoning, see, e.g., Johnson-Laird and Bara (1984), and Johnson-Laird, Oakhill and Bull (1986).

CHAPTER 13

Induction, concepts and probability

The discovery of penicillin began with a single observation. Sir Alexander Fleming noticed that bacteria had been destroyed on a culture plate which had been lying around for a couple of weeks. In fact, a chain of coincidences had led to their destruction. 'Chance', as Pasteur said, 'favours the prepared mind.' Fleming was prepared. He knew that the bacteria were hardy, and so he reasoned that something must have killed them:

> Events of this type do not normally happen.
> An event of this type has happened.
> Therefore, there is some agent that caused the event.

The inference increases semantic information, ruling out more states of affairs than its premises do (see the previous chapter). It is an *induction*. The invocation of a causal agent is an explanatory conjecture, but you cannot get something for nothing, and the price for increasing semantic information is that the step may be unwarranted. Induction should come with a government warning.

A baby girl of sixteen months hears the word 'snow' used to refer to snow. Over the next months, as Melissa Bowerman has observed, the infant uses the word to refer to: snow, the white tail of a horse, the white part of a toy boat, a white flannel bed pad, and a puddle of milk on the floor. She is forming the impression that 'snow' refers to things that are white or to horizontal areas of whiteness, and she will gradually refine her concept so that it tallies with the adult one. The underlying procedure is again inductive. We all continue to make inductions throughout our lives as we form impressions about classes of people, events and the meanings of expressions.

Under the tutelage of a helpful doctor, you study some cases of smallpox. You notice that each patient had a prior contact with someone suffering from the disease. You reason thus:

Patient *a* was in contact with a case of smallpox and *a* has smallpox.
Patient *b* was in contact with a case of smallpox and *b* has smallpox.
And so on . . .
Therefore, if anyone is in contact with a case of smallpox, they are likely to catch the disease.

The inference is an induction: it goes from a finite number of instances to a conclusion about every member of a class.

The physiologist Horace Barlow has proposed that the human cortex is able to build models of the environment because its cells can detect 'suspicious coincidences' amongst the messages they receive: they can carry out inductive inferences. Induction is important, and this chapter is about its basic operations, its study in the psychological laboratory, and its implementation in computer programs. The concept of semantic information will provide a framework that clarifies the basic inductive operations. It will also suggest a general constraint that people may use in thinking inductively. Another source of constraints is knowledge of a specific domain, and the final topic of the chapter is what happens when people lack knowledge – in particular, knowledge of the theory of probability.

GENERALIZATION AND SPECIALIZATION IN INDUCTION

Philosophers are greatly exercised about the justification of induction. Your induction about smallpox seems reasonable, but, to borrow an argument from Nelson Goodman, your evidence also supports the conclusion:

If anyone is in contact with a case of smallpox, then until the year 2000 they are likely to catch the disease, and thereafter they are likely to catch measles.

Obviously this inference is silly, but why? You may say: because we know that diseases no more change their spots than leopards do. But how do we know that? If you are not careful, you may reply, 'Because all our observations support this claim.' Alas, all our observations are equally consistent with the claim that smallpox will remain smallpox until the year 2000 when it will become measles.

One reaction to the problem of justification is to reject induction altogether. Sir Karl Popper argues that science is not based on induction but on explanatory conjectures that are open to empirical falsification. And where do conjectures come from? Popper says it doesn't matter: they can come from anywhere. Since not all conjectures are equally sensible, and since many of them appear to be based on induction, the problem does not go away. So what are the psychological mechanisms of induction?

There are many possible procedures, but their essentials can be traced back to John Stuart Mill's canons of induction, which in turn go back to Sir Francis Bacon's formulation. They boil down to two main ideas. First, if positive instances of a phenomenon have only one characteristic in common, then it may play a crucial role. Second, if positive and negative instances differ in only one characteristic, then it is critical.

An inductive conjecture may be remote from the truth because it is not even based on appropriate notions, e.g. 'smallpox is a punishment for blasphemy'. But, where the hardest problem has been cracked – that is, relevant notions *are* amongst the set of available ideas – then there are two main ways in which an induction may need to be revised. They can be illustrated in terms of your hypothesis that contact with smallpox leads to the disease. On the one hand, the hypothesis may be too general. Indeed, vaccination provides protection, and so your hypothesis needs to be more specialized:

If anyone is in contact with a case of smallpox and has not been vaccinated, they are likely to catch the disease.

On the other hand, your original conjecture was also too specific: contact with infected clothes can lead to the disease. Your conjecture needs to be generalized:

If anyone is in contact with a case of smallpox or with infected clothes, they are likely to catch the disease.

This form of generalization adds a disjunctive clause. Another form, which is used in many programs including Patrick Winston's and Ryszard Michalski's, drops part of a conjunction. Thus, the conjecture:

If anyone is in contact with a case of smallpox and is elderly, they are likely to catch the disease

becomes

If anyone is in contact with a case of smallpox, they are likely to catch the disease.

Hence, induction calls for both generalization and its converse, specialization. A concept should be general enough to include all positive instances but specific enough to exclude all negative instances.

There are two outstanding questions. First, what is the underlying nature of generalization (and specialization), and, second, how many distinct operations of generalization (and specialization) are there? The answers to both questions can be derived from the concept of semantic information.

SEMANTIC INFORMATION AS A FRAMEWORK FOR INDUCTION

The more possible states of affairs that a hypothesis eliminates from consideration, the greater its semantic information. Hence, generalization is any action that increases the semantic information of a hypothesis by ruling out at least some additional state of affairs. Specialization has the opposite effect: it admits some additional state of affairs, and so it is a valid deduction from a hypothesis that reduces it semantic information.

There are many possible forms of generalization. Consider, for instance, a rule used in a program devised by Ryszard Michalski. It turns a conjunction:

If anyone is in contact with a case of smallpox *and* with the clothes of an infected person, then they are likely to catch the disease

237

into a disjunction:

> If anyone is in contact with a case of smallpox *or* with the clothes of an infected person, then they are likely to catch the disease.

This action, however, can be achieved by combining the two earlier rules of generalization. The first rule drops part of a conjunction to yield:

> If anyone is in contact with a case of smallpox, then they are likely to catch the disease.

The second adds a disjunction:

> If anyone is in contact with a case of smallpox *or* with the clothes of an infected person, then they are likely to catch the disease.

In fact, there are only three basic operations that are needed in order to construct any form of generalization in the predicate calculus. The first operation consists in conjoining the negation of any description to the current hypothesis so as to rule out an additional state of affairs. The second operation moves from a finite number of observations to a universal claim, as in the inference from a small number of patients to the conclusion that contact with smallpox suffices to catch the disease. The third operation, not yet exploited in any computer program, is exemplified by the step from:

> Every one of those diseases is cured by some drug

to:

> There is some particular drug that cures every one of those diseases.

These three basic operations suffice for any generalization in the ordinary predicate calculus, provided that the relevant concepts are amongst those available to the operations.

Unless a hypothesis has a very high information content, the number of its possible generalizations increases exponentially with the number of concepts that may be relevant to framing the generalization. Hence, any procedure based on eliminating putative hypotheses will be unable to examine them all in a reasonable amount of time. How, then, is one to find the correct generalization?

A SEMANTIC CONSTRAINT ON INDUCTION

The solution to the exponential problem is, once again, to impose constraints, and there is a plausible general constraint based on semantic information. When people try to induce a novel concept or hypothesis, they concentrate on its positive exemplars. In this case, the constraint is to formulate a hypothesis that has the largest amount of semantic information based directly on the evidence. If you examine a patient with Ebstein's disease, and this individual has a cyclical fever, a rash and a sore throat, your maximally informative hypothesis about the signs of this disease is:

cyclical fever and rash and sore throat.

If you examine another patient with the same disease, who has a cyclical fever, a sore throat but no rash, you will realize at once that your first hypothesis eliminated too much. You will modify your conjecture to the maximally informative one based on the evidence:

cyclical fever and sore throat.

Suppose, however, that you had started off with the hypothesis:

cyclical fever or rash or sore throat.

It would remain unaffected by the second patient. If the real sign of the disease is merely a cyclical fever, you will never home in on it from positive exemplars alone, because your initial hypothesis will always accommodate them. Hence, when you are trying to acquire a concept from positive instances, you must advance the most semantically informative hypothesis based on the data. It may rule out too much, but if so, sooner or later you will encounter a positive instance that allows you to correct it.

When children develop their taxonomies of the world, they appear to be guided by this principle. Frank Keil has shown that they organize their concepts in hierarchies like the one in Figure

239

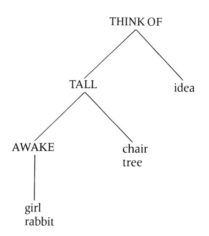

Figure 13.1: A tree representing the typical judgements of a five-year-old in Keil's study.

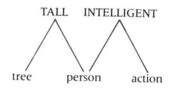

Figure 13.2: An artificial tree showing the sort of overlap that does not occur in children's judgements. The overlap exists because of an ambiguity: an intelligent action does not possess intelligence as a person does.

13.1. Overlapping arrangements like the one in Figure 13.2 are rare, and probably arise from ambiguities. Keil derives the children's classifications from the pattern of their answers to such questions as: does it make sense to say that a tree is an hour long? A child may have the taxonomic rule:

If something is living, then it is a person.

An older child, however, distinguishes two classes:

240

If something is living, then it is a person or a plant (but not both).

This way of refining a taxonomy suggests that children are sensitive to semantic information. If a category is to be divided, the semantically strongest division is one that yields two mutually exclusive subcategories, where no entity can belong to both. Perhaps it is this semantic principle that leads children to avoid overlapping taxonomies.

Consider, now, a domain that Peter Wason has investigated experimentally. I give you as an initial instance of a concept the series of digits:

2 4 6

Many people suppose that the concept is:

any series of numbers increasing by two

which assumes, plausibly, that the concept concerns a general property. Given a pair of such conjectures, it may be possible to order them in terms of their semantic informativeness. For example, the hypothesis:

a series of *even* numbers increasing by two

is stronger than the previous one because it rules out, for example, 3 5 7. Unfortunately, you cannot count up the relative numbers of possibilities since there are infinitely many of them. What is worse, you have no obvious procedure for generating conjectures in the order of their relative semantic informativeness. There are infinitely many possible concepts governing a series, and it is easy to overlook one, e.g. successive multiples of the same number.

The subjects in Wason's experiment generated their own test instances, and he observed a striking bias. They persisted in generating positive instances of their hypotheses. For example, they tried out many such instances as:

4 6 8
20 22 24
100 102 104

to corroborate the conjecture of any three adjacent ascending

241

even numbers. Of course, it would have been much more informative had they produced *negative* instances, such as:

1 2 3

They would then have learned that these items were also positive instances of the concept, which was in fact:

any three ascending numbers.

Why are people biased towards confirming their hypotheses? Some direct corroboration of a hypothesis is necessary, and the process is easier than an attempted refutation. Perhaps the bias is a hangover from domains like natural language which are primarily learned from positive exemplars.

There is a theorem in formal learning theory due to Dana Angluin, which I can re-express in terms of semantic information: there are certain concepts (or languages) that can be acquired from positive evidence alone, namely, those where one can ensure that no hypothesis that is advanced is semantically weaker than some other hypothesis based on the data so far. Eventually, the procedure will arrive at a hypothesis that does not rule out too much and so it will never need to be abandoned. People may be able to put this procedure into practice in certain domains but not others. Where a domain is infinite, as in Wason's experiment, it is difficult to assess semantic informativeness, and impossible to ensure that one advances hypotheses of the maximum informativeness. Robert Berwick, who drew attention to Angluin's procedure, argues that children use it in acquiring language, since they seldom knowingly confront ungrammatical sentences. What has yet to be determined is whether it is feasible to order conjectures about grammar according to their semantic informativeness, particularly if there are no innate constraints on the set of possible conjectures.

THE NATURE OF CONCEPTS

Until recently, following Mill and other Empiricist philosophers, psychologists assumed that people acquire concepts by a process of abstraction that drops idiosyncratic details differing from one exemplar to another and leaves behind only what holds in common. Hence, most experiments have used a technique in which the subjects have to discover the common element underlying a concept. In the 1930s, the Russian psychologist Lev Semenovich Vygotsky devised a sorting task in which wooden blocks differing in shape, colour, size and thickness are laid out on a table, and one is turned over to reveal a nonsense label, such as 'MUR', stuck beneath it. The subject then has to sort together all those blocks likely to have the same label. Young children lump together an unorganized heap of blocks, perhaps because they make a nice pattern. At a later age, they select one block, which suggests another, and so on, in a chain of interdependent selections reminiscent of Bowerman's observations on the use of 'snow'. Children at the next stage sort together appropriate blocks, but when the experimenter turns one of them over to reveal that it lacks the label, 'MUR', they remove it from the pile but do nothing about other similarly offending selections. Vygotsky claimed that they are not capable of the abstract thought needed to infer the full concept, and that they achieve this ability only from interacting with adults.

In the 1950s, Jerome Bruner, Jacqueline Goodnow and George Austin introduced an improvement on Vygotsky's procedure. They used a large array of diagrams from which the subject selected a series; and after choosing each diagram the subject was told whether or not it was an instance of the concept. Different subjects appeared to use different strategies in selecting the diagrams: some focused closely on the initial instance picked out by the experimenter and varied one characteristic of it at a time, others were prepared to gamble by choosing items that differed on several characteristics. Bruner and his collaborators also observed that disjunctive concepts are difficult to discover, which appeared to vindicate the 'common element' thesis, since a concept such as *large or green* embraces both large red objects and small green ones that have neither colour nor shape in common.

Everyday concepts, however, do not consist in the conjunction or disjunction of characteristics, but rather in *relations* amongst them. A table, for example, is not a mere conjunction of legs and a top: the legs *support* the top. Moreover, when relational concepts are introduced into the laboratory, they can yield a significant improvement in performance. Ellen Markman and her colleague Jeffrey Seibert showed kindergarten children some toy frogs – two big frogs and four baby ones. They asked, echoing a famous experiment carried out by Jean Piaget: 'Are there more frogs or more baby frogs?' The children, as in Piaget's study, replied: 'More baby frogs' – a response that is wrong, though the question is misleading. But when children were told that there was a *family* of frogs, and were asked the same question, they got the answer right.

Another aspect of everyday concepts is that their exemplars may not have a common element. Kenneth Smoke had this worry in the 1930s: 'As one learns more about dogs, his concept of "dog" becomes increasingly rich, not a closer approximation to some bare "element". . . . No learner of "dog" ever found a "common element" running through the stimulus patterns through which he learned.' The same worry was made famous by Wittgenstein's *Philosophical Investigations*:

> Consider for example the proceedings that we call 'games'. I mean board-games, card-games, Olympic games, and so on. What is common to them all? – Don't say: 'There *must* be something common, or they would not be called "games"' – but *look and see* whether there is anything common to all. – For if you look at them you will not see something that is common to *all*, but similarities, relationships, and a whole series of them at that.

Wittgenstein argued that concepts depend, not on common elements, but on networks of similarities that are like the resemblances among the members of a family. This idea gained popularity in the 1970s. Theorists argued that the world is conceptualized in terms of stereotypes (Hilary Putnam in philosophy), prototypes (Brant Berlin and Paul Kay in anthropology), frames (Marvin Minsky in artificial intelligence), or scripts (Roger Schank and Robert Abelson in artificial intelligence and psychology). The terminology differs but the underlying theories are remarkably similar: a concept specifies the typical characteristics of members of the class; it does not have necessary and sufficient conditions; and it does not have clear-cut boundaries. Hence, when you teach someone a new concept, you begin with typical cases. You say, for example, that a bird is a small creature that has wings and a tail, it flies, it lays its eggs in a nest and it sings. Then you tell them about the exceptional cases. Eleanor Rosch and her colleagues showed experimentally that not all instances of everyday concepts are deemed equally representative. A robin is a prototypical bird, whereas a chicken is not. Even people's times to respond vary appropriately: they are faster to judge that a robin is a bird than to judge that a chicken is a bird.

What is the logic of a prototype? Wittgenstein spoke of *criteria* in place of necessary and sufficient conditions. Minsky had the similar idea of a *default value*, that is, a characteristic of an object that can be taken for granted unless there is evidence to the contrary. The defaults of birdhood, for instance, include having two wings, feathers, a tail and the ability to sing. Hence, if I refer to a bird, you can infer by default that it has these characteristics – unless there is evidence to the contrary. The characteristics are not necessary conditions – a bird can be one-winged, bald, tailless and mute – but the prototype can be mentally represented by a model that incorporates all of the defaults.

There has perhaps been an overemphasis on prototypes. One check to this bias is the recent observation that many apparently prototypical phenomena also occur with concepts that really do have necessary and sufficient conditions. The number 3, for example, is judged to be more representative of an odd number than the number 23. Variations in typicality, or in the speeds of judgements, are not enough to demonstrate that a concept depends on a prototype. The only certain evidence is that it supports inferences by default, not necessity.

Everyday concepts are not isolated, independent entities; they are related to one another. Their boundaries are set, in part, by the taxonomy in which they occur. Whether or not something is judged to be a dog depends on its similarity to typical dogs, typical cats, typical wolves, and so on. This idea goes back to the *structuralism* of Saussure (see Chapter 1); the variety of taxonomic relations was studied by George Miller and myself.

245

The most clear-cut relations are hierarchies generated by the inclusion of one concept within another, e.g. a canary is a bird, a bird is an animal, an animal is a living thing. Other relations, as Miller and I found, are more complex. The contrasts between English spatial prepositions, such as *at* and *with* are a good example. We argued:

> to say 'x is at y' is to say that x is included in the region of y, that is, x is where it can interact with y socially, physically, or in whatever way x's conventionally interact with y's.

Often such regions depend on what a person is able to do. Thus, the sentence 'The chair is at the table' is a less appropriate description where the chair is facing away from the table. The converse sentence, 'The table is at the chair', is odd unless one thinks of a small table next to a chair so that the table can be included within the region of interaction of a person sitting in the chair. Some sentences are hardly idiomatic at all, such as 'Mary is at Anne', though one person can be within the region of interaction with another. The reason is that there is a symmetrical relation between the two individuals, and English has another preposition, 'with', which is more appropriate in this case. In the chapter on meaning, I shall describe the organization of the mental lexicon in more detail.

PROGRAMS FOR INDUCTION

One of the first computer programs for learning concepts inductively was developed in the 1960s by Earl Hunt and his colleagues. It assumed that concepts consist in conjunctions or disjunctions of characteristics. Its strategy was to focus on the positive instances of a concept, and to build up a tree of decisions that categorized any item as a member of the concept or not. Given the shapes in Figure 13.3, it first checks whether there are any characteristics common to all the positive and negative instances of the concept, and eliminates them as irrelevant. There are none in the Figure. Next, it checks whether there is any characteristic common to all the positive instances but to none of the negative instances. If so, a decision about this characteristic categorizes any item. The shapes in the Figure have no such characteristic, and so the program passes to the next step. It finds a characteristic that occurs frequently in the positive instances. Where several are equally frequent, it chooses one at random. In the present case, it chooses, say, the characteristic, large, and sets it up as the first decision in the tree (see Figure 13.4). The decision divides the shapes into two classes, which are then treated as categorization problems in their own right. The full program is then used to solve each of them in turn. This recursive use of the procedure is similar in design to Newell and Simon's general problem-solving program that I discussed in Chapter 9. The end result is the decision-tree shown in Figure 13.4.

Kenneth Smoke observed that negative instances discourage snap judgements about a concept. His subjects came to wrong conclusions less readily, and less often, than when they were learning from positive instances alone. Patrick Winston has used the same intuition to design a program for acquiring concepts. It begins by forming a representation (in a suitable descriptive language) of an initial positive instance of a concept. Given the

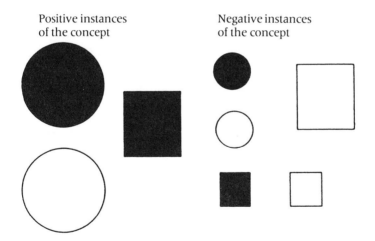

Positive instances of the concept   Negative instances of the concept

Figure 13.3: A set of materials for a concept attainment study.

247

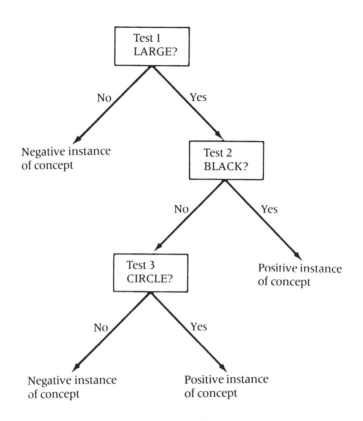

Figure 13.4: A decision-tree constructed by Hunt's program for the concept governing the materials in Figure 13.3.

first item in Figure 13.5 as an example of an arch, it constructs the hypothesis:

An arch consists of a right-hand column and a left-hand column which support a lintel.

As usual, I ignore the syntax of the program. A helpful teacher then presents a series of positive and negative instances of the concept in a sequence designed to make learning easy. The second item in the Figure is therefore a 'near miss', i.e. a negative instance that is close enough to the concept to be informative.

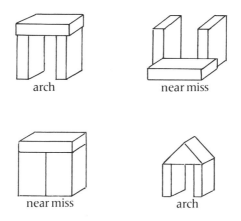

Figure 13.5: An arch training sequence for Winston's program.

The program uses the near miss to modify its current hypothesis. If the hypothesis contains a relation that is lacking in a near miss, this relation is marked as a necessary part of the concept. Hence, the columns *must* support the lintel. Conversely, if the negative instance contains a relation that is missing from the hypothesis, as in the third item in the Figure, then this relation is marked as forbidden in the concept: the two columns must not be touching each other. A positive instance may contain something that fails to match the current hypothesis, e.g. the fourth item in the Figure does not have a rectangular brick as a lintel. If the two items have a common superordinate, it is substituted for the term in the hypothesis; otherwise, a disjunction of them must be used. But, if there are only bricks and wedges in the universe of discourse, there is plainly no need to specify that the lintel must be either a brick or a wedge.

Winston's program depends on the teacher to present the instances in a helpful order. A more powerful procedure developed by Michalski and his collaborators chooses its own sequence of instances from the complete set. A program based on this approach induced the descriptions of soybean diseases from a large number of previously identified examples, and outperformed a human expert in diagnosis.

249

KNOWLEDGE AND PROBABILISTIC JUDGEMENT

Some theorists, notably Noam Chomsky, have suggested that there may be no general inductive procedures, only specific procedures based on innate knowledge of particular domains. Certainly, a major source of constraints on induction is knowledge of the particular area under scrutiny. Most of the inferences that you make go beyond the information given to you, and they do so, like Fleming's inference about the destruction of the bacteria, because they exploit your background knowledge. The point is easily demonstrated by asking people to make judgements about matters on which they have little knowledge. For example, I attach a ball to a piece of string and spin it horizontally in a circle. The string snaps. What is the trajectory of the ball afterwards? People who do not know Newton's laws often say: 'It moves off in a spiral that gradually straightens out,' and they appeal to an almost medieval notion of impetus: something that a moving object is supposed to have. The correct answer, ignoring gravity, is that the ball moves in a straight line (see Chapter 11).

Knowledge of the variability of properties is critical for induction. As Richard Nisbett and his colleagues have shown, if a single sample of a rare element conducts electricity, we are likely to conclude that any sample will. But, if a single member of an exotic tribe is obese, we are much less likely to generalize. We know that the properties of chemical elements vary much less than a property such as obesity.

A full grasp of the concept of variation calls for knowledge of the theory of probability. The theory is so different from its intuitive precursors that at least one commentator, Ian Hacking, has remarked that anyone who had played dice armed with it in ancient times would soon have won the whole of Gaul. In a magisterial series of experiments, Amos Tversky and Daniel Kahneman have demonstrated that people make egregious errors of judgement because of their ignorance of the workings of probability. The burden of Tversky and Kahneman's findings is that the errors of the naive are reproduced at a sophisticated level by the experts. Here are some of the phenomena:

Problem 1. Which are more frequent: words beginning with the letter 'R' or words in which 'R' is the third letter? Most people answer: words beginning with 'R'. They are wrong.

Problem 2. A group of subjects is asked the result of the calculation: $1 \times 2 \times 3 \times 4 \times 5 \times 6 \times 7 \times 8$. Their estimates fall around the value of 512. Another group is asked the result of: $8 \times 7 \times 6 \times 5 \times 4 \times 3 \times 2 \times 1$. Their estimates fall around the value of 2,250. Both estimates are woefully small: the correct answer is 40,320.

Tversky and Kahneman argue that what happens is that people are biased by the *availability* of information. Words beginning with 'R' are easier to think of than words in which 'R' is the third letter – presumably because the mental lexicon is organized primarily by initial letters. The difference affects the estimates of frequency. Similarly, a subject begins to calculate $1 \times 2 \times 3 \times \ldots$ and the availability of answer suggests that the overall result will not be large, whereas someone who begins to calculate $8 \times 7 \times 6 \times \ldots$ rapidly arrives at a larger number. Both groups fail to appreciate the explosive growth of the calculation.

Problem 3. You are playing roulette and observe the sequence: Red Red Red Red Red Red. What colour should you bet on next? The 'gambler's fallacy' is to bet on black because it will have to come up soon to balance the probabilities: equal proportions of reds and blacks are more *representative* of a random process. In fact, the outcomes of a truly random process are independent of one another: the probability of 0.5 for red does not change from one spin to the next. The only winning system is therefore to detect a bias in the wheel that favours some numbers at the expense of others (by carrying out a statistical test on the frequencies of the numbers). Unfortunately, even if there is a bias, it can take a long time to discover, and the owners of casinos take the precaution of changing the wheels from one session to the next.

Problem 4. A certain town has two hospitals: one is large and has about forty-five births per day, and the other is small and has about fifteen births per day. Assuming that boys are equally likely as girls, is there any difference between the hospitals in the

251

number of days on which 60 per cent or more of the babies born are boys?

Most people say: no. In fact, the outcome is likely to happen about twice as often in the small hospital. Both hospitals are samples from the total number of births, but a small sample is more affected by chance fluctuations, and so it departs more often from the true proportion of 50 per cent of male births. As Socrates might have said: You knew that all along. It just seemed that the two hospitals were equally *representative* of the population.

Representativeness is like the typicality of an exemplar, or its closeness to the prototype. It can lead to an even more startling effect:

Problem 5. Bill is thirty-four years old. He is intelligent, but unimaginative, compulsive and generally lifeless. In school, he was strong in mathematics but weak in social studies and humanities. How likely would you rate (on a scale from 1 to 7) each of the following propositions?

Bill is an accountant.
Bill is an accountant who plays jazz for a hobby.
Bill is a physician who plays poker for a hobby.
Bill is an architect.
Bill is a reporter.
Bill climbs mountains for a hobby.
Bill surfs for a hobby.
Bill plays jazz for a hobby.

Tversky and Kahneman's subjects rated the second of these assertions as more probable than the last of them in direct violation of the principle that the conjunction of two states (being an accountant and playing jazz) cannot be *more* probable than just one of them (e.g. playing jazz). The description of Bill is, of course, more representative of an accountant than of a jazz musician. The conjunction of the two properties thus lies between these two extremes, and was judged as such by nearly 90 per cent of the subjects: representativeness overrides the laws of probability. Let the buyer beware: the detail in any prediction may add verisimilitude but it must reduce its probability of coming true.

Tversky and Kahneman propose an explanation of thinking about probabilities that dovetails neatly with the account of reasoning by mental models that I offered in the previous chapter. They write:

> Some events are perceived as so unique that past history does not seem relevant to the evaluation of their likelihood. In thinking of such events we often construct *scenarios*, i.e. stories that lead from the present situation to the target event. The plausibility of the scenarios that come to mind, or the difficulty of producing them, then serve as a clue to the likelihood of the event. If no reasonable scenario comes to mind, the event is deemed impossible or highly unlikely. If many scenarios come to mind, or if the one scenario that comes to mind is particularly compelling, the event in question appears probable.

Further reading

Fleming's discovery of penicillin is recounted in Macfarlane (1984). Black (1967) discusses the philosophy of induction; Nisbett and Ross (1980) and Holyoak and Nisbett (1987) describe its psychology; and programs for induction are presented in Hayes-Roth and McDermott (1978), Michalski, Carbonell and Mitchell (1983, 1986), and Holland, Holyoak, Nisbett and Thagard (1986). Smith and Medin (1981) review psychological studies of concepts; Armstrong, Gleitman and Gleitman (1983) report the result that odd numbers yield 'prototypical' judgements. Keil derives his constraint on children's taxonomies from Sommers (1959). A source book for studies of naive physics is *Mental Models* edited by Gentner and Stevens (1983), which includes McCloskey's study of predictions about the trajectories of rotating objects. Tversky and Kahneman's major papers are included in Kahneman, Slovic and Tversky (1982).

CHAPTER 14

Creation

The tricky problem in induction is to have access to the right ideas in the first place. If they are not amongst your available repertoire, you will have to *create* them out of whatever building blocks are at your disposal. Many people believe that creation is mysterious and magical, and that it neither can nor should be analysed. In this chapter, however, I am going to advance a computational theory of it. I will argue that any creative process must fall into one of three classes of computation. Finally, I will consider this theory in the light of several case histories – procedures for generating ideas in mathematics, music and science.

Psychologists have studied creativity in many ways: they have designed tests to measure it, experiments to explore it, exercises to enhance it, and investigations to reveal it in the lives of gifted individuals. Yet they have formulated few theories of its underlying processes. Those that do exist are far from providing a complete account of how the mind comes up with novel ideas, and they often seem to yield an outcome that would not normally be judged as creative. One classic theory proposed by Graham Wallas, for example, argues that while you are busy doing one thing, unconscious processes can be working on solving an entirely different problem. There is no good evidence to support this hypothesis, and it cannot be used as a basis for a computational model without going far beyond what is in its original formulation. Other theories, such as that creativity depends on unusual associations, are too simplistic to yield genuine works of the imagination. Much more is at stake in writing a poem, painting a picture or composing a sonata than merely producing a chain of remote associations. There are constraints to be met within these genres, and a work consisting merely of a series of remote associations would be more likely to be judged crazy than creative. The masters of Dada and their modern descendants aim, however, to provoke this reaction.

Some theories fall into both traps: they are incomplete and they fail to specify the right sort of computation. The late Arthur Koestler, for instance, argued that creativity depends on 'bisociation', that is, an associative link from one frame of reference to another. On the one hand, this hypothesis cannot be readily modelled, since it is not clear how to represent a frame of reference. On the other hand, a musical composition may derive from entirely within one frame of reference – the frame provided by the constraints of the composer's style.

A WORKING DEFINITION OF CREATIVITY

What does count as creative? Although the psychological problems will not be solved by framing a definition, it is useful to delimit the domain of study. A creative process, I shall assume, has three characteristic properties.

First, like all mental processes, it starts from some given building blocks. One cannot create out of nothing.

Second, the process has no precise goal, but only some pre-existing constraints or criteria that it must meet. One creates pictures, poems, stories, sonatas, theorems, theories, principles, procedures, inventions, games, jokes, problems, puzzles and so on. One creates within genres or paradigms, and even the creation of a new genre must meet certain criteria.

Third, a creative process yields an outcome that is novel for the individual, not merely remembered or perceived, and not constructed by rote or by a simple deterministic procedure. Creation calls for more than imitation or calculation. Thus, if you multiply two numbers together, their product may be a number that you have never thought of before. Yet your response is hardly creative – especially if you obtained the correct answer. Unlike calculation and other similar procedures, the process of creation is not deterministic.

Of course, the result may not be truly original: a mental process can be creative even if other people have had the same idea. Genuine originality matters to society, but it is not a purely psychological notion. What is valuable about a creative process is that its results are judged as striking, brilliant, and not banal. These judgements depend on the mental processes of many people, and they might be explicable in general terms by cognitive science. They do, however, depend on historical, cultural and scientific events. And they will never be predictable – if only because, as I shall argue, the products of creative mental process themselves are not predictable. Hence, the immediate goal for cognitive science is to explain how mental processes create ideas that are novel for the creator; a more remote goal is to explain how a critical consensus can be reached by society; and a goal that will be for ever out of reach is a model that generates only genuinely original and excellent outcomes. Not even human beings can do that.

CREATION AS A PROCESS THAT IS NOT DETERMINISTIC

Is the mind really not deterministic? Consider, for example, Picasso as he is painting a particular picture. At any moment, there are probably several alternative brush strokes that he could make – all of which would yield a perfectly recognizable Picasso picture. Whatever the abstract principles that define the Platonic notion of a Picasso, they do not legislate for just one possible brush stroke at each point in the painting process. If they did, there would be only as many works as there are beginnings, since everything thereafter would be determined. One could argue that the particular choice of brush stroke depends on some minuscule aspect of Picasso or his environment, e.g. the state of his digestion, or the prevailing direction of the wind. If a causal account could be given of such factors, his mental processes would be deterministic, and it would be only our ignorance that forced us to deny determinism. Alternatively, one could argue that even when such factors have been explained, the mind is able to make arbitrary decisions – perhaps by the mental equivalent of flipping a coin. If particular situations could be reinstated exactly, the decision would sometimes be different the second time around.

In what follows, I shall be agnostic about these various interpretations. The crux is that a theory of creation must allow for more than one possible continuation, and cannot state how the decision is made amongst them. Hence, by definition it will not be deterministic (see Chapter 3). Real computers are deterministic, but they can simulate arbitrary choices.

THREE MINIMAL COMPUTATIONAL ARCHITECTURES

There is a close relation between creating and learning. When you learn a new task, you assemble existing skills into a novel arrangement that meets the constraints of the task. When you create a new idea, you assemble existing elements into a novel arrangement that meets the constraints of the task. The difference between the two is that when you learn, you absorb information from a teacher or the environment; but when you create, the essential constraints are those that you provide yourself. There are only three classes of program for learning (see Chapter 7), and they therefore have exact analogues for creation: there are only three classes of program that can create.

The first class have what I refer to as a 'neo-Darwinian' architecture by analogy with the theory of evolution. New species evolve as a result of the shuffling of genes followed by the constraints of natural selection, which eliminate organisms that are not viable. This architecture for creativity has the same design: its first stage arbitrarily combines elements to generate putative products; its second stage uses constraints to filter out the products that are not viable. It is the only mechanism available if there are no constraints that can guide the initial generation of ideas, but it is highly inefficient because most of its products will not be viable. The only way in which a neo-Darwinian program can produce a creative product is by apeing the evolution of species. It will have to rely on a series of gradual steps, in which appropriate constraints are used after each arbitrary shuffling, so that there is a reasonable probability of at least one putative product surviving for the next generation. The architecture has sometimes been advocated as the only possible mechanism for creativity, but people are not likely to create by combining ideas purely arbitrarily, that is, with no constraints whatsoever on the process.

There is a second possible architecture for creativity, one which I refer to as 'neo-Lamarckian' by analogy with Lamarck's theory of evolution. This theory postulates that an organism adapts to its environment and can convey these adaptive constraints to its progeny, which are generated under their guidance. The creative architecture works analogously: a set of constraints is used to generate *viable* possibilities, and if at any step there is more than one possibility, an arbitrary choice is made from amongst them. Since all the available constraints govern the generative stage, there is only a relatively small number of products, all of which meet the criteria of the genre or paradigm. Hence, the architecture is highly efficient, though it is feasible only if there is some way for previous experience to govern the generative stage.

The third architecture has what I refer to as a 'multi-stage' design. It uses some constraints to generate ideas and some to select viable ones from amongst them. Because creativity is not deterministic, there may at some point be more than one possibility – even after the use of all the constraints – and, if so, an arbitrary choice is made from amongst them. The constraints may be spread over many stages, or products may be fed back for modification to the generative stage.

THE PARADOX OF CREATIVITY

Multi-stage creativity uses constraints both generatively and selectively. You might wonder why there is this division of labour, since it would be more efficient to apply all the constraints in the generative stage (as in the neo-Lamarckian architecture). In fact, as David Perkins has remarked, the paradox of creativity is that people are better critics than creators: their knowledge is more readily available to them for judgement than for generation. Many creative achievements thus depend on a multi-stage process in which an initial idea is generated and then goes through a progressive series of revisions guided by constraints.

The design of the mind may account for the paradox, since it appears to consist in a set of separate processors that communicate data one from another but that are not privy to each other's internal operations. As an example, consider the ability to sing a tune. It depends on a mental representation of the sequence of musical intervals in the tune, which must be available to the processor controlling the process. The ability to write down the tune in musical notation is similar: the processor controlling the movements of the hand must have access to a representation of the sequence of intervals. Yet there are many musically literate individuals who are unable to write down tunes that they can sing. This accomplishment is mastered by only a few of those who can read music. It is difficult because the melodic representation for singing is not automatically available to other processes, such as writing music. Similarly, the criteria for evaluating acts of creation are not automatically available to the generative process. Since these criteria are easy to communicate to other people, whereas generative abilities tend to be ineffable, critical judgement is in advance of the ability to generate ideas.

A CASE HISTORY IN MATHEMATICS

Most theories of creativity, as I have already remarked, are too vague to be modelled. Douglas Lenat, however, has developed a program called 'AM' that generates mathematical conjectures (see Davis and Lenat, 1982). It starts with a set of concepts and a large number of criteria to guide its search for new ideas. It finds theorems that may be worth proving, but is not itself able to prove anything. A crucial feature of AM is that the human user interacts with it so as to push it in the right direction. The program suggests a new concept, Lenat works on this concept, and feeds his results back to the program. 'By and large,' he writes, 'other concepts which AM developed were either already known, or real losers.' The program is only really successful when it is guided by the human user. Moreover, the longer it runs, the greater is its tendency to generate what Lenat calls a 'mud' of uninteresting ideas.

How is AM to be classified in terms of the three sorts of architecture? The program is large and complex, but in essence it generates ideas by combining given elements according to a set of deterministic constraints. The human user finds the jewels in the mud and polishes them up for further use. Together, program and user are an example of a multi-stage architecture; it is impossible to assess their respective merits from the accounts of the work.

A CASE HISTORY IN MUSIC: MUSICAL IMPROVISATION

Musical improvisation is a form of creation in which the criteria must be represented within the musician's mind, and must suffice for the generation of satisfactory music. Many great composers – Bach, Mozart and Liszt, for example – were consummate improvisers. Beethoven improvised with such brilliancy that his extempore works were sometimes considered to be superior to his compositions. Yet he composed with the greatest of difficulty. The two skills evidently depend in part on different underlying processes – as shown by the existence of composers who cannot improvise, and improvisers who cannot compose.

The greatest improvisers are now to be found in modern jazz, Indian classical music and in the music of other cultures. What is common to most forms of improvisation is a reliance on two quite separate components: first, a long-term memory for a set of basic structures, such as the chord sequences of modern jazz or the ragas (scalic patterns) of Indian classical music; and, second, a set of principles that underlie the improvisatory skill. The basic structures are accessible to consciousness: they can be written down, taught explicitly and described in detail. The improvisatory principles, however, are inaccessible to consciousness. Some musicians are aware of a few aspects of them. No one, however, has introspective access to them all. Musicians learn to improvise by imitating virtuosos, and by experimenting. They learn to improvise by improvising; the process takes years to master.

Jazz musicians improvise melodies to fit a large variety of different chord sequences. These chord sequences are known by heart, and the same basic sequence is used over and over throughout a piece. The computational problem is therefore to produce in real time an acceptable melody that fits the chord sequence; and the tempi of modern jazz may call for melodies to be extemporised at an extremely rapid rate of up to ten or twelve notes per second. A plausible conjecture about the solution to this problem can be based on the difference between the basic structures and the improvisatory principles. The chord sequences are not made up during performance, and they may be the work of several musicians over a long period of time; the improvisatory principles, however, must operate very rapidly. Hence, a sensible solution is to do as much work as possible in the construction of the chord sequences. They carry the piece, and a considerable amount of computational power can go into their making. For the improvisatory principles to work efficiently, they should embody as little computational power as possible, that is, they should produce notes using the smallest possible amount of memory for intermediate results (see Chapter 3).

Since one cannot get inside musicians' heads, the way in which I have explored this conjecture is by developing a program that generates tonal chord sequences of the sort used in modern jazz, and programs for improvising melodies given such chord sequences.

Most Western music is based on tonal chord sequences. Theories of tonality from Rameau to Forte have implied that chord sequences can be produced with a minimum of computational power. When one attempts to make such theories explicit, they translate into finite-state devices (with no memory for the results of intermediate computations). A simple example is illustrated in Figure 14.1. The Roman numerals denote the root of the chord: I = the tonic, V = the dominant, and so on. (Non-musicians need not worry about the interpretation of these symbols, and should treat them as strings in an abstract symbolic language.) A chord sequence is generated by starting in the initial state, S_0, and making transitions from one state to another. As each transition along an arrow is made, the symbol above the arrow is generated. Thus, the finite-state device generates, for example, the following sequence of symbols: I II V I, which corresponds to the standard tonal sequence of tonic, supertonic, dominant, tonic. A more realistic device would specify the type of chord on each of these roots. The device shown in the figure is not deterministic, e.g. there are three different choices available in state S_1.

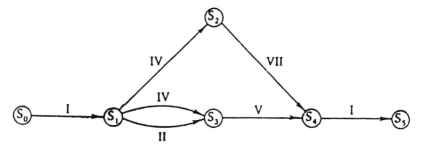

Figure 14.1: A finite-state device for generating chord sequences.

In fact, finite-state devices are not powerful enough to generate the chord sequences used in modern jazz (or other Western music). The program that I have developed has a multi-stage architecture. Stage 1 employs a grammar, containing such rules as:

TWO-BARS → | I | V_D |

to generate an *underlying* chord sequence. Many of the rules contain more than one option and the program makes an arbitrary choice in such cases. There are many possible variations on the underlying sequence, I V, including the following three:

	Imj7	VIm7		IIm7	V7	
	Imj7	bIII7		bVImj7	bII7	
	Imj7	IVm7 bVII7		bIIIm7 bVI7	IIm7 V7	

which are also shown in Figure 14.2. Mark Steedman has outlined a set of rules that take an underlying sequence and map it into a set of superficial variations, and Stage 2 of the program uses similar rules that are sensitive to context and interpolate chords into an underlying sequence according to the 'cycle of fifths'. Hence, given as input the sequence:

| I | V_D |

the program, on detecting a chord containing the symbol D, can transform the chord into a seventh (symbolized as '7') and insert a previous chord that is related to it by the cycle of fifths:

| I | II7 V7 |

262

Figure 14.2: Three variants for piano of the underlying chord sequence: tonic dominant.

A further step of the same sort can be used to insert a chord in front of II7.

    | I | VIm7 II7   V7 |

By working backwards in this way, the final result of Stage 2, depending on the choices of expansion, might be:

    | Imj   VIIm7 III7 | VIm7 II7   V7 |

Stage 3 employs a further set of rules sensitive to context in order to substitute one sort of chord for another and to make another sort of interpolation. Given the previous string as input, and depending on its choices, it can produce:

    | Imj7   IVm7 bVII7 | bIIIm7 bVI7   IIm7 V7|

Thus, the program uses considerable computational power, because each stage depends on a memory for the results of the previous stage, and because the interpolations must be made in particular contexts and so require a memory for the previous state of the chord sequence. The results could not be produced by the finite-state devices implicit in music theory. Because musicians who devise new chord sequences can write them down, there is no reason for them to use their working memories in the same way as the program. Notation is a substitute for memory, and so computational power exacts no psychological price.

The double bass player in modern jazz improvises a bass line to fit a given chord sequence (of the sort generated by the previous program). Figure 14.3 presents a fragment from a typical bass line, together with the chords on which it is based. It is rhythmically simple – a steady four-four beats to the bar – though other styles are more complex. The actual timing of the notes depends on an exquisite sense of the metrical pulse of jazz. Nevertheless, the base line allows us to approach melody without the complications of rhythm.

Figure 14.3: A fragment from a typical bass line.

How do bass players decide what to play next? One possibility is that they weave together sequences of existing melodies, modifying them to fit the chord sequence. Although both J. Ulrich and David Levitt have devised programs based on this idea, it is easier in the long run, as any competent performer will tell you, to make up new melodies than to remember a vast array of motifs and to modify them to fit the chord sequence (see, for example, the reminiscences of David Sudnow, a well-known sociolinguist who learned to play jazz piano). A grammar is a device for generating melodies, and it will generate many that the musician has never played before. Some such device is necessary even on Ulrich's or Levitt's account, since the motifs to be learned must be invented by someone.

I have developed a neo-Lamarckian program in which a grammar is used to generate the 'contours' of acceptable bass lines. Its general principle is that after a series of small steps in pitch, a step of a rather larger interval, and *vice versa*, make for a pleasing melody. (A separate program for melodies also employs a grammar to generate rhythms.) Bass players must also choose their notes to meet the constraints of harmony, which allow notes that are concordant with the current chord and those that are used in 'passing' between such notes. The various constraints are used in generating the bass line, and when there is more than one possible note that meets them the program makes an arbitrary choice. Figure 14.4 presents a fragment from a typical output of the program. The output, which also contains a rudimentary accompaniment based on the chord sequence, is played by a further program, devised by Roy Patterson and Rob Milroy, which synthesizes the sound of bass and accompaniment.

Figure 14.4: A fragment from a typical output of the bass program.

The program functions as a finite-state device, which is psychologically plausible because it would enable a musician to improvise a melody as quickly as possible with barely any need to compute intermediate representations. However, it lacks two abilities of the jazz player. It makes no specific use of chromatic runs of several passing notes (see the second bar of Figure 14.3), and it makes no use of motifs, which do occasionally feature in bass performances. It also commits a solecism that revealed the existence of a special category of passing notes of which I was hitherto unaware. The modifications to rectify these shortcomings do not require a larger memory for intermediate computations, but a slightly larger memory for what has just been played. Even though the program is well understood, it is impossible to predict its output on any particular occasion. It simulates processes that use the criteria of a genre in a way that is not deterministic.

265

ANALOGY AND SOLVING SCIENTIFIC PROBLEMS

A scientific problem can be illuminated by the discovery of a profound analogy, and a mundane problem can be solved in a similar way. In a series of studies, M. L. Gick and Keith Holyoak have demonstrated the phenomenon using a well-known puzzle devised by Karl Duncker. The task is to think of a way in which to use X-rays to destroy an internal tumour without at the same time damaging the healthy surrounding tissue. People tend not to discover the solution spontaneously, but they are likely to do so if they are given an explicit hint to make use of a story that provides a helpful analogy. It recounts that an army could not capture a fortress in a single frontal attack, but succeeded when the general divided it into separate bands that attacked the fortress from all sides. Thus, many sources of weak X-rays are placed round the body, with their beams focused so that they converge on the tumour and destroy it without harming the normal tissue.

Paul Thagard and Keith Holyoak have proposed a theory of analogy, which they have also modelled as part of a more general computer program for solving problems. The human user provides an initial set of definitions of the various concepts and rules of a particular domain (such as the fortress problem) together with a statement of a target problem (such as the X-ray puzzle). Given that the program solves the fortress problem, the solution is associated with each of its component concepts. If the program fails to solve the X-ray problem, then an analogical mechanism comes to life. In the current implementation, the mechanism depends on the user defining rules that relate the concepts in the X-ray problem to those in the fortress problem, e.g. rules that establish links from *rays* to *army*, from *tumour* to *fortress*, and so on. When at least two concepts in the fortress problem are activated by the rules, it itself becomes activated, and the program is able to establish a mapping from one domain to the other:

$$
\begin{array}{lcl}
\text{rays} & \longleftrightarrow & \text{army} \\
\text{tumour} & \longleftrightarrow & \text{fortress} \\
\text{destroy} & \longleftrightarrow & \text{capture}
\end{array}
$$

It can then transfer the actions that solved the fortress problem to the X-ray problem.

The theory lying behind the program makes two main claims. First, what is transferred in an analogy is the sequence of actions generated by the rules of inference used in solving the first problem. Dedre Gentner and her colleagues have also devised a computational model of analogy that stresses the transfer of 'high-level' relations from one domain to another. Second, the creation of the mappings depends on content-specific rules of inference – on facts, which at present have to be given to the program.

The discovery of a profound scientific analogy is unlikely to depend on pre-existing rules that establish mappings from one domain to another. An innovation depends on the invention of new mappings. The domains of knowledge – knowledge of the solar system, of atoms, of waves, of clocks, and so on – make up a vast 'space', and the task of creating a profound analogy consists in linking two regions within the space. The more remote they are from one another, the longer the chain of links, and granted that in its construction there are always different possible continuations leading to different domains, the harder it will be to construct: the number of possible mappings will grow exponentially with the number of links. Once again, we have run into a process that is not tractable in a reasonable amount of time, though it will be perfectly feasible to check the correctness of a mapping when it has been established. Indeed, the task of discovering a profound analogy defeats all but a handful of individuals: the number of concepts that might be relevant is too large for us to be able to consider all their implications. The exceptional thinker has mastered more constraints, and can use them in the generative stage of a multi-stage procedure. Those of us who can use them only in an evaluative stage therefore have much less of a chance of discovering the analogy, though once it is pointed out to us we may have no difficulty in grasping its force.

CONCLUSIONS

Musical improvisation and other extempore performances such as spontaneous speech are good examples of the use of a neo-Lamarckian architecture. This design guarantees that the output is always at least satisfactory, and it also allows the process to be weak in computational power and so make minimal demands on working memory.

Critics are sometimes sceptical about the use of grammars. They claim that people 'often break the rules' in order to produce a more original work of art. They also say that although a grammar may capture a genre, individuals have their own unique styles. Both objections are instructive. If a creative process breaks the rules, then it must either make an arbitrary choice regardless of the consequences or else be governed by yet further criteria. If an individual has a unique style, then it must depend on idiosyncratic biases in choosing alternatives, or on additional or different criteria governing the creative process. A grammar can be framed to capture the output of any computational process, whether it is random, probabilistic or of maximal computational power (see Chapter 3). It follows that the breaking of a rule can be described by yet another rule, and that individual styles can be described by grammars. Yet perhaps the use of explicit rules does do violence to the underlying *mechanism* of spontaneous creation. Musicians may have no such rules in their heads, but rather a vast distributed representation of latent possibilities that they have acquired by merging together many experiences.

The creation of a novel, painting or tonal chord sequence is typically carried out within the conventions of an existing genre. Likewise, the creative processes of a scientist normally occur, as Thomas Kuhn has argued, within the constraints of an existing paradigm. These types of creativity depend, I believe, on multi-stage algorithms. The creator generates ideas, making use of at least some initial constraints. The outcome, however, calls for revision or elaboration, and the process may be governed by constraints that cannot be used in the generative stage. In the case of scientific hypotheses, a major constraint to be used at a later stage is a set of empirical observations.

The invention of a new genre or scientific paradigm is ranked above all other forms of creation. Such revolutionary transitions are so rare, and so disparate in content, that they are unlikely to be governed by a neo-Lamarckian procedure. There will be no set of principles guaranteed to produce only viable revolutions. Like the case of a profound analogy, the only procedure that can be used in this type of creativity must therefore have a multi-stage architecture. There will be no simple, tractable procedure for innovation.

Further reading

The best review of creativity is Perkins (1981). Theories include Freud (1908), Mednick (1962) who favours associations, and Skinner (1953) and Campbell (1960) who favour neo-Darwinianism. The measurement of creative ability is described in Getzels and Jackson (1962). An attempt to increase creativity was made by Haddon and Lytton (1968). Creative scientists have been investigated by Roe (1952), and Darwin has been studied by Gruber (1974). Sonneck (1967) includes accounts of Beethoven's improvisations. Hiller and Isaacson (1959) report an early program that generates music. Moles (1966) uses finite-state devices to analyse music, and they are discussed by Eigen and Winkler (1983). Informal grammatical analyses of music are reported by Perlman and Greenblatt (1981) and Lerdahl and Jackendoff (1983). More formal computer models have been made by Sundberg and Lindblom (1976), Longuet-Higgins (1979) and Longuet-Higgins and Lee (1982). The three architectures for creativity and the programs for improvisation are reported in Johnson-Laird (1987).

PART V

COMMUNICATION

Every human group that anthropologists have studied has spoken a language. The language always has a lexicon and a grammar. The lexicon is not a haphazard collection of vocalizations, but is highly organized; it always has pronouns, means for dealing with time, space, and number, words to represent true and false, the basic concepts necessary for propositional logic. The grammar has distinguishable levels of structure, some phonological, some syntactic. The phonology always contains both vowels and consonants, and the phonemes can always be described in terms of distinctive features drawn from a limited set of possibilities. The syntax always specifies rules for grouping elements sequentially into phrases and sentences, rules governing normal intonation, rules for transforming some types of sentences into other types.

GEORGE A. MILLER

CHAPTER 15

The nature of communication

In a beautiful series of experiments, Karl von Frisch established that when bees return to the hive after finding a source of pollen or nectar, they carry out a wiggling dance on the vertical surface of the honeycomb. The number of wiggles is proportional to the distance of the food source, and, still more remarkably, the portion of the dance containing the wiggles is at an angle to the vertical that corresponds to the direction of the food in relation to the sun's position. Other worker bees closely attend the dancing bee, and are then able to fly unerringly to the food source.

The honey bee's dance illustrates the minimum that is required for one organism (or robot) to communicate with another. One bee discovers a source of food, and forms an internal symbolic representation of its direction and distance. The dance depends on such a representation rather than a mere record of behaviour, because if the bee is forced by the terrain to fly a path that makes a dog-leg, it nevertheless signals the direct angle of the food source from the hive. The bee's representations are an instance of an internal symbolism, since they satisfy the criteria of a symbolic system, which I set out in Chapter 2: there is a set of symbols, a domain that is symbolized, a method of relating symbols to what they symbolize, and, lying behind the system, some purpose that it serves. Granted that an organism (or a robot) has such internal symbols, then it may be able in addition to communicate them to other entities of the same kind by using some form of external symbolic behaviour.

The simplest form of interaction between organisms occurs when the behaviour of one organism has a causal effect on the behaviour of another. If the behaviour of the first organism has no function other than to bring about the behaviour of the second, then some theorists speak of a communication as having occurred, e.g. an ant lays down a chemical trail that can be

273

followed by other ants. However, such an interaction may occur in the absence of any independent representation of the world, and therefore the communicating behaviour has no symbolic significance. It does not designate or refer to a state of the world, but merely causes an innate reaction in other organisms.

It is often hard to assess whether an interaction depends on a genuine symbolic communication. Vervet monkeys, for example, make three different sorts of alarm call. As Cheney and Seyfarth have observed, one call occurs when a leopard is in the vicinity, and monkeys who hear it immediately climb trees; a second occurs in the presence of a snake, and monkeys who hear it examine the ground; and a third occurs when an eagle is overhead, and monkeys who hear it take cover and look upwards. The behaviours of the monkeys who hear the calls do not appear to be simple stereotyped responses, but it is difficult to determine the status of the calls. It has proved to be just as difficult to establish whether the chimpanzees that have been taught various sign languages use them in a truly symbolic way to refer to states of the world or merely as an instrumental means to bring about certain states of affairs.

In general, symbolic communication requires the communicator to have formed a perceptual representation of the world:

$$\text{world} \xrightarrow{\text{perception}} \text{representation of world}$$

which sets up the instructions for a symbolic action:

$$\text{representation of world} \xrightarrow{\text{formulation}} \text{instructions}$$

These instructions then govern the behaviour of the animal:

$$\text{instructions} \xrightarrow{\text{action}} \text{behaviour}$$

The animal perceiving the communication first has to form a representation of that behaviour:

$$\text{behaviour} \xrightarrow{\text{perception}} \text{representation of behaviour}$$

Next, it has to interpret the behaviour, that is, to use its representation to form a representation of the world. This process of comprehension yields a representation like the one that initiated the communication:

$$\text{representation of behaviour} \xrightarrow{\text{comprehension}} \text{representation of world}$$

Finally, this representation of the world is used by the receiver as a guide to action. The whole chain of symbolic communication is summarized in Figure 15.1:

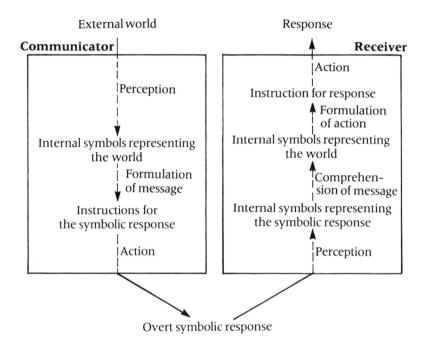

Figure 15.1: The main stages in animal communication.

THE NATURE OF LANGUAGE

Human communication is more complex than any other because it can use language. Although human beings can communicate in other ways – by gesture, by facial expression, by emotional cries

275

– and although language can be used for purposes other than communication – for the externalization of thought, for self-expression – no system of communication is as rich as natural language. What makes it so powerful is the combination of three principal abilities: first, the means to produce a large repertoire of distinct symbols (words); second, the syntactic competence to combine these basic elements (words) so as to yield a potentially infinite number of different messages (sentences); third, the semantic competence to communicate messages that are not under the immediate control of the local environment but that can intentionally refer to other states of affairs including hypothetical or imaginary ones.

Nearly everyone masters these three abilities effortlessly in a few years of childhood – so effortlessly that many people are inclined to think that language presents only two psychological problems: learning to read and learning to speak a foreign language. In fact, a more profound problem is to explain the facility with which language is used in daily life and the ease with which children acquire it.

Linguists believe that language is governed by rules, and that there are different sets of rules for its different levels of organization. There are rules that govern what counts as an acceptable English speech sound, e.g. the vowel 'ee' in the word 'feet', but not the vowel in the French word 'rue'. There are rules that govern what can count as an acceptable English word. New words are coined all the time, and it is simple to make up possible English words that do not yet exist, e.g. 'platch', 'snorp' and 'brell'. When people are asked to invent new words, they automatically obey the rules. They do not make up words like 'tchpla', 'spnor' or 'blree', though such sequences of consonants do occur in other languages. There are rules governing the grammatical arrangements of words that can occur in English sentences. Violations of acceptable English are immediately obvious. You notice that something is wrong, for example, when a visiting foreigner explains: 'My works is many and my salary are few.' There are rules governing the meanings of expressions. Violations of acceptable usage are again obvious. The sentence, 'The invisible stain believes the sky' is grammatically well formed, but semantically odd.

These examples also illustrate the hierarchical structure of language. It is organized at the level of speech sounds (and by

276

conventions governing alphabets), at the level of words (and by conventions governing spelling), at the level of grammar, and at the level of meaning. The organization is intricate: despite two millennia of study by philosophers and theoretical linguists, no complete account yet exists of any of the three thousand or more known human languages. The reader who is sceptical about the power of rules to describe the different levels of language, or who regards them as too precise for the vagaries of the everyday tongue, should recall one of the lessons of Chapter 3: rules can be made powerful enough to capture any computable output, and it does not matter whether that output is probabilistic, vague or not deterministic.

Perhaps, as many linguists suppose, the mind is organized so that it can acquire rules, and follow them, without being consciously aware of what they are. The unconscious nature of linguistic knowledge and the tacit process of acquiring it provide us with a clue to the nature of human mentality – a clue to which I shall return later in the book. Meanwhile, I shall end this brief introduction to language with an example of how much of it is ordinarily hidden from us. You might suppose that the pronunciation of a word consists in articulating one speech sound after another – just as writing a word consists in spelling it out one letter after another. This assumption is commonly held, but wholly false: the elements of speech sounds overlap each other in time.

The fundamental linguistic skills are the ability to speak and the ability to listen and understand. To explain these abilities therefore calls first for a grasp of how speech is produced and decoded. The following chapter is about these processes. At the heart of linguistic communication, however, are the levels of grammar and meaning. I shall devote two further chapters to them. Hence, the next three chapters concern the three unique components of natural language: speech, syntax and semantics.

CHAPTER 16

Speech and hearing

THE NATURE OF SOUNDS

All sounds, whether speech, music or noise, are vibrations in a medium, typically air. An object that vibrates causes a series of compressions (as it moves outwards) and decompressions (as it moves inwards) of nearby molecules, and these disturbances are transmitted from particle to particle through the air. The oscillations in pressure can differ in their size and in their frequency – how fast they occur. Roughly speaking, loudness depends on the size of the oscillation: the larger it is, the louder the sound. And the pitch of the sound depends on the frequency of the oscillation: the faster it is, the higher the pitch.

The variation of pressure over time can be plotted as a wave (see Figure 16.1). Any sound, whether a speech or a symphony, is a single wave of pressure, which causes the ear drum to move in and out. This mechanical energy is converted into nerve impulses that ultimately give rise to hearing. It is as though someone pushes a pencil up and down in the palm of your hand with a varying pressure and frequency. Since neither speech nor symphony seem to be so simple an experience, something rather interesting must be going on.

Figure 16.1: An example of a wave of variation in pressure, produced by the speech sound 's'.

(From D. B. Fry, *The Physics of Speech*. Cambridge: Cambridge University Press, 1976, p. 84)

Figure 16.2: A complex wave can be built up from, or equivalently decomposed into, a set of simple waves. Add waves (a), (b) and (c) together point by point and you obtain the complex wave (d).

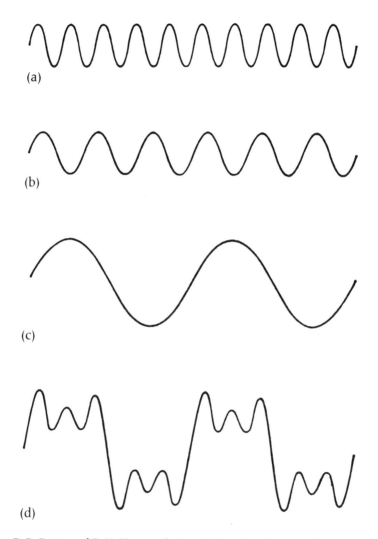

(a)

(b)

(c)

(d)

(From P. B. Denes and E. N. Pinson, *The Speech Chain.* New York: Anchor Books, 1973, p. 37. Copyright © 1963 by Bell Telephone Laboratories, Inc. Reprinted by permission of Bantam, Doubleday, Dell Publishing Group, Inc.)

The answer is that sound is another instance of a 'linear system': if separate variations in air pressure are combined, they have additive effects. Hence, if three adjacent loudspeakers produce waves (a), (b) and (c) of Figure 16.2, the result will be equivalent to wave (d). Conversely, three filters tuned to the appropriate frequencies will recover waves (a), (b) and (c) from an input of wave (d). What you hear if you listen to the three waves is a single note with a pitch of the slowest vibrating wave (c), which is the *fundamental* frequency, and a timbre that depends on the other waves, which are the *harmonics*. The harmonics consist of progressively faster vibrations – all exact multiples of the frequency of the fundamental – that are usually smaller in size (see Figure 16.3). When separate notes or sounds are combined, the result is a single complex and irregular wave formed from their sum. That is why any combination of sounds can be created by a single vibrating object, such as a gramophone needle.

Figure 16.3: The amplitude (or size) of the changes in air pressure of the three waves making up the complex wave in the Figure 16.2. Wave (c) on the left of the figure is the fundamental, and waves (b) and (a) to its right are harmonics.

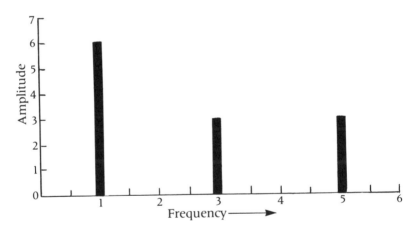

(From P. B. Denes and E. N. Pinson, *The Speech Chain*. New York: Anchor Books, 1973, p. 39. Copyright © 1963 by Bell Telephone Laboratories, Inc. Reprinted by permission of Bantam, Doubleday, Dell Publishing Group Inc.)

The simple 'sine' waves into which all sounds can be decomposed are readily produced by tuning forks or electronic synthesizers. The shimmering beauty of, say, Ravel's *Daphnis and Chloe* or the raucous excitement of Charlie Parker's *Ko Ko*, could all be created by a team of musicians wielding nothing more than tuning forks if only they could control them with unerring super-human precision.

THE NATURE OF HEARING

The human ear decomposes complex waves into simpler constituents. The vibrations of the ear drum are conveyed by three small bones to the oval window in the side of the cochlea – the part of the inner ear that connects to the semi-circular canals, which are important for the sense of balance (see Figure 16.4). The salty water in the cochlea is set in motion and transmits the vibrations to a membrane that runs down the middle of the cochlea, curled up within its snail-like shape. Hearing probably developed from the more primitive sense of touch, and this 'basilar membrane' is essentially a piece of skin lined by several rows of hairs, which in turn are attached to nerve cells. When the basilar membrane moves upwards, it bends the hairs, and thereby causes the nerve cells to fire. The nerves do not respond as the membrane moves downwards. The different frequencies of vibration of a complex sound cause different parts of the membrane to vibrate. The frequencies are spread out in an orderly fashion from one end to the other, with high frequencies vibrating the end nearest to the bones of the middle ear. Hence, the membrane acts like a bank of filters – each tuned to a narrow band of frequencies – that covers the audible range.

The note an octave below middle C on a piano has a frequency of just under 131 vibrations per second. The nerve cells mediating this pitch fire in synchrony with the vibrations, but they do not each respond to every vibration. Nerve cells do not fire for sustained periods at rates much above 200 impulses per second. So how do they respond to a note two octaves above middle C with a frequency of about 1046 vibrations per second? And how do they respond to different intensities? In fact, a large

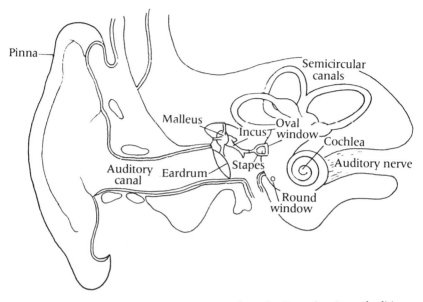

Pinna

Semicircular canals

Malleus

Incus

Oval window

Cochlea

Stapes

Auditory nerve

Auditory canal

Eardrum

Round window

(After P. Lindsay and D. Norman, *Human Information Processing*. Second edition, New York: Academic Press, 1977, p. 126)

number of cells monitor each region of the basilar membrane; none fires on every pulse of a rapid vibration, but when a cell does fire it is in synchrony with the vibration, and it fires more often to more intense vibrations. Hence, each cycle causes some cells to fire and the frequency is maintained by different cells firing on adjacent cycles – like a company of soldiers firing volleys faster than any individual could, because some fire whilst others reload. The volleys from different parts of the basilar membrane decompose sounds into their separate frequencies.

MUSICAL SOUNDS

Streams of nerve impulses pass down the auditory nerve from the ear to the cortex. Its task is to analyse them, to recognize sounds, and to locate their source. A sound with a repeating pattern in its wave is perceived as having a definite pitch, e.g. a musical note, a vowel sound in speech, and many communicative cries of animals. A striking feature of musical notes is that when their frequency is doubled (i.e. raised by an octave), they sound much the same. This psychological phenomenon lies at the heart of all music: a musical scale, such as the familiar European 'doh ray me fah soh lah te doh', repeats itself over and over in a cyclical fashion from the lowest to the highest notes in the audible range. This cycle can be represented graphically by a spiral, which is a figure generated by a rotation around an axis combined with a shift along that axis. A logarithmic spiral (to the base 2) has the property that the distance round the spiral doubles on each successive circuit. Roy Patterson has recently proposed that the auditory system might use a computational model of a spiral to detect periodicity in sound waves, and he has modelled his theory in a program. The basic idea is simple, but intriguing, and I will describe it in terms of the computer program.

Impulses corresponding to a given pitch enter one after another at the centre of a logarithmic spiral (of base 2), and move round it at a constant velocity. At a certain moment of time, say, after eight impulses have been sent into the spiral, they will be in the positions shown in Figure 16.5. Once in every cycle of the sound, the geometry of the spiral guarantees that regular impulses will line up with each other in straight lines emanating from the centre of the spiral like the spokes of a wheel. Such a configuration is shown in the Figure. The angles between the spokes are always the same, regardless of the pitch of the note. But the position of the spokes rotates clockwise as pitch increases; when the pitch is double that of the original note, the spoke pattern is back to where it started. Thus, notes an octave apart yield very similar patterns. If a procedure monitors the position of the spokes, then it will distinguish notes of different pitches, but those an octave apart will seem similar. The spokes in the spiral arise because of the correlations between one part of a regular stream of impulses and another. The auditory system must use some such method for detecting correlations.

Certain combinations of musical notes sound consonant, others sound dissonant. Each note produces the characteristic four-spoke pattern, and the orientation of the pattern depends on

Figure 16.5: The pattern of spokes in Patterson's spiral processor after eight impulses have entered at the centre and moved around the spiral, at a constant velocity. The spokes arise from correlations between one part of a regular stream of impulses and another.

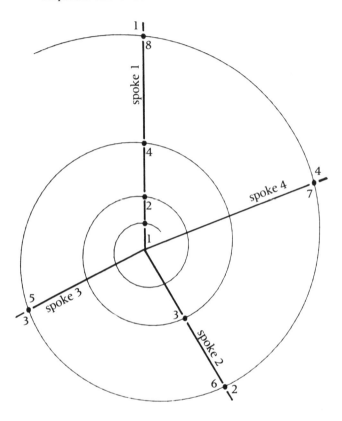

(From R. D. Patterson, Spiral detection of periodicity and the spiral form of musical scales. *Psychology of Music,* 1986, p. 47)

the pitch of the note. If you play middle C on the piano together with the note E that is three notes above, the result is consonant. The two patterns produced by the notes have one spoke in common, and this coincidence occurs with other consonant pairs of notes. Dissonant pairs (e.g. two adjacent notes, such as middle C and the B below it) produce patterns with no spokes in

Figure 16.6: The harmonics of a note on the piano and a note an octave higher on the clarinet. The horizontal axis is frequency in cycles per second.

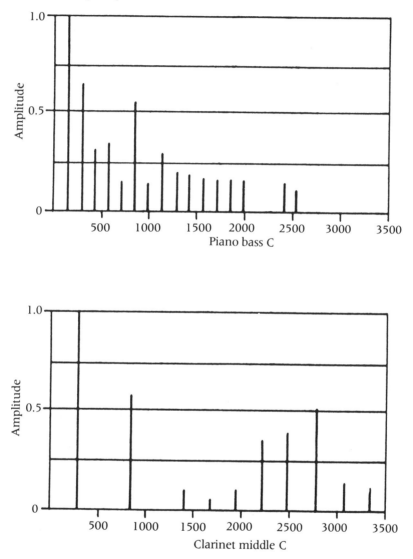

(From D. B. Fry, *The Physics of Speech*. Cambridge: Cambridge University Press, 1976, p. 59)

285

common. Insofar as consonance has an auditory foundation, it may depend on the coincidence of spoke patterns. Since cultures differ in what they find consonant, there must also be effects of experience on judgement.

A note played on a musical instrument has a fundamental and many harmonics, but what you perceive is not each separate frequency but rather a single pitch, usually that of the fundamental, with a particular timbre. The timbre depends on the harmonics and their intensities. Figure 16.6 shows the different harmonics produced by a note on a piano and a note on a clarinet. Timbre is also affected by the speed with which the various harmonics come on during the first fraction of a second at the beginning of a note: without hearing the start of a note, it is difficult to identify a musical instrument. Quite how these transitions are mentally represented is not yet known.

SPEECH SOUNDS

The human voice is like a complicated musical instrument. Air expelled from the lungs vibrates the vocal cords of the larynx. If you put your fingers on your Adam's apple and say 'aaah', you can feel the vibrations. If you whisper the same sound, you will not feel any vibrations: the air whistles through the open larynx and vocal tract to produce a turbulent rushing noise. Once air has been set in motion by either of these means, the vocal tract can modify it in various ways.

One form of modification is 'resonance'. You can experience this phenomenon by singing in the bath. If you sing various notes, you should discover that the loudness of some of them is enhanced by the acoustics of the bathroom. The amplification occurs only for certain pitches: their wavelength, i.e. the distance between the maximal pressures, fits exactly into the length of the bathroom and so they are reinforced. It is resonance that enables you to hear that a bottle is being filled with liquid; as the amount of air diminishes, so the resonating pitch rises – together with the rising liquid. The larynx produces a wave, which, as Figure 16.7 shows, is composed of a fundamental and many harmonics. The shape of the vocal tract causes some of the harmonics to resonate

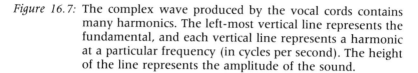

Figure 16.7: The complex wave produced by the vocal cords contains many harmonics. The left-most vertical line represents the fundamental, and each vertical line represents a harmonic at a particular frequency (in cycles per second). The height of the line represents the amplitude of the sound.

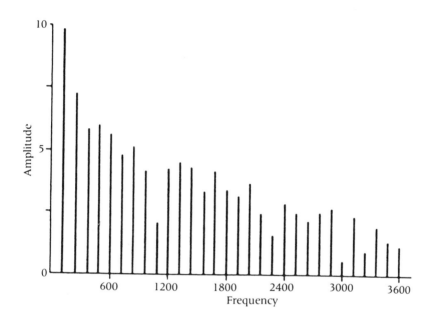

(From D. B. Fry, *The Physics of Speech*. Cambridge: Cambridge University Press, 1976, p. 66)

and others to be dampened. By moving your tongue, lips, soft palate, or opening up your nasal passage, you change the shape of the tract and thus the particular bunches of adjacent harmonics that resonate. These bunches of resonating frequencies are called 'formants'. Their pattern is displayed by an instrument known as a spectrograph, which produces a picture of the amount of energy in each band of frequencies from the lowest to the highest (see Figure 16.8). What distinguishes one vowel (e.g. 'ee') from another (e.g. 'oo') is the pattern of formants created primarily by the position of the tongue.

Figure 16.8: A spectrogram of the utterance 'She began to read her book' (shown in phonetic notation below the horizontal axis). The vertical scale is frequency in thousands of cycles per second (kilohertz), and the horizontal scale is time in seconds. The filter allows a relatively wide band of adjacent frequencies through in this case: nearby harmonics are therefore no longer distinguishable and so give rise to the broad bands corresponding to the 'formants', e.g. after the fairly broad distribution of energy for the initial 'sh' sound, the first two formants of 'e' in 'she' are clearly visible. The vertical striations are registering the opening and closing of the vocal cords as they vibrate: each time they open there is a little puff of energy which diminishes when they close.

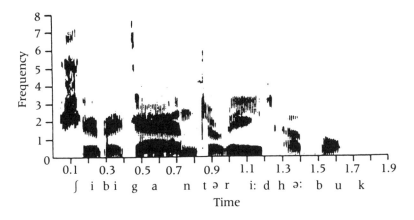

(From D. B. Fry, *The Physics of Speech.* Cambridge: Cambridge University Press, 1976, p. 107)

Figure 16.9 shows the typical formants of various vowels in the standard pronunciation of British English. The frequencies of the formants remain much the same regardless of the pitch of the fundamental frequency of the larynx's vibration. This stability explains why you can say 'ee' in a low-pitched voice or in a high-pitched voice and still be recognized as saying the same vowel. The fundamental pitch changes, but not the pattern of formants.

Figure 16.9: A spectrogram of the words 'heed', 'hid', 'head', 'had', 'hod', 'hawed', 'hood', and 'who'd', as spoken in a standard British accent.

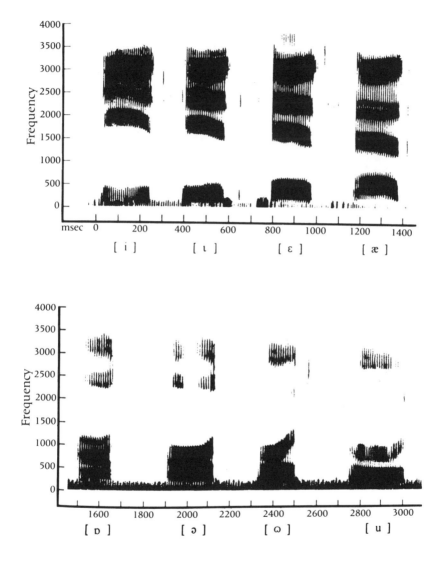

(From P. Ladefoged, *A Course in Phonetics*. New York: Harcourt Brace Jovanovich, 1975, p. 171)

289

Languages differ, as do dialects, in their vowel sounds. Anyone who has struggled to learn French knows the difficulty of pronouncing the vowel in 'rue': you have to get your tongue and lips into a position that does not correspond to any English vowel.

Consonants are created by interrupting the flow of air. The consonants 'b' and 'p' are produced by bringing the lips together, the consonants 't' and 'd' are produced by bringing the tip of the tongue up behind the teeth, obstructing the flow of air until the pressure mounts, and then allowing its explosive release. Other consonants, such as the 'ss' sound, are produced by restricting the flow of air so as to cause turbulence. These obstructions or constrictions may, or may not, be accompanied by the larynx vibrating, as in the contrast between a 'zz' and an 'ss' sound. (Try to whisper 'zz'!)

Figure 16.10: The consonant 'd' has a different pattern of formants depending on which vowel follows it, as shown here for *di* ('dee') versus *du* ('doo'). These artificial spectrographic patterns suffice to give rise to the two sounds from a device that produces synthetic speech.

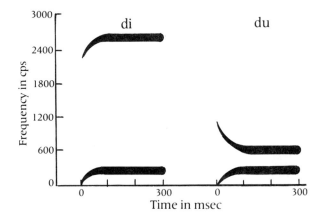

(From A. M. Liberman *et al.*, Perception of the speech code. *Psychological Review*, 74, 1967. Copyright © 1967 by the American Psychological Association. Reproduced by permission of the authors.)

Writing is a sequence of one letter after another, but, as I said in the previous chapter, speech is *not* a simple sequence of one sound after another. This fact has been demonstrated by Alvin Liberman and his colleagues at the Haskins Laboratories in New Haven. What they have shown is that the vocal apparatus does several things simultaneously. Look into a mirror and compare the difference in your lip position when you say, 'dee', with the position when you say, 'doo'. You will see that even while you are pronouncing the initial consonant your lips are taking up a position appropriate to the subsequent vowel. Although you hear the same consonant in both cases, its pattern of formants is very different, as shown in Figure 16.10.

There are some strange aspects of this phenomenon. You do not hear the shift in the pitch of the formants shown in the Figure. You might expect to hear a sort of chirp or glissando, and you *do* hear it if a single formant is played in isolation. Otherwise, what you hear, of course, is 'dee' or 'doo'. If you attempt to snip off the end of recordings of these sounds to leave only the initial 'd' consonant on the tape, you will discover that the task is impossible! As long as you can hear anything, you hear 'dee' and 'doo', though the durations of the vowels get shorter and shorter as you snip away.

Instead of speech sounds following each other like beads on a string, they run alongside each other like trains on separate tracks, because the vocal apparatus articulates one sound as it is articulating others (see Figure 16.11). These *co-articulations* enable speech to be produced up to speeds of 25 sounds per second, and sometimes more rapidly. This rate is much faster than a string of discrete sounds could be made or identified – much faster than morse code can be transmitted or received by human beings. The corollary, however, is that the cues to a speech sound depend on context, and a feature such as a particular formant can simultaneously carry information about different speech sounds. The unconscious integration of cues is borne out by a demonstration devised by Henry McGurk and J. MacDonald. If you watch a film of someone saying 'ga' but on the soundtrack the speaker says 'ba', then what you hear is 'da'. The visual and auditory cues are integrated into a unitary perception – a com-

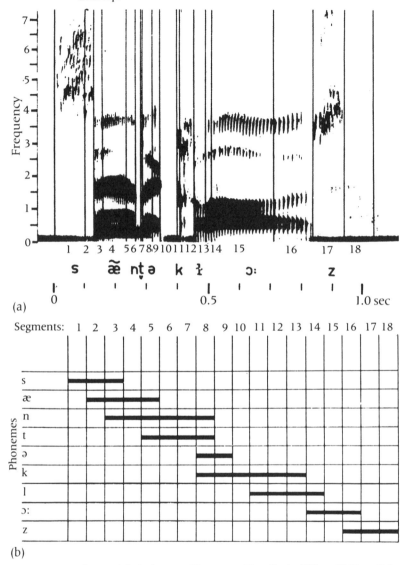

Figure 16.11: The cues for speech sounds overlap each other in time: (a) a spectrogram of the utterance 'Santa Claus'; and (b) a diagram showing how the cues to the different phonemes overlap.

(a)

(b)

(From E. Lenneberg, *Biological Bases of Language*. New York: Wiley, 1967, p. 94) promise – and you are wholly unaware of the conflict. The perceptual apparatus makes available to consciousness something that appears to correspond neither to the sound wave itself nor to the articulatory movements that produced it, but to more abstract categories of speech. To clarify this notion, we must turn to phonology – the linguistics of speech sounds.

THE LINGUISTICS OF SPEECH SOUNDS

You can make two distinct sorts of 'p' sounds: one yields a considerable puff of air, and the other does not. If you hold your hand up to your mouth and say 'pit', you will feel the puff of air. If you say 'spit', you will feel much less. In English, it makes no difference which of the 'p' sounds you use. You could pronounce 'spit' using the aspirated sound, and no one except a phonetician would notice. In some languages, however, the difference does matter, and if you use the wrong 'p' you will utter a different word.

Any language contains only some of the sounds that humans can produce, and it treats physically different sounds as instances of the same category. Indeed, no two instances of the same vowel produced by the same speaker are precisely alike. The significant categories of sound in a language, which are known as 'phonemes', depend on contrasts in the way in which they are articulated – an idea that goes back to Structuralism (see Chapter 1). Thus, vowels can be distinguished by the position of the highest point of the tongue, its closeness to the palate, and the duration of the sound; consonants can be distinguished by the part of the vocal tract in which an obstruction to the air-flow occurs, and by the manner in which the obstruction takes place.

The linguist Morris Halle has established that an English speaker's unconscious representation of the language must be sensitive to such articulatory features. Consider, for instance, the way in which you form plurals of the following nouns:

bus	bush	buzz	garage	finch	badge		
lip	pit	pick	cough	sixth			
cab	lid	cove	rogue	scythe	cam	call	car.

293

The first row of nouns form plurals by the addition of 'ez', e.g. the plural of 'bus' is pronounced 'busez'. The second row form plurals by the addition of a simple 'ss' sound, e.g. the plural of 'lip' is pronounced 'lipss'. The third row form plurals by the addition of a 'z' sound, e.g. the plural of 'cab' is pronounced 'cabz'.

How do you pronounce the plurals of the imaginary English words: 'platch', 'snorp' and 'brell'? Unless you are being deliberately contrary-minded, you probably pronounce them as, 'platchez', 'snorpss' and 'brellz'. Since there are no such words in English, then as Halle points out you must use unconscious principles to form these plurals. You might depend on rules about the final phonemes of words, e.g. if a singular noun ends with an *s, sh, z, zh, ch* or *dge* sound, then form its plural by adding an *ez* sound. Such rules are complicated and *ad hoc*. Halle has formulated much simpler and more principled rules in terms of articulatory features:

1. If a singular noun ends with a sound made by raising the blade of the tongue and making a strident hiss, then add the *ez* sound.

2. If a singular noun ends with a sound that does not involve the larynx vibrating, then add the *ss* sound.

3. In any other case, add the *z* sound.

What is the plural of 'Bach'? I imagine that, like most speakers of English, you would say 'Bachs', using the 'ss' sound. The 'ch' sound, which is not in English, is not a strident hiss made by the blade of the tongue, but it does fit the second of Halle's rules, and thus calls for the plural 'Bachs'.

WORDS, WORDS, WORDS . . .

When you listen to a familiar language, you hear words rather than sounds. How you identify words is a puzzle because the problem of identifying phonemes would seem to be aggravated by casual everyday pronunciation and by the differences from speaker to speaker. Moreover, as a spectrogram shows, speakers do not delimit each word by a pause, and there are often no obvious cues to where one word ends and another starts. How then do listeners segment speech into separate words?

One hypothesis is that they are guided by .the stress pattern of syllables. In English, syllables differ in stress, e.g. the word 'melted' is normally pronounced with a stressed and full vowel in its first syllable and a shorter and weaker vowel in its second syllable. Since stressed syllables are easier to identify than unstressed syllables, Anne Cutler and Denis Norris have conjectured that each syllable containing a stressed vowel is treated as the potential start of a word. They tested this hypothesis in an experiment in which listeners heard a series of two-syllable items, such as 'larmage, meltive, bozzen, abnidge . . .', and had to respond as soon as they recognized an initial syllable that was a word, e.g. 'meltive'. This item has two syllables, 'mel' and 'tive', which each have a stressed vowel. If stressed syllables are perceived as the potential beginnings of words, listeners should segment 'meltive' between the two syllables, and therefore take longer to detect the embedded word 'melt'. They should be faster with 'meltesh', which will not be segmented, because its second syllable, 'tesh', is unstressed and so not perceived as the potential beginning of a word. The results confirmed this prediction.

People very rapidly identify words and understand what is being said to them. William Marslen-Wilson, Lorraine Tyler and their colleagues have devised some remarkable demonstrations of this phenomenon. Certain individuals can listen to a tape-recording of a speaker and repeat aloud the same words with a lag of only about a syllable, i.e. about a quarter of a second. Yet, they understand what they hear: their errors almost always make sense in the context, and when the experimenters insert deliberate mistakes into the recordings, the subjects spontaneously correct them.

Listeners can indeed identify words before they have heard their endings. Tyler has demonstrated this ability using a technique invented by François Grosjean: a listener hears progressively larger fragments of a word and attempts to identify it on each presentation. In the context of a sensible sentence, the listener succeeds after less than half of the word has been presented, e.g. after its first syllable. Since there are typically some thirty words starting with the same syllable, the context clearly aids the process of identification; a nonsensical or ungrammatical context slows the process down.

One of the most influential theories of word recognition was formulated by John Morton. He proposed that each word is represented by a separate mental processor, or 'logogen', which collects positive evidence for the occurrence of the word. There are separate systems of logogens for hearing and for reading. When the evidence pushes a particular logogen over its threshold, it fires and the word that it represents is recognized. Logogens accumulate evidence both 'bottom up' from the sensory input and 'top down' from the context.

Marslen-Wilson and his colleagues have proposed an improved version of the theory. As information from the start of a word – its articulatory features, say – enters the system, it activates those processors representing words that match its beginning: the better the match, the greater the degree of activation, though there is a bias favouring words in more frequent use. As further information about the word arrives, it reduces the activation of those members of this initial 'cohort' that no longer match the word. When the mismatch reaches a certain size, processors switch themselves off and disappear from the cohort. Hence, unlike Morton's logogens, a critical role is played by evidence counting *against* the occurrence of certain words. A word is recognized as soon as there is only one reasonably active processor left, but the context of a word may enable a short cut to occur. Context does not affect activation – it can neither introduce nor eliminate candidates from the cohort, but it can select an item from the active words that matches the sense and syntax of the utterance, and in this way speed up the process of recognition.

The cohort theory assumes that a representation of the articulatory features of a word is compared with similar representations of words in the mental lexicon. Perhaps bundles of features are first identified as phonemes. Such a level of representation would explain how you can rapidly adjust to the different vowel sounds of a different dialect, as when someone with a South African accent says, 'I lift the book on my disk.' You adjust the bundle of features required for the vowels, and recognize the utterance as, 'I left the book on my desk.'

If words can be recognized prior to their endings, why haven't their endings gradually atrophied and disappeared from the language? Perhaps a predictable ending guards against the effects of noise, and makes it easier to find the beginning of the next word. If the cohort theory is correct, the perception of speech on a noisy telephone line will be much harder when the noise obliterates the beginnings of words rather than those parts that occur beyond the theoretical recognition point. If stressed syllables function as potential beginnings of words, however, then the obliteration of unstressed syllables at the start of words as in 'enrage' should be less disruptive than the obliteration of stressed syllables. The experiment has yet to be performed.

INTONATION AND TONE OF VOICE

Leo Rosten tells the story of Stalin receiving a telegram from Trotsky and reading it to the assembled masses: 'You were right and I was wrong. You are the true heir of Lenin. I should apologize. Trotsky.'

A Jewish tailor steps up from the crowd and says, 'Such a message, Comrade Stalin. For the ages! But you read it without the right *feeling*!'

And this is how the tailor reads it: 'You were right and I was *wrong*? *You* are the true heir of Lenin? *I* should apologize???!!'

A speaker's tone of voice can indeed convey important information. It can make a remark dogmatic, questioning, ironical, bored, good-humoured, irritated, ill-mannered or even downright sarcastic. These effects depend on the prosody of the utterance – its rhythm and intonation – and on the quality of the speaker's voice – whether it is gruff, husky, creaky and so on.

An important function of prosody is to emphasize particular words. Someone asks you: 'Is that a pink tie?'

And you reply: 'No, it's a RED tie'.

If you had been asked instead: 'Is that a red handkerchief?'

You might have replied: 'No, it's a red TIE'.

As Michael Halliday and other linguists have noted, the

emphasis draws attention to the new information in your utterance and contrasts it with the information presupposed by the question. It also makes a word easier to perceive: Cutler and her colleagues have shown that listeners who have to detect any word beginning with a certain phoneme, say 'd', respond faster if such a word is emphasized. They also respond faster if the prosody of the sentence indicates that the word is going to be emphasized, even if in fact it is not.

Many people imagine that emphasis is created by speaking a word louder. Although there is some truth in this idea, it overlooks other more important cues. There is no simple or direct cue to stress, but it often depends on raising (or lowering) the pitch of the fundamental by comparison with the context, or on prolonging the duration of the syllable.

There appears to be only a small number of significant intonational gestures, such as a rise in the fundamental pitch of the voice, a fall, or a fall immediatcly followed by a rise. The use of these gestures, however, differs from language to language. In English, the sentence, 'Can you open the window?' can be used either to ask a question requiring the answer 'yes' or 'no', or else to make a request. A rise in pitch at the end of the utterance signals a question; a fall often signals a slightly peremptory request. But not every language follows these conventions.

Is intonation a separate and independent channel of communication? Some linguists, such as Mark Liberman and Ivan Sag, have suggested that it may be. If you hear someone say:

Would you mind cleaning my boots for me?

and then the door slams and you hear only a muffled reply with the following pitch contour:

you will think that the response was an indignant objection. Liberman and Sag demonstrate the point by playing the same contour on a kazoo. Unfortunately, there are no set interpretations for each intonation contour. As Anne Cutler and Steve Isard observe, the contour above could be used by an irate individual making the request:

Go and see what the fellow wants!

Hence the same contour can be used for assertions or requests.

Speech sets words to a 'melody', but the interpretation of an utterance does not merely add the meaning of one to the meaning of the other. The effects of intonation contour depend on the content of the utterance, as Klaus Scherer and his colleagues have established. If 'Can you open the window?' ends with a fall in pitch, the utterance is interpreted as an impatient command but only by listeners who can identify the form of the interrogative. If it does not require the answer 'yes' or 'no', such as, 'Who was that lady I saw you with last night?', then it normally ends with a fall. Thus, the same intonation may sound polite for one sentence but peremptory for another. The emotional state of the speaker, however, does appear to overlay speech like a separate channel of communication. It is conveyed by the quality of the voice, and Scherer and his colleagues found that emotional cues can be identified even when a tape-recording of speech is cut up into small pieces and randomly spliced together – an operation that destroys the original intonation contour.

Cognitive scientists have discovered much about the production and perception of speech, the recognition of words, and the function and realization of different tones of voice. They have so far been unable to construct a complete theory of how speech is produced and perceived. A good test of progress is to examine how far the ability to speak and to hear can be implemented in computer programs.

PROGRAMS THAT SYNTHESIZE SPEECH SOUNDS

If a robot is to communicate, it needs to be able to map its model of the world or its own internal milieu into words, and then to translate them into speech sounds. The words should be represented in an unambiguous phonological code, like the pronunciation instructions of a dictionary, which can be converted into actual sounds. But how should the sounds be produced?

In 1779, Christian Kratzenstein made a set of resonators that produced simple vowel sounds; twenty years later, Wolfgang von Kempelen constructed a machine that could produce some vowels and consonants; subsequent workers, including Alexander Graham Bell, built still better machines. Of course a gramophone can reproduce speech, but a record encodes the complete sound wave – a vast amount of information. The first electrical method that *synthesized* speech, the Voder system of the 1930s, generated a periodic buzz (akin to the vibrations of the larynx) and random noise (akin to turbulence), and used a bank of filters to act like the resonances of the vocal tract. The machine needed a skilled operator if it was to produce anything like real speech. In the early 1950s, various devices were constructed that could play back sounds from spectrograms or other similar representations. These two methods – modelling the vocal tract or simulating the speech waveform – are both used in computer programs for speech synthesis.

Programs based on the physics of the vocal tract use anatomical and physiological data to simulate the way it makes sounds. Thus, for example, the instructions for a 'b' sound specify that the larynx vibrates, the lips close to build up air pressure, and then open abruptly. The advantage of this method is that co-articulations of speech sounds will occur automatically. However, even modern phonetic recording techniques, such as microbeam X-rays, have yet to reveal how all the various parts of the vocal apparatus change their shapes. Moreover, the acoustic consequences of many shapes are still not predictable, and so this method has yet to produce good synthetic speech.

Instead of directly modelling the vocal tract, other methods generate signals corresponding to laryngeal vibrations and

300

turbulent noise, and then pass them either through a series of computationally realized filters that act like the vocal tract or else into a small number of parallel circuits that each synthesize a formant. A major distinction here is between systems that specify the required resonances on the basis of analyses of actual formants produced by speakers – a technique pioneered by James Flanagan at the Bell Telephone Laboratories – and those that compute them from rules based on a theory of speech.

The rule-based methods of synthesis have yet to match the naturalness of resynthesis, but they are necessary if the computer is to model human performance. They take as input a transcription of the phonemes in the words making up an utterance, and the program then attempts to work out a feasible stress and phrasing of the sentence as a whole, and assigns a pitch and duration to the individual phonemes of the words in the sentence. This string of symbols is passed to the synthesis procedure. It may rely on a table of target frequencies for formants, and compute the transitions from one phoneme to the next – as in the programs devised by Lawrence Rabiner at Bell Laboratories, and by John Holmes and his colleagues at the Joint Speech Research Unit in Cheltenham. Alternatively, the string of symbols may control a model of the vocal tract – as in the program devised by Jonathan Allen at MIT.

At the other extreme, the programmer can forget about the vocal tract and simulate the speech waveform by concatenating stored samples of speech waves. This technique is an advanced version of the old, but impractical, idea of recording separate words and then reproducing them in any required order. Such utterances sound highly unnatural and the individual words are difficult to recognize within them. The original 'speaking clock' on British telephones was an exception: hours, minutes and seconds were recorded on separate glass disks and rotated at speeds synchronized with a clock. Nowadays computers can be used to store digital *samples* of waves. One method treats speech a little like the opening stages of visual analysis (see Chapter 4). It is passed through a bank of filters covering the audible frequencies, and the number of zero-crossings in each unit of time is computed for the output of each filter. This procedure converts waves into streams of pulses that are economical to store in the computer's memory.

Such a vocabulary of phonemes can be used to synthesize sounds. Of course, information must also be stored about the co-articulation of one phoneme with another if the speech is to be intelligible. Unfortunately, the technique ignores stress and intonation.

A currently popular technique is a compromise. It is based neither on emulating the movements of the vocal apparatus nor on reproducing actual waves, but on an *abstract* model of speech production. If the air pressure of a speech wave is measured every ten thousandth of a second, then it is possible to predict the value of the next measurement. The prediction depends on weighting the values of the immediately preceding twelve measures of air pressure in order to capture the filtering effects of the vocal tract, which changes shape relatively slowly. The prediction must also take into account the current source of energy for the speech — either a train of pulses at the frequency of the fundamental (when the larynx vibrates) or random noise (when the larynx is open). This technique is known as 'linear prediction', and it was first applied to speech by B. Atal in the early 1970s. It enables utterances to be resynthesized with a different intonation contour — the pitch of the fundamental is set to different values. One of the first synthesizers to be marketed on a single microchip, Texas Instruments' 'Speak-n-Spell' toy, used a linear predictive method.

In short, there is no difficulty in equipping a robot with some powers of speech, and most methods are commercially available on microchips. The speech, however, may sound monotonous and unnatural; it may be difficult to understand, especially if there is background noise. The way human beings produce speech is still not completely understood.

PROGRAMS FOR THE PERCEPTION OF SPEECH SOUNDS

Most programs for speech perception require an initial training session with the speaker, and most can recognize only a limited number of words that must be spoken with pauses between them. The speaker has to address the machine like a dog-owner uttering instructions to a dog, except that if the machine fails to identify a word and the speaker reacts by talking too carefully or by descending to 'baby talk', its performance becomes catastrophically bad. The programs work by building up a separate 'template' for each word that is spoken during the training session. There are various ways of constructing the templates, which usually encode information about the relative intensities of the sound at each frequency – rather like a spectrogram. The timing of the word that is to be recognized may differ from that of the template, and so the matching process is carried out by stretching the template in some places and compressing it in others. Likewise, the word to be recognized may match more than one template, and so there is a procedure that chooses between rival candidates. The programs work in a different way from human perception and are inferior to it.

Although templates for words have been used to try to identify continuous speech, they cannot cope with rapid articulation, with large vocabularies, or with a variety of different speakers. The only solution is to devise a system that operates at the level of speech sounds. The cues to phonemes concern the place and manner in which a sound is articulated, and they are relatively independent of the particular characteristics of a speaker's voice. Ken Stevens and his colleagues have for many years been searching – with some success – for invariances in them. But the cues often overlap because of the co-articulation of speech. A psychologically plausible procedure should therefore attempt to identify the features of articulation, taking into account their possible overlap. The waveform should be sampled, and analysed into formants and other acoustic cues to articulation that can aid the identification of phonemes. This information can be used to access the mental lexicon.

The representation of a word in the mental lexicon must be abstract so that it can be matched with any reasonable pronunciation. Variations in stress and prosody can be accommodated by rules. Thus, alternative pronunciations of the word can be captured by a finite-state device that specifies the acceptable sequences of sounds in any realization of the word. There are various methods by which the lexicon can be addressed: the psychological evidence, which I discussed earlier, implies that the human system calls for the activation, and subsequent deactivation, of a cohort of words.

Since the early 1970s, when the Advanced Research Projects Agency (ARPA) of the US Department of Defense sponsored the automatic recognition of continuous speech, a number of systems have been developed on the lines I have described. They make use of syntactic and semantic analyses to try to overcome the deficiencies in their identification of speech sounds. Their performance, however, is poorer than that of human beings. The programs do not use prosody to direct their attention to the most important, and hence most clearly articulated, parts of utterances. The perception of these parts makes it easier to perceive those that are slurred or incoherent.

CONCLUSION

This chapter should have convinced the reader that many aspects of speech are governed by unconscious principles (in the Helmholtzian sense of unconscious, see Chapter 1). Some of these principles are built into the mechanisms for speech; others vary from language to language and so cannot be inborn, though there may be innate constraints on the form they take. The chapter should also have convinced the reader that these principles work in parallel and at different levels from articulatory features up to words and to the intonation contour of the utterance as a whole. Most theoretical analyses have assumed that these unconscious principles are explicitly structured rules. They may, in fact, be represented in a distributed format.

Further reading

Denes and Pinson (1973) is a good introductory guide to speech and hearing; Fry (1976) is an advanced treatment of the physics of speech. Garnham (1985) is an excellent introduction to psycholinguistics and considers the problems of recognizing words. The views of the Haskins group are reported in Liberman (1982). The attempts to make machines that speak are described by Flanagan (1972b). Computer speech processing is surveyed in Fallside and Woods (1985), Linggard (1985) and Witten (1982).

CHAPTER 17

Grammar

Although the speakers of a language know only a finite number of words, they can put them together in different ways to express an unlimited number of different ideas. These combinations depend on grammatical principles that govern the formation of sentences, but the grammatical structure of a sentence is also a recipe for deriving its meaning from the meanings of its parts. Highly inflected languages, such as Russian, convey much of this information by the endings of words; languages such as English convey much of it by word order.

Native speakers of a language have an unconscious knowledge of its grammatical principles. Speakers of English appreciate, for instance, that there is something missing from the utterance, 'He decided Bill would take'. Of course, many ungrammatical sentences are easy to understand, e.g. 'This sentence no verb', and many grammatical sentences are hard to understand, e.g. 'It was the patient the doctor was cured by' – one has to stop to work out who cured whom. For the moment, however, I shall ignore these issues and concentrate on what sort of grammar is represented in the mind.

THE FORMAL THEORY OF GRAMMAR

A grammar is a finite set of rules that characterizes all the sentences in a language. Grammars cannot *do* anything, they are simply descriptions – blueprints for the structure of sentences. Thus, there have to be programs that use a grammar to produce sentences, or to parse them into their constituents. An increase in the power of the grammar, as I showed in Chapter 3, calls for a correspondingly more powerful program.

This analysis of grammar owes much to the linguist Noam Chomsky, who in 1957 created a revolution in linguistics with his book *Syntactic Structures*. He insisted on three fundamental points:

1. People speak and understand a language because they have a knowledge of its grammar.

2. A theory of the grammar of a natural language must specify the rules in an entirely explicit way so that the set of sentences that they characterize can be determined without the theorists exercising intuition or guesswork.

3. A theory of language must explain how children acquire the grammars of their native tongues.

Chomsky's impact on psychology was considerable. He demonstrated a fundamental shortcoming in the Behaviourists' conception of grammar. Their theories implicity assumed that the sentences of natural language could be produced and analysed by a finite-state device, that is, by a device that needs no working memory. This hypothesis, as we shall now see, is false.

FINITE-STATE DEVICES ARE NOT POWERFUL ENOUGH FOR LANGUAGE

Consider the following simple way in which you might try to construct a device that produces English. You have an array of pigeon-holes, such as the one shown in Figure 17.1, with rows and columns labelled with the different grammatical categories of English words. You use this array to record the transitions from one part of speech to another in a representative sample of English sentences. In the sentence, 'The old man left the large house suddenly', the first transition is from 'the' to 'old'. Hence, you add 1 to the number in the pigeon-hole representing the transition from an article to an adjective. The next transition is from 'old' to 'man', and so you add 1 to the number in the pigeon-hole with the row labelled 'adjective' and the column labelled 'noun'. You continue in this way until you have recorded all the transitions in the sentence. The result is shown in Figure 17.1.

If the array is to be of any use, it should contain a more comprehensive set of grammatical categories, and it should be

The next word in the transition

		Noun	Adjective	Verb	Adverb	Article
The first word in the transition	Noun	0	0	1	1	0
	Adjective	2	0	0	0	0
	Verb	0	0	0	0	1
	Adverb	0	0	0	0	0
	Article	0	2	0	0	0

Figure 17.1: An array for representing the transitions from one grammatical category of word to the next in English sentences. The grammatical categories in the rows represent the first word in the transition and the categories in the columns represent the next word. The numbers in the cells represent the frequency of the different transitions in the sentence, 'The old man left the large house suddenly.'

based on the transitions within many sentences. You can use the array to *construct* strings of words. First, you choose a word to start the string, and so you take into account the relative frequencies of the different sorts of initial words in your sample of sentences (something that is not shown in Figure 17.1). You might select, for example, an adverb, and so you go to your dictionary and choose an adverb at random, say, 'fortunately'. Second, you go to the array and examine the row that is labelled 'Adverb', and since you need to generate the next word, you select a pigeon-hole from that row at random, taking into account the relative frequencies of the different transitions. You toss a dice, as it were, but one that is biased by the frequencies, so that you are more likely to select a pigeon-hole with a large number in it than one with a small number in it. The result, say, is the pigeon-hole in the column labelled 'Noun', and so you choose a noun at random, e.g. 'honesty'. Third, you return to the row labelled 'Noun', and choose yet another pigeon-hole to generate the next word. And so the process continues.

This rudimentary device does not do a good job. It constructs such examples as:

Fortunately honesty shook the boy obtained a big fault of them all things go away for Nirvana ahead . . .

Each transition is fine, but stringing together acceptable pairs of words does not produce acceptable English. It will be better to construct acceptable triplets of words, which can be represented in an array where each row is labelled with an acceptable pair of words, such as:

article adjective

and the pigeon-holes contain the frequencies of the different categories that occur next.

There is no reason to stop here. The construction of an array that takes, say, four words of context into account prior to a transition calls for considerable labour. Because there are many different sorts of acceptable sequences of four words, the array will have many rows. Yet, the task can be done. The result, which represents the grammatical choices for the fifth word after a context of four, generates such strings as:

All of the nomads slept on sand coloured by the setting sun hauntingly disappeared . . .

Yet again, not enough context has been taken into account, though the approximation to English is improving. With a context of six words, the following example is constructed:

Only the very best of people will go to the country places only if you capitulate after the war of devastating proportions . . .

You might imagine that at some point, as you increase the amount of context, the array will converge completely on English. Indeed, many Behaviourists took for granted that language was based on some such finite system. They were wrong.

One decisive practical objection was raised by George Miller, the founder of the modern study of the psychology of language. If children are to acquire a mental array of pigeon-holes, they will have to learn the frequencies stored in each pigeon-hole. Miller pointed out that on average there are about four acceptable choices for the grammatical category of the next word in a sentence. Hence, to acquire an array for one-word contexts, children will need to learn the contents of 4^2 pigeon-holes (4 contexts x 4 next words). In order to acquire an array for two-word contexts, they will need to learn the contents of 4^3 pigeon-holes (4^2 contexts x 4 next words), and so on. Grammatical dependencies, however, can easily extend over fourteen words or more:

> The man who met the clerk that made the loan that saved the old firm is in prison

where the verb 'is' must agree in number with its subject, 'the man'. It follows that children will have to acquire an array for contexts of at least fourteen words, and so they will need to learn the contents of 4^{15} pigeon-holes. This number is approximately a billion. Even if children could learn one pigeon-hole entry per second, the task would still take them over thirty years!

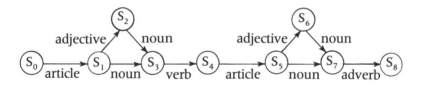

Figure 17.2: The representation of a pigeon-hole device as a finite-state device for constructing strings of English words. Each circle represents a state of the device, each arrow a transition, and the label on an arrow is the category of the word produced when the transition is made.

Figure 17.2 is an alternative representation of a pigeon-hole array, which makes clear that it is a finite-state device. Its output, in turn, can be characterized by a grammar. Each transition is captured by a grammatical rule with the initial state on its left-hand side and the category of the next word on its right-hand side, followed, where necessary, by the next state of the device:

$$S_0 \rightarrow \text{article } S_1$$
$$S_1 \rightarrow \text{adjective } S_2$$
$$S_1 \rightarrow \text{noun } S_3$$
$$\ldots$$
$$S_7 \rightarrow \text{adverb}$$

Figure 17.3 shows the sort of tree-diagram that these rules can be used to construct. It has the simplest imaginable grammatical structure – a series of binary divisions that branch away in one direction. This structure might be adequate for the restricted grammatical ability of chimpanzees who have been taught sign languages, but, in an argument that I will sketch in the next section, Chomsky demonstrated that it is wholly inadequate for natural language.

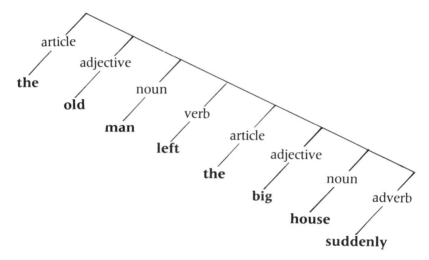

Figure 17.3: A tree-diagram of a sentence constructed by a grammar corresponding to a finite-state device.

PHRASE-STRUCTURE RULES

Consider the following expressions:

John
The old man
The man who met the clerk

310

They and many others like them can each serve as the subject of a sentence:

> John
> The old man   } robbed the bank.
> The man who met the clerk

They can also occur in many other sorts of sentence:

> The bank was robbed by { John.
>   the old man.
>   the man who met the clerk.

> Did { John
>   the old man   } rob the bank?
>   the man who met the clerk

Each expression evidently belongs to the same higher order grammatical category of *noun phrases*. Moreover, the members of this category have a common expressive function: they each can be used to refer to something.

A grammar can be simplified by specifying rules for noun phrases, and rules for where noun phrases can occur within sentences. The rules for noun phrases include:

> Nounphrase   →   article noun
> Nounphrase   →   propernoun

Figure 17.4: A tree-diagram of a sentence constructed from a phrase-structure grammar.

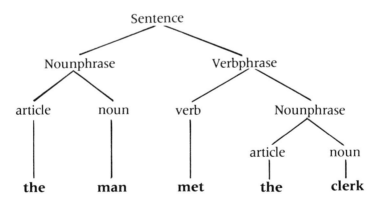

The rules for the positions of noun phrases include:

Sentence	→ Nounphrase Verbphrase
Verbphrase	→ verb Nounphrase

(I have used initial capital letters to symbolize higher order categories, and initial lower case letters to symbolize the categories of individual words.) Such a grammar groups words together into higher order categories, which in turn are grouped together into still higher categories. This bracketing of words and phrases can be represented in a tree-diagram (see Figure 17.4). The resulting *phrase structure* is richer than anything that can be constructed by a finite-state device.

One way to construct sentences from the phrase-structure grammar is to use a *set* of finite-state devices such as the two shown in Figure 17.5. The *sentence* device constructs the high-level structure of sentences. Whenever it needs a noun phrase, it calls on the services of the *noun-phrase* device to construct one. Together, the devices produce sentences 'top down' (see Chapter 5) in a procedure that reflects the organization of the grammar: noun phrases are constructed independently and plugged into sentences where they are needed.

Figure 17.5: Two finite-state devices that together construct simple sentences using a phrase-structure grammar.

A Sentence device:

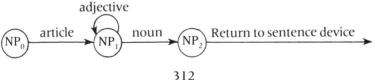

A Nounphrase device:

Suppose the noun-phrase device has just finished constructing a noun phrase, such as:

the man

It now passes the control of the constructive process back to the sentence device, but where exactly should the sentence device continue from? Is the noun phrase the subject of the sentence or the object? The only way to find the correct point to continue is, of course, to have kept a record of where the sentence device had got to when it called on the services of the noun-phrase device. This record can be kept in a working memory.

Certain noun phrases in English contain relative clauses:

The man who met the clerk . . .

and there is no limit on the number of them that can occur within a single noun phrase (other than the stamina of the speaker and the patience of the listener):

The man who met the clerk that made the loan . . .

The grammar must therefore contain certain additional rules for relative clauses, such as:

Nounphrase   → article noun Relativeclause
Relativeclause   → relativepronoun verb Nounphrase

Hence, *Nounphrase* can lead to *Relativeclause*, which in turn can lead to *Nounphrase* again – just what is needed to characterize an unlimited number of relative clauses within a single noun phrase.

A separate device can be used to construct relative clauses according to the rule that analyses them as:

relativepronoun verb Nounphrase.

The construction of a noun phrase containing several relative clauses proceeds as follows:

The noun-phrase device constructs the initial noun phrase:

The man

and calls the relative-clause device. It produces the relative pronoun and the verb:

who met

313

but then has to call the noun-phrase device. It produces:

the clerk

and calls the relative-clause device. It produces:

that made

and calls the noun-phrase device. It produces:

the loan

and returns it to the relative-clause device, which then passes the relative clause:

that made the loan

back to the noun-phrase device. It passes the noun phrase:

the clerk that made the loan

back to the relative-clause device. It passes the relative clause:

who met the clerk that made the loan

back to the noun-phrase device. It completes the noun phrase:

The man who met the clerk that made the loan.

And, at last, passes it to the sentence device.

This example demonstrates that one device needs to call another, which in turn can call the device that called it, and so on *ad libitum*. The simplest possible way to keep track of all these recursive calls requires a stack-like memory of the sort that I described in Chapter 3. It piles up records of the current state of the process when devices call one another, and takes them off the stack as each task is completed. The recursive ability to embed one structure within another demonstrates convincingly that finite-state devices cannot cope with the grammar of natural language, because recursion requires this powerful form of working memory.

TRANSFORMATIONAL GRAMMAR

The sort of grammar needed for natural language continues to be intensely debated in modern linguistic theory. It must be at least as powerful as a phrase-structure grammar, but are these the only rules that are necessary? I can illustrate the problem by considering a particular sort of sentence, which contains a *topicalized* noun phrase, e.g.:

Denis, I like.

Such sentences seem odd in isolation, but they often occur in certain contexts:

What do you think of Denis and Maggie?
Denis, I like. But Maggie . . .

The verb 'like' is transitive, that is, it takes a direct object, and so it cannot occur in contexts that lack such a noun phrase. An intransitive verb, such as 'laugh', can occur without an object:

I laughed

but a transitive verb cannot:

I liked.

This information about the categorization of verbs has to be captured in the lexicon to ensure that sentences are correctly formed, e.g. 'like' is represented as occurring only in contexts that contain a following noun phrase. Now, however, we can see the problem that topicalization creates. A sentence of the form:

Denis, I *verb*

has no following noun phrase. It fails to meet the specification for 'like', but it does meet the specification for 'laugh'. Hence, it ought to be grammatical to say:

Denis, I laugh

and ungrammatical to say:

Denis, I like.

These are exactly the wrong predictions.

In 1965, Chomsky argued that the most natural way in which to specify the structure of sentences is to use a grammar with two components: phrase-structure rules that specify the underlying structures of sentences (the so-called 'deep' or 'D' structures), and *transformation* rules that transform one structure into another. More recently, he has proposed that there are also deletion rules that act on the output of the transformations (the so-called 'S' structures) and delete various abstract elements from them to yield the 'surface' grammatical structure of the sentence.

The phrase-structure rules, like those of the previous section, specify underlying structures, such as:

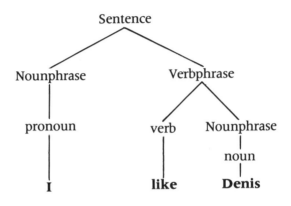

A transformation rule can move the noun phrase, *Denis*, to the front of the tree:

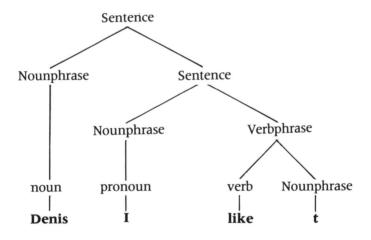

The symbol 't' stands for trace: a moved constituent leaves a ghostly trace of its former presence. This analysis solves the problem of inserting verbs into their correct contexts: there *is* a noun phrase following the verb and so a transitive verb such as 'like' is correct here, and an intransitive verb such as 'laugh' is incorrect.

The example demonstrates another essential point about a transformation rule: it takes a tree (equivalently a labelled bracketing) of symbols as its input and delivers a new tree as output. Transformation rules are therefore more powerful than phrase-structure rules, which merely analyse one symbol in terms of others. Indeed, it can be proved that transformational grammars in general are equivalent in computational power to a universal Turing machine.

GOVERNMENT AND BINDING

Although Chomsky's most recent theory – 'government and binding' – is a form of transformational grammar, it is a radical reorientation of the earlier account. The grammar now consists of a set of separate modules, each acting in a general way on the basis of simple principles. Any sentence, particularly a complicated one, is a result of an interaction between the modules. In place of specific rules, such as a transformation to topicalize a noun phrase, the new theory depends on general rules. There is, for instance, only one transformational rule, which can move any constituent anywhere. An important role is therefore played by constraints that severely restrict the power of the grammar by ruling out ungrammatical sentences. Thus, for example, it is not possible to topicalize 'Denis' in the sentence:

Maggie knows someone who likes Denis

since the result is ungrammatical:

Denis, Maggie knows someone who likes.

The constraints on transformations prevent this and many other unacceptable derivations.

What lies behind the constraints is not just the goal of formulating a grammar that describes the language, but, as

Chomsky stresses, the need to explain how children are able to discover the grammar of their native tongue from a corpus of adult utterances. Although there are studies of the theoretical learnability of classes of grammars, a factor that overrides the power of a grammar is the ease of isolating it within the set of grammars accessible to human beings (see Chapter 7). If few grammars have to be tried out and the choice amongst them is easy, then even a grammar with the power of a universal Turing machine could be acquired.

For Chomsky, a grammar develops like the growth of a bodily organ, since both are under control of an innate program. The constraints on rules reflect what is *not* possible in a language, or in any language, and so it is difficult to see how they could be learned – you cannot easily learn from what does not occur. Hence, there must be an innate 'universal grammar' of constraints that apply to all human languages, e.g. that their rules govern structures, not just strings of words. Children acquire a grammar for their particular language by using the utterances they hear to set the values of each of a finite number of choices in the universal grammar. These choices govern the possible orders of constituents in the underlying structures of sentences, and the scope and constraints on transformations, e.g. from which structural positions a constituent cannot be moved. Since each choice offers only a certain number of alternatives, there are only finitely many possible grammars for natural language.

Whether this theory is correct is not known, and there is as yet no definitive account of universal grammar. What is indubitable is that language cannot be acquired without access to some innate constraints. The late Jean Piaget argued that they are not specific to language, but underlie general intellectual development. Alas, it is hard to see how constraints of that sort could determine which noun phrases in a sentence can be topicalized. Hilary Putnam, and others, have argued that what children are really trying to do is to understand their language: the acquisition of grammar depends on the acquisition of meaning. This hypothesis is plausible. Most current linguistic theories (including government and binding) agree that if you know the meaning of a word, you can predict many aspects of its syntactic

318

behaviour. But there does remain a residue of syntactic facts that are independent of meaning.

PSYCHOLINGUISTICS AND TRANSFORMATIONAL GRAMMAR

Throughout the major stages in the evolution of transformational grammar – the initial theory of 1957, the 'standard' theory of 1965, and the recent theory of 'government and binding' – Chomsky has always maintained that linguistics is a branch of cognitive psychology because a grammar is a description of tacit linguistic knowledge. Whether this knowledge takes the form of a transformational grammar, however, is open to doubt. Modern psycholinguistics began with George Miller's idea that although phrase-structure rules probably have nothing to do with mental processes, transformations might explain a number of aspects of linguistic performance. The first results did indeed suggest that a sentence such as:

Wasn't the apple eaten by the horse?

is harder to understand and to remember than the sentence:

The horse ate the apple

because the former has a more complicated transformational structure than the latter. Gradually, it became clear that transformational complexity is not a reliable guide to psychological complexity, and at the same time there were growing pains and growing changes in linguistic theory. Chomsky himself wrote in 1965: 'When we say that a sentence has a certain derivation with respect to a particular generative grammar, we say nothing about how the speaker or hearer might proceed, in some practical or efficient way, to construct such a derivation.' The claim implies that the device which contructs sentences is not affected by the complexity of the rules it has to use in any particular case: nothing observed in the psycholinguist's laboratory was likely to put the linguistic theory at risk.

And so it proved. A collaboration at MIT among a philosopher, a linguist and a psychologist – Jerry Fodor, Tom Bever and Merrill Garrett – held fast to the linguistic theory but abandoned

319

the idea that transformation rules had any direct part to play in comprehension. Yet the MIT group insisted on a role for deep structure. For instance, they examined the perception of clicks presented to one ear whilst tape-recorded sentences were being played to the other ear. Thus, when people heard the sentence:

John expected Bill to leave

accompanied by a click in the middle of 'Bill', they characteristically erred in reporting the position of the click, tending to relocate it between 'expected' and 'Bill'. This position corresponds to a boundary between two clauses (i.e. parts of the tree-diagram labelled 'sentence') in the deep structure of the sentence, though there is no obvious boundary in its surface structure.

The MIT investigators proposed that deep structure is recovered by a number of rules of thumb, e.g. any sequence of the form *noun . . . verb . . . noun* is treated as a potential underlying clause. The idea seemed plausible because when such an analysis turns out to be wrong, as in a sentence that begins:

The boy told the story . . .

and continues:

passed it on to us

the sentence leads the reader up the garden path by creating the wrong expectation. What was strange about the MIT theory was that rules of grammar should be implanted in the mind only to play no direct part in parsing sentences.

There was a further problem. Evidence began to accumulate that perhaps people do not represent the deep structure of sentences. Deep-structure clauses are syntactic units that need a semantic interpretation. Studies of memory showed that people remember meaning, not deep structure. Thus, they readily confuse, as Rosemary Stevenson and I observed, such sentences as:

John bought the picture from the duchess

and:

The duchess sold the picture to John.

These sentences have similar meanings, but the same noun phrases play very different roles in their deep structures. Hence, the status of deep structure in psychological processes became somewhat suspect. Indeed, there is still no definite evidence that its recovery plays any part in the comprehension of sentences.

GENERALIZED PHRASE-STRUCTURE GRAMMAR

If neither transformations nor deep structure have a role in mental processes, the psychology of language seems to need a grammar that makes no use of them. Just such grammars have been advocated on linguistic grounds by a number of linguists, notably Michael Brame, Gerald Gazdar, Ron Kaplan and Joan Bresnan, and (in unpublished work) Stanley Peters.

Gazdar has shown how a generalization of phrase-structure grammar can cope with sentences that had once been thought to require transformations. In the case of topicalization, the phrase-structure rules directly insert both the initial topicalized noun phrase and the trace that is necessary for interpreting the sentence. A rule such as:

Sentence → Nounphrase   Sentence/Nounphrase

signifies that a sentence can consist of an initial noun phrase followed by a sentence minus a noun phrase, i.e. a sentence with a hole in it corresponding to a missing noun phrase. Once such a hole is introduced into a structure, then special rules allow it to percolate down the tree until finally, as in the earlier transformational derivation, it is replaced by the trace element, t. Thus, a topicalized sentence has the following structure:

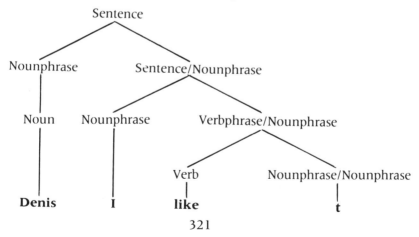

Gazdar's grammar accounts for this and other sentences without using transformations.

Which positions can a constituent such as a noun phrase occur in? A provocative conjecture made by Tony Ades and Mark Steedman is that there are basic forms of sentences, and the only permissible variations on them are those that can be analysed using some special rules governing a stack-like memory. The basic forms are captured by simple phrase-structure rules. Since the rules cannot cope with the initial noun phrase of a topicalized sentence, such as 'Denis, I like', the noun phrase is put on the stack. The interpretation of 'I like' as the start of a basic sentence proceeds smoothly but then runs into a problem because 'like' is a transitive verb and there are no further words in the sentence. The missing noun phrase, however, is still waiting on the stack and so it can now be incorporated into the interpretation of the sentence. Once again, no transformations are needed.

THE DESIGN OF THE MENTAL PARSER

Even if we knew for certain that there was a particular sort of grammar in the mind, we would still need to discover how it is used to parse sentences. There is no experimental procedure that isolates the process. Psycholinguists can observe, say, the time it takes to understand a sentence or to carry out some operation on it, but they cannot with any certainty insulate performance from the effects of meaning and interpretation. Nevertheless, I want to consider three major issues that concern the design of the mental parser.

The first question is the nature of the parser's general operations. It could use the rules to work top down like the system in Figure 17.5. A version of such a system (a so-called 'augmented transition network') has been developed to parse transformational grammars. It has been used by Bill Woods in a program that answers questions about the samples of moon rock; and Ron Kaplan, Eric Wanner and their colleagues have argued that the mental parser may have a similar design. Another possibility is that the parser uses the rules to construct an analysis of a sentence working bottom up. It starts by identifying the syntactic categories of words and then attempts to use the rules to construct the analysis upwards towards the higher level constituents.

The beginnings of phrases cannot be predicted top down, but once the start of a phrase has been identified, the rules of the grammar can be used to make predictions, e.g. an occurrence of 'the' indicates the start of a noun phrase and so a subsequent occurrence of a noun can be predicted. Hence, the parser may operate according to this principle: it starts in bottom-up mode, but once it has recognized the left-hand corner of a phrase, it attempts to make a top-down prediction. Certainly, there is a need to make predictions because, as Lyn Frazier and Janet Fodor point out, the holes (or traces) corresponding to noun phrases often have no explicit cue to their presence, e.g.:

Denis, I like to tell jokes.

This example is ambiguous and could correspond either to:

I like to tell Denis jokes

or to:

I like Denis to tell jokes.

The second question is how the parser copes with ambiguity, and with those ambiguities that are local to the earlier part of a sentence, e.g. 'The firm drives me mad', and 'The firm drives were not affected by the flash flood', where the correct analysis only becomes clear later in each sentence. Local ambiguities arise whenever there is more than one possible grammatical rule that can be used in the analysis. They can be dealt with in several different ways. One strategy is to use 'backtracking', which I discussed in Chapter 9. The parser tries one choice, and if ultimately it leads nowhere, it returns to the choice point and tries another. The only time that people are aware of any process resembling backtracking is when a sentence has led them up the garden path like the earlier example, 'The boy told the story passed it on to us'. However, they may not be reparsing the sentence. Stephen Crain and Mark Steedman have argued that these sentences mislead the processes which interpret meaning.

An alternative method is to try to resolve any decision about which rule to use by looking ahead at the rest of the sentence.

This idea inspired Mitch Marcus to design a parser for transformational grammars that never has to change its mind. It works deterministically, and so as soon as it encounters an ambiguity, it holds off a decision until it has gone on to make a preliminary analysis of the next three constituents of the sentence. For instance, a sentence that begins:

Have the boys . . .

may be an imperative:

Have the boys take the exam today

or an interrogative:

Have the boys taken the exam today?

Once the parser has looked ahead, it can decide what sort of sentence it is dealing with. Although Marcus restricts his claims to those sentences that people can grasp without conscious difficulty, there are some apparent counterexamples. The sentence:

Denis, I like to tell jokes to

is readily understood, but the role of 'Denis' does not become clear until after the first three constituents. Similarly, William Marslen-Wilson's discovery that certain people can repeat and understand a tape-recorded discourse with a lag of only a syllable (see Chapter 16) implies that the parser may not wait to analyse subsequent parts of a sentence.

The most efficient method of dealing with a local ambiguity is to construct all of its alternative analyses in parallel. People may be able to use this strategy, at least for certain sorts of ambiguity. However, when they read sentences containing a local ambiguity, then, as Lyn Frazier and her colleagues have observed, their eyes move back to the ambiguous portion just as though it is going to be reparsed. Of course, reading is different from listening, if only because there is no intonation contour to guide the parser.

The third question is how the parser dovetails with the procedures that interpret the meaning of the sentence. One practitioner of artificial intelligence, Roger Schank, argues that grammatical analysis takes second place to meaning. Another,

Terry Winograd, who devised an impressive program for interpreting natural language, argues that the parser is sometimes guided by semantic decisions. He noted that a request such as:

Put the blue pyramid on the block in the box

is ambiguous. Is the object to be moved the blue pyramid or the blue pyramid on the block? Winograd's program uses a special procedure that interrupts the parser to check whether there is a blue pyramid on the block.

At the other extreme, Jerry Fodor, Ken Forster and other erstwhile members of the MIT school have defended the autonomy of grammatical analysis. They view the parser as a module that develops analyses of sentences that are, at least initially, independent of the procedures for interpreting meanings. There have been no experiments sensitive enough to resolve this controversy to everyone's satisfaction. There may be no need, however, for the parser to hand over an explicit tree structure of a sentence to the semantic processor. The parser could directly control the process of combining the elements of meaning. If there are signposts all the way, a destination can be reached without a map.

CONCLUSION

Modern theories of grammar are so complicated that they take years of study to master. There is a paradox here, because in theory such grammars have already been mastered effortlessly in childhood. I mentioned in the opening chapter of the book the danger of imposing a theory on the mind, and Stuart Sutherland has pointed out that the grammar of a language may not be explictly represented in the minds of speakers: they may have other means of speaking and understanding. A grammar can provide an accurate description of performance and yet, as in the case of the navigational robot (of Chapter 3), play no part in the production of that performance. When one attempts to analyse how the mind works, there is a strong tendency to postulate theories that depend on a manipulation of explicit symbols by explicit rules. This assumption is a projection from the way in which theorists, like everyone else, tend to think *consciously* in terms of clear-cut categories. But what evidence is there for a mental representation of explicit grammatical rules? The answer is: people produce and understand sentences that appear to follow such rules, and their judgements about sentences also appear to be guided by them. But that is all. What is left open is the possibility that the formal rules of grammar are not to be found inside the head, just as the formal rules of logic are not to be found there. If connectionism is correct, for example, the mind behaves as if it were rule-governed, but contains only parallel distributed representations. Some linguists regard this possibility as reducing their science to a sort of alchemy. Not so. Linguistics remains as a theory of what is computed by mental processes, but not an account of how they compute it. We will not know how the computations occur until we discover the form of our unconscious knowledge of language.

Further reading

A good introduction to Chomsky is Lyons (1970). Exchanges of views between Chomsky, Piaget and other leading figures are reported in Piattelli-Palmarini (1980). The problem of generating approximations to English from data on transitions is discussed in Miller, Galanter and Pribram (1960, Ch. 11). The remaining references here are technically demanding.

The best introductions to recent theories are Radford (1981) and Sells (1985). The main study of generalized phrase-structure grammar is by Gazdar, Klein, Pullum and Sag (1985). This topic and the design of the mental parser are described in Johnson-Laird (1983, Chs. 12 and 13). A set of studies of natural language parsing are to be found in Dowty, Karttunen and Zwicky (1985).

There is an enormous literature on children's acquisition of language, but few formal or computational models of how the process might proceed (but cf. Anderson, 1976; Power and Longuet-Higgins, 1978; Wexler and Culicover, 1980; Pinker, 1984; and Berwick, 1985).

CHAPTER 18

Meaning

If I blindfold you and take you into your kitchen, you can probably find your way around. But if I have rearranged the furniture, you will be in trouble. I can warn you: 'Watch out – the table is on the right of the dresser', and you should be able to avoid it. You may form a vivid image of the table in its new location, or you may have no such experience – you just *know* where the table is, though you cannot fathom how this knowledge is represented. If cognitive scientists are to make a robot that can also use verbal warnings to guide its path, then they need answers to two main questions:

What do people construct when they understand discourse?
How do they carry out the process of construction?

This chapter uses work from most of the disciplines in cognitive science to outline answers to these two questions.

SEMANTIC NETWORKS

In the beginning there was not the word, but the association. According to the 'old testament' psychologists, a word is an associative stimulus that elicits the corresponding object. I say 'table' and so you think of a table. If a word does not denote anything tangible, e.g. the word 'is', then its meaning consists of associations to other words.

There is a decisive objection to this ancient dogma. A link from a word to an object says nothing about the nature of the relation between them; still less can it indicate that the word is a symbol standing for the object. Moreover, the meaning of an utterance usually depends on combining the meanings of its parts according to the grammatical relations between them. But how can associative links be combined grammatically?

One proposed solution to these problems is that the links should have labels on them. This idea was mooted by Otto Selz in 1913, but it has flourished only since the advent of computers and the invention of so-called 'semantic networks', which are the basis of most computational and psychological theories of meaning.

There are many forms of semantic network, but they all go back to Ross Quillian's seminal account in 1968. Like Selz, he recognized the importance of the relations between words. Unlike Selz, he had access to a programming language that made it possible to build a working network. In LISP, a symbol can be a string of letters such as TABLE. By itself, this symbol is meaningless, but it appears to become more meaningful if several labelled associations are linked to it:

> TABLE   superordinate: FURNITURE
> parts: LEGS
> parts: WORKTOP

and further associations established between them:

> support: LEGS WORKTOP

When one describes the theory, it is natural to use a network to show how the information is organized:

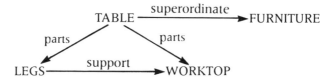

Network theorists have adopted many of Quillian's assumptions. They suppose that networks can represent the meanings of words and sentences, and that the format is powerful enough to handle any idea. (In fact, it has the power of a universal Turing machine.) They have also introduced a notational distinction between general concepts (e.g. TABLE) and specific instances of them (e.g. the table in your kitchen). They have recognized a small set of ubiquitous relational links: *superordinate, property, parts.* But they allow, of course, that many other terms can be labels on a link. They have usually been committed to a parsimonious organization in which general information is represented only at a superordinate level. The fact, say, that tables are physical objects does not need to be represented by a direct link from TABLE to OBJECT, but can be inferred from the following chain of superordinate links:

TABLE ⟶ FURNITURE ⟶ OBJECT.

Certain words, such as 'tiger', 'lemon' and 'water', challenge analysis because they depend on prototypes rather than sets of necessary conditions (see Chapter 13). The challenge can be met by a semantic network. It can distinguish between a link that represents a necessary relation, e.g. a tiger is an animal, and a link that represents a characteristic one, e.g. a tiger has a tail. A prototype has many characteristic properties and relations, and few necessary ones. Some philosophers would say there are *no* necessary conditions.

Quillian also initiated certain assumptions about the processing of information in semantic networks. His program establishes a relation between any given pair of words. It puts 'tags' representing activity into the network at the points corresponding to the words, and then uses a procedure that propagates tags down all the links that emanate from these two points. The two patterns of spreading activity stop as soon as they intersect one another – something that happens sooner for 'table' and 'furniture' than for 'table' and 'object'. Early experimental results suggested that human beings are also faster to establish a link in the first case. Subsequent work has qualified this picture: the time to make a judgement is not always related to the length of the path in a semantic network, and, as Doug Herrmann and Roger Chaffin have argued, some relations like the relative squashability of substances are unlikely to be represented by a link at all.

DECOMPOSITION INTO ATOMS OF MEANING

Some proponents of networks have adopted a theory of meaning designed for transformational grammar by Jerry Katz and Jerry Fodor. The theory assumes that the meanings of words can be decomposed into atoms of meaning universal to all languages.

Figure 18.1 shows such atoms in a representation of the sentence, 'John gave Fido to Mary', according to a network devised by Don Norman, Dave Rumelhart and their colleagues.

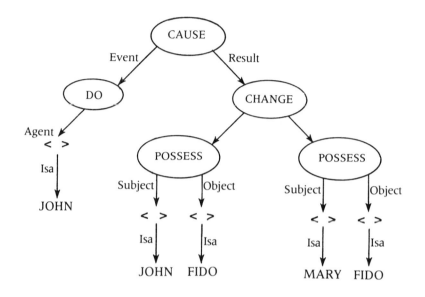

Figure 18.1: A semantic network proposed by Norman and Rumelhart. The angle brackets < > are nodes representing specific instances of concepts.

The concept of decomposition led to a quest for the ultimate set of atoms. Roger Schank, for example, proposed eleven primitive actions: to propel, to move a body part, to ingest, to expel, to grasp, to speak, to attend, to change location, to change an abstract relation such as possession, to create a thought, and to construct new information. Thus, the meaning of:

John ate a frog

is represented by a complex structure that captures the information that John *moved* his hand *grasping* a frog to his mouth and *ingested* the frog. Schank's program even makes the inference that John's health was adversely affected by this action. The primitives, however, are not truly elemental, e.g. a general concept of movement must underlie propel, move, ingest and several other of the actions.

George Miller and I offered a comprehensive psychological analysis of the meanings of words in our book *Language and Perception*. Our starting point was perception. The *idéologues* of the French Revolution, inspired by Locke's empiricism, had essayed an analysis of words into their primitive, allegedly perceptual, components. This analysis, they believed, would establish which ideas were *sensible* and which were not, and society could then be rebuilt on solid foundations. (Napoleon had other ideas.) The Logical Positivists attempted a similar though more sophisticated programme of research. It too failed, and so we knew from the outset that language could not be reduced to perceptible predicates. The strategy at least allowed us to consider the relations between words and perception. Hence, we built up a list of representative properties that people can attend to and make judgements about. They range from simple to complex, e.g. from *red* to *vertical*.

There are many predicates that go beyond perception. You can perceive that one object collides with another and *causes* it to move, but the perception is not identical to the concept of cause. The concept is often taken to be primitive (see Figure 18.1), but it can be broken down still further. One event *causes* another if it is impossible for the first event to occur without the second occurring, i.e. causation can be analysed in terms of a matrix of possibilities between the antecedent and consequent states of affairs. But, worlds-that-might-have-been are not perceptual objects.

At this point, we introduced the idea of a 'procedural semantics'. We assumed that when, say, you understand my warning about the new position of the table, the initial product of your understanding is a mental process. The procedure can be for the construction of a mental representation, for a test on a mental representation, for the retrieval of information, or for a number of other operations. I will describe some procedures in more detail presently. The meaning of 'table' in my warning is therefore not an image of a table, but rather conceptual elements that can contribute to whatever procedure you construct in interpre-

331

ting a sentence containing the word 'table'. These elements come from your concept of a table, which includes knowing how to identify tables, but which goes beyond the perceptible because it concerns the relations of tables to other entities and their function – matters of human intention and aspiration.

Armed with this theory, Miller and I analysed the meanings of over two thousand words. We found that the mental dictionary is organized, as many theorists had believed, in fields of related words. What is at the core of a field is a basic concept – a tacit theory of the domain. For example, there are fields of motion ('move', 'propel', 'expel', . . .), possession ('own', 'buy', 'give', . . .), perception ('see', 'hear', 'glimpse', . . .). Certain other concepts crop up in many fields to provide the framework of ideas in which one thinks about experience. The most notable cases of such concepts are: space, time, possibility, permissibility and intention. They modulate the concept at the core of the field so as to yield a variety of relations, many of which have been dignified by a word of their own. The following paraphrases illustrate the ubiquitous role of *cause* in verbs of motion, possession and perception:

To propel an object	=	to cause an object to move.
To give an object to someone	=	to cause someone to possess an object.
To show an object to someone	=	to cause it to be possible for someone to see an object.

Such paraphrases may not be completely synonymous with the verbs they characterize, and they are not substitutable for those words without doing violence to meaning (and syntax). Yet they reveal the concepts implicit in words.

MEANING POSTULATES

Are there good definitions of words? Jerry Fodor and his colleagues give a resounding 'no' to this question. There are no definitions, they claim, that state the conditions which suffice to capture the complete meaning of a word. If this claim is correct, it is impossible to analyse meanings into more primitive elements.

(Fodor has relinquished his earlier theory.) But, if the meaning of 'table' does not depend on the concept of worktop, the question arises of how one can infer:

He made a table.
Therefore, he made something with a worktop.

The answer according to Fodor and others is to rely on 'meaning postulates', i.e. rules of inference that express the necessary consequences of specific words. Thus, the meaning postulate:

if x is a table, then x has a worktop

enables the inference to be drawn. The logical properties of other words are similarly postulated, e.g.:

if x is on the right of y
and y is on the right of z,
then x is on the right of z.

The meaning postulants – as I call them – assume that comprehension consists in translating utterances into a mental language, and then, if need be, using meaning postulates to make inferences from them. There is no process of decomposition into atoms; the words of natural language correspond virtually one-to-one with the words of the mental language. John Anderson has developed a semantic network that similarly does not decompose meanings but instead uses productions – the computational equivalent of meaning postulates (see Chapter 9) – to make inferences. As Figure 18.2 illustrates, these networks are close to the grammatical structure of sentences.

THE SYMBOLIC FALLACY

When I tell you that your table is on the right of the dresser, you can imagine the new arrangement and navigate your way around the room. Even if you did not form an image, your success in avoiding the obstacle shows that your movements are guided by a *model* of the spatial arrangement of the furniture. Semantic networks, whether based on decomposition or meaning postulates, cannot explain your performance. They can tell you that two words are related, or that one sentence is a paraphrase of

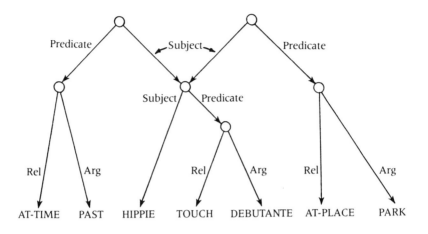

Figure 18.2: The semantic network for the sentence 'In a park a hippie touched a debutante'. Following Anderson, this diagram has omitted the nodes representing words. 'Rel' stands for Relation and 'Arg' stands for Argument.

another, but they are as circular as dictionaries. They perpetrate the 'symbolic fallacy' that meaning is merely a matter of relating one set of verbal symbols to another. As the philosopher David Lewis says, to translate a sentence into such a representation provides no more of an account of its significance than does a translation into Latin. It does not say anything about how words relate to the world.

Why have so many theorists ignored the relation between language and the world? Perhaps they have assumed that this relation is independent of the problem that they have concentrated on – the relations amongst expressions. In fact, the two are not independent. A theory that relates words to the world, as I will argue, willy-nilly relates words to one another, and renders superfluous those theories that carry out only the latter task. My strategy will therefore be to show how linguistic expressions relate to models – beginning with the clear case of formal semantics – and then to show how models relate to the world, and thus how to avoid the symbolic fallacy.

FORMAL SEMANTICS

In the last century, the logician Gottlob Frege drew a distinction between the *reference* of an expression and its *meaning*. The reference is what it stands for in the world, while the meaning connects it to its reference. To take Frege's example, the reference of the two noun phrases 'the Morning Star' and 'the Evening Star' is the same, namely, the planet Venus. But the meanings of the two expressions are different, since one means the 'star' observed in the morning and the other the 'star' observed in the evening. The same distinction can be drawn about a statement, such as:

The Morning Star is identical to the Evening Star.

It is true, but it is easy to imagine a world just slightly different from ours in which it is false. Its meaning in such a world, however, would remain the same.

The distinction between meaning and reference has been illuminated by the development of formal semantics. The logician Alfred Tarski showed how to give a rigorous account of the truth of sentences in a formalized language. They are interpreted in relation, not to the real world, but to a *model*. The rules that provide these interpretations are of two sorts. The first sort provides a referent for each basic word in the language. Thus, given a calculus for dealing with sets of individuals, which has the vocabulary of proper nouns:

Anne, Charles, Diana, Elizabeth, Mark, Philip

there will be a rule that picks out a specific individual in the model for each name to refer to. If the calculus also has the following predicates for sets of individuals:

female, male, feminist, horselover, anarchist

then another basic rule assigns each of them a reference consisting of the appropriate set of individuals, if any, in the model, e.g.:

female = (Anne, Diana, Elizabeth)
male = (Charles, Mark, Philip)
feminist = (Anne, Charles)
horselover = (Anne, Elizabeth, Mark, Philip)
anarchist = ()

The second sort of rules build up the reference of complex expressions from the reference of their parts, and these rules are designed to operate in parallel with the grammar of the calculus. Thus, if there is a grammatical rule that allows sentences of the form, 'Charles is a feminist':

Sentence → Propernoun *is a* Predicate

there is a corresponding semantic rule which stipulates that:

A Sentence is *true* if and only if the individual who is the interpretation of the Propernoun is a member of the set that is the interpretation of the Predicate.

Hence, the interpretation of 'Charles is a feminist' is true if the person named 'Charles' is a member of the set denoted by 'feminist' (which in the model above he is).

Suppose that there is another grammatical rule that permits expressions of the form 'female horselover' to be constructed:

Predicate → Predicate Predicate

then it too has a matching semantic rule:

The interpretation of the Predicate on the left-hand side of the rule is the set of individuals, if any, who are members of both sets denoted by the Predicates on the right-hand side of the rule.

Hence, the interpretation of 'female horselover' is the set of those individuals in the model who are in both the set of females and the set of horselovers, i.e. (Anne, Elizabeth).

The interpretation of a sentence, such as 'Anne is a female horselover', can be built up as the sentence is parsed. The first word, 'Anne', denotes a particular individual in the model. The next constituent stipulates that the individual is a member of a set, which turns out to depend on the interpretation of 'female horselover'. The grammatical rule that parses these terms is matched by a semantic rule calling for the individuals in both sets. Anne is indeed a member of this set, and so the sentence is true in the model.

I won't continue this sketch any further since the idea of interpreting sentences in relation to a model should now be clear.

The advantage of having a sementic rule for each grammatical rule is that each step in parsing a sentence can yield a step in its interpretation. To devise such a system for natural language, however, is a work of frightening complexity. It has been successfully undertaken only for fragments of languages, principally under the aegis of Richard Montague.

In the example above, the semantic rules build up the referents of expressions, but for several reasons this strategy is impossible for natural language. For instance, some adjective-noun combinations call for a simple operation like the one I described for the predicates above, e.g. 'red apples' are things that are members of the set of red objects *and* members of the set of apples. But other cases cannot be handled in this way. 'Good apples' are not things that are good *and* apples, but things that are good *as* apples – ripe, crisp and tasty, perhaps. Even an apparently simple combination, such as 'pet fish', as Dan Osherson and Ed Smith have shown, is not just the conjunction of two sets, since people judge a guppy to be a better exemplar of a pet fish than an exemplar of either the category of fish or the category of pets. Similarly, James Hampton in a monumental series of studies has demonstrated that an item can be judged to be a member of a complex concept but not a member of one of its components. Thus, people judge that chess is *a game that is a sport*, but they say that chess is *not a sport*. This phenomenon is analogous to the 'conjunctive fallacy' of Chapter 13, except that it is not a fallacy, because the rule combining game and sport is not a conjunction. In short, the rules for combining interpretations operate, not on the referents of expressions, but on their meanings – and in ways that are not yet properly understood.

Another problem is that the interpretation of many sentences depends on the particular context in which they are uttered. For example, the interpretation of:

I am not a horselover

depends on who the speaker is. From the standpoint of psychology, however, the major problem is that an assertion such as 'The table is on the right of the dresser' can be true of many different tables, dressers and positions of the objects. A picture may be worth a thousand words, but a proposition is worth an infinity of pictures. Indeed, assertions in natural language call for an infinite number of models corresponding to each of the possible states of affairs in which they can be true.

MENTAL MODELS OF SENTENCES

An infinity of possible worlds, as the linguist Barbara Partee has observed, is too big to fit inside anyone's head. The theory of mental models that I have developed therefore assumes that the initial mental representation of an assertion – a procedure close to its linguistic form – is used to construct just *one* model. But, how can one model stand for all the different possible states of affairs compatible with the truth of an assertion? The problem is a descendant of a traditional puzzle in philosophy: how can an image, or a diagram in a geometric proof, stand for many different things? In his *Critique of Pure Reason*, Immanuel Kant wrote that the task is impossible and that concepts must be represented by schemata, not images. Wittgenstein, however, argued that there might be objects that function as schemata – say, a schematic leaf, or a sample of green. A slip of pure green can be understood as a sample, he said, depending on the way that it is used. Perhaps one of the secrets of his reputation is illustrated by his not giving us any clue about *how* a sample should be used to serve this purpose. But a clue is to be found in David Hume's *Treatise of Human Nature*:

> . . . after the mind has produced an individual idea, upon which we reason, the attendant custom, revived by the general or abstract term, readily suggests any other individual, if by chance we form any reasoning that agrees not with it. Thus, should we mention the word triangle, and form the idea of a particular equilateral one to correspond to it, and should we afterwards assert, *that the three angles of a triangle are equal to each other*, the other individuals of a scalenum and isosceles, which we overlooked at first, immediately crowd in upon us, and make us perceive the falsehood of this proposition . . .

338

This view contains the germ of an idea that I shall exploit: the single mental model is provisional, and it can be revised in the light of subsequent information.

A PROCEDURAL SEMANTICS FOR MENTAL MODELS

Theories that deal only with the relations between expressions may do so, as we have seen, without postulating any semantic atoms or elements. This strategy is not workable, however, for a theory that purports to explain how words relate to the world. Many different scenes can be described by the same words, and many different words can describe the same scene. Hence, the relations between words and scenes must depend on elements at a lower level than either of them. These semantic elements will be ineffable – they cannot be expressed in the language under analysis, but only in a special theoretical terminology. They cannot therefore be analysed by meaning postulates, or any other apparatus that contains only terms that directly correspond to the words of ordinary language.

Formal semantics finesses this problem, since it stipulates merely that words have interpretations in models. A psychological theory, however, needs to explain how elements of meaning are used in procedures for constructing and interpreting mental models. I will illustrate such a theory, which exploits Hume's insight, in terms of a program that interprets spatial descriptions.

The program builds two-dimensional models. If you assert:

The dishwasher is on the right of the cupboard

it constructs a model by putting tokens into a spatial array in a way that fits your assertion. The model therefore has the same general structure as one formed by seeing or imagining the kitchen. It needs information in this case about dishwashers and cupboards, but I shall concentrate on spatial relations. Their meanings are represented in such a way that they can be used by all the program's procedures that construct, manipulate and interpret models. Thus, the meaning of 'on the right' specifies where one object must be located in relation to another so as to satisfy a description of the form: 'X is on the right of Y'. It is represented in a definition:

ONRIGHT: hold the value of the depth axis constant and increment the value of the horizontal axis

which is couched in primitive components that are ineffable in the spatial language under analysis. The program uses this definition to construct the following model of your assertion:

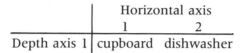

which corresponds to a view of the objects. It can be enlarged if necessary so as to accommodate objects in front of it or to either side.

Discourse uses noun phrases to refer to things, and comprehension hinges on establishing that a noun phrase refers to something that has already been mentioned. If your description continues:

The oven is on the left of the dishwasher

the program discovers that the model contains the representation of the dishwasher. In actual discourse, the business of establishing co-reference is often complicated and can depend on inferences of many sorts. The program is satisfied by a corresponding item in the model. It calls a procedure that uses the definition of 'on the left of' to insert the new item into the model in an appropriate position. However, the assertion is problematic since it does not establish a definite relation between the oven and the cupboard. Everyday discourse is riddled with such indeterminacies, but normally they do not matter and so one does not notice them. Faced with such an indeterminacy, the program plumps for one particular interpretation:

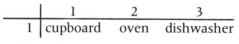

Suppose at this point, you assert:

The oven is on the left of the cupboard

then the program establishes that both oven and cupboard are already in the model. Since there are no new items referred to in the sentence, the program calls a procedure to verify your assertion. This procedure checks whether the relation between the objects satisfies the meaning of 'on the left'. Since it does not, the assertion is false in the current model. Whenever a sentence is falsified in this way, the program calls a recursive procedure, which, based on Hume's advice, checks whether there is any other possible model of the previous discourse in which the latest assertion turns out to be true. If it fails to find such an alternative, then it indicates that you have contradicted yourself. In the present case, however, the model:

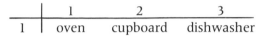

	1	2	3
1	oven	cupboard	dishwasher

satisfies all three assertions. The model originally embodied an assumption that was made by default; subsequent information conflicted with that assumption, and the procedure has revised the model so that it is consistent with the discourse as a whole. Hence, the program shows in principle how to solve Wittgenstein's problem: one model can serve as a representative sample from the potentially infinite set of models that satisfy a discourse, because the model can be revised to satisfy any subsequent consistent information.

The program is also able to make valid inferences. If you begin a description with the following two assertions:

A cupboard is on the right of an oven.

A dishwasher is on the right of the cupboard.

the interpretation is straightforward:

	1	2	3
1	oven	cupboard	dishwasher

If you now assert:

The dishwasher is on the right of the oven

then the verification procedure establishes that the assertion is *true* in the current model. Whenever something is verified in this way, the program calls a recursive procedure that is the mirror-image of the one for dealing with indeterminacies. It searches for

341

an alternative model of the previous discourse that renders the latest assertion *false*. If there is no such model, then your latest assertion follows necessarily from what has gone before, and the program announces that it is a valid deduction. In this way, the program implements the theory of reasoning described earlier in the book: it makes valid deductions without recourse to formal rules of inference, meaning postulates, or any other such devices. The logical transitivity of 'on the right' is an emergent property of its meaning – the way it relates to models – and is nowhere represented as an explicit rule.

We can define a sense of 'on X's right' in terms of scanning in a roughly rectilinear way outwards from the intrinsic right-hand side of X. This definition will capture the vagaries in the logical properties of the relation. It is transitive when, for example, people are seated along one side of a rectangular table. But, when they are seated at a round table, transitivity may break down – there comes a point after a certain number of assertions of the form:

> Arthur is on Lancelot's right
> Lancelot is on Guinevere's right
> Guinevere is on Merlin's right

where one says, not that Arthur is on Merlin's right, but that he is opposite Merlin. Such vagaries emerge entirely naturally from the definition: Arthur is not in the region demarcated by scanning outwards from Merlin's right-hand side. Networks and meaning postulates are superfluous: the relations between words emerge from their relations to models of the world.

Do people build such models when they understand discourse? The evidence suggests that they do, but the process is under a degree of voluntary control. When you understand my warning about the rearrangement of your furniture, you must build some such representation, which you can retain for some time, though you rapidly forget the verbatim details of the discourse on which it was based. Such phenomena are readily replicable in the laboratory. Unlike the program, you have only a limited ability to revise a model if you plump for a wrong choice with an indeterminate description. Kannan Mani and I found that the gist of determinate descriptions of spatial layouts is much easier to retain than the gist of indeterminate descriptions. It seemed that our subjects abandoned the attempt to construct a model for an indeterminate description – an hypothesis that is corroborated by their better memory for the verbatim details of these descriptions. Similarly, Kate Erhlich, Alan Garnham and his colleagues, and Valentina d'Urso and I, have obtained abundant evidence that disruptions in referential coherence retard and impair the comprehension of discourse.

MENTAL MODELS AND THE SYMBOLIC FALLACY

Models are symbolic structures, and I have shown how they can be constructed from verbal descriptions, and how statements can be true or false in relation to them. The relation of a model to the world, however, cannot simply be read off from the model. So how can a sentence be true or false in relation to the world? How, in other words, do models avoid the symbolic fallacy? The answer to these questions can best be framed by returning to our robot.

If the robot is equipped with a program for interpreting spatial discourse, it can build a model of an assertion such as: 'The table is on the right of the dresser.' Since it already possesses programs for using vision to construct three-dimensional models of the world and to identify *what* is *where* (see Chapter 6), it can in principle verify statements in relation to such models. In this case, words are related to the world by way of models, and there is no symbolic fallacy. However, as I have stressed, much of language goes beyond the perceptible. Some words refer to mental states, processes and feelings, and the robot could be provided with a vocabulary for referring to its own internal milieu. What is more problematic is discourse about such abstract matters as possibility, permissibility and causation.

Suppose that we provide the robot with a program that starts from a given model, derived from perception or discourse, and then uses statements of general knowledge to construct a model of a course of future events. If a certain statement is true in this model, then the statement designates a *possible* outcome of affairs in relation to the initial situation. If no such model can be constructed, the statement designates an *impossible* outcome. If the initial model derives from an actual state of affairs, these scenarios tell the robot about the truth or falsity of such statements in relation to the world. It will be able to understand and to evaluate assertions about what is possible and impossible.

An analogous program will allow the robot to cope with assertions about what is permissible and impermissible, but now its general knowledge will have to embrace certain principles regulating behaviour. Starting from a given model, the robot will be able to use these principles to construct a model of a course of future events. If it can construct such a model in which a certain statement is true, the statement designates a *permissible* state of affairs in relation to the initial model. If not, the statement designates an *impermissible* state of affairs in relation to the initial model. The latter state may be possible but the principles will stipulate that the robot must avoid it. Of course, there can be no real concept of permissibility unless the robot interacts with others according to certain regulatory principles. My aim is not to isolate the essence of morality, but rather to show that given the requisite concepts, models of situations enable statements of permissibility to be evaluated as true or false. These concepts do not correspond to anything in the physical or perceptible situation. They depend for their existence on conceptual abilities, and on the occurrence of certain behaviours that have a symbolic significance in relation to these conceptions.

THE NATURE OF DISCOURSE

Discourse is more than a string of co-referential sentences. The following passage, for example, is co-referential but hardly a satisfactory discourse:

> Furtively he dragged a package out of the reeds towards him. Out of curiosity, he opened the package and hid it beneath the bank in safety. He struggled with a youth who killed him. Then they stretched out indolently on the bank . . .

344

The following passage has exactly the same chain of references but makes much better sense:

> Furtively he watched a package drift into the reeds beneath him. Out of curiosity, he tried to climb down to the package but it was too far down the bank for safety. He called to a passing youth to help him. Then they carefully descended the bank . . .

When people read texts of this sort, then as my colleagues Alison Black and Paul Freeman have shown, they understand and remember the more plausible sequences of events rather better. Discourse is only a blueprint for states of affairs: it relies on the reader to flush out the missing details. Thus, when you were reading the sentence:

> He called to a passing youth to help him

you almost certainly inferred that the youth was going to help the old man *to climb down the bank*. Such 'bridging' inferences, as Herb Clark calls them, are rapid and automatic. You are seldom aware of making them, though they may show up in your recall of the discourse. They depend on your general knowledge, but, because the first of the passages above violates this knowledge, it is harder to understand and to remember.

Roger Schank and Robert Abelson have written computer programs that represent the 'scripts' of certain stereotyped activities, such as dining in a restaurant, and that use this information to infer details missing from stories. Scripts are prototypes for sequences of events: they allow a speaker to leave many things unsaid because a listener can fill in the gaps by default. It is unnecessary, for instance, to state explicitly that a customer in a restaurant eats the food he has ordered.

The use of general knowledge goes beyond discourse – you use it to interpret actual events, too. It also calls for mechanisms other than 'scripts'. The plausibility of a sequence of events, whether described or experienced directly, depends on how readily it can be construed within a temporal, spatial, causal and intentional framework – just the framework that Miller and I detected in all semantic fields.

Is discourse merely a string of co-referential sentences interpretable in the light of general knowledge? Plainly not. The following passage meets both criteria, yet it is not proper discourse:

> My daughter works in a library in London. London has a museum of natural history. It is organized cladistically. This theory concerns the classification of living things. All living things die . . .

What is wrong with this passage is its lack of theme. As you read it, you gradually realize that the writer has no global intention to communicate anything. The passage is not going anywhere. Normally, communication has a purpose, because it is governed by an intention.

INTENTION AND COMMUNICATION

You have finished navigating your way around your rearranged kitchen, and you say to me: 'Could you move the table back?' I reply: 'Yes, I think I could,' and do nothing. I have taken your interrogative to be a question, when obviously you intended it to be a request. You may think I'm crazy. (Schizophrenics have a talent for taking remarks literally – a certain patient would always knock on a particular door every time he passed it; it bore the sign, 'Please knock'.) What I failed to do was to infer your communicative intention.

The philosopher Paul Grice has argued that listeners have not understood a remark until they know the speaker's intention in uttering it. The only problem with this hypothesis is to demarcate the relevant intentions. When the prime minister evades the thrust of a question by answering in a diversionary manner, do you fail to understand her unless you have grasped this aspect of her intentions? What seems to be true is that you do not understand her reply until you recover its intended referents and determine whether she intends to make a statement, ask a question, or issue a command. The doyen of the 'ordinary language' philosophers, J. L. Austin, postulated a variety of such 'illocutionary acts', including in addition promising, advising and naming; and various theorists have analysed their usage.

There are several manifest cues to illocutions. The intonation of an utterance often distinguishes it (see Chapter 16). Similarly, the presence of certain words in an interrogative immediately signals a request: 'Could you move the table back, *please.*' Even grammatical structure plays a role, since an illocutionarily ambiguous clause can inherit the force of a clause to which it is conjoined: 'Please shut the door and could you move the table back?' Yet in many cases a speaker's intentions can be determined only from the context in which an utterance is made and from a knowledge of the cooperative conventions of conversation. According to a psychological theory proposed by Herb Clark and his collaborators, the intended force of a sentence is derived from an initial construction of its literal meaning. The fact that misreadings of illocutionary force do occur lends weight to this hypothesis, though certain turns of phrase perhaps no longer call for a literal interpretation. When an English gentleman begins an utterance, 'Would you be so kind as . . .', almost certainly he is making a request.

Discourse can be organized so that the force of utterances is made transparent:

> May I ask you a question?
> *Yes.*
> Is the door open?

Such a stratagem, relying on a set of standardized manoeuvres, is used in a program devised by Richard Power that allows two robots to communicate with each other in order to solve a problem. Human beings, however, generally converse more informally. They share social conventions about how to conduct a conversation cooperatively, and Grice has summarized these conventions in four maxims:

Quantity:	Make your contribution as informative as is required – neither too much nor too little information.
Quality:	Don't say what you believe to be false. Don't say what you lack evidence for.
Relation:	Be relevant.
Manner:	Avoid obscurity and ambiguity. Be orderly and brief.

347

These are not cast-iron principles. Indeed, the best evidence for their existence comes from their violations. If there were no convention to tell the truth, lies would seldom succeed. The blatant flouting of a convention also has its own rhetorical effect. When you assert a self-evident truth:

That's my table you've moved!

I can infer the reason for your flouting the maxim of quantity.

CONCLUSIONS

Logicians have related language only to models in various ways; psychologists have related it only to itself. The real task, however, is to show how language relates to the world through the agency of the mind. Semantic networks and meaning postulates are not sufficient for this task. Once it has been carried out, however, these theories are strictly speaking no longer necessary. Human beings perceive the world and construct models of it. They can evaluate assertions about the perceptible world in relation to these models, and they can manipulate them in order to conceive and to evaluate assertions about abstract matters. They can map such models into speech, that is, they can produce symbolic behaviours – linguistic expressions – that are intended to convey them to someone else. The individual who decodes the linguistic expressions constructs a model that resembles the state of the world that the speaker experienced and intends to convey. Hence, language enables us both to experience the world by proxy and to communicate certain abstract conceptions of it.

A mental model represents the particular state of affairs to which a sentence refers, but because the model can be revised as a result of subsequent information, it functions as a representative sample from the set of all possible models of the sentence. Hence, the initial linguistic representation of the sentence captures its meaning.

Human communication, however, depends upon intentions. The full significance of a remark may be beyond the listener's grasp, but speakers have communicative intentions and these must be recovered if the listener is to understand an utterance.

The notion of an intention is one of many related problems that cognitive science has yet to elucidate. It is to these problems that I shall turn in the final section of the book.

Further reading

Semantic networks are discussed in Findler (1979) and Johnson-Laird, Herrmann and Chaffin (1984), meaning postulates in Kintsch (1974), and models of discourse in Stenning (1978), Webber (1978), Kamp (1981), Johnson-Laird (1983) and Van Dijk and Kintsch (1983). Procedural semantics has its origins in Davies and Isard (1972), Longuet-Higgins (1972), Woods (e.g. 1981) and Steedman and Johnson-Laird (1977). Introductions to formal semantics and Montague's work include Partee (1975) and Dowty, Wall and Peters (1981). Experiments on reference and other aspects of discourse are described in Sanford and Garrod (1981). The theory of illocutionary acts has been developed by Searle (1969), Bach and Harnish (1979), and many others. Cohen and Perrault (1979) have modelled some aspects of the theory computationally. The area is reviewed comprehensively by Levinson (1983). Sperber and Wilson (1986) attempt to reduce Grice's conventions to one: be relevant.

PART VI

THE CONSCIOUS AND THE UNCONSCIOUS MIND

. . . you deduce the whole range of human satisfactions as averages from statistical figures and scientifico-economic formulas. You recognize things like wealth, freedom, comfort, prosperity and so on as good, so that a man who deliberately went against the tabulation would be . . . an obscurantist or mad, wouldn't he? But . . . how does it come about that all the statisticians and experts and lovers of humanity, when they enumerate the good things of life, always omit one particular one? . . .

Furthermore, you say, science will teach men . . . that they have not, in fact, and never have had, either will or fancy, and are no more than a sort of piano keyboard or barrel-organ cylinder; and that the laws of nature still exist on earth, so that whatever man does he does not of his own volition but, as really goes without saying, by the laws of nature. . . . All human actions, of course, will then have to be worked out by those laws, mathematically, like a table of logarithms, and entered in an almanac. . . .

One's own free and unfettered volition, one's own caprice, however wild, one's own fancy, inflamed sometimes to the point of madness – that is the best and greatest good, which is never taken into consideration because it will not fit into any classification, and the omission of which always sends all systems and theories to the devil.

FYODOR DOSTOYEVSKY

CHAPTER 19

Self-reflection, free will and intentions

Cognitive science can account for many faculties of mind. In equipping our robot with rudimentary powers of vision, memory and thought, we have explained them in terms that are computational rather than mystical. But, as opponents of cognitive science from Descartes to Dostoyevsky never cease to remark, an automaton does not have a will of its own, it does not have feelings, it does not have consciousness. Indeed, are these 'greatest goods' computable at all?

Philosophers have answered this question both positively and negatively. Some, such as Paul Ziff, have argued that only beings made out of flesh and blood can have feelings. Others, such as Hilary Putnam, have argued that a subjective experience is like a state in an automaton – a view that goes back to Craik and Turing. Both views, however, rely on intuitions, and such grounds have been discredited by the success of theories, such as quantum electrodynamics, that run counter to intuition.

No one knows what consciousness is or whether it serves any purpose. There are many psychological theories. Nick Humphrey has argued that it serves to cope with that most complex of problems – social interactions with other people: it helps you to imagine what they might be thinking, since it provides you with direct access to what you yourself are thinking. George Mandler has argued that it depends on a particular mode of processing that affects the mental structures governing actions. Tim Shallice goes further and argues that it determines what actions to take and what goals to seek – it is the court of last appeal for resolving internal conflicts. All these accounts are plausible; none of them is the whole story.

In this final section of the book, I am going to outline a theory of the conscious and unconscious mind that is based on a computational framework. I will begin with a conjecture about the architecture of the mind, and then I will develop the concept of a mental model of the self. I will show how the theory can account for what we can and cannot be aware of, and for the phenomena of subjective experience including self-reflection, free will and intentionality. In the final chapter I will extend the theory to motives and emotions.

PARALLEL PROCESSING AND
THE ARCHITECTURE OF THE MIND

Some theorists identify mental phenomena solely with consciousness – everything else, they say, is a matter of neurophysiology. If so, then one is bound to wonder about the status of the neurophysiological events giving rise to conscious experience, and also about the mysterious power by which, say, a telephone number stored in memory can be transformed into consciousness when it is called to mind. Since both states represent the same content, it seems preferable to talk of mental representations that can be conscious or unconscious.

Other theorists, notably Freud, have postulated an unconscious repository of primitive instinctual drives and other matters that are repressed because they create too much anxiety to be admitted into consciousness. But, as Helmholtz argued and as I have tried to show in this book, there are also many benign unconscious processes that underlie perception and cognition. Their existence implies that different mental processes occur in parallel: different processors operate in the mind at the same time.

These parallel processors control the events that occur simultaneously when we talk or walk, or walk and talk. They also cope with the hierarchical organization of skills. To understand discourse, for instance, there are separate processors for identifying speech sounds, recognizing words, parsing grammatical structure, constructing a representation of meaning, and making inferences. Each of these activities calls for an exquisite timing and interrelation with the others. The processors must operate together like workers on a factory production line that takes in the speech waveform as the raw material and transforms it into the finished product of comprehension.

354

The most general design for a parallel architecture is a network of processors – finite-state devices – wired up to each other so as to allow for communication. One processor cannot observe, or interfere with, the detailed workings of another. They merely pass information to one another. There is no central clock that synchronizes them: each processor springs to life as soon as it receives an adequate input.

There are many variations on this design. The channels of communication may transmit explicitly structured symbolic messages on which the processors carry out distinct rule-governed operations like those of a production system (see Chapter 9). The processors may all carry out the same synchronized procedure simultaneously like the 'array' computers constructed during the last decade. They may communicate only levels of activation, and each respond according to the same simple procedure based on the sum of their input activations (cf. the connectionist systems in Chapter 10).

Whatever form parallel processing takes, it cannot compute anything that could not be computed by a single serial processor, such as the universal Turing machine. Nor can it make intractable search problems tractable: they are to computation what Malthus's doctrine of population growth is to civilization. What parallel processing can do is to speed up tractable procedures, to allow several processors to carry out the same task so that it is less affected by noise or damage to the system, and to enable different groups of processors to specialize in particular tasks – to form dedicated 'modules'. As several cognitive scientists have observed, the brain could hardly have evolved without splitting into separate modules.

Speed, reliability and specialization have obvious evolutionary advantages. But parallel computation has dangers, too. If one processor is waiting for an input from another, which in turn is waiting for an input from it, then the two are paralysed in a deadly embrace from which neither can escape. Likewise, if one processor says *move left* and another processor says *move right*, then the unfortunate organism may tear itself apart in trying to move in opposite directions. Such problems do not occur in intact organisms: natural selection weeds out pathological connections

355

among processors. Human beings, however, are not dependent just on behaviours wired into their nervous systems. They can learn. Hence, they must have mechanisms to deal with novel pathologies when programs are distributed over many processors. A simple principle here is to promote one processor to monitor the operations of others and to override them if they get locked into a pathological configuration. If this design is replicated on a large scale, the result, once again, is a hierarchy – an architecture for the nervous system that has been proposed by neuroscientists since the nineteenth century.

THE CONSCIOUS MIND AS AN OPERATING SYSTEM

Simple consciousness – the bare awareness of events such as pain – may owe its origin to the emergence of a high-level monitor from the web of parallel processes. This 'operating system' at the top of the hierarchy sets goals for lower level processors and monitors their performance. Since it is at the top, its instructions can specify a goal in explicitly symbolic terms, such as to get up and walk. It does not need to send detailed instructions about how to contract muscles. They will be formulated in progressively finer detail by the processors at lower levels right down to the contractions of muscle spindles (see Chapter 11). It receives the results of computations from the lower processors, but again in a high-level and explicitly symbolic form. Thus, the tangible world is so vivid that Dr Johnson thought he could refute Berkeley's Idealism merely by kicking a stone.

The experience of reality is a triumph of the architecture of the mind: the operating system has no access to the processes on which it is based. There are good evolutionary reasons for this arrangement: if you could scrutinize the whole process of perception, it would have to be much slower since it could not depend on parallel processes. You might also be likely to doubt its veridicality – a fatal flaw in the case of danger.

A robot can also have a parallel computational architecture. Its operating system at the top of the hierarchy can be responsible for planning its actions, and for monitoring them under the guidance of feedback from its model of the world. Depending on the operating system's computations, the contents of its working memory will consist sometimes of a goal, sometimes of a particular portion of its model of the world, sometimes a signal from its internal milieu, and sometimes information retrieved from long-term memory. These contents function as its consciousness: they are what it is aware of at any moment as it carries out computations at the highest level in the hierarchy. The theory implies that there is a split between consciousness and the unconscious processes lower in the hierarchy. Such *dissociations* occur in human beings.

DISSOCIATIONS BETWEEN CONSCIOUS AND UNCONSCIOUS PROCESSES

If someone says to you, 'Look at that bird', you can search for a bird in your visual world, or you can refrain from doing so; the decision can be conscious. But, involuntary eye-movements and shifts of attention can also be brought about by unconscious processes. If, for example, your name occurs in a nearby conversation at a cocktail party, it attracts your attention involuntarily – a phenomenon (see Chapter 8) that establishes the existence of a processor that lies dormant until the right pattern of sound brings it to life.

On some occasions you can consciously control your behaviour; there are other occasions when, much as you would like to, you cannot control yourself. You may genuinely intend to give up smoking, for instance, but be unable to put your intention into practice. Some people can usually control themselves; others, as Oscar Wilde said, can resist everything except temptation. The majority of us vary from situation to situation. We are similarly often unable to control our feelings: we may suppress their expression, but the feeling itself will not go away. What underlies such phenomena are internal conflicts. A serial processor such as the operating system cannot be in conflict, but it can be in conflict with other processors: it has one goal, they have another. The conflict is resolved by the interactions amongst them. If it is resolved in favour of the operating system, you succeed in carrying out an intended action.

357

Otherwise, you fail, and some other unintended behaviour may occur.

Self-deception is another form of dissociation. It occurs most profoundly in hysterical paralyses, which arise not from damage to the nervous system but from unconscious motives. Those who are sceptical of Freud's case histories should consult Lord Adrian's account of how he cured neurotic paralyses brought on by 'shell shock' during the First World War. Adrian, who subsequently won the Nobel Prize for his work in physiology, realized that his patients were not malingering. They truly believed themselves to be paralysed, and did not recover if he tried to persuade them otherwise. He had to outwit the unconscious processes responsible for the malady, and so he treated the paralysis as genuine, and convinced the patients that it would be cured by a special treatment. He stroked the affected limb with a wire brush that gave a slight electrical tingle. The procedure worked for over ninety per cent of the cases. Cognitive forms of psychotherapy rest on the same idea – the need to bring about a change in unconscious processes.

A striking dissociation is the phenomenon of 'blindsight' described by Larry Weiskrantz and his collaborators, and confirmed by my colleague Tony Marcel. After damage to part of the brain concerned with vision, some patients report that they have become blind in a large area of the visual field. Their blindness is apparently confirmed by clinical tests. Yet, if the patients are forced to guess the location of a spot of light shining within the blind region, they are able to do so remarkably well. Some low-level visual processes continue to function, but no longer yield a symbolic output to consciousness.

A surgical intervention that creates subtle dissociations is the so-called 'split-brain' operation. Its consequences have been studied by Mike Gazzaniga of the Cornell Medical Center in New York. If you fixate a point in the scene in front of you, everything to the left of that point is projected to the right half of your brain, and everything to the right is projected to the left half of your brain. Information is rapidly transferred from one half of the brain to the other by a massive bundle of nerve fibres, the corpus callosum. The split-brain operation is carried out to control extreme forms of epilepsy. The surgeon cuts the corpus callosum so as to isolate the left cerebral cortex from the right. The operation is often highly beneficial, but it has some strange side-effects.

The first effect that Gazzaniga observed was the patients' inability to name any object in the left visual field: the object is projected to the right half of the brain, but the main language centres are in the left half. Information can no longer be transmitted from one half to the other, and so the patients deny seeing the object. However, when they are asked to make guesses about it, their emotions are almost identical to those that they have when they can see it. They become frightened by terrifying pictures, but they attribute their fear to the demeanour of the experimenter. Similarly, if the command 'walk' is flashed to the right half of the brain, the patient gets up and starts to walk. If asked why, the left half, which is unaware of the command, concocts a confabulatory explanation.

If I remove the cooling fan from my microcomputer, the machine is soon incapable of carrying out any computations. Someone who knows little about computers might therefore infer that the fan plays a central role in computation. Analogous errors are an ever-present danger in the study of brain damage. Gazzaniga wisely resists them and repudiates the one-time vogue for alleged dichotomies between left-brain thinking (analytical) and right-brain thinking (intuitive).

The dissociations between the conscious and unconscious mind have implications for the way we theorize in psychology. Unconscious mental processes may depend, not on rule-governed manipulations of symbols, but on some form of distributed representation, like those, perhaps, of the connectionist schemes of Chapter 10. Conscious thought, however, will try to accommodate them within its explicitly symbolic mode of operation. Thus, we think of speech as composed of sounds strung together like the letters of the alphabet that we can consciously apprehend. We think of concepts as having necessary and sufficient conditions like the definitions that we consciously coin. We think of thought itself as governed by formal rules of logic like those that logicians formulate explicitly. As I tried to show earlier in the book, these doctrines are delusions.

SELF-REFLECTION AND MODELS OF THE SELF

What is responsible for the subjective experience of awareness – the actual feeling of pain, sensation of thirst, or quality of redness? And why are certain states experienced consciously and others not? The theory so far provides only for a division between the conscious and unconscious mind, and not for the answers to these questions. It is logically possible, as William James held, that unconscious processes *are* separately conscious, and have no way of communicating this fact to the conscious mind. A more sensible idea, however, is that there are genuine differences between the two and that the conscious mind is the result of a special mode of processing that creates the subjective experience of awareness. Once an operating system had evolved, it could take on such a function, and this mode of processing, I believe, is our capacity for *self-awareness*. You can be deeply engrossed in some activity, such as skiing, or you can become aware of yourself as perceiving and acting. This state of self-awareness is distinct from ordinary awareness, but in my view is responsible for its particular phenomenological character.

Self-reflection is similar to self-awareness. You have a sense of your own integrity, continuity and individuality. You know about your history, predispositions, preferences and abilities. You have information, not about the inner workings of your mind, but about your high-level options and intentions. You know who you are. And you can reflect on all these matters in deciding what to do. Self-reflection, I shall argue, depends on the same mode of processing as self-awareness, but it also requires access to a particular mental representation – a representation that to some extent enables a processing system to understand itself. But what can it mean to say that a processor – a mere automaton – understands itself?

One possibility is suggested by a Turing machine which, when presented with a blank tape, prints out a description of itself in binary notation. (A universal Turing machine uses such descriptions of particular Turing machines to re-enact their computations.) To devise a self-describing Turing machine may seem a trivial task, but it is not. The obvious approach is to use instructions to print out each of the Turing machine's instructions, but then these 'print' instructions will need to be printed out too, and so on *ad infinitum*. The solution depends on a special procedure which when given a binary numeral prints out the description of a machine that would produce that numeral.

Some computer scientists believe that a self-describing Turing machine has the power of introspection. It produces a description of itself that is useful for self-reproduction. However, it no more understands this description than a molecule of DNA understands genetics. Marvin Minsky once suggested that a self-describing Turing machine could contain an interpretative program that would use its own description to calculate what it itself would do in some hypothetical situation. The idea is ingenious, but it does not correspond to the human capacity for self-reflection. The machine would imitate itself perfectly because it would have access to a complete and accurate description of its own inner workings. Our self-reflection, however, is imperfect and incomplete. It depends, I assume, on a *mental model* rather than on a complete description.

What makes a model a *model* is that it can be used by an interpretative system: a robot has a model of the world if its behaviour is guided by an internal representation that corresponds to some useful extent to the world. The robot can avoid falling down holes because it has a representation of them that it uses in deciding which way to go. The robot's operating system similarly can use a model of itself – its history, options, preferences and workings – to guide its decisions.

There is a whiff of paradox about this idea, because one of the operating system's options is to use its model of itself in tackling a problem, and this option in turn must be in the model, too. The circle is not vicious, but leads to the special mode of processing that is crucial for self-reflection and self-awareness. It consists in the operating system calling for the construction of a model of its own operations, which it uses to guide its processes. This 'self-reflective' procedure can be applied to its own output so that the system can construct a model of its own use of such models, and so on, in a series of ever-ascending levels of representation. Similarly, the same mode of processing can be applied to the contents of the operating system's working memory. Normal perception yields a model of the world, and the robot has a bare awareness of these contents in its working memory. But the operating system can replace those contents with a model of itself processing those contents: it perceives itself perceiving the world. It can call for a model of this experience, too, and so perceive that it is perceiving itself perceiving the world. The self-reflective procedure resembles the recursive embedding of one structure within another – a matter that I discussed in relation to grammatical rules – except that the operating system must be able to move freely from one level to another, e.g. when it has decided what to do at one level, it must be able to exploit this knowledge at a lower level. A potentially infinite regress is brought to a halt by the limited capacity of working memory.

So much for the theory of self-reflection, but is there any evidence to support it? The hypothesis could be mistaken, as some materialists would argue. It assumes that the framework of reflections and intentions, which we use to reason about our behaviour and to explain it, is no epiphenomenon but plays a causal role in guiding our thoughts and actions. In fact, as we shall see, the theory makes sense of a variety of phenomena.

SELF-REFLECTION, FREE WILL AND INTENTIONALITY

The hypothesis that the operating system has access to a model of itself, which it can use in a self-reflective mode, is corroborated by a number of observations about conscious experience. You do indeed have the capacity to reflect upon what you are doing – at a higher level than actual performance – and as a result of this reflection to modify your performance. For example, if you are successful in solving a series of problems, and then are stumped by one, you can ask yourself: what am I doing when I solve these problems? Your answer is based on your ability to scrutinize your own performance, that is, to raise yourself up one level so that you become a spectator of your own thoughts and behaviour. And your answer may help you to reformulate how you should proceed at the level of actual performance.

Your ability to use models of your own performance is the basis of all your 'meta-cognitive' skills. You can think about how you remember things, and take remedial steps to try to improve your ability. You can think about how you get on with people, and work out a plan to cope with a difficult social situation. You can think about a practical skill, such as driving a car, and try to adopt a conscious strategy to avoid a persistent error. As the concept of self-reflective processing predicts, you can even think about your own meta-cognitive thoughts. Thus, when you think about how you deal with certain problems, you may realize what you are doing and say to yourself, 'This is one of those problems that I can tackle by thinking about how I have solved them in the past, but *whenever I use this ability, I tend to concentrate too much on previous successes.'*

When you follow a plan, you do not carry out a rigid sequence of actions, but rather you observe the outcomes of your actions, and may as a result modify your plan. You may even abandon it. You often have the freedom to choose between several options at various points in its execution, particularly if you are exercising your imagination (cf. Chapter 14).

The concept of freedom that I am refering to here is freedom of will – the propensity that Descartes and Dostoyevsky invoked in order to cast doubt on a science of the mind. Scientists often retort that free will is an illusion. Yet its existence is compatible with the capacity for self-reflecting thinking. The argument can be illustrated by asking the reader a simple question:

What are you going to do next?

You could choose – sensible individual that you are! – to continue reading this book, if only to discover my solution to the riddle of free will. But you could decide that you have had enough cognitive science for the time being, and go out for a walk. There are many, many possibilities. Sometimes, you adopt a course of action without conscious thought. On other occasions, when you are stuck between two equally appealing alternatives, you say to yourself: 'This is ridiculous: I'll have to choose one of them.' And you may then, as a result of this higher order reflection, make an arbitrary decision. You may even ensure that it is arbitrary by recourse to external means. You spin a coin, or, like the hero of Luke Rhinehart's novel *Dice Man*, you throw dice.

At the lowest level, you do not make a conscious choice at all. You just continue to read, or you go for a walk, or whatever:

Level 0:   Continue to read
           Go for a walk.

At the meta-level, you think about what to do and make a decision based, say, on a simple preference:

Level 1:   By assessing preferences, you choose from:
Level 0:   Continuing to read
           Going for a walk.

How did you arrive at this method of choice? You didn't think consciously about all the different ways in which you could make a choice, and then choose the assessment of preferences from amongst them. It simply came to mind as the right way to proceed. Perhaps most methods of choice are selected this way. But, as the theory allows, they need not be. You can confront the issue consciously (at the meta-meta-level), and reflect on which of the various methods of choice you will use. Perhaps you try to choose rationally from amongst them:

Level 2:   Making a rational assessment, you choose from:
Level 1:   Assessing preferences
           Taking your spouse's advice } to choose from:
           Spinning a coin
Level 0:   Continuing to read
           Going for a walk.

Why did you decide to choose rationally from amongst the various methods of choice? Once again, it just came to mind as the right way to proceed. The method of decision at the highest level is always chosen tacitly. If it were chosen consciously, there would be a still higher level at which that decision was made. In theory, there need be no end to the hierarchy of decisions about decisions about decisions, but the business of life demands that you *do* something rather than get lost in speculation about how to decide what to do. The buck must stop somewhere.

We are free, not because we are ignorant of the roots of many of our decisions, which we certainly are, but because our models of ourselves enable us to choose how to choose. Amongst the range of options are even those arbitrary methods that free us from the constraints of an ecological niche or a rational calculation of self-interest. This fact lies behind Dostoyevksy's deepest beliefs, epitomized in the quotation at the head of this section, and behind the Existentialists' fascination with gratuitous acts: one demonstrates freedom (if not imagination) in acting arbitrarily.

When you have decided what to do and planned how to do it, you can act intentionally to try to achieve your goal. There are computer programs that also try to achieve a stated goal (see Chapter 9). Some cognitive scientists, such as John McCarthy, have argued that these programs have intentions. It seems more accurate to say that they act *as though* they had intentions. What is missing from them is self-reflection. Most of us recognize, for instance, that the road to hell is paved with good intentions. We know that our having an intention, such as to give up smoking, is not necessarily sufficient to achieve the goal. In the light of this knowledge, we sometimes take special steps to try to ensure an intended outcome.

At the lowest level (like the computer programs), human beings can:

Level 0: Construct a model of a possible future state of affairs.
Compute what to do to try to bring about that state of affairs.
Carry out this plan.

Unlike a computer program, human beings have access to a model of these abilities, and they can use it:

Level 1: Determine what to do by consulting a model of:
Level 0: Constructing a model of a possible future state of affairs.
Computing what to do to try to bring about that state of affairs.
Carrying out this plan.

People know that they can act to try to achieve some goal, and they can use this knowledge in determining what to do.

Once again, as the theory allows, people know that they can take into account their self-knowledge in making decisions. They can:

Level 2: Determine what to do by consulting a model of:

Level 1: Determining what to do by consulting a model of:

Level 0: Constructing a model of a possible future state of affairs.

Computing what to do to try to bring about that state of affairs.

Carrying out this plan.

People know that they know that they can act to try to achieve some goal, and they can use this knowledge in determining what to do. Even this level is not necessarily the top of the hierarchy.

CONCLUSIONS

The architecture that I have proposed consists of a hierarchy of parallel processors. The operating system at the highest level has access to the contents of its working memory: they are all that it can use directly in determining its course of action. It also has access to a partial model of itself, and the self-reflective machinery to embed models within models. These conditions appear to be necessary to give rise to the phenomena of self-awareness and self-reflection. It is an open question whether they are sufficient; it is also an open question whether cognitive scientists will be able to construct programs that are self-reflective.

In Don Siegal's terrifying 1956 film, *The Invasion of the Body Snatchers*, the inhabitants of a small town are transformed one by one into perfect replicas that lack free will and are apparently under the control of an alien force. But how does one know that an individual lacks free will? How does one know that another person is a conscious agent? This problem for the film's hero is still more serious for cognitive scientists. Of course there are many clear signs that a person is *not* functioning as a conscious agent, e.g. a failure to respond to any external stimuli. But the mere absence of these signs is not enough to establish consciousness. Everybody could be an unconscious robot from Mars except for you and me (and I'm not so sure about you). The theory that I have proposed implies that consciousness is a property of a class of particular computational procedures. The results of these procedures can in principle be obtained from serial procedures that cannot give rise to consciousness. Hence, there can be no decisive observation of behaviour which establishes that an organism is conscious: it ain't what you do, it's the way that you do it!

Yet this difficulty may not be insuperable. Members of the forensic professions recognize cases of diminished responsibility; psychiatrists recognize cases of compulsive behaviour; lay people recognize cases of involuntary action. The best tell-tale sign of consciousness is the ability to engage in discourse that explicitly concerns the individual's use of self-reflective judgement. Because the contents of consciousness are identical to the highest level of current reflection, this method allows the investigator to assess the degree of self-reflection that an individual can achieve. People who can tell you that they are choosing a particular course of action because they weighed up the pros and cons of several alternatives and it seemed to be the best, and that they chose this way of choosing as a result of reflection about a number of methods, should be judged to be responsible, conscious agents capable of exercising free will. Patients suffering from mental illness, brain damage or the effects of other traumas, may no longer have access to models of themselves or to the reflective procedure. They will act with diminished responsibility, and they will be unable to engage in self-reflective discourse. Psychological studies have shown that anxiety, stress and other such factors, increase the tendency for normal individuals to make mistakes in performance. These factors may also adversely affect the self-reflective capacity in daily life.

The contents of consciousness fall into two categories: symbolic and non-symbolic. The symbolic contents are perceptions, ideas, beliefs, hypotheses and all those mental entities that philosophers

367

refer to as having a propositional content. They range from the transcendental to the trivial – from the tenets of ethics to the headlines of your daily newspaper. They can be mapped into words, as when you describe to someone a belief that you hold. They can be deliberately manipulated by structural rules that are accessible to consciousness, as when you deliberately check whether a sentence contains a split infinitive. The non-symbolic contents of consciousness are feelings and sensations. You can feel an emotion such as fear, or a physical sensation such as pain. They are not symbols for anything, and they do not have any internal propositional structure. There is an intimate relation between the symbolic and the non-symbolic contents of consciousness, and I shall give an account of this relation in the next chapter.

Further reading

An earlier version of the theory was proposed in Johnson-Laird (1983, Ch. 16), which also gives the details of the construction of the self-describing Turing machine (following Thatcher, 1963). Similar ideas can be found in Hofstadter and Dennett (1981). Studies of consciousness appear in Bisiach and Marcel (1987), and of self-deception in Martin (1985). Self-reflection, in one guise or another, has a long philosophical history – see, for example, Dennett (1984), who defends the existence of free will. Skinner (1971) denies its existence. Oatley (1978) describes the history of the idea that the nervous system is hierarchically organized. Its organization in modules is defended by Simon (1981), by Marr (1982), and with great panache by Fodor (1983). Theories of errors in performance are proposed by Norman (1981) and by Reason and Mycielska (1982). For accounts of modern cognitive psychotherapy, see Beck (1976) and Oatley (1984). Erdelyi (1985) tries to reconcile the Freudian unconscious with the findings of cognitive psychology.

CHAPTER 20

Needs and emotions

We can construct a robot with rudimentary cognitive powers – with the ability to perceive the world, to cogitate, and to act. But, what should the robot do? Not everything that it can see will be worth remembering; not every inference that it can draw will be worth making; not every action that it can perform will be worth taking. If it is to act usefully and independently, we must wire into its circuitry some fundamental goals. Isaac Asimov in his science-fiction novels proposes three laws of robotics:

1. A robot may not injure a human being, or, through inaction, allow a human being to come to harm.
2. A robot must obey the orders given it by human beings except where such orders would conflict with the First Law.
3. A robot must protect its own existence as long as such protection does not conflict with the First or Second Law.

These laws have the wrong order of priority for autonomous organisms with 'selfish genes'. They appear to be governed by the following principles, which I am tempted to ascribe to that little known Soviet sociobiologist, I. Vomisa:

1. An organism must reproduce and ensure the survival of its genes.
2. An organism must protect its own existence as long as such protection does not conflict with the First Law.
3. An organism may cooperate with members of its species and help them from coming to harm as long as such cooperation does not conflict with the First or Second law.

Evolution, however, has equipped living creatures with highly specific goals. The question is: how do they get translated into behaviour?

THE FUNCTION OF FEELINGS

Primitive organisms, such as insects, rely on an innate set of responses for coping with their environment: the occurrence of a particular event triggers a particular response. Complex organisms, such as human beings, are able to use powerful inferential machinery and explicit symbolic principles in order to determine what to do. Wired-in responses are inflexible; inferences are costly in time and resources. Is there, perhaps, some middle way? The answer that Keith Oatley and I give is: yes. A complex organism has *feelings* of both bodily sensations such as pain and of emotions such as anxiety, and they are an independent means of guiding behaviour. They prepare the organism, not for a specific innate response, but for a general course of action appropriate to the situation. They do not require complex inferential processes. Indeed, they are an evolutionarily older method of control and their effects can be rapid and effective.

Consider the facts of life for a social mammal. Survival depends on food, water, air, maintenance of body temperature, and avoidance of predators, toxins and disease. The animals may cooperate both in hunting for prey and in defending against predators. Their reproduction also depends on social relations. There are potential mates and potential rivals, and much of the organization of society hinges on a hierarchy of power and status amongst rivals. There may be a need for territory for conceiving and raising offspring, and this territory may have to be defended against competitors. Finally, offspring need nurturing until they can fend for themselves.

Some of these goals concern bodily needs, whereas others concern external events and especially relations to other members of the species. Bodily needs have physical causes, e.g. an animal deprived of food becomes hungry. They can be terminated by other physical causes, which in turn produce further bodily states. Relations to other members of the species, however, have psychological causes. They are created and terminated by cognitive evaluations, e.g. the perception of a predator creates fear, and this fear can be communicated to other members of the species by an alarm, that is, by a ritualized behaviour that no longer serves any function other than to communicate the emotion to other members of the species. Hence, Oatley and I assume that emotions have their evolutionary origin as a control mechanism for interaction with other members of the species.

If emotions originated in social mammals in order to guide their behaviour, then we can begin to understand the diversity of emotions by examining their function in the organization of social life. The important situations in the life of a species can be mapped into a relatively small number of emotions. There are, as we saw above, only a small class of significant events in the social life of animals:

the making or breaking of attachments between caretakers and offspring,

the acceptance or rejection of bonds between mates,

aggression towards or flight from rivals, and analogous relations to prey and predators.

This ontology is also evident in the lives of human beings, and it suggests the following set of evolutionarily basic emotions:

Happiness, which occurs in successful attachments, but which may have distinct modes depending on whether the attachment is parental or sexual.

Sadness as a result of separation from an attached individual.

Anger as a precursor to aggression, which may have distinct modes depending on whether it is directed towards rivals, competitors for territory, predators or prey.

Fear as a precursor to submission to dominant rivals, to flight from predators, and to the 'freezing' response in unfamiliar situations: again these categories may call for distinct modes.

Disgust as a precursor to rejection.

371

The origin of disgust is presumably the bodily feeling of nausea induced by bad food and toxins. But, in the 1940s, the Canadian psychologist Donald Hebb reported that chimpanzees showed every sign of disgust when they were shown such things as an isolated eyeball. They had even developed a somewhat ritualized communication of the feeling. Hence, since its causes can be psychological, it can function as an emotion.

Ever since Descartes proposed a list of basic emotions in the seventeenth century, theorists have speculated about the members of the set. These five families of emotions, however, can all be found in social mammals. Their innate basis in human emotional life has been confirmed by Paul Ekman and his colleagues, who have discovered that the same facial expressions are used to convey these emotions across a wide variety of different cultures. Surprise has a similarly universal expression, but it can play a part in the genesis of any emotion. It should not be confused with the startle reflex – the fixed pattern of response that occurs in mammals, though not reptiles, to loud noises such as a pistol shot: the animal blinks its eyes and makes a rapid defensive reaction, which in human beings is certainly involuntary. Ekman and his colleagues have also shown that the basic emotions (and surprise) yield distinct patterns of physiological activity, including differences in heart rate, skin temperature, sweating and muscle tension.

Human emotions are complicated and dependent on personal, historical and cultural experience. They have transcended their evolutionary origins. Before I deal with this aspect of them, however, I shall consider how bodily feelings and emotions control behaviour.

INTERNAL SIGNALS OF BODILY NEEDS AND EMOTIONS

When a mammal, such as the humble rat, loses water from its body, its blood changes in volume and saltiness. Its kidneys, which excrete water into the urine, react by producing an enzyme that in turn leads to a release of a substance made up from a chain of eight amino acids, angiotensin II. If this substance reaches a certain concentration in the blood, its presence is detected by nerve cells in the hypothalamus – an organ in the middle of the brain of all vertebrates. We know that these cells control drinking, because when they are electrically stimulated, the rat begins to drink if there is water available. The cells do not trigger a fixed sequence of responses like those of an insect, but a flexible set of procedures designed to lead eventually to drinking: the rat may have to find some water. The intake of water begins to offset the depletion, and when the system has returned to normal, the animal stops drinking. The bodily need is satisfied by behaviour governed by a feedback loop that Fred Toates and Keith Oatley have modelled in a computer program.

Some forms of feedback are directly controlled by the amounts of certain substances in the body, whereas other forms depend on an internal representation (see Chapter 11). What about bodily needs – does a rat, for example, *feel* thirsty or is its behaviour solely governed by angiotensin II and other such substances? Since a thirsty rat will lick at a source of cool air, which causes the evaporation of still more water from its tongue, the rat may have bodily sensations. In this case, they mislead it. Such feelings could serve as a signal to the operating system of the brain so that behaviour is coordinated to achieve a relevant biological goal.

Rats in the wild are social animals with hierarchies of dominance in both males and females. They behave emotionally, exhibiting fear and rage. James Olds and Peter Milner showed thirty years ago that the electrical stimulation of certain points in the rat's brain close to the hypothalamus, and elsewhere, evidently yields a pleasurable sensation: the rat will press a lever continuously to receive such stimulation. A recent discovery is that these points of the brain also produce a specific chemical, dopamine, a so-called 'neurotransmitter' that helps to transmit nerve impulses across synapses between one nerve cell and another. Cocaine and other drugs which give human beings pleasure seem to operate like this neurotransmitter. The stimulation of other areas of the hypothalamus gives rise to angry behaviours. The detection of a rival presumably activates these same cells, and the flight of the rival inhibits them. The social goal of dominance is achieved by an emotional behaviour governed by perceptual feedback.

The theory of mental architecture which I described in the previous chapter posited consciousness as an operating system at the top of a hierarchy of processors. It receives messages that represent the world from the processors in the hierarchy; it sends messages to them that communicate its plans. Processors lower in the hierarchy form modules that may use distributed representations, but communications with the operating system depend on explicitly structured symbols with a propositional content. The internal signals of needs and emotions, Oatley and I propose, are a distinct mode of signalling within this architecture. They are transmitted by a small number of innate signals. There is not a separate chemical message for each signal, but specific neurotransmitters may be used at certain points in the system. Unlike the sentences of a language, the signals do not have an explicit symbolic structure – they do not have an interpretation that depends on the meanings of their separate parts, since their separate parts have no meaning. Each signal is more like an alarm call – one with a complex pattern unlikely to be confused with any other.

One processor initiates a signal and transmits it to other processors, and they can then call others by sending the same signal, and so on, until a significant proportion of the processors have entered the same mode and triggered the relevant physiological responses and suite of programs governing behaviour. The whole hierarchy can thus make a rapid transition from one mode to another, interrupting other activity to respond appropriately, without the need for symbolic computation. The hierarchy can also be set for a prolonged period into one of the modes with an intensity that depends on the number of processors that are recruited. Different processors, however, may be in different modes and the conflict may take time to be resolved.

There are signals for all the innate goals in the life of the animal: those that arise from bodily needs and from emotional goals. The operating system is equipped with a built-in knowledge of the significance of each signal: it does not have to learn that the signal for pain signals pain, or that the signal for anger signals anger. This form of interpretation is not a semantic one, since the signal has no internal structure.

374

If you are deprived of water, you begin to feel thirsty: the operating system receives a signal that has its origins in the processors monitoring the loss of water. The feeling may be accompanied by various localizable bodily sensations, such as a dry mouth. At first, you can ignore the signal and choose some other course of action, but as it grows in intensity it comes to preoccupy your conscious thoughts so that its demands cannot be ignored. Hence, any potential conflict between a higher order intention formulated by the operating system and the lower order need will eventually be resolved in favour of the need. The signal that reaches consciousness, however, has no parts to be interpreted according to an internal structure. It *is* thirst.

Emotional feelings that emanate from processors lower in the hierarchy work in the same way. They too have no internal symbolic structure; they too may be accompanied by specific bodily sensations; they too predispose the individual to certain sorts of behaviour. But, their origin is a cognitive interpretation of events. If the symbolic message capturing the cognitive evaluation fails to reach consciousness, the signal is a disembodied emotion that will be experienced for no particular reason. If some other symbolic message happens to impinge on consciousness and to have a relevant content, the feeling conveyed by the signal may be misattributed to the event it represents. If the right cognitive message reaches consciousness, but instead the emotional signal does not, there will be an inappropriate lack of feeling – a numbness that we experience when we know that we ought to be feeling a particular emotion but for some reason are not. The cognitive evaluations that create emotions may occur within the operating system itself, in which case the feeling cannot lack a cognitive evaluation, though the converse is still possible. I will come back to these complex emotions that originate in consciousness.

The signals of needs and emotions are adaptive because they can influence intentional behaviour without relying on symbolic processing or on a rigid set of responses like those of insects and other primitive organisms. The conscious experience may in turn lead to further cognitions and perhaps to another emotion or to attempts to suppress the feeling if it is judged to be unworthy.

These conflicts cannot be settled by conscious acts alone, since they require the mode of the majority of the processors to be resolved one way or another. As Paul Valéry remarked: 'Consciousness reigns, but it does not rule.'

EXTERNAL SIGNALS OF EMOTION

Charles Darwin wrote that the expression of emotions is advantageous to many species including human beings. He also argued that expressive behaviours had evolved from those of simpler animals. His arguments have been vindicated by the observations of ethologists such as Konrad Lorenz, Niko Tinbergen and Irenäus Eibl-Eibesfeldt. In many species, defence against predators depends on emotional signals of alarm. Some species even have different signals for different predators, like the cries of the vervet monkeys that I described in Chapter 15.

Alarm signals have the evolutionary advantage that many individuals can monitor the environment for signs of danger, and all benefit from a sighting by any one individual. The signals propagate rapidly and set all the individuals in the community into the same state. They are thus formally similar to the signals that propagate within the brain: they have no internal symbolic structure, but mobilize appropriate responses in others. Indeed, both the internal and external events happen together, since an individual emitting an alarm cry will be aroused and frightened, and will pass this state on to others.

The signals that occur as a preliminary to mating are complex and ritualized in many species. Sexual rivalry, social dominance and the defence of territory all produce social conflicts. They are settled by displays of hostility, ritualized combat, or fighting in earnest. Fighting typically continues until one individual flees or engages in a submissive ritual, e.g. a dog turns over on its back and urinates a little. Submission helps to control aggression if it can be recognized before a mortal injury occurs.

There are characteristic expressions of attachment between caretakers and offspring, and behaviours apart from giving food are important to the relationship. Even simple physical contact, as Harold Harlow has demonstrated, plays a critical role: infant monkeys survive the trauma of separation from their mothers much better if they have a terry-cloth surrogate to cling to, as opposed to a wire frame. Hence, the perception of a bodily state can create an emotion. Contact and warmth may lead to attachment; pain may lead to fear. The bodily sensations are produced by physical stimuli and can be experienced without the emotion, but they can be important to the emotion, which may act to amplify them.

ARE HUMAN FEELINGS INDEPENDENT OF COGNITION?

The thesis that emotions arise as a result of cognitive evaluations is contrary to the view of the eminent social psychologist R. B. Zajonc, who has argued that preferences and feelings do not depend on inferences. While they may not always arise from *conscious* inferences, some sort of cognitive appraisal appears to be crucial in creating emotions – a thesis proposed by Aristotle and defended by modern students of emotion such as Stanley Schachter and George Mandler.

If emotions are a non-symbolic way of guiding behaviour, it follows that they have a causal effect on behaviour. They are not an irrelevant by-product or a form of magical thinking – a view once urged by the Existentialist philosopher, Jean-Paul Sartre. (Strange if something so central to human life had turned out to be like appendicitis: the inflammation of a superfluous mental organ.) Emotions can indeed affect perception. In the 1950s, Jerome Bruner and his colleagues observed that when words are flashed briefly in front of people, the exposure-time necessary for their recognition is longer for emotionally charged words, such as 'bitch', 'anger', 'cancer'. Norman Dixon has even found that the detection of a spot of light shown to one eye can be influenced by emotional words shown so dimly to the other eye that the sub-jects in the experiment are not even aware of them. These studies have always created controversy, but processors lower in the hierarchy could act to censor the materials that make up the contents of consciousness.

There are similar phenomena showing that emotions can affect memory. The classic study was carried out by the nineteenth-century polymath, Francis Galton. He compiled lists of words which he put away in a desk drawer and forgot. Later, he worked through the list making free associations to each word, i.e. he read the word and responded with the first word that it called to mind. Often his responses shocked him so much that in his report of the study he passes briefly over them, saying only that they revealed the otherwise 'hidden plumbing' of the mind. Carl Jung observed that words that are emotionally laden take longer to respond to in free association: he was thereby able to unmask a thief from her slow responses to words relating to details of the crime. Recently, Gordon Bower and his colleagues have shown that people recall events that happened to them in an emotional state more readily if they are currently experiencing the same feeling. When you are sad, you remember the occasions of sadness rather than of happiness – as Billie Holiday used to sing, 'It's easy to remember and so hard to forget.'

The burden of these studies is that cognition and emotion are causally interlinked, and must be integrated within the same theory. If the computational framework cannot accommodate feelings, then it will have to be abandoned for cognition too. The humble rat, one supposes, has no model of itself and no self-reflective apparatus. It operates at level zero (in the terminology of the previous chapter): it constructs a model of its environment that guides its behaviour. It has a 'bare awareness' of the world, and it has feelings that affect its operating system. But, it has no awareness of its self in relation to the world. The crucial question is how the internal signals of needs and emotions are embodied within an organism that does have self-awareness – that does have a self-reflective operating system. The integration must avoid irreconcilable conflicts and other pathologies, and it must show how cultural factors enter into emotional life.

A THEORY OF HUMAN FEELINGS

Human beings are social mammals; they have all the bodily and social goals of social mammals. They therefore experience the five main classes of basic emotion: happiness, sadness, anger, fear and disgust. There may be distinct modes within these classes corresponding to the particular role of the individual, e.g. love is a species of happiness that arises from an attachment to another, but the happiness of a sexual attachment may depend on an internal signal that is distinct from the happiness of a parental attachment. Similarly, hate is a species of disgust. It can lead to anger, but there is no necessary connection: you can feel hatred for someone without feeling anger; you can feel angry with someone you do not hate. Human beings do not appear to have any basic emotions other than those that occur in simpler social mammals. Humour, for instance, leads to an innate response of laughter, which is unique to human beings, but the underlying emotion is a species of happiness.

A basic emotion can be created by a cognitive evaluation anywhere in the hierarchy of processors. If such an evaluation occurs lower in the hierarchy, then its content may fail to impinge on consciousness. Hence, the emotion will be experienced for no apparent reason. The individual will feel happy, sad, angry, frightened or nauseated, and be unable to discern any particular cause for the feeling. Analogously, the emotion may have an object, but again be engendered for no apparent reason. The individual will feel love, sorrow, anger, fear or hate towards someone, but be unable to attribute the cause.

The ethologist Eckhart Hess has a nice demonstration of this point: people given two seemingly identical pictures of the same person reliably prefer one picture to the other, though they cannot say why. In fact, the person in the preferred picture has eyes with dilated pupils. The dilation of the pupils is itself involuntary and unconscious, and one reason for it is a preoccupation with something of interest. It even occurs, as Patricia Wright and Danny Kahneman have observed, when people try to remember sentences. When you see someone with dilated pupils it may be a sign that they are taking an interest in you, and your perceptual system can unconsciously register the fact, but signal to consciousness only an emotion with the person as its object. You therefore find the person more attractive without knowing the reason for your feeling. That perhaps is why Spanish women once used belladonna as a cosmetic: it made their pupils dilate.

Basic emotions can, of course, arise consciously so that the individual experiencing them can give a correct account of their origin. A good example, which also demonstrates the role of culture in consciously created emotions, occurs in one of Darwin's anecdotes. A native of Tierro del Fuego touched some preserved meat that Darwin was eating and showed disgust at its softness; Darwin felt disgust that someone had touched his food. This incident shows that although disgust contains the bodily sensation of nausea as a major component, it can be a culturally determined reaction.

Human beings experience many other emotions apart from the basic ones. Their origin, Oatley and I argue, is in the cognitive evaluations of consciousness – of the operating system that has access to a model of the self.

CONSCIOUSNESS AND COMPLEX EMOTIONS

Feelings are the meeting place of mind, body and behaviour. They can bring together a conscious experience – often with thoughts about its perceived cause – various bodily and hormonal changes, and characteristic expressions and behaviours. Why is it important for you to be conscious of your feelings? Part of the answer, as we have seen, is that consciousness is the root of your voluntary, intentional behaviour, which depends on access to your model of your self. Hence, a feeling can affect your intentions only if you are aware of it. Another part of the answer is that certain emotions have their origins in consciousness since they depend on the model of the self. These emotions are complex, because they integrate an emotional signal and a cognitive evaluation emanating from the operating system. The two cannot be separated and so, unlike emotions arising elsewhere in the hierarchy, you cannot experience a complex emotion, such as remorse, pity or jealousy, without being aware of the relevant cognitive evaluation.

The fundamental distinction within complex emotions is between those that have you yourself as their object and those that have other people as their object. Those for which you are the object can arise from evaluating your situation in relation to your model of your self. Thus, for instance, you may feel proud of yourself: the emotional signal is happiness, but the subjective experience is an awareness that you have done something well – at least by the canons of your model of your self. You may instead feel remorse (sad with yourself), cross with yourself, frightened of yourself, or self-hatred. A feeling for which you are the object can also arise from an evaluation of your self in relation to other people. Thus, for example, you may feel a sense of belonging (happiness), abandonment (sadness), bitterness (anger), embarrassment (mild fear that you are making a fool of yourself), or shame (self-disgust) in comparing yourself with them. Complex emotions that have other people as their objects arise from evaluations of your self in relation to them. You may feel, say, reverence, pity, indignation, awe or jealousy.

The model that you form of your self, and the models that you form of other people and of the world at large, depend on many aspects of the particular society in which you live. Thus, you acquire a cultural background for the genesis of complex emotions. The underlying emotional signals remain the same as those of the basic emotions, but they can be engendered by events that depend on the details of your cultural experience – as filtered through your cognitive apparatus. What causes, say, jealousy in one culture may be innocuous in another.

THE CONCEPT OF FEELINGS

Feelings depend on bodily and emotional signals, but they can be cognitively elaborated by cultural experience into a large number of states that have many descriptive labels in human languages. But, you do not just experience feelings, you have *concepts* of feelings too. A concept is a mental construct – a symbolic representation – that enables you to categorize your experiences.

The Polish linguist Anna Wierzbicka has tried to define basic emotional terms, such as 'sadness':

> X feels sad = X feels as one does when one thinks that what one has desired to happen has not happened and will not happen.

381

As she admits, however, feelings do not have a structure that can be rendered in words. Moreover, one can feel sad for no conscious reason, or fail to feel sad when one has exactly the thoughts in Wierzbicka's definition. Since basic feelings are signals that have no symbolic structure, there cannot be analytical concepts of them. There can be concepts only of the scenarios into which they typically enter — their causes, concomitants and consequences. What children learn, for instance, is that the absence of an individual to whom they are strongly attached produces a particular feeling, and that as a result they are likely to cry and want to withdraw from the world. They learn that the feeling is called 'sadness' in English. When they observe other people in similar situations displaying similar signs, they attribute the same subjective experience to them. Although the observable signs and behaviours are necessary for learning how to use emotional terms, they are not part of their meaning. If they were, one could not say: 'I feel sad for no reason,' or 'I feel sad even though I am not showing it.' Such remarks would be bound to be false.

There are concepts of complex emotions, and they have a full scenario as part of their analysis. Remorse, for example, is the emotion of sadness you experience when you realize that you have offended your own moral code.

CONCLUSIONS

In these two final chapters, I have presented a theory of mental architecture. The conscious mind depends on the serial processing of explicitly structured symbols. The unconscious mind depends on the parallel processing of distributed symbolic representations. The link from bodily needs to the mind is by way of processors in the hierarchy that monitor certain substances in the body, and that propagate signals which are not symbolic at all. Emotional feelings depend on a similar channel of communication within the hierarchy. They are not the perception of bodily responses. You don't feel sad, say, because you perceive yourself as crying — a hypothesis once defended by William James. Likewise, emotions are not based on a general arousal that can be modified by whatever cognitive evaluation of it that happens to occur — an hypothesis once defended by Stanley Schachter and his colleagues. Emotions are caused by cognitive evaluations that propagate distinct internal signals.

Some emotions have their origin in unconscious processes. Indeed, it is commonplace that some emotions can be experienced for no known reason. But, if emotions can arise unconsciously, why should they ever be experienced consciously? This question is troubling because any evolutionary advantage might have accrued solely to their bodily and behavioural accompaniments. However, when an emotional signal impinges on the operating system, it gives rise to a distinct feeling and so the underlying motive can influence intentional behaviour. Moreover, certain emotions arise from the operating system because they depend on the model of the self.

Human beings are right to assign a pre-eminent role to feelings in their daily lives. Contrary to the arguments of certain materialists, the subjective component of mental life is, not an irrelevant 'ghost in the machine' to be exorcised by the study of physiology, but an important mainspring of behaviour. Feelings affect actions. The way in which people think and talk about them makes sense, and it is not, as some sceptics suppose, an incoherent assemblage of myths from 'folk' psychology. Lay concepts are incomplete, because many aspects of the mind lie beyond introspection, and because basic feelings have no meaningful internal structure. But everyday conceptions of the causes of feelings are often correct, as are the conceptions of jealousy, remorse and other complex emotions.

Feelings can be explained within a framework that brings together natural selection and a computational view of the mind. And so perhaps a robot could have feelings. It could be equipped with processors that monitor its internal milieu – detecting, say, that its supply of energy is low – and with other processors that detect important events in its environment, such as the presence of danger. These processors would transmit a particular signal to others in the hierarchy. Depending on the number of processors that a signal recruits, it might impinge on the operating system that determines the robot's actions by reference to a model of its capabilities. The signal would be an instruction that directly affects processors, but it would have no high-level symbolic structure. Computer programmers are familiar with a similar device. A routine in the low-level code that directly controls a computer can be called up from within a program in a high-level language when there is no way of eliciting the required operations in the high-level language. The analogous point about conscious mental processes is that they can be translated into the low-level code of the brain, but not all the instructions in that code correspond to instructions in the high-level symbols.

When the robot's operating system registers a signal that it is low on energy, would it *feel* a sort of hunger for energy? The signal could recruit more and more processors in the hierarchy, so that any conflict between them and some alternative high-level plan would be resolved in favour of finding a source of energy. The operating system would accordingly register something that functions as a specific warning to adopt intentional plans for satisfying the need. But the warning is – at least for the operating system – a signal without any interpretable structure. In that sense, it would function like a feeling. The only way in which a robot could experience the same feelings as we do would be if it had the same needs and social goals and was controlled by the same internal codes as we are. But are your subjective experiences the same as mine? The only way that we could ever know is if it became possible to send signals directly from one nervous system to another. This possibility is remote.

Further reading

This chapter is based in part on Oatley and Johnson-Laird (1987). Oatley (in press) examines the social aspects of emotions, and Power and Champion (1986) argue that a defective model of the self may lead to chronic depression. There are other attempts to integrate emotions and cognition, and starting points to their study include Strongman (1982), Mandler (1984), and Ortony, Clore and Foss (1987). Simon (1967), Sloman (1987) and Mellor (1987) present different conceptions of the relation between computation and emotions. Eibl-Eibesfeldt (1971) describes the ethology of human emotions; Changeux (1985) describes neurotransmitters and the brain.

ENVOI

Human beings are animals.   (Darwin)
Animals are machines.   (Descartes)
∴ Human beings are machines.   (La Mettrie)

You may resist this 'mechanomorphic' syllogism. You may reject one or other of its premises or argue that human beings are a special sort of animal – one whose actions are governed by conscious judgements and feelings. No matter what argument is adduced, you may persist: *But people have free will, they have moral and spiritual values, they aren't machines! The very idea reduces the mystery of life. It's demeaning. If people were machines, we would be able to understand completely how they worked. But to understand why, say, you love someone would destroy your love. To understand your imagination would annihilate it. If people were machines, then, as Dostoyevsky said, we would be able to predict what each individual would do. And that would be horrible, because we would no longer be free. In fact, the idea is impossible, since I can always act to refute any prediction about my behaviour. Cognitive science is trying in vain to destroy freedom, imagination and individuality.*

To that cry can be added a chorus of Existentialists, Phenomenologists and Hermeneuts. Cognition, they say, is not based on mental representations. There is no world independent of us: the only world is the one we create through our language. Our discourse, however, is not the transmission of information. It is a form of social action. There is, as hermeneutic doctrine has it, no objective standpoint from which we can examine our beliefs. There are no literal meanings: everything depends on context, that is, on the background knowledge shared by speaker and hearer. This knowledge, by which human beings render the world intelligible, cannot be made exhaustively explicit.

These claims have been repeated and amplified by others.

385

Thus, Hubert Dreyfus, a persistent Heideggerian critic of artificial intelligence, says that the basic problem facing workers trying to use computers to simulate human behaviour is that 'all alternatives must be made explicit'. The erstwhile artificial intelligencer Terry Winograd and his colleague Fernando Flores similarly argue that background knowledge is not a set of propositions, but 'our basic orientation of "care" for the world'. John Searle, a philosopher of language, has pointed out that a computer program cannot understand anything, or have any other cognitive states, because the binary numerals with which it operates have no interpretation other than that provided by human users. Only machines that have the causal powers of the human brain, he says, can perceive, understand and display the full properties of human mentality. Joseph Weizenbaum, a computer scientist, argues that there are many things that human beings know that cannot be made accessible to a computer. They know things as a result of having a body, and of having been treated as a human being by other human beings. They also have intuitions, hunches and creative processes, which depend on the unconscious mind, and – says Weizenbaum – the unconscious cannot be treated in 'information-processing' terms. 'Man is not a machine. . . . although man most certainly processes information, he does not necessarily process it in the way computers do.'

The sceptics may be right. Their criticisms are valuable because they pose challenges to cognitive scientists and curb their hubris. But one must be sceptical about the sceptics too. They don't produce the ideas they feed on, and they are sometimes wrong, as I shall try to show. Their criticisms are of three kinds: the moral, the metaphysical and the scientific.

The moral issue has been sharply stated by Weizenbaum: 'however intelligent machines may be made to be, there are some acts of thought that *ought* to be attempted only by humans'. I agree. I don't mind if bank statements are prepared by computers, but I do object if they have the responsibility of starting World War III. In fact, they play a central part in calculating the odds that the Russians have launched missiles against the West, and they are less conservative in their estimates than human beings would be. Moral decisions should be made by people, not computers. What of the morality of building computational models of theories of the mind? Weizenbaum finds no project in computer science repugnant, but he does condemn certain projects in artificial intelligence. He objects to the automatic recognition of speech on the grounds that it is obviously an irreversible step towards automated surveillance. But his case is hardly a strong one – does he object to micro-chips because they are an irreversible step to automated weapons?

During the decade since Weizenbaum delivered these judgements, the research to which he objected has not achieved the results he feared, and there are now projects in computer science to which he might object, such as those in the Strategic Defense Initiative. There are no grounds for singling out artificial intelligence for special opprobrium. Moreover, the quest to understand the mind should be distinct from the question of how to treat human beings and from any attempt to supplant them by computers.

Consider next the sceptical denial of a world independent of language and thought. Cognitive science – to echo William James's words of nearly a century ago – is the study of finite individual minds, and it assumes that there is a physical world in space and time, and that mental processes enable people to perceive that world, to have thoughts and feelings, and to be aware of themselves. These assumptions can be challenged, but, as James observed, their discussion is called metaphysics and lies outside the scope of science.

Science proceeds by making simplifying assumptions about the world, and by explaining the resulting idealized picture. Any scientific theory, as far as we know, can be modelled in a computer program. Whether that program *embodies* the phenomenon in question is quite a different matter. Meteorology, as I remarked previously, can be modelled in a program, but the weather itself cannot be produced by a program. The sceptics do not argue that cognitive science is impossible. They do not argue – for the most part – that programs cannot model theories of the mind. (A counterexample would be tantamount to a refutation of Turing's conjecture described in Part I.) Their main case is against the 'mechanomorphic' syllogism and the notion that a suitably programmed machine could possess mentality.

John Searle's argument about language allows that a theory of meaning could be modelled in a computer program, but asserts that computers do not thereby understand language. The argument repeats a point due to David Lewis, and often emphasized by others: a formal language is meaningless until it is assigned an interpretation. The point is well-taken, and indeed it has been made more than once during the course of this book (see Part V). Computers will not understand natural language until they are able to relate it to its proper domain of interpretation. Robots equipped with electronic sensory organs and perceptual programs have some ability to relate language to the world (see Part II), but discourse about morality, feelings and abstract matters eludes them. There is nothing that we know for certain, however, that renders it impossible to equip them with the mechanisms needed for motives, internal sensations and consciousness (see Part VI).

Because science makes simplifying assumptions about the world, the thesis that knowledge can never be made completely explicit does not threaten the science of the mind. Yet, in the long history of this thesis, it has often been mistakenly said to do so. In the 1920s, the linguist Leonard Bloomfield argued that there could never be a scientific analysis of meaning, because it would require all knowledge to be taken into account. In the 1960s, the philosophers Jerry Katz and Jerry Fodor proposed a theory of literal meaning, but argued that there could never be a scientific analysis of the effects of context, because it would require all knowledge to be taken into account. In fact, subsequent workers have formulated theories of how context guides interpretation. The overwhelming nature of knowledge may make it difficult – even impossible – for us to construct intelligent machines (other than by the original biological method). It has no direct bearing on the feasibility of cognitive science.

Yet, is it true that knowledge cannot be made completely explicit? One answer is that human beings are a living proof of the feasibility of the operation: they have finite brains, and they acquire only a finite amount of knowledge. And some cognitive scientists have begun to spell out its content. There are studies of lexical knowledge by George Miller, Ray Jackendoff, and others, studies of the naive physics of everyday life by Pat Hayes, and many investigations of the knowledge required for computer programs that function as 'expert systems'. The enterprise is enormously time-consuming, but if there are any insuperable barriers to it, they have yet to be discovered.

A more radical possibility is that there will be no need for an *explicit* representation of knowledge in order to construct intelligent machines. The brain itself may represent much of its knowledge in an implicit representation based on parallel distributed processing (see Part III). Programs for acquiring such knowledge would obviate the need for explicit analyses. Distributed processing may also be the answer to Weizenbaum's claim that the unconscious mind does not work like a computer. It may not work like a conventional digital computer, but there are no grounds to suppose that its mode of operation cannot be modelled computationally.

Some sceptics argue that cognitive science is impossible because people behave in ways that cannot be predicted. The same case, however, could be made against physics. Many simple deterministic systems, from a dripping tap to billiard balls bouncing off one another, behave in ways that rapidly become impossible to predict. Yet no one seriously supposes that physics is impossible. Indeed, the impossibility of prediction is adumbrated by that branch of physics known as the theory of chaos. It is a mistake to confuse two sorts of prediction: those that concern the specific details of what is going to happen next, and those that concern the testing of scientific hypotheses. The modern synthesis of genetics and natural selection explains how species evolve, and the theory's predictions have survived many empirical tests, but it cannot predict what new species will evolve next.

Most people, as I remarked at the start of the book, believe that their conscious feelings and judgements govern their actions, and that they have free will. Perhaps the most surprising aspect of cognitive science is that there is no need to abandon this belief: feelings and free will can be explained from within a computational framework. Even a system that is not deterministic can be completely understood though its specific behaviour cannot be predicted (see Part IV). The compatibility of free will with computational explanation reveals the crassness of the assumption that psychology is a means for the prediction and control of individual behaviour. No science can predict the products of your imagination, or what you will feel about everyone you meet, or what you will do on every occasion. Cognitive science does not threaten your freedom or dignity.

An important lesson from the study of the mind is the need for separate levels of explanation. It is necessary to formulate a general theory of what the mind computes, a theory of the program that is used to carry out the computations, and a theory of how the program is implemented in the nervous system. This lesson runs counter to the view that all psychological explanations will ultimately be couched in terms of neurophysiology (or biochemistry (or chemistry (or physics))). Conversely, cognitive science does not threaten to reduce social and cultural phenomena to explanations in its terms. It admits the need for economic, sociological and cultural levels of theorizing. Such theories should not violate what is known about the workings of the mind – no more than they should violate the laws of physics, but they cannot be replaced by accounts of mental operations.

When Behaviourism came in, it seemed that at last psychology was moving in the right direction. Forty years passed before the majority of psychologists realized that they were in a cul-de-sac. Will cognitive science suffer a similar demise? It is possible. Its researchers will never be certain about the true nature of the human mind: their understanding, like that of any scientists, will always be provisional. Yet they have had some success, as I hope the contents of this book have shown, in treating the mind as a machine. Each chapter of the endeavour (and the book) has its own remaining mysteries and puzzles – what mechanism, for example, is used to perceive the function of an unfamiliar object, to bring an associated idea to mind, to recognize a speech sound, or to acquire a grammar? At present, we have no satisfactory working models of any of these abilities. The nature of theory and experiment may have to change beyond recognition before we do possess them. However, if Turing was right when he conjectured that any effective procedure can be reduced to the operations of one of his simple automata, then, whatever the changes, I am happy to predict that the concept of computation will not be replaced by any other framework.

Cognitive science is already affecting the world we live in. Its most immediate applications are to the development of intelligent software and a humane technology. I hope that it will yield new ideas about psychopathology, and that it will be able to replace Freud's essentially nineteenth-century view of neurosis with an explanation that provides more effective forms of psychotherapy. The computational view of the mind, however, is likely to unfold in other, more surprising ways. It may even affect the way in which we think about what it is to be a human being. Certainly, it will change our conception of machines. Once upon a time a machine was a clock, or an engine, or a dynamo – a device for converting energy from one form to another. The computer is very different from the clanking monsters of the mechanical era, and the concept of computation in cognitive science goes beyond the conventional operations of a digital computer. The cognitive computer is a device for converting energy into symbols, symbols into symbols, and symbols into actions.

Cognitive computation raises many philosophical problems. It suggests an alternative to the traditional philosophies of mind: mental processes are the computations of the brain. This thesis is incompatible with the Dualistic philosophy that holds mind and matter to be independent domains. It is also incompatible with both Materialism and Idealism – the traditional attempts to abandon one domain or the other. It implies that certain organizations of matter enable processes to occur that represent events elsewhere in the world. It also implies that the fabric of a computer does not matter. The way in which it realizes its computations is – almost in both senses of the word – immaterial. What matters is the organization of these processes. This philosophy replaces the concept of the immortal soul with an alternative form of immortality. There is a remote possibility that the computations of a human mind might be captured within a medium other than a brain. A facsimile of a human personality could be preserved within a computer program. All living things pass on to their offspring a self-reproducing program in their genes. Human beings, in addition, can leave behind them some traces of their personalities in books, in pictures, in theories, and in other cultural artefacts. We are familiar with the idea of interacting with such artefacts in order to glean some understanding of a long-dead person. The concept of interacting with a dynamic representation of an individual's intellect and personality is sufficiently novel to be disturbing. It raises moral, metaphysical and scientific issues of its own.

ACKNOWLEDGEMENTS

This book would not have existed without the help of many people. Helen Fraser of Fontana and Patricia Williams of Harvard University Press convinced me that it was a feasible project for me to undertake. They and their respective colleagues, Stuart Proffitt and Michael Aronson, have all read portions of the book and given me valuable advice and encouragement.

Six people read the entire first draft of the book. My colleague Ruth Byrne went through it with the finest of combs and caught many mistakes; she has also helped with many other jobs from checking references to testing subjects. Geoffrey Hawthorn's enthusiasm for my efforts was a tonic at just the point I needed it. Keith Oatley saw more clearly than I the theme of the book, and helped me to make it more explicit. Stuart Sutherland, as ever, pounced on many infelicities in style and content, corrected my vision of vision, and convinced me that problems that I had thought I had solved, I had not. Steven Pinker forced me to think yet again about 'connectionism', to clarify the exposition of formal learning theory, and to recast my account of transformational grammar. And Bernard Williams, who taught me logic twenty-five years ago, taught me some new lessons by revealing all sorts of nasty philosophical problems that I had glibly skated over. My thanks to all of these readers. The final version of the book is better for their efforts, but there are points where I have been unable (and very occasionally unwilling) to follow their advice, and so the book should not be taken to have their imprimatur.

I have also benefited enormously from the advice of a number of experts, who have read one or more chapters dealing with the topics of their expertise. They have saved me from an embarrassing number of blunders, though doubtless I have inserted many more in trying to correct those they found. As scholarly journals sometimes do, I shall list the names of these reviewers:

ACKNOWLEDGEMENTS

John R. Anderson	William Marslen-Wilson
Tony Anderson	Don Norman
Alan Baddeley	Roy Patterson
Alison Black	Kim Silverman
Donald Broadbent	Lolly Tyler
Anne Cutler	John Wann
John Gammack	Roger Watt
Geoff Hinton	Alan Wing
Ben Johnson-Laird	Richard Young
Christopher Longuet-Higgins	

Many other colleagues have helped in innumerable ways, and I am grateful to Jeremy Butterfield, Martin Conway, Thomas Green, Hugh Mellor, Tony Marcel, Denis Norris, Karalyn Patterson and Tim Shallice for many stimulating discussions over the years. My thanks also to Peter Wason, my original supervisor, who took a keen interest in the project, and to four long-standing groups of collaborators: Bruno Bara of the University of Florence, Alan Garnham and Jane Oakhill of the University of Sussex, Paolo and Maria Legrenzi of the Universities of Trieste and Padova, and Patrizia Tabossi of the University of Bologna. I am also indebted to my brother Andy Johnson-Laird of Johnson-Laird, Inc., Portland, Oregon, who remains a one-man surgical team for computational problems, hardware or software.

I am grateful to the Medical Research Council and to Alan Baddeley, the Director of Applied Psychology Unit in Cambridge, for providing me with a congenial atmosphere and all the facilities I need to pursue my own research in cognitive science and to write this book. The staff at the Unit have been most helpful. Alan Copeman took the photographs; Carmen Frankl drew the original figures (my son Ben and the 'Mac' prepared many initial versions of them); Ann Edwards and Jill Ethridge slaved over a hot photocopier; Sharon Gamble coped with the correspondence; and Lillian Astell ensured that everything ran smoothly.

The impetus for the book came from two graduate courses that I taught, one at Stanford University in 1985, and the other at Princeton University in 1986. One teaches to learn, of course; and the students convinced me that the subject had an underlying coherence. I am grateful to Ewart Thomas, Chairman of the Department of Psychology at Stanford, and to Joel Cooper, Chairman of the Department of Psychology at Princeton, for inviting me. Many people in these two departments worked hard to make me feel at home, and to provide me with a wonderful intellectual experience. There isn't room to thank everyone, but I must record my gratitude to Gordon Bower, Herb and Eve Clark, and Barbara and Amos Tversky at Stanford, and to Carol Colby, Bob Friedin, Sam Glucksberg, Steve and Catherine Hanson, Marcia Johnson, Judy Kegl, Carl Olson, Sue Sugarman and Paul Thagard at Princeton. I must thank one other Princeton friend: George Miller. He is one of the founders of cognitive science, and it was he who generously took me on my first guided tour through the subject some fifteen years ago, and who continues to educate me. I owe him an immense debt.

Finally, despite a collective groan when the project was announced, my family have borne with me, and they have all read chapters, checked references, and, most important of all, administered brief psychotherapy whenever it was called for. Thanks to Mo, Ben and Dorothy.

Phil Johnson-Laird

REFERENCES
and citation index

Numbers in brackets refer to pages in the text.

Ades, A.E., and Steedman, M.J. (1982) On the order of words. *Linguistics and Philosophy*, 4, 517–58. (322)

Adrian, E.D., and Yealland, L.R. (1917) The treatment of some common war neuroses. *Lancet*, June, 3–24. (358)

Aleksander, I., and Burnett, P. (1983) *Reinventing Man: the Robot becomes Reality*. London: Kogan Page. (214)

Allen, J. (1985) Speech synthesis from unrestricted text. In F. Fallside and W.A. Woods, eds., *Computer Speech Processing*. London: Prentice-Hall. (301)

Anderson, J.R. (1976) *Language, Memory, and Thought*. Hillsdale, NJ: Lawrence Erlbaum. (326, 333–4)

Anderson, J.R. (1983) *The Architecture of Cognition*. Cambridge, Mass.: Harvard University Press. (166–8, 169, 171–2)

Angluin, D. (1980) Inductive inferences of formal languages from positive data. *Information and Control*, 45, 117–35. (242)

Aristotle. *De Memoria*. In Sir D. Ross, ed., *The Works of Aristotle*. Oxford: Oxford University Press, 1959. (130)

Aristotle. *Rhetoric*. In ibid. (377)

Armstrong, S.L., Gleitman, L.R., and Gleitman, H. (1983) What some concepts might not be. *Cognition*, 13, 263–308. (253)

Asimov, I. (1968) *I, Robot*. St Albans, Herts: Granada. (369)

Atal, B.S., and Hanauer, S.L. (1971) Speech analysis and synthesis by linear prediction of the speech wave. *Journal of the Acoustical Society of America*, 50, 637–55. (302)

Austin, J.L. (1962) *How to Do Things with Words*. Oxford: Clarendon Press. (346–7)

Bach, K., and Harnish, R.M. (1979) *Linguistic Communication and Speech Acts*. Cambridge, Mass.: MIT Press. (349)

Bacon, F. (1620) *Novum Organum*. Edited by T. Fowler. Oxford: Oxford University Press, 1889. (236)

Baddeley, A.D. (1983) *Your Memory: a User's Guide.* Harmondsworth, Middx: Penguin Books. (157)

Baddeley, A.D., and Hitch, G. (1974) Working memory. In G. Bower, ed., *The Psychology of Learning and Motivation,* Vol. 8. London: Academic Press. (151–2)

Bar-Hillel, Y., and Carnap, R. (1952) An outline of a theory of semantic information. In Y. Bar-Hillel, *Language and Information.* Reading, Mass.: Addison-Wesley, 1964. (233)

Barlow, H.B. (1985) Cerebral cortex as model builder. In D. Rose and V.G. Dobson, eds., *Models of the Visual Cortex.* London: Wiley. (235)

Barthes, R. (1972) *Mythologies.* London: Jonathan Cape. (28)

Bartlett, F. C. (1932) *Remembering: a Study in Experimental and Social Psychology.* Cambridge: Cambridge University Press. (22, 181)

Beck, A. T. (1976) *Cognitive Therapy and the Emotional Disorders.* New York: Meridian. (368)

Berkeley, G. (1975) *Philosophical Works.* London: Dent. (356)

Berlin, B., and Kay, P. (1969) *Basic Color Terms: Their Universality and Evolution.* Berkeley: University of California Press. (244)

Bernstein, N. (1967) *The Coordination and Regulation of Movement.* London: Pergamon Press. (201)

Berwick, R.C. (1985) *The Acquisition of Syntactic Knowledge.* Cambridge, Mass.: MIT Press. (142, 326)

Berwick, R.C. (1986) Learning from positive-only examples: the subset principle and three case studies. In Michalski, Carbonell and Mitchell (1986). (242)

Biederman, I. (1987) Recognition-by-components: a theory of human image understanding. *Psychological Review,* 94, 115–47. (126)

Bisiach, E., and Luzzatti, C. (1978) Unilateral neglect of representational space. *Cortex,* 14, 129–33. (123)

Bisiach, E., and Marcel, A.J., eds. (1987) *Consciousness in Contemporary Science.* Oxford: Oxford University Press. In press. (368)

Black, A., Freeman, P., and Johnson-Laird, P.N. (1986) Plausibility and the coherence of discourse. *British Journal of Psychology,* 77, 51–62. (345)

Black, M. (1967) Induction. In P. Edwards, ed., *The Encyclopedia of Philosophy.* New York: Macmillan. (253)

Blakemore, C. (1970) The representation of three-dimensional visual space in the cat's striate cortex. *Journal of Physiology*, 209, 155–78. (97)

Block, N., ed. (1981) *Imagery*. Cambridge, Mass.: MIT Press. (126)

Bloomfield, L. (1926) A set of postulates for the science of language. *Language*, 2, 153–64. (388)

Boakes, R.A. (1984) *From Darwin to Behaviourism: Psychology and the Minds of Animals*. Cambridge: Cambridge University Press. (142)

Boden, M. (1977) *Artificial Intelligence and Natural Man*. Hassocks, Sussex: Harvester. (27)

Bower, G.H., and Cohen, P. (1982) Emotional influences in memory and thinking: data and theory. In Clarke and Fiske (1982). (378)

Bowerman, M. (1977) The acquisition of word meaning: an investigation of some current concepts. In Johnson-Laird and Wason (1977). (234, 243)

Brady, J.M. (1983) Representing shape. In L. Gerhardt and J.M. Brady, eds., *Robotics*. New York: Springer. (105)

Brady, J.M., Hollerbach, J.M., Johnson, T.L., Lozano-Pérez, T., and Mason, M.T., eds. (1982) *Robot Motion: Planning and Control*. Cambridge, Mass.: MIT Press. (214)

Braine, M.D.S. (1978) On the relation between the natural logic of reasoning and standard logic. *Psychological Review*, 85, 1–21. (224)

Brame, M.K. (1978) *Base Generated Syntax*. Seattle: Noit Amrofer. (321)

Broadbent, D.E. (1958) *Perception and Communication*. Oxford: Pergamon. (22, 147–8, 152)

Broadbent, D.E. (1971) *Decision and Stress*. London: Academic Press. (127)

Broadbent, D.E. (1984) The Maltese cross: a new simplistic model for memory. *Behavioral and Brain Sciences*, 7, 55–94. (152)

Broadbent, D.E. (1985) Simple models for experimental situations. Unpublished paper, Department of Experimental Psychology, Oxford. (154–5)

Brown, R., and McNeill, D. (1966) The 'tip of the tongue'

phenomenon. *Journal of Verbal Learning and Verbal Behavior*, 5, 325–37. (194)

Bruner, J. S. (1983) *In Search of Mind: Essays in Autobiography.* New York: Harper and Row. (377)

Bruner, J.S., Goodnow, J.J., and Austin, G.A. (1956) *A Study of Thinking.* New York: Wiley. (22, 243)

Bryan, W.L., and Harter, N. (1897) Studies in the physiology and psychology of the telegraphic language. *Psychological Review*, 4, 27–53. (210)

Byrne, R.M.J. (1987) The contextual nature of conditional reasoning. Unpublished Ph.D. thesis, Trinity College Dublin. (232)

Campbell, D. (1960) Blind variation and selective retention in creative thought as in other knowledge processes. *Psychological Review*, 67, 380–400. (269)

Chaffin, R., and Herrmann, D.J. (1984) The diversity and similarity of semantic relations. *Memory and Cognition*, 12, 134–41. (329)

Changeux, J–P. (1985) *Neuronal Man: the Biology of Mind.* New York: Pantheon. (384)

Cheney, D.R., and Seyfarth, R.M. (1981) Selective forces affecting the predator alarm calls of vervet monkeys. *Behavior*, 76, 25–61. (*See also* Seyfarth, Cheney and Marler, 1980.) (274)

Chomsky, N. (1957) *Syntactic Structures.* The Hague: Mouton. (23, 137, 305–6, 310 *et seq.*, 319)

Chomsky, N. (1959) On certain formal properties of grammars. *Information and Control*, 2, 137–67. (45, 52, 310 *et seq.*)

Chomsky, N. (1963) Formal properties of grammars. In R.D. Luce, R.R. Bush and E. Galanter, eds., *Handbook of Mathematical Psychology*, Vol. II. New York: Wiley. (310 *et seq.*)

Chomsky, N. (1965) *Aspects of the Theory of Syntax.* Cambridge, Mass.: MIT Press. (315, 319)

Chomsky, N. (1980) *Rules and Representations.* New York: Columbia University Press. (250)

Chomsky, N. (1982) *Some Concepts and Consequences of the Theory of Government and Binding.* Linguistic Inquiry Monograph 6. Cambridge, Mass.: MIT Press. (141, 316–19)

Church, A. (1936) A note on the Entscheidungsproblem. *Journal of Symbolic Logic*, 1, 40–1 and 101–2. Reprinted in M. Davis, ed., *The Undecidable.* Hewlett, NY: Raven Press, 1965. (222–3)

Churchland, P.M., and Churchland, P.S. (1981) Functionalism, qualia, and intentionality. *Philosophical Topics*, 12, 1. (16)

Clark, H.H. (1977) Bridging. In Johnson-Laird and Wason (1977). (345)

Clark, H.H. (1979) Responding to indirect speech acts. *Cognitive Psychology*, 11, 430–77. (347)

Clark, H.H., and Lucy, P. (1975) Understanding what is meant from what is said: a study in conversationally conveyed requests. *Journal of Verbal Learning and Verbal Behavior*, 14, 56–72. (347)

Clark, H.H., and Schunk, D.H. (1980) Polite responses to polite requests. *Cognition*, 8, 111–43. (347)

Clowes, M. (1971) On seeing things. *Artificial Intelligence*, 2, 79–116. (107–10)

Cohen, P.R., and Perrault, C.R. (1979) Elements of a plan-based theory of speech acts. *Cognitive Science*, 3, 177–212. (349)

Coltheart, M., Patterson, K., and Marshall, J.C., eds. (1980) *Deep Dyslexia.* London: Routledge and Kegan Paul. (191)

Craik, K. (1943) *The Nature of Explanation.* Cambridge: Cambridge University Press. (26, 35, 215, 227, 353)

Craik, K. (1947) Theory of human operator in control systems. 1. The operator as an engineering system. *British Journal of Psychology*, 38, 56–61. (206)

Crain, S., and Steedman, M.J. (1985) On not being led up the garden path: the use of context by the psychological syntax parser. In Dowty, Karttunen and Zwicky (1985). (323)

Crick, F., and Asanuma, C. (1986) Certain aspects of the anatomy and physiology of the cerebral cortex. In McClelland, Rumelhart and the PDP Research Group, Vol. 2 (1986). (194)

Cutler, A. (1976) Phoneme-monitoring reaction time as a function of preceding intonation contour. *Perception and Psychophysics*, 20, 55–60. (298)

Cutler, A., and Foss, D.J. (1977) On the role of sentence stress in sentence processing. *Language and Speech*, 20, 1–10. (298)

Cutler, A., and Isard, S.D. (1980) The production of prosody. In

B. Butterworth, ed., *Language Production*, Vol I. London: Academic Press. (299)

Cutler, A., and Norris, D. (1985) Syllable boundaries and stress in speech segmentation. Paper presented to the 109th meeting of the Acoustical Society of America, Austin, Texas. (295)

Darwin, C. (1871) *The Descent of Man.* London: Murray. (385)

Darwin, C. (1872) *The Expression of the Emotions in Man and the Animals.* London: Murray. (376)

Darwin, C.J., Turvey, M.T., and Crowder, R.G. (1972) An auditory analogue of the Sperling partial report procedure: evidence for brief auditory storage. *Cognitive Psychology*, 3, 255–67. (*See* Sperling, 1960)

Davies, D.J.M., and Isard, S.D. (1972) Utterances as programs. In D. Michie, ed., *Machine Intelligence*, Vol. 7. Edinburgh: Edinburgh University Press. (349)

Davis, R., and Lenat, D.B. (1982) *Knowledge-based Systems in Artificial Intelligence.* New York: McGraw-Hill. (259–60)

Denes, P.B., and Pinson, E.N. (1973) *The Speech Chain.* New York: Anchor Books. (279, 280, 304)

Dennett, D.C. (1984) *Elbow Room: the Varieties of Free Will Worth Wanting.* Cambridge, Mass.: Bradford Books, MIT Press. (368)

Descartes, R. (1637) *A Discourse on Method.* In E.S. Haldane and G.R.T. Ross (trans.), *The Philosophical Works of Descartes*, 2 Vols. Cambridge: Cambridge University Press, 1967. (14, 353, 363, 385)

Descartes, R. (1649) *The Passions of the Soul.* In Haldane and Ross, ibid. (372)

de Vries, J.V. (1604) *Perspective.* New York: Dover, 1968. (108)

Dickinson, A. (1980) *Contemporary Animal Learning Theory.* Cambridge: Cambridge University Press. (142)

Dixon, N. (1971) *Subliminal Perception: the Nature of a Controversy.* London: McGraw-Hill. (377)

Dostoyevsky, F.M. (1864) *Notes from Underground.* Trans. by J. Coulson. Harmondsworth, Middx: Penguin, 1972. (351, 353, 363, 365, 385)

Dowty, D.R., Karttunen, L., and Zwicky, A.M., eds. (1985) *Natural Language Parsing: Psychological, Computational, and*

Theoretical Perspectives. Cambridge: Cambridge University Press. (326)

Dowty, D.R., Wall, R.E., and Peters, S. (1981) *Introduction to Montague Semantics.* Dordrecht: Reidel. (349)

Dreyfus, H.L. (1972) *What Computers Can't Do: a Critique of Artificial Reason.* New York: Harper and Row. (386)

Duncker, K. (1945) On problem-solving. *Psychological Monographs,* 58, whole no. 270. (266)

d'Urso, V., and Johnson-Laird, P.N. (1987) Referential cohesion and memorability. Mimeo, MRC Applied Psychology Unit, Cambridge. (343)

Ehrlich, K., and Johnson-Laird, P.N. (1982) Spatial descriptions and referential continuity. *Journal of Verbal Learning and Verbal Behavior,* 21, 296–306. (343)

Eibl-Eibesfeldt, I. (1971) *Love and Hate: On the Natural History of Basic Behaviour Patterns.* London: Methuen. (376, 384)

Eigen, M., and Winkler, R. (1983) *Laws of the Game: How the Principles of Nature Govern Chance.* Harmondsworth, Middx: Penguin. (269)

Ekman, P., ed. (1982) *Emotion in the Human Face.* Second edition. Cambridge: Cambridge University Press. (372)

Ekman, P., Levenson, R.W., and Friesen, W.V. (1983) Autonomic nervous activity distinguishes among emotions. *Science,* 221, 1208–10. (372)

Erdelyi, M.H. (1985) *Psychoanalysis: Freud's Cognitive Psychology.* New York: Freeman. (368)

Evans, J.St B.T. (1982) *The Psychology of Deductive Reasoning.* London: Routledge and Kegan Paul. (233)

Fallside, F., and Woods, W.A., eds. (1985) *Computer Speech Processing.* London: Prentice-Hall (UK). (304)

Farah, M.J. (1984) The neurological basis of mental imagery: a componential analysis. *Cognition,* 18, 245–72. (126)

Feigenbaum, E.A., and McCorduck, P. (1984) *The Fifth Generation: Artificial Intelligence and Japan's Computer Challenge to the World.* London: Pan Books. (233)

Feldman, J.A., and Ballard, D.H. (1982) Connectionist models and their properties. *Cognitive Science,* 6, 205–54. (194)

403

Findler, N.V., ed. (1979) *Associative Networks: Representation and Use of Knowledge by Computers.* New York: Academic Press. (349)

Flanagan, J.L. (1972) The synthesis of speech. *Scientific American,* February, 226, 48–58. (301)

Flanagan, J.L. (1972) Voices of men and machines. In J.L. Flanagan and L.R. Rabiner, eds., *Speech Synthesis.* Stroudsberg, Penn.: Dowden, Hutchinson and Ross. (304)

Fodor, J.A. (1980) Fixation of belief and concept acquisition. In Piattelli-Palmarini (1980). (134–6)

Fodor, J.A. (1983) *The Modularity of Mind: an Essay on Faculty Psychology.* Cambridge, Mass.: Bradford Books, MIT Press. (105, 325, 368)

Fodor, J.A., Bever, T.G., and Garrett, M.F. (1974) *The Psychology of Language.* New York: McGraw-Hill. (319–20)

Fodor, J.A., Garrett, M.F., Walker, E.C.T., and Parkes, C.H. (1980) Against definitions. *Cognition,* 8, 263–367. (332–3)

Fodor, J.D., Fodor, J.A., and Garrett, M.F. (1975) The psychological unreality of semantic representations. *Linguistic Inquiry,* 4, 515–31. (332–3)

Fogel, L., Owens, A., and Walsh, M. (1966) *Artificial Intelligence through Simulated Evolution.* New York: Wiley. (142)

Forster, K.I. (1979) Levels of processing and the structure of the language processor. In W.E. Cooper and E.C.T. Walker, eds., *Sentence Processing: Psycholinguistic Studies Presented to Merrill Garrett.* Hillsdale, NJ: Lawrence Erlbaum. (325)

Forte, A. (1979) *Tonal Harmony in Concept and Practice.* Third edition. New York: Holt, Rinehart and Winston. (261)

Frazier, L., Clifton, C., and Randall, J. (1983) Filling gaps: decision principles and structure in sentence comprehension. *Cognition,* 13, 187–222. (324)

Frazier, L., and Fodor, J.D. (1978) The sausage machine: a new two-stage parsing model. *Cognition,* 6, 291–325. (323)

Frege, G. (1879) *Begriffsschrift, eine der Arithmetischen nachgebildete Formelsprache des reinen Denkens.* Halle: Nebert. Trans. by T.W. Bynum: *Conceptual Notation and Related Articles.* Oxford: Clarendon Press, 1972. (221, 233)

Frege, G. (1892) Über Sinn und Bedeutung. *Zeitschrift für*

Philosophie und philosophische Kritik, 100, 25–50. Translated as: On sense and reference. In P.T. Geach and M. Black, eds., *Philosophical Writings of Gottlob Frege*. Oxford: Basil Blackwell, 1952. (335)

Freud, S. (1908) Creative writers and day-dreaming. In J. Strachey, ed., *Standard Edition of the Complete Psychological Works of Sigmund Freud*, Vol. 9. London: Hogarth Press, 1959. (269)

Freud, S. (1909) *The Interpretation of Dreams*. Second edition. Harmondsworth, Middx: Penguin, 1976. (28)

Freud, S. (1933) *New Introductory Lectures on Psychoanalysis*. In J. Strachey, ed., *Standard Edition of the Complete Psychological Works of Sigmund Freud*, Vol. 22. London: Hogarth Press, 1964. (15, 354, 358, 368, 391)

Frisby, J.P. (1979) *Seeing: Illusion, brain and Nind*. Oxford: Oxford University Press. (74–5, 80, 95)

Frisby, J.P., and Clatworthy, J.L. (1975) Learning to see complex random-dot stereograms. *Perception*, 4, 173–8. (84)

Frisch, K. von (1966) *The Dancing Bees*. Second edition. London: Methuen. (273)

Fry, D.B. (1976) *The Physics of Speech*. Cambridge: Cambridge University Press. (278, 285, 287, 288, 304)

Gabriel, R.P. (1986) Massively parallel computers: the connection machine and the NON-VON. *Science*, 231, 975–8. (194)

Galton, F. (1883) *Inquiries into Human Faculty and its Development*. London: Macmillan. (378)

Gardner, H. (1985) *The Mind's New Science: a History of the Cognitive Revolution*. New York: Basic Books. (27)

Garnham, A. (1985) *Psycholinguistics: Central Topics*. London: Methuen. (304)

Garnham, A., Oakhill, J., and Johnson-Laird, P.N. (1982) Referential continuity and the coherence of discourse. *Cognition*, 11, 29–46. (343)

Gazdar, G. (1981) On syntactic categories. *Philosophical Transactions of the Royal Society*, B, 295, 267–83. Reprinted in H.C. Longuet-Higgins, J. Lyons and D.E. Broadbent, eds., *The*

Psychological Mechanisms of Language. London: The Royal Society and the British Academy. (321–2)

Gazdar, G., Klein, E., Pullum, G., and Sag, I. (1985) *Generalized Phrase Structure Grammar*. Oxford: Basil Blackwell. (326)

Gazzaniga, M.S. (1985) *The Social Brain: Discovering the Networks of the Mind*. New York: Basic Books. (358–9)

Geman, S., and Geman, D. (1984) Stochastic relaxation, Gibbs distributions, and the Bayesian restoration of images. *IEEE Transactions of Pattern Analysis and Machine Intelligence*, PAMI, 6, 721–41. (194)

Gentner, D. (1987) The mechanisms of analogical learning. In A. Ortony, ed., *Similarity and Analogy in Reasoning and Learning*. In press. (267)

Gentner, D., and Stevens, A.L., eds. (1983) *Mental Models*. Hillsdale, NJ: Lawrence Erlbaum. (253)

Getzels, J.W., and Jackson, P.W. (1962) *Creativity and Intelligence: Explorations with Gifted Students*. New York: Wiley. (269)

Gibson, J.J. (1950) *The Perception of the Visual World*. Boston: Houghton Mifflin. (97–8, 101)

Gibson, J.J. (1966) *The Senses Considered as Perceptual Systems*. Boston: Houghton Mifflin. (61, 125)

Gick, M.L., and Holyoak, K.L. (1983) Schema induction and analogical transfer. *Cognitive Psychology*, 15, 1–38. (266)

Gold, E.M. (1967) Language identification in the limit. *Information and Control*, 16, 447–74. (138–41)

Goodman, N. (1965) *Fact, Fiction, and Forecast*. Second edition. Cambridge, Mass.: Harvard University Press. (235)

Goodman, N. (1968) *Languages of Art: an Approach to a Theory of Symbols*. Indianapolis, Indiana: Bobbs-Merrill. (36)

Gregory, R.L. (1970) *The Intelligent Eye*. London: Weidenfeld and Nicolson. (126)

Gregory, R.L. (1981) *Mind in Science: a History of Explanations in Psychology and Physics*. London: Weidenfeld and Nicolson. (126)

Gregory, R.L., and Heard, P.F. (1983) Visual dissociation of movement, position, and stereo depth: some phenomenal phenomena. *Quarterly Journal of Experimental Psychology*, 35A, 217–37. (97)

Grice, H.P. (1968) Utterer's meaning, sentence-meaning, and word-meaning. *Foundations of Language*, 4, 1–18. (346)

Grice, H.P. (1975) Logic and conversation. In P. Cole and J.L. Morgan, eds., *Syntax and Semantics*. Vol. 3: *Speech Acts*. New York: Seminar Press. (347, 349)

Grimson, W.E.L. (1981) *From Images to Surfaces*. Cambridge, Mass.: MIT Press. (97)

Grosjean, F. (1980) Spoken word recognition and the gating paradigm, *Perception and Psychophysics*, 28, 267–83. (295)

Gruber, H.E. (1974) *Darwin on Man: a Psychological Study of Scientific Creativity*. New York: Dutton. (269)

Haber, R.N. (1983) The impending demise of the icon: a critique of the concept of iconic storage in visual information processing. *Behavioral and Brain Sciences*, 6, 1–54. (149)

Hacking, I. (1975) *The Emergence of Probability*. Cambridge: Cambridge University Press. (250)

Haddon, F.A., and Lytton, H. (1968) Teaching approach and the development of divergent thinking abilities in primary schools. *British Journal of Educational Psychology*, 38, 171–80. (269)

Halle, M. (1978) Knowledge unlearned and untaught: what speakers know about the sounds of their language. In M. Halle, J. Bresnan, and G. A. Miller, eds., *Linguistic Theory and Psychological Reality*. Cambridge, Mass.: MIT Press. (293–4)

Halliday, M.S. (1967) *Intonation and Grammar in British English*. The Hague: Mouton. (297–8)

Halsall, F., and Lister, P.F. (1980) *Microprocessor Fundamentals*. London: Pitman Education. (157)

Hampton, J.A. (1987) Inheritance of attributes in natural concept conjunctions. *Memory and Cognition*. In press. (337)

Hampton, J.A. (1987) Overextension of conjunctive concepts: evidence for a unitary model of concept typicality and class inclusion. *Journal of Experimental Psychology: Learning, Memory and Cognition*. In press. (337)

Harlow, H.F., and Zimmermann, R.R. (1959) Affectional responses in the infant monkey. *Science*, 130, 421–32. (376)

Harmon, L.D. (1973) The recognition of faces. *Scientific American*, November, 229, 70–82. (77–8)

Hayes, P.J. (1985) The second naive physics manifesto. In J.R. Hobbs and R.C. Moore, eds., *Formal Theories of the Commonsense World*. Norwood, NJ: Ablex. (389)

Hayes-Roth, F., and McDermott, J. (1978) An interference matching technique for inducing abstractions. *Communications of the Association for Computing Machinery*, 21, 401–11. (253)

Hebb, D.O. (1949) *The Organization of Behavior*. New York: Wiley. (22, 182, 372)

Helmholtz, H. von (1897) *Treatise on Physiological Optics*. Third edition trans. J.P.C. Southall. Optical Society of America, 1924. (15, 59, 114, 354)

Herrmann, D.J. (1980) An old problem for the new psychosemantics: synonymity. *Psychological Bulletin*, 85, 490–512. (*See also* Chaffin and Herrmann, 1984.) (329)

Hess, E.H. (1965) Attitude and pupil size. *Scientific American*, April, 212, 46–54. (379)

Heuer, H., and Wing, A.M. (1984) Doing two things at once: process limitations and interactions. In Smyth and Wing (1984). (212)

Hilgard, E.R., and Bower, G.H. (1974) *Theories of Learning*. Fourth edition. New York: Appleton-Century-Crofts. (142)

Hiller, L.A. Jr, and Isaacson, L.M. (1959) *Experimental Music*. New York: McGraw-Hill. (269)

Hinde, R.A. (1982) *Ethology: Its Nature and Relations with Other Sciences*. London: Fontana. (142)

Hinton, G.E. (1979) Some demonstrations of the effects of structural descriptions in mental imagery. *Cognitive Science*, 231–50. (124)

Hinton, G.E. (1984) Parallel computations for controlling an arm. *Journal of Motor Behavior*, 16, 171–94. (201–3, 209)

Hinton, G.E., and Anderson, J.A., eds. (1981) *Parallel Models of Associative Memory*. Hillsdale, NJ: Lawrence Erlbaum. (178, 194)

Hinton, G.E., McClelland, J.L., and Rumelhart, D.E. (1986) Distributed representations. In Rumelhart, McClelland and the PDP Research Group, Vol. 1 (1986). (190–1)

Hinton, G.E., Sejnowkski, T.J., and Ackley, D.H. (1986) Learning and relearning in Boltzmann machines. In Rumelhart, McClelland and the PDP Research Group, Vol. 1 (1986). (194)

Hodges, A. (1983) *Alan Turing: the Enigma.* London: Burnett. (11, 36)

Hodges, W. (1977) *Logic.* Harmondsworth, Middx: Penguin. (233)

Hofstadter, D.R. (1979) *Gödel, Escher, Bach: an Eternal Golden Braid.* New York: Basic Books. (53)

Hofstadter, D.R., and Dennett, D.C., eds. (1981) *The Mind's I: Fantasies and Reflections on Mind and Soul.* New York: Basic Books. (368)

Hogg, D. (1983) Model-based vision: a program to see a walking person. *Image and Vision Computing,* 1, 5–20. (118–19)

Holland, J., Holyoak, K.J., Nisbett, R.E., and Thagard, P. (1986) *Induction: Processes of Inference, Learning, and Discovery.* Cambridge, Mass.: Bradford Books, MIT Press. (253)

Holmes, J.N., Mattingly, I.G., and Shearme, J.N. (1964) Speech synthesis by rule. *Language and Speech,* 7, 127–43. (301)

Holyoak, K.J., and Nisbett, R.E. (1987) Induction. In R.J. Sternberg and E.E. Smith, eds., *The Psychology of Human Thinking.* New York: Cambridge University Press. (253)

Horn, B. (1984) *Robot Vision.* Cambridge, Mass.: MIT Press; New York: McGraw-Hill. (61)

Hubel, D.H., and Wiesel, T.N. (1962) Receptive fields, binocular interaction and functional architecture in the cat's visual cortex. *Journal of Physiology,* 160, 106–54. (73)

Huffman, D.A. (1971) Impossible objects as nonsense sentences. In B. Meltzer and D. Michie, eds., *Machine Intelligence 6.* Edinburgh: Edinburgh University Press. (107–9)

Hume, D. (1896) *A Treatise of Human Nature.* Edited by L.A. Selby-Bigge. Oxford: Clarendon Press. (16, 121–2, 338–9, 341)

Humphrey, N. (1983) *Consciousness Regained: Chapters in the Development of Mind.* Oxford: Oxford University Press. (353)

Hunt, E.B., Marin, J., and Stone, P.J. (1966) *Experiments in Induction.* New York: Academic Press. (246–8)

Hunter, I.M.L. (1977) Mental calculation. In Johnson-Laird and Wason (1977). (233)

Inhelder, B., and Piaget, J. (1958) *The Growth of Logical Thinking from Childhood to Adolescence.* London: Routledge and Kegan Paul. (222)

Inhelder, B., and Piaget, J. (1964) *The Early Growth of Logic in the Child: Classification and Seriation.* New York: Harper and Row. (173)

Jackendoff, R. (1983) *Semantics and Cognition.* Cambridge, Mass.: MIT Press. (389)

Jackson, J.H. (1931) *Selected Writings of John Hughlings Jackson.* Edited by J. Taylor. London: Hodder and Stoughton. (210)

James, W. (1890) *The Principles of Psychology.* New York: Holt. (217, 360, 382, 387)

Johansson, G. (1975) Visual motion perception. *Scientific American*, June, 232, 76–88. (100)

Johnson-Laird, P.N. (1975) Models of deduction. In R.J. Falmagne, ed., *Reasoning: Representation and Process in Children and Adults.* Hillsdale, NJ: Lawrence Erlbaum. (224)

Johnson-Laird, P.N. (1983) *Mental Models: Towards a Cognitive Science of Language, Inference, and Consciousness.* Cambridge: Cambridge University Press; Cambridge, Mass.: Harvard University Press. (157, 233, 326, 349, 368)

Johnson-Laird, P.N. (1987) Freedom and constraint in creativity. In R.J. Sternberg, ed., *Creativity.* Cambridge: Cambridge University Press. In press. (269)

Johnson-Laird, P.N., and Anderson, A. (1986) Common-sense inference. Mimeo, MRC Applied Psychology Unit, Cambridge. (221)

Johnson-Laird, P.N., and Bara, B. (1984) Syllogistic inference. *Cognition*, 16, 1–61. (233)

Johnson-Laird, P.N., Herrmann, D.J., and Chaffin, R. (1984) Only connections: a critique of semantic networks. *Psychological Bulletin*, 96, 292–315. (349)

Johnson-Laird, P.N., Oakhill, J., and Bull, D. (1986) Children's syllogistic reasoning. *Quarterly Journal of Experimental Psychology*, 38A, 35–58. (233)

Johnson-Laird, P.N., and Stevenson, R. (1970) Memory for syntax. *Nature*, 227, 412. (320)

410

Johnson-Laird, P.N., and Wason, P.C., eds. (1977) *Thinking: Readings in Cognitive Science.* Cambridge: Cambridge University Press. (233)

Joyce, J. (1922) *Ulysses.* Paris: Shakespeare and Company. Reprinted Harmondsworth, Middx: Penguin, 1969. (16, 217)

Julesz, B. (1971) *Foundations of Cyclopean Perception.* Chicago: University of Chicago Press. (84)

Jung, C. (1919) *Studies in Word Association.* New York: Moffat Yard. (378)

Just, M.A., and Carpenter, P.A. (1976) Eye fixations and cognitive processes. *Cognitive Psychology,* 8, 441–80. (121–2)

Kahneman, D., Slovic, P., Tversky, A., eds. (1982) *Judgement Under Uncertainty: Heuristics and Biases.* Cambridge: Cambridge University Press. (253)

Kahneman, D., and Tversky, A. (1982) On the study of statistical intuitions. *Cognition,* 11, 123–41. Reprinted in Kahneman, Slovic and Tversky (1982). (251–2)

Kamp, J.A.W. (1981) A theory of truth and semantic representation. In J. Groenendijk, T. Janssen and M. Stokhof, eds., *Formal Methods in the Study of Language.* Amsterdam: Mathematical Centre Tracts. (349)

Kandel, E.R., and Schwartz, J.H. (1981) *Principles of Neural Science.* New York: Elsevier. (194)

Kant, I. (1787) *The Critique of Pure Reason.* Second edition. Trans. J.M.D. Meiklejohn, London: Dent, 1934. (16, 338)

Kaplan, R.M. (1972) Augmented transition networks as psychological models of sentence comprehension. *Artificial Intelligence,* 3, 77–100. (322)

Kaplan, R.M., and Bresnan, J.W. (1982) Lexical-functional grammar: a formal system for grammatical representation. In J.W. Bresnan, ed., *The Mental Representation of Grammatical Relations.* Cambridge, Mass.: MIT Press. (321)

Katz, J.J., and Fodor, J.A. (1963) The structure of a semantic theory. *Language,* 39, 170–210. (329, 333, 388)

Keil, F.C. (1979) *Semantic and Conceptual Development: an Ontological Perspective.* Cambridge, Mass.: Harvard University Press. (239–40, 253)

411

Kelso, J.A.S., ed. (1982) *Human Motor Behavior: an Introduction.* Hillsdale, NJ: Lawrence Erlbaum. (201, 214)

Kintsch, W. (1974) *The Representation of Meaning in Memory.* Hillsdale, NJ: Lawrence Erlbaum. (349)

Klahr, D., Langley, P., and Neches, R., eds. (1986) *Production System Models of Learning and Development.* Cambridge, Mass.: MIT Press. (173)

Kneale, W., and Kneale, M. (1962) *The Development of Logic.* Oxford: Clarendon Press. (233)

Koenderink, J.J. (1984) What does the occluding contour tell us about solid shape? *Perception,* 13, 321–30. (105)

Koestler, A. (1964) *The Act of Creation.* London: Hutchinson. (255)

Koffka, K. (1935) *Principles of Gestalt Psychology.* New York: Harcourt Brace. (19)

Köhler, W. (1929) *Gestalt Psychology.* New York: Liveright. (19)

Kohonen, T. (1977) *Associative Memory: a System-Theoretical Approach.* Berlin: Springer. (178)

Kolers, P.A. (1975) Memorial consequences of automatized encoding. *Journal of Experimental Psychology: Human Learning and Memory,* 1, 689–701. (169)

Koshland, D.E. Jr (1977) A response regulator model in a simple sensory system. *Science,* 196, 1055–63. (24)

Kosslyn, S.M. (1980) *Image and Mind.* Cambridge, Mass.: Harvard University Press. (123–4, 126)

Kosslyn, S.M. (1983) *Ghosts in the Mind's Machine.* New York: Norton. (123–4, 126)

Kuhn, T.S. (1970) *The Structure of Scientific Revolutions.* Second edition. Chicago: University of Chicago Press. (268)

La Mettrie, J.O. de (1747) *L'homme machine.* Trans. by G.C. Bussey as *Man a Machine.* Chicago: University of Chicago Press, 1912. (385)

Ladefoged, P. (1975) *A Course in Phonetics.* New York: Harcourt Brace Jovanovich. (289)

Lashley, K.S. (1951) The problem of serial order in behavior. In L.A. Jeffress, ed., *Cerebral Mechanisms in Behavior.* New York: Wiley. (23, 158)

Lenneberg, E. (1967) *Biological Bases of Language.* New York: Wiley. (292)

Lerdahl, F., and Jackendoff, R. (1983) *A Generative Theory of Tonal Music.* Cambridge, Mass.: MIT Press. (269)

Levinson, S.C. (1983) *Pragmatics.* Cambridge: Cambridge University Press. (349)

Lévi-Strauss, C. (1963) *Tristes Tropiques.* New York: Atheneum. (20, 28)

Levitt, D.A. (1981) A melody description system for jazz improvization. M.Sc. thesis, Department of Electrical Engineering and Computer Science, MIT. (264)

Lewis, C. (1981) Skill in algebra. In J.R. Anderson, ed., *Cognitive Skills and their Acquisition.* Hillsdale, NJ: Lawrence Erlbaum. (170)

Lewis, C.I. (1946) *An Analysis of Knowledge and Valuation.* La Salle, Ill.: Open Court. (195)

Lewis, D.K. (1972) General semantics. In D. Davidson and G. Harman, eds., *Semantics of Natural Language.* Dordrecht: Reidel. (334, 388)

Liberman, A.M. (1982) On finding that speech is special. *American Psychologist,* 37, 148–67. Reprinted in M.S. Gazzaniga, ed., *Handbook of Cognitive Neuroscience.* New York: Plenum Press, 1984. (304)

Liberman, A.M., Cooper, F.S., Shankweiler, D.P., and Studdert-Kennedy, M. (1967) Perception of the speech code. *Psychological Review,* 74, 431–61. (290–1)

Liberman, M., and Sag, I. (1974) Prosodic form and discourse function. *Papers from the Tenth Regional Meeting of the Chicago Linguistic Society,* 416–27. (298–9)

Lindsay, P., and Norman, D. (1977) *Human Information Processing.* Second edition. New York: Academic Press. (175–6, 282)

Linggard, R. (1985) *Electronic Synthesis of Speech.* Cambridge: Cambridge University Press. (304)

Locke, J. (1690) *An Essay Concerning Human Understanding.* New York: Dover, 1959. (331)

Longuet-Higgins, H.C. (1972) The algorithmic description of natural language. *Proceedings of the Royal Society of London,* B. 182, 255–76. Reprinted in Longuet-Higgins (1987). (349)

Longuet-Higgins, H.C. (1979) The perception of music. *Proceedings of the Royal Society,* B, 205, 307–22. Reprinted in Longuet-Higgins (1987). (269)

Longuet-Higgins, H.C. (1981) A computer algorithm for reconstructing a scene from two projections. *Nature,* 293, 133–5. Reprinted in Longuet-Higgins (1987). (61)

Longuet-Higgins, H.C. (1984) The visual ambiguity of a moving plane. *Proceedings of the Royal Society of London,* B, 223, 165–75. Reprinted in Longuet-Higgins (1987). (102)

Longuet-Higgins, H.C. (1987) *Mental Processes: Studies in Cognitive Science.* Cambridge, Mass.: MIT Press. (61, 102, 269, 349)

Longuet-Higgins, H.C., and Lee, C.S. (1982) The perception of musical rhythms. *Perception,* 11, 115–28. (269)

Longuet-Higgins, H.C., and Prazdny, K. (1980) The interpretation of a moving retinal image. *Proceedings of the Royal Society of London,* B, 208, 385–97. Reprinted in Longuet-Higgins (1987). (102)

Lorenz, K. (1970) *Studies in Animal and Human Behaviour,* 2 Vols. Cambridge, Mass.: Harvard University Press. (131, 376)

Lyons, J. (1970) *Chomsky.* London: Fontana/Collins. (326)

Macfarlane, G. (1984) *Alexander Fleming: the Man and the Myth.* London: Hogarth Press. (253)

Mackworth, A. (1976) Model driven interpretation in intelligent vision systems. *Perception,* 5, 347-70. (113)

Mallarmé, S. For his views on poetry, see P. Valéry, *Leonardo Poe Mallarmé.* London: Routledge and Kegan Paul, 1972. (32)

Malthus, T.R. (1978) *An Essay on the Principle of Population, as it Affects the Future Improvement of Society.* London: J. Johnson. (355)

Mandler, G. (1984) *Mind and Body: Psychology of Emotion and Stress.* New York: Norton. (353, 377, 384)

Mani, K., and Johnson-Laird, P.N. (1982) The mental representation of spatial descriptions. *Memory and Cognition,* 10, 181-7. (342–3)

Marcel, A.J. (1986) Cortical blindness: a problem of visual function or visual consciousness. Mimeo, MRC Applied Psychology Unit, Cambridge. (358)

Marcus, M. (1980) *A Theory of Syntactic Recognition for Natural Language.* Cambridge, Mass.: MIT Press. (324)

Markman, E.M., and Seibert, J. (1976) Classes and collections: internal organization and resulting holistic properties. *Cognitive Psychology,* 8, 561-77. (244)

Marr, D. (1982) *Vision: a Computational Investigation into the Human Representation and Processing of Visual Information.* San Francisco: W.H. Freeman. (59 *et seq.*, 70–4, 76, 86, 91 *et seq.*, 113, 126, 368)

Marr, D., and Nishihara, H.K. (1978) Representation and recognition of the spatial organization of three-dimensional shapes. *Proceedings of the Royal Society of London,* B, 200, 269-94. (115–18)

Marr, D., and Poggio, T. (1976) Co-operative computation of stereo disparity. *Science,* 194, 283-7. (91, 167)

Marr, D., and Poggio, T. (1979) A computational theory of human stereo vision. *Proceedings of the Royal Society of London,* B, 204, 301-28. (96)

Marroquin, J.L. (1976) Human visual perception of structure. Master's thesis, Department of Electrical Engineering and Computer Science, MIT. (77)

Marslen-Wilson, W.D. (1973) Linguistic structure and speech shadowing at very short latencies. *Nature,* 224, 522-3. (295, 324)

Marslen-Wilson, W.D. (1975) Sentence perception as an interactive parallel process. *Science,* 189, 226-8. (295, 324)

Marslen-Wilson, W.D. (1987) Functional parallelism in spoken word-recognition. *Cognition,* 25, 71-102. (296–7)

Marslen-Wilson, W.D., and Tyler, L.K. (1980) The temporal structure of spoken language understanding. *Cognition,* 8, 1-71. (296–7)

Martin, M.W., ed. (1985) *Self-Deception and Self-Understanding: New Essays in Philosophy and Psychology.* Lawrence: University of Kansas Press. (368)

Mayhew, J.E.W., and Frisby, J.P. (1981) Psychophysical and computational studies towards a theory of human stereopsis. In J.M. Brady, ed., *Computer Vision.* Amsterdam: North-Holland. (97)

415

Mayhew, J.E.W., and Frisby, J.P. (1984) Computer vision. In T. O'Shea and M. Eisenstadt, eds., *Artificial Intelligence*. London: Harper and Row. (80, 113)

McCarthy, J. (1979) Ascribing mental qualities to machines. In M. Ringle, ed., *Philosophical Perspectives in Artificial Intelligence*. Atlantic Highlands, NJ: Humanities Press. (365)

McClelland, J.L., and Rumelhart, D.E. (1981) An interactive activation model of context effects in letter perception: I. An account of basic findings. *Psychological Review*, 88, 375-407. (176–8, 179)

McClelland, J.L., Rumelhart, D.E., and the PDP Research Group (1986) *Parallel Distributed Processing. Explorations in the Microstructure of Cognition*, Vol. 2: *Psychological and Biological Models*. Cambridge, Mass.: Bradford Books, MIT Press. (194)

McCloy, D., and Harris, M. (1986) *Robotics: an Introduction*. Milton Keynes: Open University Press. (211, 214)

McGurk, H., and MacDonald, J. (1976) Hearing lips and seeing voices. *Nature*, 264, 746-8. (291–3)

McLeod, P. (1980) What can probe RT tell us about the attentional demands of movement? In G.E. Stelmach and J. Requin, eds., *Tutorials in Motor Behaviour*. Amsterdam: North-Holland. (213)

Mednick, S.A. (1962) The associative basis of the creative process. *Psychological Review*, 69, 220-32. (269)

Mellor, D.H. (1987) How much of the mind is a computer? In P.P. Slezak and W.R. Albury, eds., *Computers, Brains and Minds: Essays in Cognitive Science*. Dordrecht: Reidel. In press. (384)

Michalski, R.S., Carbonell, J.G., and Mitchell, T.M., eds. (1983) *Machine Learning: an Artificial Intelligence Approach*. Vol 1. Palo Alto, Calif.: Tioga Press. (253)

Michalski, R.S., Carbonell, J.G., and Mitchell, T.M., eds. (1986) *Machine Learning: an Artificial Intelligence Approach*. Vol. 2. Los Altos, Calif.: Morgan Kaufmann. (253)

Michalski, R.S., and Chilausky, R.L. (1980) Learning by being told and learning from examples: an experimental comparison of the two methods of knowledge acquisition in the context of developing an expert system for soybean disease diagnosis.

International Journal of Policy Analysis and Information Systems, 4, No. 2. (237, 249)

Michie, D., ed. (1979) *Expert Systems in the Micro-Electronic Age.* Edinburgh: Edinburgh University Press. (233)

Mill, J.S. (1843) *A System of Logic,* Book III. London. (236, 242)

Miller, G.A. (1956) The magical number seven, plus or minus two. *Psychological Review,* 63, 81-97. (22, 147, 169)

Miller, G.A. (1962) Some psychological studies of grammar. *American Psychologist,* 17, 748-62. (319)

Miller, G.A. (1966) *Psychology: the Science of Mental Life.* Harmondsworth, Middx: Penguin. (27)

Miller, G.A. (1968) *The Psychology of Communication: Seven Essays.* Harmondsworth, Middx: Penguin. (271)

Miller, G.A. (1986) Dictionaries in the mind. *Language and Cognitive Processes,* 1, 171-85. (389)

Miller, G.A., and Chomsky, N. (1963) Finitary models of language users. In R.D. Luce, R.R. Bush and E. Galanter, eds., *Handbook of Mathematical Psychology,* Vol. 2. New York: Wiley. (308 *et seq.*)

Miller, G.A., Galanter, E., and Pribram, K. (1960) *Plans and the Structure of Behavior.* New York: Holt, Rinehart and Winston. (23, 158, 308 *et seq.*, 326)

Miller, G.A., and Johnson-Laird, P.N. (1976) *Language and Perception.* Cambridge: Cambridge University Press; Cambridge, Mass.: Harvard University Press. (120, 245–6, 331–2, 345)

Milner, B. (1970) Memory and the medial temporal regions of the brain. In K.H. Pribram and D.E. Broadbent, eds., *Biology of Memory.* New York: Academic Press. (150)

Minsky, M.L. (1968) Mind, matter, and models. In M.L. Minsky, ed., *Semantic Information Processing.* Cambridge, Mass.: MIT Press. (361)

Minsky, M.L. (1975) Frame-system theory. In R.C. Schank and B.L. Webber, eds., *Theoretical Issues in Natural Language Processing.* Pre-prints of a conference at MIT. Reprinted in Johnson-Laird and Wason (1977). (244, 245)

Minsky, M.L., and Papert, S. (1969) *Perceptrons.* Cambridge, Mass.: MIT Press. (184)

Moles, A.A. (1966) *Information Theory and Aesthetic Perception.* Urbana, Ill.: University of Illinois Press. (269)

Montague, R. (1974) *Formal Philosophy: Selected Papers.* New Haven, Conn.: Yale University Press. (337, 349)

Morton, J. (1969) Interaction of information in word recognition. *Psychological Review,* 76, 165-78. (296)

Neisser, U. (1981) John Dean's memory. *Cognition,* 9, 1-22. (182)

Newell, A. (1973) You can't play 20 questions with nature and win. In W.G. Chase, ed., *Visual Information Processing.* New York: Academic Press. (157)

Newell, A. (1973) Production systems: models of control structures. In W.G. Chase, ed., *Visual Information Processing.* New York: Academic Press. (173)

Newell, A., and Rosenbloom, P.S. (1981) Mechanisms of skill acquisition and the law of practice. In J.R. Anderson, ed., *Cognitive Skills and their Acquisition.* Hillsdale, NJ: Lawrence Erlbaum. (168–70)

Newell, A., and Simon, H.A. (1972) *Human Problem Solving.* Englewood Cliffs, NJ: Prentice-Hall. (22, 27, 158–62, 165, 247)

Newell, A., and Simon, H.A. (1976) Computer Science as empirical inquiry: symbols and search. *Communications of the Association for Computing Machinery,* 19 113–26 (36)

Nisbett, R.E., Krantz, D.H., Jepson, D., and Kunda, Z. (1983) The use of statistical heuristics in everyday inductive reasoning. *Psychological Review,* 90, 339-63. (250)

Nisbett, R.E., and Ross, L. (1980) *Human Inference: Strategies and Shortcomings of Social Judgement.* Englewood Cliffs, NJ: Prentice-Hall. (250, 253)

Norman, D.A. (1981) Categorization of action slips. *Psychological Review,* 88, 1-15. (368)

Norman, D.A., Rumelhart, D.E., and the LNR Research Group (1975) *Explorations in Cognition.* San Francisco: Freeman. (330)

Norman, D.A., and Shallice, T. (1980) Attention to action: willed and automatic control of behaviur. University of California San Diego CHIP Report 99. In R.J. Davidson, G.E. Schwartz and D. Shapiro, eds., *Consciousness and Self-Regulation: Advances in Research, IV.* New York: Plenum Press. In press. (157)

418

Oatley, K. (1978) *Perceptions and Representations: the Theoretical Bases of Brain Research and Psychology.* London: Methuen. (115, 126, 205, 368)

Oatley, K. (1984) *Selves in Relation: an Introduction to Psychotherapy and Groups.* London: Methuen. (368)

Oatley, K. (1987) *Best Laid Plans.* Cambridge, Mass.: Harvard University Press. In press. (384)

Oatley, K., and Johnson-Laird, P.N. (1987) Towards a cognitive theory of emotion. *Cognition and Emotion,* 1, 29-50. (Ch. 20 *passim*)

Olds, J., and Milner, P. (1954) Positive reinforcement produced by electrical stimulaton of septal area and other regions of rat brain. *Journal of Comparative and Physiological Psychology,* 47, 419-27. (373)

Ortony, A., Clore, G., and Foss, M.A. (1987) The referential structure of the affective lexicon. *Cognitive Science,* 11, 341–64. (384)

Osherson, D.N. (1975) Logic and models of logical thinking. In R.J. Falmagne, ed., *Reasoning: Representation and Process in Children and Adults.* Hillsdale, NJ: Lawrence Erlbaum. (224)

Osherson, D.N., and Smith, E.E. (1982) Gradedness and conceptual conjunction. *Cognition,* 12, 299-318. (337)

Osherson, D.N., Stob, M., and Weinstein, S. (1986) *Systems that Learn: an Introduction to Learning Theory for Cognitive and Computer Scientists.* Cambridge, Mass.: Bradford Books, MIT Press. (142)

Partee, B.H. (1975) Montague grammar and transformational grammar. *Linguistic Inquiry,* 6, 203-300. (349)

Partee, B.H. (1979) Semantics – mathematics or psychology? In R. Bäuerle, U. Egli and A. von Stechow, eds., *Semantics from Different Points of View.* Berlin: Springer. (338)

Patterson, R.D. (1986) Spiral detection of periodicity and the spiral form of musical scales. *Psychology of Music,* 14, 44–61. (283–6)

Pavlov, I. (1927) *Conditioned Reflexes.* Trans. by G.V. Anrep. Oxford: Oxford University Press. (17, 131)

Perkins, D.N. (1981) *The Mind's Best Work.* Cambridge, Mass.: Harvard University Press. (258, 269)

Perky, C.W. (1910) An experimental study of imagination. *American Journal of Psychology*, 21, 422-52. (122)

Perlman, A.M., and Greenblatt, D. (1981) Miles Davis meets Noam Chomsky: some observations on jazz improvisation and language structure. In W. Steiner, ed., *The Sign in Music and Literature*. Austin: University of Texas Press. (269)

Piaget, J. (1950) *The Psychology of Intelligence*. London: Routledge and Kegan Paul. (244)

Piaget, J. (1952) *The Child's Conception of Number*. New York: Humanities Press. (162–3, 173)

Piaget, J. (1980) The psychogenesis of knowledge and its epistemological significance. In Piattelli-Palmarini (1980). (21, 318)

Piattelli-Palmarini, M., ed. (1980) *Language and Learning: the Debate between Jean Piaget and Noam Chomsky*. London: Routledge and Kegan Paul. (326)

Pinker, S. (1979) Formal models of language learning. *Cognition*, 7, 217-83. (142)

Pinker, S. (1984) Visual cognition: an introduction. *Cognition*, 18, 1-63. (126)

Pinker, S. (1984) *Language Learnability and Language Development*. Cambridge, Mass.: Harvard University Press. (142, 326)

Pinker, S., and Prince, A. (1987) On language and connectionism: analysis of a parallel distributed processing model of language acquisition. Occasional Paper No. 33, Center for Cognitive Science, MIT. (194)

Poggio, T. (1984) Vision by man and machine. *Scientific American*, April. (62–3, 80)

Polya, G. (1957) *How to Solve it*. Second edition. New York: Doubleday. (160)

Polyani, M. (1958) *Personal Knowledge*. Chicago: University of Chicago Press. (195)

Popper, K.R. (1972) Conjectural knowledge: my solution to the problem of induction. In *Objective Knowledge: an Evolutionary Approach*. Oxford: Clarendon Press. (236)

Porter, A. (1969) *Cybernetics Simplified*. London: English Universities Press. (214)

Post, E. (1941) Absolutely unsolvable problems and relatively undecidable propositions: account of an anticipation. Reprinted in M. Davis, ed., *The Undecidable: Basic Papers on Undecidable Propositions, Unsolvable Problems and Computable Functions.* Hewlett, NY: Raven Press, 1965. (162)

Power, M.J. (1986) A technique for measuring processing load during speech production. *Journal of Psycholinguistic Research,* 15, 371–82. (150–1)

Power, M.J., and Champion, L.A. (1986) Cognitive approaches to depression: a theoretical critique. *British Journal of Clinical Psychology,* 25, 201-12. (384)

Power, R.J.D. (1979) The organization of purposeful dialogues. *Linguistics,* 17, 107-52. (347)

Power, R.J.D., and Longuet-Higgins, H.C. (1978) Learning to count: a computational model of language acquisition. *Proceedings of the Royal Society.* B, 200, 391-417. (326)

Putnam, H. (1960) Minds and machines. In S. Hook, ed., *Dimensions of Mind.* New York: New York University Press. (353)

Putnam, H. (1975) The meaning of 'meaning'. In K. Gunderson, ed., *Language, Mind and Knowledge.* Minnesota Studies in the Philosophy of Science, Vol. 7. Minneapolis: University of Minnesota Press. (244)

Putnam, H. (1980) What is innate and why: comments on the debate. In Piattelli-Palmarini (1980). (318)

Pylyshyn, Z.W. (1984) *Computation and Cognition: Toward a Foundation for Cognitive Science.* Cambridge, Mass.: Bradford Books, MIT Press. (124, 126, 193)

Quillian, M.R. (1968) Semantic memory. In M.L. Minsky, ed., *Semantic Information Processing.* Cambridge, Mass.: MIT Press. (328–9)

Rabiner, L.R. (1969) A model for synthesizing speech by rule. *Institute of Electrical and Electronic Engineers, Transactions,* AU-17, 7- 13. (301)

Radford, A. (1981) *Transformational Syntax: a Student's Guide to Chomsky's Extended Standard Theory.* Cambridge: Cambridge University Press. (326)

Raibert, M.H., and Sutherland, I.E. (1983) Machines that walk. *Scientific American*, January, 248, 32-41. (214)

Rameau, J.P. (1722) *Treatise on Harmony.* Reprint, New York: Dover, 1971. (261)

Reason, J., and Mycielska, K. (1982) *Absentminded? The Psychology of Mental Lapses and Everyday Errors.* Englewood Cliffs, NJ: Prentice-Hall. (157, 368)

Reichardt, W.E., and Poggio, T. (1981) Visual control of flight in flies. In W.E. Reichardt and T. Poggio, eds., *Theoretical Approaches in Neurobiology.* Cambridge, Mass.: MIT Press. (79)

Rhinehart, L. (1971) *Dice Man.* London: Talmy, Franklin. (364)

Rips, L.J. (1983) Cognitive processes in propositional reasoning. *Psychological Review*, 90, 38-71. (224)

Roberts, L.G. (1965) Machine perception of three-dimensional solids. In J.T. Tippett, D.A. Berkowitz, L.C. Clapp, C.J. Koester and A. Vanderburgh, eds., *Optical and Electro-Optical Information Processing.* Cambridge, Mass.: MIT Press. (114, 118)

Robinson, J.A. (1979) *Logic: Form and Function, the Mechanization of Deductive Reasoning.* Edinburgh: Edinburgh University Press. (233)

Roe, A. (1952) *The Making of a Scientist.* New York: Dodd Mead. (269)

Rosch, E. (1977) Classification of real-world objects: origins and representations in cognition. In Johnson-Laird and Wason (1977). (245)

Rosenblatt, F. (1961) *Principles of Neurodynamics: Perceptrons and the Theory of Brain Mechanisms.* New York: Spartan. (182–4)

Rosten, L. (1970) *The Joys of Yiddish.* London: W.H. Allen. (297)

Rumelhart, D.E., Hinton, G.E., and Williams, R.J. (1986) Learning internal representations by error propagation. In Rumelhart, McClelland and the PDP Research Group, Vol.1 (1986). (185, 186–8)

Rumelhart, D.E., McClelland, J.L., and the PDP Research Group (1986) *Parallel Distributed Processing: Explorations in the Microstructure of Cognition*, Vol 1: *Foundations.* Cambridge Mass.: Bradford Books, MIT Press. (194)

Russell, B.A.W. (1917) *Mysticism and Logic.* New York: Barnes and Noble. (34)

Russell, B.A.W. (1927) *An Outline of Philosophy*. London: Allen and Unwin. (19)

Sacks, O. (1985) *The Man who Mistook his Wife for a Hat*. London: Duckworth. (157)

Sanford, A.J., and Garrod, S.C. (1981) *Understanding Written Language: Explorations of Comprehension beyond the Sentence*. Chichester: Wiley. (349)

Sartre, J-P. (1939) *Sketch for a Theory of the Emotions*. London: Methuen, 1962. (377)

Saussure, F. de (1916) *Course in General Linguistics*. London: Peter Owen ,1960. (20, 245)

Schachter, S., and Singer, J. (1962) Cognitive, social and physiological determinants of emotional state. *Psychological Review*, 69, 379-99. (377, 383)

Schank, R.C. (1975) *Conceptual Information Processing*. Amsterdam: North-Holland. (324, 330–1)

Schank, R.C., and Abelson, R.P. (1977) *Scripts, Plans, Goals and Understanding*. Hillsdale, NJ: Lawrence Erlbaum. (244, 345)

Scherer, K.R., Ladd, D.R., and Silverman, K.E.A. (1984) Vocal cues to speaker affect: testing two models. *Journal of the Acoustical Society of America*, 76, 1346-56. (299)

Schneider, W., and Shiffrin, R.M. (1977) Controlled and automatic human information processing: I. Detection, search, and attention. *Psychological Review*, 84, 1-66. (154, 155)

Searle, J.R. (1969) *Speech Acts: an Essay in the Philosophy of Language*. Cambridge: Cambridge University Press. (349)

Searle, J.R. (1980) Minds, brains, and programs. *Behavioral and Brain Sciences*, 3, 417-24. (386, 388)

Sejnowski, T.J., and Rosenberg, C.R. (1986) NETtalk: a parallel network that learns to read aloud. The Johns Hopkins University Electrical Engineering and Computer Science Technical Report JHU/EECS-86/01. (188–9)

Sells, P. (1985) *Lectures on Contemporary Syntactic Theories: an Introduction to Government-binding Theory, Generalized Phrase Structure Grammar, and Lexical-functional Grammar*. Stanford, Calif.: Center for the Study of Language and Information, Stanford University. (326)

423

Selz, O. For an account of his work, see G. Humphrey, *Thinking: an Introduction to its Experimental Psychology*. London: Methuen, 1951. (328)

Seyfarth, R.M., Cheney, D.L., and Marler, P. (1980) Vervet monkey alarm calls: semantic communication in a free-ranging primate. *Animal Behavior*, 28, 1070-94. (274)

Shallice, T. (1972) Dual functions of consciousness. *Psychological Review*, 79, 383-93. (353)

Shallice, T. (1978) Neuropsychological research and the fractionation of memory systems. In L-G. Nilsson, ed., *Perspectives in Memory Research*. Hillsdale, NJ: Lawrence Erlbaum. (157)

Shallice, T., and Warrington, E.K. (1970) Independent functioning of the verbal memory stores: a neuropsychological study. *Quarterly Journal of Experimental Psychology*, 22, 261-73. (150)

Shaw, G.B. (1932) *The Adventures of the Black Girl in Search of God*. London: Constable. (131)

Shepard, R.N., and Cooper, L.A. (1982) *Mental Images and their Transformations*. Cambridge, Mass.: Bradford Books, MIT Press. (121–2, 126)

Simon, H. (1967) Motivational and emotional controls of cognition. *Psychological Review*, 74, 29-39. (384)

Simon, H. (1981) *The Sciences of the Artificial*. Second edition. Cambridge, Mass.: MIT Press. (170, 173, 368)

Simon, H. (1983) Why should machines learn? In Michalski, Carbonell and Mitchell (1983). (168)

Skinner, B.F. (1953) *Science and Human Behavior*. New York: Macmillan. (17, 131, 269)

Skinner, B.F. (1971) *Beyond Freedom and Dignity*. New York: Knopf. (368)

Sloman, A. (1987) Motives, mechanisms and emotions. *Cognition and Emotion*. 1, 217–33. (384)

Smith, E.E., and Medin, D.L. (1981) *Categories and Concepts*. Cambridge, Mass.: Harvard University Press. (253)

Smoke, K.L. (1932) An objective study of concept formation. *Psychological Monographs*, 42, whole No. 191. (244, 247)

Smolensky, P. (1986) Information processing in dynamical

systems: foundations of harmony theory. In McClelland, Rumelhart and the PDP Research Group, Vol.1 (1986). (194)

Smyth, M.M., and Wing, A.M., eds. (1984) *The Psychology of Human Movement.* London: Academic Press. (214)

Solomons, L.L., and Stein, G. (1896) Normal motor automatisms. *Psychological Review,* 3, 492-512. (212)

Sommers, F. (1959) The ordinary language tree. *Mind,* 68, 160-85. (253)

Sonneck, O.G., ed. (1967) *Beethoven: Impressions by his Contemporaries.* New York: Dover. (269)

Spelke, E., Hirst, W., and Neisser, U. (1976) Skills of divided attention. *Cognition,* 4, 215-30. (214)

Sperber, D., and Wilson, D. (1986) *Relevance: Communication and Cognition.* Oxford: Basil Blackwell. (349)

Sperling, G. (1960) The information available in brief visual presentations. *Psychological Monographs,* 74, whole No. 498, 1-29. (*See also* Darwin, Turvey and Crowder, 1972.) (149)

Standing, L. (1973) Learning 10,000 pictures. *Quarterly Journal of Experimental Psychology,* 25, 207-22. (182)

Steedman, M.J. (1982) A generative grammar for jazz chord sequences. *Music Perception,* 2, 52-77. (262–3)

Steedman, M.J., and Johnson-Laird, P.N. (1977) A programmatic theory of linguistic performance. In P.T. Smith and R.N. Campbell, eds., *Advances in the Psychology of Language: Formal and Experimental Approaches.* New York: Plenum. (349)

Stenning, K. (1978) Anaphora as an approach to pragmatics. In M. Halle, J. Bresnan and G.A. Miller, eds., *Linguistic Theory and Psychological Reality.* Cambridge, Mass.: MIT Press. (349)

Sternberg, S. (1975) Memory scanning: new findings and current controversies. *Quarterly Journal of Experimental Psychology,* 27, 1- 32. (153–5, 157)

Stevens, K.N., and Blumstein, S.E. (1981) The search for invariant acoustic correlates of phonetic features. In P.D. Eimas and J.L. Miller, eds., *Perspectives on the Study of Speech.* Hillsdale, NJ: Lawrence Erlbaum. (303)

Strongman, K.T. (1982) *The Psychology of Emotion.* Second edition. Chichester: Wiley. (384)

425

Sudnow, D. (1978) *Ways of the Hand.* London: Routledge and Kegan Paul. (264)

Sundberg, J., and Lindblom, B. (1976) Generative theories in language and music descriptions. *Cognition,* 4, 99-122. (269)

Sutherland, N.S. (1966) Discussion of 'Some reflections on competence and performance' by J.A. Fodor and M.F. Garrett. In J. Lyons and R.J. Wales, eds., *Psycholinguistic Papers.* Edinburgh: Edinburgh University Press. (325)

Sutherland, N.S. (1973) Intelligent picture processing. In N.S. Sutherland, ed., *Tutorial Essays in Psychology,* Vol. I. Hillsdalc, NJ: Lawrence Erlbaum. (113–14)

Sutherland, N.S., and Mackintosh, N.J. (1971) *Mechanisms of Animal Discrimination Learning.* New York: Academic Press. (36)

Tarski, A. (1956) The concept of truth in formalized languages. In *Logic, Semantics, Metamathematics: Papers from 1923 to 1938.* Translated by J.H. Woodger. Oxford: Oxford University Press. (335)

Thagard, P., and Holyoak, K.J. (1985) Discovering the wave theory of sound: inductive inference in the context of problem solving. *Proceedings of the Ninth International Joint Conference on Artificial Intelligence,* 610-12. Palo Alto, Calif.: William Kaufmann. (266)

Thatcher, J.W. (1963) The construction of a self-describing Turing machine. In J. Fox, ed., *Mathematical Theory of Automata.* Microwave Research Institute Symposia, No. 12. Polytechnic Institute of Brooklyn. New York: Polytechnic Press. (368)

Thurstone, J., and Carraher, R.G. (1966) *Optical Illusions and the Visual Arts.* New York: Litton (Van Nostrand). (119)

Tinbergen, N. (1951) *The Study of Instinct.* Oxford: Oxford University Press. (376)

Toates, F.M., and Oatley, K.J. (1970) Computer simulation of thirst and water balance. *Medical and Biological Engineering,* 8, 71-87. (373)

Touretzky, D.S., and Hinton, G.E. (1985) Symbols among the neurons: details of a connectionist inference architecture.

426

Ninth International Joint Conference on Artificial Intelligence, 238-43. Palo Alto, Calif.: William Kaufmann. (192)

Trakhtenbrot, B.A. (1963) *Algorithms and Automatic Computing Machines.* Trans. and adapted from second Russian edition by J. Kristian, J.D. McCawley and S.A. Schmitt. Boston: D.C. Heath. (52)

Treisman, A.M. (1964) Verbal cues, language, and meaning in selective attention. *American Journal of Psychology,* 77, 206-19. (149)

Treisman, A.M., and Gelade, G. (1980) A feature-integration theory of attention. *Cognitive Psychology,* 12, 97-136. (149)

Tulving, E. (1983) *Elements of Episodic Memory.* Oxford: Oxford University Press. (166)

Turing, A. (1936) On computable numbers, with an application to the Entscheidungsproblem. *Proceedings of the London Mathematical Society,* 2nd Series, 42, 230-65. Correction, ibid, 43, 544-546. Reprinted in M. Davis, ed., *The Undecidable: Basic Papers on Undecidable Propositions, Unsolvable Problems and Computable Functions.* Hewlett, NY: Raven Press, 1965. (49–52, 191, 387, 391)

Turing, A. (1950) Computing machinery and intelligence. *Mind,* 59, 433-60. (22, 26, 52, 353)

Turvey, M.T., Fitch, H.L., and Tuller, B. (1982) The Bernstein perspective: I. The problems of degrees of freedom and context-conditioned variability. In Kelso (1982). (201, 202, 214)

Tversky, A., and Kahneman, D. (1973) Availability: a heuristic for judging frequency and probability. *Cognitive Psychology,* 4, 207-32. Reprinted in Kahneman, Slovic and Tversky (1982). (253)

Tversky, A., and Kahneman, D. (1974) Judgement under uncertainty: heuristics and biases. *Science,* 185, 1124-31. Reprinted in Kahneman, Slovic and Tversky (1982). (250–2)

Tyler, L.K., and Wessels, J. (1983) Quantifying contextual contributions to word-recognition processes. *Perception and Psychophysics,* 34, 409-20. (295)

Ullman, S. (1979) *The Interpretation of Visual Motion.* Cambridge, Mass.: MIT Press. (99–101, 105)

Ulrich, J.W. (1977) The analysis and synthesis of jazz by computer. *Fifth International Joint Conference on Artificial Intelligence*, 865-72. (264)

Valéry, P. (1970) *Analects*. London: Routledge and Kegan Paul. (376)

van Dijk, T.A., and Kintsch, W. (1983) *Strategies of Discourse Comprehension*. New York: Academic Press. (349)

von Neumann, J. (1958) *The Computer and the Brain*. New Haven, Conn.: Yale University Press. (22, 146, 191)

Vygotsky, L.S. (1962) *Thought and Language*. Edited and trans. by E. Hanfmann and G. Vakar. Cambridge, Mass.: MIT Press. (243)

Wallas, G. (1926) *The Art of Thought*. London: Jonathan Cape. (254)

Waltz, D. (1975) Understanding line drawings of scenes with shadows. In Winston (1975). (107, 111–13)

Wanner, E. (1980) The ATN and the sausage machine: which one is baloney? *Cognition*, 8, 209-25. (322)

Wanner, E., and Maratsos, M.P. (1978) An ATN approach to comprehension. In M. Halle, J.W. Bresnan and G.A. Miller, eds., *Linguistic Theory and Psychological Reality*. Cambridge, Mass.: MIT Press. (322)

Warrington, E.K., and Taylor, A.M. (1973) The contribution of the right parietal lobe to object recognition. *Cortex*, 9, 152-64. (120–1)

Wason, P.C. (1968) 'On the failure to eliminate hypotheses . . .' . . . a second look. In Johnson-Laird and Wason (1977). (241–2)

Wason, P.C. (1983) Realism and rationality and the selection task. In J.St B.T. Evans, ed., *Thinking and Reasoning: Psychological Approaches*. London: Routledge and Kegan Paul. (225)

Wason, P.C., and Johnson-Laird, P.N. (1972) *Psychology of Reasoning: Structure and Content*. London: Batsford. Cambridge, Mass.: Harvard University Press. (225, 233)

Watson, J.B. (1913) Psychology as the behaviorist views it. *Psychological Review*, 20, 158-77. (16–19)

Watt, R.J. (1988) *Visual Processing: Computational, Psychophysical and Cognitive Research.* Hillsdale, NJ: Lawrence Erlbaum. (80)

Watt, R.J., and Morgan, M.J. (1985) A theory of the primitive spatial code in human vision. *Vision Research,* 25, 166–74. (74–5, 97)

Webber, B.L. (1978) Description formation and discourse model synthesis. In D.L. Waltz, ed., *Theoretical Issues in Natural Language Processing,* 2. New York: Association for Computing Machinery. (349)

Weiner, N. (1947) *Cybernetics.* Cambridge, Mass.: MIT Press. (206, 214)

Weiskrantz, L. (1986) *On Blindsight.* Oxford: Oxford University Press. (358)

Weizenbaum, J. (1976) *Computer Power and Human Reason: from Judgment to Calculation.* San Francisco: Freeman. (386–7, 389)

Wertheimer, M. (1961) *Productive Thinking.* Enlarged edition. London: Tavistock. (19)

Wexler, K. and Culicover, P. (1980) *Formal Principles of Language Acquisition.* Cambridge, Mass.: MIT Press. (326)

Wheeler, D. (1970) Processes in word recognition. *Cognitive Psychology,* 1, 59-85. (194)

Whitehead, A.N. (1911) *Introduction to Mathematics.* London. (130)

Wierzbicka, A. (1972) *Semantic Primitives.* Frankfurt: Athenäum. (381–2)

Willshaw, D.J., Buneman, O.P., and Longuet-Higgins, H.C. (1969) Nonholographic associative memory. *Nature,* 222, 960-2. (194)

Winograd, T. (1972) *Understanding Natural Language.* New York: Academic Press. (325)

Winograd, T., and Flores, F. (1986) *Understanding Computers and Cognition: a New Foundation for Design.* Norwood, NJ: Ablex. (386)

Winston, P.H., ed. (1975) *The Psychology of Computer Vision.* New York: McGraw-Hill. (111, 126)

Winston, P.H. (1984) *Artificial Intelligence.* Second edition. Reading, MA: Addison-Wesley. (173, 237, 247–9)

Witten, I.H. (1982) *Principles of Computer Speech.* London: Academic Press. (304)

Wittgenstein, L. (1953) *Philosophical Investigations.* New York: Macmillan. (244–5, 338, 341)

Woods, W.A. (1977) Lunar rocks in natural English: explorations in natural language question-answering. In A. Zampolli, ed., *Linguistic Structure Processing*. Amsterdam: North-Holland. (322)

Woods, W.A. (1981) Procedural semantics. In A.K. Joshi, I. Sag and B.L. Webber, eds., *Elements of Discourse Understanding*. Cambridge: Cambridge University Press. (349)

Woolf, V. (1925) *Mrs. Dalloway*. London: Chatto and Windus. (16)

Wright, P., and Kahneman, D. (1971) Evidence for alternative strategies of sentence retention. *Quarterly Journal of Experimental Psychology*, 23, 197-213. (379)

Young, R.M. (1979) Production systems for modelling human cognition. In Michie (1979). (162–6)

Zajonc, R.B., (1980) Feeling and thinking: preferences need no inferences. *American Psychologist*, 35, 151-75. (377)

Zhang, G., and Simon, H.A. (1985) STM capacity for Chinese words and idioms: chunking and acoustical loop hypotheses. *Memory and Cognition*, 13, 193-210. (152)

Ziff, P. (1959) The feelings of robots. *Analysis*, 19, 64-8. (353)

Zuriff, G.E. (1985) *Behaviorism: a Conceptual Reconstruction*. New York: Columbia University Press. (19)

NAME INDEX

431

433

SUBJECT INDEX